Revolutionary Justice

Revolutionary Justice

SPECIAL COURTS AND THE FORMATION OF REPUBLICAN EGYPT

Yoram Meital

OXFORD
UNIVERSITY PRESS

OXFORD
UNIVERSITY PRESS

Oxford University Press is a department of the University of Oxford. It furthers the University's objective of excellence in research, scholarship, and education by publishing worldwide. Oxford is a registered trade mark of Oxford University Press in the UK and certain other countries.

Published in the United States of America by Oxford University Press
198 Madison Avenue, New York, NY 10016, United States of America.

Library of Congress Cataloging-in-Publication Data
Names: Meital, Yoram, author.
Title: Revolutionary justice : special courts and the formation of republican Egypt / Yoram Meital.
Description: New York, NY : Oxford University Press, 2016. |
Includes bibliographical references and index.
Identifiers: LCCN 2016010378 | ISBN 9780190600839 (hardcover : alk. paper)
Subjects: LCSH: Courts of special jurisdiction—Egypt—History—20th century. |
Trials (Political crimes and offenses)—Egypt—History—20th century. |
Egypt—History—Revolution, 1952 | Egypt—Politics and government—1952–1970.
Classification: LCC KRM1588 .M45 2016 | DDC 347.62/04—dc23
LC record available athttp://lccn.loc.gov/2016010378

To Alice, my lighthouse

CONTENTS

ACKNOWLEDGMENTS

Now that this work has been completed and before a much hoped-for dialogue begins with its readers, it is appropriate to reflect on how it all began and to express gratitude to those who helped me along the journey. The idea of this book was planted in Cairo ten years ago, when over dinner with friends I was asked about my work. I described my interest in the study of the revolution of July 23, 1952, and particularly the transitional phase that laid the foundations for the authoritarian regime that has remained in place for more than six decades since. What were the circumstances that quickly turned the widespread public support for the Free Officers into opposition by key parties? What were the measures taken by the new regime to quell dissent during this critical moment of the revolution? The vibrant conversation around the table at the Greek Club in the heart of the Egyptian capital challenged some of my premises.

In the following days I filled page after page, drafting the framework of the study. I was most troubled by one fundamental question: Where could I find first-hand information about the relations between the interim government, the Revolution Command Council (RCC), and its opponents? Several days later, in a used bookshop in al-Azbakiyya, I stumbled across the third volume of *Mahkamat al-Thawra* (The Revolution's Court). While leafing through its pages, I realized suddenly that the official sphere of the courts offers a rare opportunity to hear the voices that the RCC toiled to silence in the critical stages of the revolution. Thus, a visit to a bookstore became a constitutive moment in a study, which turned into a journey through many spaces and times. Confronted by experiences and challenges, I was beset en route by uncertainty and even fear that I would not be able to bring this ship to its destination.

It is now clear that assistance and support from colleagues, friends, and family were crucial to the completion of this intricate study. First and foremost, I would like to express my gratitude to two friends who are no longer with us: the brilliant Egyptian playwright ʿAli Salem and the renowned historian ʿAbd al-ʿAzim Ramadan. Their insights helped me to understand better the nuances of Egyptian politics and the spirit of the Nasserite period. Other Egyptian colleagues helped me on return visits to Cairo and Alexandria, and with complete understanding I respect their requests not to be named in a study by an Israeli scholar. The manner in which they shared with me their thoughts and first-hand experience reflects their intellectual openness. Their concern is an explicit comment on the growing danger posed by the current political climate in Egypt.

My deepest gratitude goes to several colleagues and friends who spared no time or energy in commenting on my half-baked ideas and drafts of this study. I have been most fortunate in having the benefit of their wisdom, invaluable knowledge, and long study of the Middle East: Roger Owen, a distinguished historian of the modern Middle East, shared his vast knowledge of modern Egypt and accompanied this study from its inception to its conclusion. Duncan Kennedy, professor of law at Harvard University, has been a rich source of knowledge on the legal aspects, and his incisive remarks often led me to recalculate my route. Israel Gershoni of Tel Aviv University, a world authority on modern Egypt, has been a constant source of support and an intellectual mentor. He read the final draft carefully and offered dozens of suggestions and insightful comments that demonstrated his exceptional familiarity with the literature in a wide range of areas. Avi Rubin, of Ben-Gurion University, enriched my knowledge of the legal-political circumstances of the late Ottoman era. He read parts of the manuscript and offered observations that are evident in the final text. I greatly value the support of two friends, Zvi Ben-Dor Benite of New York University and Amnon Raz-Krakotzkin of Ben-Gurion University. The former is a leading scholar of Islam and Muslims in China; the latter focuses on the history of the Jewish people. They read different parts of the manuscript and devoted hours to discussing my arguments. Their thoughtful comments and ideas encouraged me to expand the discussion beyond the context of Egypt. I owe special gratitude to the anonymous readers assigned by OUP, whose reviews are a model of constructive academic critique. I wish I could name them in expressing my appreciation for their valuable suggestions, but such are the rules of academic publishing. Nancy Toff, my editor at OUP, believed in the book project and has skillfully led it to completion. Her meticulous revision and insightful comments ushered me through the editing process and added clarity and precision to the last draft. I am also grateful to Elda Granata, editorial assistant at OUP, who was very helpful in the production of this book.

The generous fellowship of the Islamic Legal Studies Program allowed me to spend the 2011–2012 academic year at Harvard University and take advantage of the unique collection of the library of Harvard Law School. I owe special thanks to Yahya Melhem, a skillful librarian who spared no effort in helping me locate Arabic sources that are difficult to obtain. I wish to thank the Center for Middle Eastern Studies (CMES) at Harvard University for awarding me affiliate research status for five years and for the opportunity to use the incredible Widener Library. I am indebted to the CMES staff and especially to the last two directors, Bill Granara and Baber Johansen. The latter, an authority on Islamic legal thought, showed great interest in my work and helped me think about continuity and change in the use of special courts during the July Revolution in comparison with Egyptian tribunals that preceded them. Following my return from Boston, I taught two advanced seminars on legalism and politics in modern Egypt. As usual, teaching is an excellent opportunity for reflection on one's own work. I am obliged to the students of the Department of Middle East Studies at Ben-Gurion University who participated in these demanding seminars and countless valuable discussions, which helped me to refine the text and make it more accessible.

Originally, I wrote drafts of this study in Hebrew and English. The fine language of the text that appears here is primarily the work of Avi Aronsky, who translated and edited substantial parts of the manuscript. In the years we have been working together on various projects we have developed a friendly relationship and often exchange ideas on the troubling situation in Israel and the Middle East. His excellent linguistic skills are evident on many pages of this book, and for that I thank him deeply. I owe deep appreciation also to Ursula Wokoeck, whose expertise as an accomplished historian and lawyer significantly improved the language of the final draft. Her sharp reading saved me from embarrassing mistakes, and for that I will always be grateful.

Throughout this journey, Hilla, my beloved wife to whom this book is dedicated, provided firm moral support. She was a true intellectual counterpart, always willing to discuss my ideas and dilemmas and to offer insightful comments. With much affection and patience she also read draft after draft and accompanied me to the final harbor.

ABBREVIATIONS

FO	Free Officers
MB	Muslim Brothers
NDP	National Democratic Party
PLO	Palestine Liberation Organization
RCC	Revolution Command Council
SCAF	Supreme Council of the Armed Forces
SA	Special Apparatus

Introduction

The overthrow of a government by force, a struggle to build a new order, and the sense that the people are embarking on a "completely new beginning" characterize the opening stages of every revolution. Whether by military coup or civil insurrection, the toppling of a regime symbolizes the start of a transition period that usually lasts for a number of years, sometimes several decades (as in the French Revolution). The transition phase is undoubtedly the moment of truth in every revolution. This juncture is informed by a collapse of the justice and law enforcement systems, heavy violence, a shortage of goods and services, and a resort to exceptional means on the part of those steering the helm. A sense of uncertainty and chaos spreads throughout society. The solidarity between political parties, sectors, and interest groups that fought to bring down the old order gives way to bitter rivalry between these same players over the contours of the new dispensation. The commonplace revolutionary step of repealing or suspending the constitution creates the illusion of a legal void. In general, the "temporary" leadership issues laws and decrees with the objective of laying the foundations for the ruling order that it is interested in constructing. Thereafter, this basic model finds expression in the new constitution.

Revolutionary Justice focuses on the critical role that the Egyptian state's justice system, especially a pair of special tribunals, filled in the struggle over the establishment of a new ruling and political order following the military coup that the Free Officers (FO) executed on July 23, 1952. It discusses the junta's intensive use of decrees, laws, and constitutional declarations during the transition stage of the July Revolution. It also analyzes the crucial role played by prominent jurists—first and foremost, the Supreme Court Judges ʿAbd al-Razzaq al-Sanhuri and Sulayman Hafiz—in the establishment of the legal foundations of the new regime. The lion's share of the book discusses a selected number of trials held by two special tribunals, which prosecuted more than one thousand of the junta's opponents.

The Revolution's Court (*Mahkamat al-Thawra*) was set up about a year after the coup. Pursuant to the government decree establishing the tribunal, the latter was given jurisdiction over the following areas: "Actions deemed to be treason against the homeland [*khiyanat al-watan*]"; domestic and foreign threats to the country's "wellbeing"; "actions directed against the present government, or against the foundation upon which the revolution was instituted"; and individuals accused of corrupting the government and allowing "imperialism" to thrive in Egypt. "[All] this has caused the rotting of the political life," as influence was exploited "without taking into account the good of the homeland."[1] Within this framework, dozens of senior and low-level position holders from the previous regime were tried. In the wake of the failed attempt on Gamal ʿAbd al-Nasser's life (October 26, 1954), the FO established the People's Court (*Mahkamat al-Shaʿb*), another tribunal with extraordinary powers, which passed judgment on over eight hundred of the Muslim Brothers (MB) movement's activists and its entire leadership. Once again, the judges and prosecutors—members of the revolution's vanguard and the attorney general's office, respectively—were vested with exceptional powers that allowed them to reach quick verdicts and impose onerous penalties on those found guilty.

The establishment of the two special tribunals under review coincided with the most serious political crisis between the new regime and the mélange of groups comprising the opposition, led by the Wafd and the MB. By this point, the euphoria surrounding King Faruq's exile and the unbridled public adoration for the revolution's heroes had worn off. Although the Revolution Command Council's (RCC) supporters were in the ascendancy and despite the tightening crackdown against the opposition, piercing criticism of the new regime was still tolerated in the public discourse. At the heart of the debate stood the legitimacy of the army's continued rule. This pivotal issue was not only a matter of controversy between the FO and the opposition but also reared up within the upper echelons of government. President Naguib was in favor of a quick transfer of power to an elected civilian leadership, whereas the majority of the RCC's members, not least ʿAbd al-Nasser, insisted on holding onto to the reins for several more years.

The trials that this book discusses indeed corresponded with the public dispute over the military government's legitimacy. The argument can be made that *Mahkamat al-Thawra* contended with the following rudimentary question: Why was it absolutely necessary for the FO to intervene and overthrow the monarchial regime? *Mahkamat al-Shaʿb* dealt with this issue in the context of the political struggle that followed in the wake of the coup. In the process, its sessions responded to another burning question: Some two years after toppling the monarchy, why had the army yet to return to the barracks?

The RCC's decision to establish the special tribunals hardly stemmed from legal considerations. The need for swift convictions and severe punishments notwithstanding, these courts had much broader goals. Above all, they were intent on advancing the regime's initial plans and priorities for the new political order in the face of a determined opposition. Although these tribunals were putatively charged with adjudicating specific defendants, they passed judgment on entire organizations and imposed collective punishment on their members. A good example is the hearings of former Prime Minister Ibrahim ʿAbd al-Hadi, which for all intents and purposes constituted a mini-trial against the entire monarchical order. Similarly, the trial of Gamal ʿAbd al-Nasser's would-be assassin, Mahmud ʿAbd al-Latif, placed the spotlight on the MB in an effort to justify the RCC's efforts to shut down the movement's operations.

Throughout the years of revolutionary experimentation, thousands of the RCC's opponents were tried before exceptional judiciary frameworks. This book concentrates on the first trials that were held in *Mahkamat al-Thawra* and *Mahkamat al-Shaʿb*, namely, the cases of ʿAbd al-Hadi, ʿAbd al-Latif and Hasan al-Hudaybi, for three primary reasons.[2] To begin, the premium that the regime placed on the opening trials and the accompanying public discourse conferred a special standing on these courts. More than anything else, the tribunals' "prestige" attested to the fact that their jurisdiction went beyond deliberating over the serious charges against the accused and sentencing the guilty. The first trials were conducted within the framework of a vast state-run propaganda campaign that netted extensive press coverage. The second reason for choosing these particular trials is the availability of pertinent documents. Unlike the other cases brought before these courts, the transcripts of these trials were published in their entirety a few months after the verdicts were released. Comparing these transcripts with other sources (mainly biographical works) indicates that the offenses imputed to the earlier defendants resurfaced time and again in later trials. Furthermore, these charges perfectly mirrored the broad goals for these tribunals that were set by the RCC.

The Courts' Transcripts

The unusual decision to publish the full transcripts of the trials against those vilified as "enemies of the people" was another key facet of the campaign to drum up pubic interest in the special tribunals. More specifically, hundreds of hours of court proceedings were recorded and transcribed, and several months after each of the two tribunals' operations had wound down, their records were published in the form of official volumes by the Information Authority (*hayat al-istiʿlamat*), a unit of the National Guidance Ministry (*wizrat al-irshad al-qawmi*).[3] This government office was established in November 1952 for the purpose of disseminating the government's positions on various topics, and its purview steadily expanded over the years of revolutionary experimentation. The three volumes of *Mahkamat al-Thawra* (1,169 pages) and the seven volumes of *Mahkamat al-Sha'b* (1,650 pages) constitute the most extensive public documentation of these trials. This singular corpus records the panoply of voices that were heard during the proceedings, beginning with the announcer's cry of "court" (*mahkama*) and ending with remarks by random people attending the sessions. The exchanges between the judges, the prosecution, the accused, the defense, and the witnesses are cited verbatim. The fact that the proceedings against the MB netted two editions speaks to the importance that the regime placed on the trials against the movement's leadership.

It bears noting that the regime published the transcripts of only those trials that it deemed to be of public interest. Several of these trials were held behind closed doors, so that only a small and truncated portion of their transcripts were brought to print. Of course, all of the published material may have been edited and even censored by the Information Authority. This possibility must be kept in the back of the scholar's mind upon examining these texts. However, it does not detract from the value of this extraordinary source, which records dialogue straight from the courtroom at an unparalleled scope. The relevance of these documents is compounded by the fact that the Egyptian state archives (from 1922 onward) are closed to researchers, especially foreigners. The regime's very decision to publish official editions of the records from *Mahkamat al-Thawra* and *Mahkamat al-Sha'b* soon after these courts had wrapped up their work was far from given. In any event, these publications attest to the importance that the government placed on infusing the special tribunals' rhetoric into the public sphere. To maximize the trials' public relations potential, so the thinking went, they had to be made public.

The documentation and circulation of the transcripts of these quasi-legal hearings was meant to publically condemn the "enemies of the revolution" on the basis of the rhetoric that was generated in the special courts. Albeit indirectly, these steps were also meant to justify the very establishment of *Mahkamat al-Thawra* and *Mahkamat al-Sha'b*. The text, along with the graphic design and photos, in the introductions and afterwords to these volumes focused on highlighting the "danger" that those convicted by the tribunals posed to the Egyptian regime and society. In turn, this threat justified the need for the courts' irregular juridical steps. The publication of the two courts records was also intended to serve as a starting point for the construction of the revolution's new hegemonic narrative, which stood in stark contradistinction to that of the opposition (the previous regime, the parties, and the MB).

The editors of these publications took the trouble to emphasize that special tribunals were an integral part of the Egyptian legal tradition. However, they also pointed to the differences between the current versions of this institution and their predecessors: "Whereas in the past Egypt had already known political trials," they were deployed by the powers that be to exact revenge rather than impart justice. The harsh punishments that were meted out in previous generations were a blatant violation of "human dignity" (*al-karama al-insaniya*). Such sentences were indeed handed down to Egyptians, who opposed the French and British occupation in the nineteenth century, including Ahmad 'Urabi. Conversely, the July Revolution's special courts, so the regime's speakers claimed, adhere to modern legal principles such as the safeguarding of defendants' rights and commensurate punishments. The establishment of the special tribunals under review was also placed in the historical context of Western revolutions during the modern era, not least the French Revolution. In the preface to the first volume of *Mahkamat al-Thawra*, the editor noted that "Goethe, the great German poet, told one of his friends on September 21, 1792 that 'On this day, in this place, was born a new epoch in the history of the world.' His words referred to the establishment of the court of the [French] Revolution, the end of the age of the monarchy, and the beginning of the age of the republic."[4] Comparisons to the French Revolution, which became a fixture in the RCC's rhetoric, offered both a local and universal contextualization for the activity of *Mahkamat al-Sha'b* and *Mahkamat al-Thawra*.

The commentary, graphic design, and photos that were integrated into the official editions of the transcripts reflect the significance that the regime placed on assimilating the court rhetoric into the public discourse. It is also worth noting that this "genre" evolved from one work to the next. While the first volume of *Mahkamat al-Sha'b* sufficed with the records and nothing else, introductions and afterwords were added to the later versions and the amount of information gradually expanded. These addenda stressed that the transcripts themselves "are not [only] the output of members of the court or the prosecution" but are also the same content that was taped and broadcast "on radio stations to every part of the world." In addition, the supplemental pages were written in a personal manner. For example, the foreword to the third volume of *Mahkamat al-Sha'b* concludes on the following note: "If you have not had a chance to obtain the first two volumes, get in touch with the publisher on 68 Qasr al-'Aini Street." This passage from the conclusion reads similiarly: "Read about the trials in this book and keep it in your home library, so that your children and grandchildren will be able to pore over them."[5]

The breadth of the accompanying material increased exponentially beginning with the fourth volume, which contained an introduction and a three-page afterword. In the preface, "the enlightened public" is invited "to read this historical record [*sijl ta'rikhi*]" that enumerates the crimes of "the Brothers' gang." The conclusion stresses that this work expounds on the offenses that were committed by "the members of [this] terrorist movement's secret apparatus." Moreover, it states that the defendants admitted their guilt "with their very [own] mouths" before the court and in the presence of "representatives of the foreign press, the local [media], and news agencies." According to the final sentence, the purpose behind this "record" is to inform "whoever does not yet know that terrorism is not a new phenomenon among the Brothers' movement, but it is a foundation among the important foundations" upon "which this movement was established."[6]

Similarly, there is an appendix titled "Some of the Incidents Carried Out by the Brothers Movement" between 1945 and 1949. On the next page is an advertisement informing readers that a limited number of the previous volumes are still available. "So if you did not get your copy," you can pick one up in Cairo's Tahrir Square at the Company for the Dissemination of the News. The preface suggests that the reader peruse through the bills of indictment, the defense's arguments, and the testimony of the accused. For those who heed this advice, "it is near certain that you will reach the same conclusion that the judges of the people reached."[7]

In light of the enormous public interest in the trials against senior MB officials, the regime published an abridged version of the minutes from *Mahkamat al-Sha'b*. Kamal 'Abd al-Hamid al-Kirah, who headed the tribunal's secretariat, was charged with editing this collection. The book is packed with information on the tribunal's work, photos of courtroom scenes, and biographical details of the state's representatives (judges and members of the prosecution and investigation offices). The vast majority of this edition is dedicated to the trials of 'Abd al-Nasser's would-be assassin and the movement's top brass. Its textual and visual content expands on the FO's rhetoric. In the dedication, for example, Kirah described the movement's leaders as egocentric individuals who "do not think about either their country or its future whatsoever. All their thoughts, activity, and struggles are centered exclusively on themselves."[8] The "true heroes" of this episode are the "internal security people" (*al-mabahith al-'ammah*) that exposed the perpetrators' intentions of strangling the July Revolution.

According to Kirah, this volume is dedicated to thoroughly exposing the MB's plans and true nature, even beyond the revelations of the court. To this end, the editor added commentaries and estimates on an array of different topics. For instance, the chapter "The Philosophy of the Brothers' Trials" grapples with the rhetorical question of "Whether Islam allows political murder?" In so doing, the book turns to a high-level authority, presenting the opinion of Shaykh Hasan al-Baquri. Once a top MB official, al-Baquri was expelled from the movement for agreeing to serve as minister of endowments in the Naguib government. At any rate, the shaykh argued in this volume that political murder is in absolute contravention of Islam. In making this point, he bolstered the court's claim that while the MB views itself to be a religious movement, its deeds run counter to the Muslim faith. Visual representations of the FO's rhetoric against the Brothers are sprinkled throughout this work. A case in point is the cover page. Foregrounding an illustration of a massive crowd are the new national flag and scales of justice—the symbol of the justice system. Atop this page is a photograph of 'Abd al-Latif, the would-be assassin. The next page is taken up by a photograph of the prime minister in full military attire; the underlying caption reads "The commander of the revolution, Lieutenant-Colonel Gamal 'Abd al-Nasser." This portrait underscores the fact that General Naguib was already stripped of power and that the helm was now firmly in 'Abd al-Nasser's hands.

The special court's transcripts also played a crucial role in their capacity as an "act." Their power rests in the fact that they are not merely another text that represents or conveys opinions, but they are also a record of direct "contact" and "dialogue" between two sides espousing antithetical views. Comparing the transcripts to the analogous press reports illuminates the differences between these sources. The lion's share of the trials was open to the public. However, most of the audience that was squeezed into the tribunal's undersized hall was comprised of radio and newspaper personnel, who reported at length from the venue. This comparison reaffirms both the importance of the full transcript and the inherent weaknesses of the media coverage. The trials indeed merited intensive coverage in the local press, but journalists were under heavy constraints. Some of these limitations stemmed from objective journalistic considerations, while others were political. To begin, the amount of space that any newspaper can devote to a single topic is limited. Furthermore, by the time the trials got underway, most of the press was already under tight government censorship and regulation. Consequently, the official state media outlets fully toed the revolution's line.[9]

Although the radio and press mediated between the regime and the public conversation, their reporting from the courtroom, the photos that they ran, and their editorial bent clearly differentiated between the "good guys" (the fomenters and supporters of the revolution) and the "bad" (the opposition). For example, an analysis of the media reports on the hearings at *Mahkamat al-Sha'b* indicates that the journalists' emphasis was on the charges brought by the state, the words of the judges and prosecutors, and the defendants or witnesses' admissions. Confessions like "I admit that I made a mistake" or "I regret what I did" became top headlines in the next day's papers. While some of the articles mentioned criticism that the accused or witnesses leveled at the court, these accounts were truncated and failed to provide enough context. In addition, *Mahkamat al-Sha'b*'s dubious juridical procedures were completely ignored. The majority of the writers simply regurgitated the government's official line that the court is a *special* tribunal and conspicuously refrained from broaching the topic of defendants' rights or the complaints as to the court's questionable procedures. For example, not one story referred to the points that were raised by Hasan al-Hudaybi. Before being elected General Guide (*al-murshid al-'amm*), Hudaybi put in many long years as a judge in a civil court. During his testimony (first as a witness and then as a defendant), he noted that the Egyptian code leaves no doubt that responsibility for a crime must be personal for the defendant to be held liable. However, in his estimation, the People's Court was seeking to convict hundreds of people who did not participate in and had no prior knowledge of the assassination plot. In sum, Hudaybi exposed a flaw in the tribunal's procedure, but the press refrained from bringing this matter to the public's attention.

This comparative textual analysis of the two courts' transcripts and the related media coverage demonstrates that the former provides a vastly more comprehensive picture than the media, which by this stage was basically a mouthpiece of the regime. The transcripts not only preserved the voices and arguments of the judges and state attorneys but also those of the accused and the witnesses. In the process, they betray the gaping differences between the official narrative, which tends to appear coherent and logical, and many of those put forth by the opposition. Put differently, competing narratives that the regime otherwise sought to exclude from the public sphere were meticulously recorded in our corpus. Consequently, the transcripts serve as a platform for voices and arguments that did not merit comparable attention in other sources. The defense and witnesses' responses to the judges and the prosecution's questions reveal shortcomings in the official narrative. Moreover, they enhance our understanding of the conceptions and patterns of the regime's opponents. For instance, the testimony of senior MB officials sheds light on the movement's deep involvement in social, political, and national matters, thereby refuting the state's claim that the MB was a radical religious cult aimed at sowing chaos in Egypt.

In addition, the transcripts repeatedly show that the MB's helmsmen were the FO's closest allies in the years before the coup. During the first year of the military regime, the collaboration between the two steadily grew. In parallel, their disagreements were mainly over political and national issues, such as whether the movement should join the coalition, the drafting of the constitution, the renewal of party and parliamentary activity, and relations with Britain. The rhetoric of *Mahkamat al-Sha'b* sought to conceal these ties, but the special court's records clearly point to tight cooperation between the two sides. The local media's inadequate coverage strengthens my hypothesis that the court transcripts are the only source that allows scholars to assay the direct dialogue between the regime's representatives and its rivals at the trials under review.

For this reason, the transcripts of *Mahkamat al-Thawra* and *Mahkamat al-Sha'b* constitute the principal source of this book. That said, I also relied on an array of other sources. To begin, I examined the official documents including decrees and laws that paved the way for the establishment of these special tribunals. A case in point is clause 8 of "the constitutional declaration" that was promulgated in February 1953. Numerous texts illuminate the work of the committee that was charged with drafting a new constitution. Moreover, *Revolutionary Justice* unveils a pair of RCC-issued decrees, which determined the courts' procedures and authority. I also drew heavily on tens of diaries, memoirs, and other texts by figures who took part in the dramatic events of the July Revolution, including jurists, defendants, and witnesses. Similar use was made of newspapers and magazines from this period as well as news reports that were screened in movie theaters before the main feature.

From a theoretical standpoint, this work leans on insights from the literature on "states of exception" (Schmidt and Agamben). The discussion on the special tribunals is set in the context of the formation of Egypt's modern legal system since the 1870s (Brown, Asad, and Esmeir). Finally, this book draws heavily on the work of micro-historians, especially those who adopt a socio-legal approach and focus on legal proceedings in modern Middle Eastern societies. From a methodological standpoint, these researchers introduced a process for assessing complex historical phenomena that does not necessarily stress the legal proceedings against their protagonists. Some of their studies are predicated on court transcripts or minutes (Iris Agmon; Leslie Pierce; Avi Rubin), whereas others employ subsequent accounts of the proceedings (Carlo Ginzburg; Natalie Zemon Davis). Following Giovanni Levi's concept on microhistory, my study deals with both individuals and the state. By delving into the trials of political dissenters, we can enhance our understanding of the 'big picture'—the complex struggle over the formation of republican Egypt following the coup of July 1952. The findings indeed validate Levi's key argument that microhistory concentrates on "fragmentation, contradictions and plurality of viewpoints."[10]

Revolutionary Justice consists of three overarching parts. In the beginning of the first part, "The Legal Dimensions of a Coup," I explore various facets of the limited and problematic discussion in the literature on the special tribunals' activities that pertain to the July Revolution's wide-ranging historiography. For the most part, the cases heard by the two courts are presented as "show trials" that offer scant insight on the political reality in Egypt during the period at hand. There is indeed little doubt that the regime wielded these tribunals like a cudgel against its opponents. More specifically, their proceedings seriously violated the defendants' rights, and the sweeping use of these frameworks was a severe blow to the Egyptian justice system. Nonetheless, these trials have considerable research value because the legal dimension of their activities was secondary. From the outset, the special courts were slated to achieve much more than convictions and punishments against particular defendants in a hasty juridical process. The trials that were conducted therein were meant to, and indeed had, a direct and substantial impact on the bitter struggle between the RCC and its domestic rivals over the contours of the new dispensation.

The first part of this book also discusses the historical context of special tribunals in Egypt. The chapter "Extraordinary Tribunals in Modern Egypt: A Genealogy" shows that the Egyptian colonial justice system inherited a model that was largely comprised of sundry French and British techniques, methods, and institutions. This heritage bestowed the country with a tangled legal framework, which included special tribunals, police, manifold intelligence services, and a prison authority. In addition, the justice system was informed by an inner contradiction between two of its principal components: an adoption of a positive law approach that strove to implement humanist values such as universal justice and exceptional legal procedures that trampled over the rights of subjects who defied the colonial regime. Prime examples of the latter are the heavy-handed juridical measures that the authorities took in the wake of both the ʿUrabi Revolt (1881–2) and the Dinshaway incident (1906) as well as the punishments imposed on the Wafd's leaders, especially Saʿd Zaghlul (1919–22). The resort to such exceptional means at the height of Egypt's colonial era indeed set the stage for the establishment of special courts in the decades to come.

The chapter "Whitewashing a Coup" assays the legal and political circumstances behind the formation and operation of the Revolution's Court and the People's Court. It also provides an in-depth analysis of the crucial legal infrastructure that was laid down by prominent jurists, especially the Supreme Court Judges Sanhuri and Hafiz, on behalf of the military regime. Furthermore, this chapter takes stock of the RCC's intensive use of decrees, laws, and constitutional declarations during the July Revolution's transition phase. While civil and criminal procedures continued to adhere formally to the existing law codes, the regime launched many of its juridical initiatives by power of fiat, such as the Treason Law and the decrees that gave rise to the two tribunals under review.

Part 2, "Judges as Historians," tracks *Mahkamat al-Thawra* over the course of the July Revolution's transition phase. The discussion focuses on this court's unique contribution to the forging and dissemination of the FO's new historical narrative. The information that the judges and prosecution extracted from defendants and witnesses constituted the raw material for the regime's negative portrayal of the Muhammad ʿAli Dynasty (1805–1952). Furthermore, the RCC used these testimonies to justify King Faruq's ouster, the abrogation of the monarchy, and the extraordinary steps it took to bury the old ruling, political, economic, and social order. The ʿAbd al-Hadi trial constitutes the focal point of this section.

The chapter "The Revolution's Court" analyzes the circumstances behind the establishment of *Mahkamat al-Thawra* and the RCC's justifications for resorting to exceptional legal means against the accused. It also scrutinizes the decree establishing the Revolution's Court, including the exceptional powers that were vested in the attorney general's office and the judges. Chapter 3 also takes stock of the legal proceedings against Ibrahim ʿAbd al-Hadi, who was charged with treason against the homeland, breach of trust, and corruption. The transcripts demonstrate how the judges and prosecutors incorporated these accusations into the RCC's official narrative of the monarchial period.

Lastly, this record captures the testy exchange between the judges and 'Abd al-Hadi's attorney, Mustafa Mar'i, who disclosed the court's serious violations of his client's basic rights.

Reconstructing the hegemonic narrative of Egypt's annals was of utmost importance to the FO. In the chapter "Who Was to Blame for the Debacle of 1948?" I contend that the judges and state prosecutors assumed the role of historians. The indictments, evidence, questioning of witnesses, the prosecution's closing arguments, and final verdicts were pieces of a puzzle that outlined the country's past and forged a new historical narrative of Egypt's defeat in the 1948 War. The king, his aides, members of government, and top generals were depicted as having ineptly prepared the army for battle, thereby throwing soldiers and officers into a campaign that was destined for failure. Furthermore, these same decision makers were accused of washing their hands of responsibility for this fiasco. The judges, who had personally taken part in the war, now spoke in the name of the combat forces. In so doing, they held the political echelon and top military brass accountable for the loss. The prosecution argued that the flawed management, such as the defective weapons episode and the launching of a campaign for which the army was ill-prepared, was just the tip of the iceberg of deep-seated venality. In sum, the court formulated a new historical narrative not only with respect to the past (e.g., the road to the War of 1948) but also the present—the revolution and its immediate aftermath—as well. The trial's rhetoric was intended, among other things, to answer the pressing questions of the day: Why should the military be allowed to continue running the state? And should it be trusted with the task of building a new order?

Chapter 5, "Rhetoric and Historical Polemics," delves into the rhetoric that was generated over the course of the 'Abd al-Hadi trial and the debate that this aroused over the rewriting of key chapters in Egyptian history. The exchanges on this topic during the trial points to *Mahkamat al-Thawra*'s ongoing correspondence with the new narrative that the FO were crafting in an effort to draw a contrast between the lax monarchial regime and the revolutionary dispensation in-the-making. The bill of indictment, the oral and written evidence, and the questioning of the accused directly linked the government's corruption under the stewardship of 'Abd al-Hadi, inter alia, to the serious damage on the nation's interests and the abuse of its citizens' rights. As part of their rhetoric, the judges and prosecutors emphasized the connection between the monarchial regime and the colonial powers. Similar to the public statements of RCC leaders, the court averred that from the first day of the coup, the July Revolution's primary objective was to extricate Egypt from the quagmire of colonialism and purify it from every last manifestation of corruption that had long hindered the people.

Part 3, "Turning Friends into Foes," shifts the spotlight onto *Mahkamat al-Sha'b*, the special tribunal that was established following the attempt on

Gamal ʿAbd al-Nasser's life on October 26, 1954. The botched assassination triggered a government crackdown that was intended to paralyze the MB, especially its upper echelons. During the preceding year, the new regime had become mired in a deep political crisis, which resulted from its attempts to force through a controversial transition plan. More than anything else, the court's trials reflected a dramatic turnaround in the junta's relations with the Islamic movement. The FO now portrayed the MB as a radical religious organization that embraces terrorism and imperils the public good. Consequently, it was imperative that the Brothers' activists are brought to justice before a special tribunal. The heavy punishments that the court imposed on the movement's leadership and thousands of its activists would indeed become a turning point in the intra-RCC struggle over the reins of power, as the dubious manner in which the accused were convicted for allegedly planning to overthrow the government ultimately resulted in President Naguib's dismissal. The helm was immediately seized by ʿAbd al-Nasser and his confederates, who proceeded to run an authoritarian regime—one that was destined to survive in various incarnations to this very day.

Chapter 6, "The Advent of the People's Court," reconstructs the circumstances behind the formation of *Mahkamat al-Shaʿb*. More specifically, it expounds on the decree that vested this tribunal with exceptional powers and established its trial procedures, which seriously curtailed the rights of the accused and witnesses. The emphasis of this chapter is on the trial of Mahmud ʿAbd al-Latif—a minor MB activist who made an attempt on the prime minister's life. Retracing the gunman's biography offers a rare glimpse of the Special Apparatus (SA)—the movement's paramilitary arm, to which the would-be assassin belonged. The court's transcripts demonstrate that the judges and prosecution's ambit was not limited to the circumstances behind the assassination bid or to securing evidence with which to convict the gunman and his superiors. To the contrary, the following topics were also broached over the course of the ʿAbd al-Latif trial: state and religion in Egypt, the relation between Islamic law (*Shariʿa*) and the Egyptian constitution and judiciary, various interpretations of jihad, and acts that are liable to provoke a civil war (*fitna*). In fact, the evidence against ʿAbd al-Latif was a mere sideshow in his own trial, which was primarily devoted to portraying the MB as an organization that skews the message of Islam for the sake of promoting a dangerous, extremist agenda.

Chapter 7, "Brothers–Officers Relations: What Went Wrong?," explores the movement's transformation from the revolutionary regime's closest ally to its main foe. The trials at *Mahkamat al-Shaʿb* offer rare documentation of how relations between the MB leadership and the army and police officers coalesced over the course of a ten-year period. It shows that contacts between the two sides were ratcheted up even further before the military coup, and, upon Faruq's disposal, the MB declared its support for the military's takeover of government and dubbed the revolution with its popular name "the blessed movement" (*al-haraka al-mubaraka*). However, the irreconcilable differences over issues that stood atop the junta's agenda, such as the drafting of a new constitution, the participation of MB representatives in the government, the agrarian reform, and the terms of Britain's withdrawal from Egypt, soon rose to the surface. 1954 was undoubtedly the RCC's year of decision, and its falling out with the MB was one of the more portentous developments. The transcripts of the People's Court expose these developments as well as the debate that raged within the MB's ranks over the movement's policy toward the regime from here onward.

Even before reading the verdict in ʿAbd al-Latif's trial, the judges began to deliberate over the serious bill of indictment that, in the meantime, was issued against Hasan al-Hudaybi. Chapter 8, "The Trial of the *Murshid*," explores this swift trial, which was indeed the culmination of *Mahkamat al-Shaʿb*'s dramatic proceedings against the MB. Among the charges against the MB leader was conspiring to overthrow the government by means of an armed insurrection that was liable to plunge Egypt into an intra-religious civil war (*fitna*). Comparing the words of the prosecution and the judges to those of the General Guide and his counsel exposes the tension between the regime's need to display a semblance of adhering to the existing law and its desire to bludgeon the MB by means of, among other things, a special tribunal.

By scrutinizing the court's records of the proceedings against various MB members who were tied to the assassination attempt, this chapter takes stock of the correspondence between the public discourse and court rhetoric. It explores how the rhetoric generated over the course of the trials against the would-be assassin and the MB's senior officials percolated into the local media, which in general labeled Hudaybi and his fellow MB helmsmen "the enemies of the people and the revolution." I contend that the rhetoric that was generated by against the movement's senior officials constitutes a unique product of *Mahkamat al-Shaʿb*, which played a critical role in stoking the e-mergency atmosphere throughout the country. In the end, this tribunal also helped tip the scales in the struggle over the RCC' continued rule.

ʿAbd al-Nasser and the FO strove to replace the monarchy with a system of government that is based on democracy and social justice. Its social and political achievements notwithstanding, the RCC laid the foundations for the establishment of an authoritarian regime that would last for decades, under the leadership of ʿAbd al-Nasser, Anwar Sadat, and Hosni Mubarak. As the recent popular uprising against the latter gained momentum, a riveting public debate examined the similarities and differences between the July 1952 and January 2011 revolutions. Drawing on insights from the present study, the final chapter, "Trapped between Two Revolutions," compares the transition phase now underway to the events of 1952.

PART I

The Legal Dimensions of a Coup

1

Extraordinary Tribunals in Modern Egypt: A Genealogy

In the historiography of modern Egypt, the July Revolution is accurately presented as a historic turning point that spawned a new ruling, political, economic, and social order in the land of the Nile. Furthermore, the policies and ideologies that were pursued under ʿAbd al-Nasser's leadership had far-reaching implications for the greater Middle East. Over the years, revolutionary Egypt has attracted researchers from manifold disciplines. For decades, scholars have focused on the Nasserite ideology as well as the domestic and foreign policies that the Egyptian government adopted between the second half of the 1950s and the president's death on September 28, 1970. Emphasis has been placed on the charismatic leader's personality.[1] The thesis whereby ʿAbd al-Nasser's personality was the driving force behind Egyptian foreign and domestic policy looms large in both academic and semi-academic publications.[2] Many of these works are not only positivistic in their approach to the sources but also put a premium on official government views.

From the early 1980s onward, historians have sought to revise the accepted narrative of the political struggles in the wake of the July Revolution. Since then, a significant shift in the historiography of the revolution took root, from an overemphasis on ʿAbd al-Nasser to the inclusion of other groups from among the elite and larger social strata. Klein examines the attitude of intellectuals toward the FO's regime, including those who supported the revolution and worked toward advancing its goals and those who were opposed to the new order.[3] In *Nasser's Blessed Movement*, Gordon debunks many of the prevalent claims with respect to the overthrow of the monarchial regime. Taking issue with Vatikiotis, Gordon convincingly argues that most of the RCC's decisions were a spontaneous reaction to events, rather than the logical outcome of a coherent ideological worldview. When the public started to get wind of the revolution's objectives, not only did an array of civil groups object to these plans but also furious power struggles erupted within the top ranks of the new regime.[4]

The "revisionists" have largely ignored the conduct of the RCC in the constitutional and legal spheres, the special courts included. In contrast, the establishment of the modern Egyptian justice system, from the latter stages of the nineteenth century until the mid-twentieth century, has commanded quite a bit of scholarly attention.[5] That said, the discussion concerning that period's special tribunals and the legal tradition on which they were founded is rather paltry. Even scanter is the literature on the juridical realm during the period of revolutionary experimentation that was ushered in by the FO. This lacuna is all the more pronounced in light of the substantial changes in this field during the July Revolution. To wit, the balance between the executive and the other branches of government was significantly altered; the *Shari'a* courts were abrogated, and a new constitution was adopted. Throughout the transition to the republican model, civil and criminal jurisprudence continued to adhere to the code that steadily took shape from the late nineteenth century onward. However, many of the RCC's steps, including the establishment of the Revolution's Court and the People's Court, were predicated on decrees that it issued.

The absence of references to legal developments is especially glaring in the writing of distinguished Egyptian jurists, particularly 'Abd al-Razzak al-Sanhuri, the chief justice of the Supreme Court (*majlis al-dawla*), and his deputy Sulayman Hafiz. These two figures played a crucial role in the July Revolution's transition phase, as they laid the juridical foundations of the new regime.[6] Both men subsequently had a falling out with the heads of the RCC, especially 'Abd al-Nasser. This turn of events reached a nadir when Sanhuri was severely beaten by thugs—who in all likelihood were operating as part of the state's security apparatus—and with Hafiz incarcerated. Sanhuri's personal diary, which was published years later under his daughter Nadya's editorship, describes the chief justice's support for the coup and his high expectations for a new social and political dispensation in Egypt. The jurist's entries do not contain much information on his involvement in the construction of the republican legal system or any direct reference to the special tribunals. However, Sanhuri excoriates the RCC-led government in *al-shahid* (the martyr), an allegorical poem that he wrote against the backdrop of the heavy punishments that the People's Court meted out to MB activists in December 1954.[7] Conversely, most of Hafiz's book, *My Memories of the Revolution*, is dedicated to the regime's juridical initiatives, including the author's input in the design of the legal/political order during the transition phase. Like his mentor (Sanhuri), though, Hafiz is silent with respect to the special tribunals.[8]

'Abd al-Rahman al-Rafi'i, an historian and jurist, penned two books and many articles lauding the July Revolution. When the FO seized power, he was putting the finishing touches on a book series called The History of the

National Movement. In light of the dramatic events in Egypt, al-Rafiʿi decided to seal the series with two more works. The first book, *Foreword to the Revolution of July 23, 1952*, offers a comprehensive version of the FO's historical narrative of the country's travails under the monarchial regime. According to this plotline, Faruq's reign was corrupt, out of touch with society, and inveterately undemocratic. Al-Rafiʿi principal argument is that the military coup was a historic turning point that liberated Egyptian society from a venal political order, which was concocted by and operated under the aegis of the British Empire. His second book, *The Revolution of July 23, 1952: Our National History over the Past Seven Years*, was a paean to the RCC government. It includes tens of decrees and laws that the regime promulgated as well as a short account of the establishment of the two special tribunals under review. All told, this uncritical survey refrains from analyzing the information that it provides. In evaluating the first seven years of the July Revolution, al-Rafiʿi asserted that there is no doubt that it "will be considered the most successful of revolutions in the modern history of Egypt."[9]

Even jurists who were critical of the revolution refrained from writing about the legal aspects and the evolution of the special tribunals. A fine example is the writing of Wahid Ra'fat, who identified with the Wafd. In fact, he represented this leading liberal party in its legal disputes with the new regime and defended a number of suspects who were prosecuted by the Revolution's Court. Although Ra'fat's legal writing and opinion pieces are characterized by a matter-of-fact style, his criticism of the FO's misuse of the justice system in its confrontations with political adversaries was unsparing.[10] In particular, he castigated Sanhuri and Hafiz for their part in the institution of the new authoritarian order. Ra'fat describes their efforts as a mortal blow to the Constitution of 1923 and to parliamentary life in Egypt. More specifically, the legal legitimacy that they imparted to the regime enabled its leaders to force their will on society and compromise the liberties that were anchored in the constitution.[11] He also exposed the deep disagreements within the upper echelons of the Egyptian legal elite in all that concerned the new regime. It bears noting that Ra'fat was dismissed from one of the Supreme Court committees on which he served; the committee was headed by none other than Hafiz. With respect to the special tribunals in question, Ra'fat served as a defense attorney in a few of their trials. As we shall see, his views on the tribunals' functioning are very clear in the relevant court minutes. However, he ignores this topic in his writing.

Fleeting references to the special courts turn up in two books that Tariq al-Bishri devoted to the RCC's struggles over the shape of the new dispensation. His basic argument is that the FO indeed aspired to bring about comprehensive change but never got around to devising a thorough plan. The laws and edicts that the RCC introduced were more often than not knee-jerk reactions to developments on the ground, and it was in this impromptu manner that the new government gradually came into being. Moreover, he argues that a substantial portion of the FO's initiatives, such as repeal of the 1923 Constitution and the call to clean up Egyptian politics was, in essence, an iteration of past proposals. That said, the revolution, according to Bishri, had infused these activities with new meaning, which engendered a different outcome. The Agrarian Reform Law was the regime's first significant initiative.[12] While noting that this legislation was predicated on a legal opinion drawn up by Sanhuri and Hafiz, he refrains from passing judgment on this issue. Bishri observes that many of the revolutionary regime's announcements were promulgated "in the name of the people." In other words, the RCC assumed that the average Egyptian supported the revolution and agreed with the steps that were being taken in his or her name. However, in the historian's estimation, this same nation was not asked for its opinion, as the RCC eschewed referendums or elections that would have enabled the people's representatives to partake in the decision-making process.[13] Bishri only mentions the special courts in passing while discussing the clear signs of torture on the bodies of MB activists who were prosecuted by the Revolution's Court.[14]

In a comprehensive study on the rule of law in Arab states, Nathan Brown discusses the role of special tribunals in the broader context of the modern Egyptian justice system. His main hypothesis is that Western imperialism played a much smaller role in this enterprise than is often believed. According to Brown, the legal reforms that were adopted in the second half of the nineteenth century were no less than acts of resistance against foreign occupation. Furthermore, they were intended to serve as the cornerstone of the nation-state's modern institutions. The reforms, he claims, were much more evolutionary than revolutionary: "There was certainly no sudden break from a system based largely on Islamic jurisprudence to the Code Napoléon; rather there was a gradual emergence of a centralized and hierarchical state-sponsored system."[15] This implies that the British did not incorporate substantial changes into the local justice system. To the intriguing question of why the Egyptian elite preferred a European-style system even though the colonial powers did not compel them to do so, Brown offers the following answer:

> While some reasons for turning to France had nothing to do with imperialism, in some other ways use of the French model could actually be a tool of resisting direct European penetration. In this limited sense, legal reform could be an indirect effect of—or more accurately, a preemptive response to—imperialism. . . . Thus the Mixed Courts were designed not to serve imperialism but to limit the effects of the capitulations.[16]

The new Egyptian legal system, Brown asserts, was driven by a desire to launch both a liberal order and a strong ruling system at the same time. In his estimation, the French civil code served as the "primary source" for the Egyptian code because it was consistent with these aspirations.[17]

The weakness of these arguments rests in the paltry role and impact that Brown ascribes to the colonial powers in the design of Egypt's modern legal system. He overlooks the asymmetrical balance of power between the colonial powers and the local authorities as well as the motives behind British imperial policy. Even if the interests of the two sides diverged with respect to the legal reforms, the assumption that the khedival regime had the wherewithal to do as it pleased cannot be reconciled with the actual circumstances, which have been meticulously documented in the literature.[18] In response to Brown's contention that the legal reform was intended to establish a strong system of government, the argument can be made that this objective coincided with the interests of Britain, whose sway over Egypt increased throughout the course of the colonial era.

Talal Asad and, more recently, Samera Esmeir have broken thematic and methodological ground on the construction of the modern order in Egypt under British colonial rule. Both improve our understanding of the deep rupture in the legal sphere due to the forced replacement of the *Shari'a*-grounded Ottoman-khedival code with positive law. In fact, Asad and Esmeir cast doubt on many of Brown's premises and arguments. The former contends that imperialism played a key role in the formulation and launching of this reform. According to Asad, the social and cultural changes that transpired during this period constituted "some of the basic preconditions for secular modernity." The ability to create a strategic buffer between the law of and society's ethical norms epitomized "the colonial situation, because it is this separation that enables the legal work of educating subjects into a new public morality."[19]

Moreover, Asad contends that Brown became over-enamored with the idea of the resistance of subalterns; namely, he believed that the Egyptians had the ability to fend off unwanted European reforms. Brown's position ignores the fact that resistance to the reforms was considered a sign of "rigidity and reaction." In addition, some of the opposition was driven by the fear that their material interests would be harmed. Asad also takes issue with Brown on the reform of the *Shari'a* legal tradition in colonial Egypt. He deftly shows that the reform did not center on restricting the use of *Shari'a* law to certain areas but on altering its standing within the framework of the modern justice system.[20]

Insofar as Esmeir is concerned, modern law is among the sources and catalysts of the colonial project. To begin, it helped the British consolidate the imperial order in Egypt. The next step in the country's physical occupation was the impairment of its local law. This objective was accomplished via a series of reforms that introduced modern positive codes and eviscerated the existing Ottoman-khedival legal tradition.[21] Like Asad, Esmeir excoriates Brown for confusing outcome with cause in his analysis of the relations between Britain and the khedival government. These flaws, Esmeir asserts, stem from his subordination of the juridical field to the political goals it was meant to serve. Missing from Brown's research is the power of the law itself and the deep impact that its centuries of service had on the social and political order.

Esmeir contends that the legal reform that was initiated in Egypt during the final decades of the 1800s revolved around a unique conception of positive law, which was informed by a "division of labor" between the local khedival government and the British colonial administration. London's representatives sought to advance a legal reform that suited their particular needs. To this end, they brought to bear the full weight of their influence as advisors to the local government and, when all was said and done, ultimately managed to dictate the content of the new legal code. Technically speaking, the British merely offered advice on the wording of orders and laws, which were then published by the khedive and the prime minister. This development gave rise to a tectonic shift. The legal tradition that was customary in khedival Egypt was abandoned in favor of a new code of law and justice system.[22]

Egyptian jurists, who had acquired their education in European universities, played an instrumental role in the implementation of this reform. These local scholars espoused positive law as well as a drastic reduction in the use of Ottoman and *Shari'a* legal traditions. Their position was grounded on the unfounded claim that the old dispensation never constituted a worthy justice system.[23] As in other societies subjected to a colonial regime, there was a profound dissonance in the Egyptian justice system: On the one hand, it featured positive legal codes, which leaned on the tenets of humanism and universal principles of law, and, on the other hand, the authorities availed themselves of exceptional juridical procedures to break the local population's resistance to the colonial regime.[24] Despite the heavy use of these measures, the fact that the exceptional component of the system was cut off from the standard codes bestowed legitimacy upon the system's positivistic elements. As Esmeir put it:

> The special tribunals operated as purifying agents for the institutions of the juridical order. Far from violating the general juridical order, they shielded it. . . . More than anything, exceptional legalities maintained the power of the general normative order, potentially revealing, for those who succeed in avoiding the seduction of law's ideality, the hybridity of the law.[25]

In their rhetoric, the British technocrats stressed that they were committed to safeguarding the rule of law and upholding the right to a fair trial, but the reality was a far cry from these lofty principles. Special courts, military tribunals, and brigandage commissions were set up, and martial law was instituted for the purpose of meeting the many challenges of defending Britain's interests in Egypt. The exceptional powers that were granted to these bodies, the trial procedures that were in force, and the punishments handed down by judges stood in stark contradistinction to the principles of justice that London ostensibly championed. Esmeir's study exposes not only the technologies of control that the colonial regime developed but also the tension and wide chasm between the humanist ideals that the British administration professed to uphold and the actual state of affairs in Egypt, especially the violence that was ingrained in the colonial regime. In fact, Esmeir argues that Britain's involvement in exceptional juridical measures preceded the physical occupation of Egypt.

Special Courts before 1952

The trials against ʿUrabi as well as dozens of military personnel and civilians who took part in the rebellion against Khedive Tawfiq (1881–2) set a legal precedent in modern Egypt for the use of special courts. The extraordinary judicial procedures, panel of judges, stern sentences, and public debates over the trials reared up time and again in tens of subsequent cases, including the cases under review.

Toward the end of the 1870s, Egypt was brought to its knees by a severe economic and political crisis. Unable to repay enormous loans from European financial institutions—the majority of which were taken to advance colossal projects that were initiated by Khedive Ismaʿil (r. 1863–79), particularly the completion of the Suez Canal—the country declared bankruptcy. Under the leadership of Britain and France, the *Caisse de la Dette Publique* (Public Debt Commission) was set up to supervise the Egyptian budget externally. From this point onward, foreign intervention in the country's affairs steadily increased, including in the field of jurisprudence. European advisors were assigned to key posts in the ruling establishment. Correspondingly, the economic pressure, particularly the tax burden on the local peasants, became intolerable. This predicament stoked rural insurrections, which were put down with a heavy hand. Several Egyptians who were charged with attacking foreigners were tried in the Mixed Courts. Established in 1875, these courts were based on the French model and adhered to an overarching civil and criminal legal code.[26] The Egyptian intelligentsia and the lower ranks of the officer corps also vented their frustration with both the khedival government and the colonial influence. In turn, the government clamped down on the press, and the senior military command took steps to silence the criticism of their subordinates.

The protest of the junior officers, the vast majority of whom were ethnic Egyptians from the lower socio-economic classes, was headed by Colonel Ahmad ʿUrabi. Their initial demand was to improve their salaries and career tracks. In other words, they sought to break the dominance of the senior officer class, almost all of whom were members of the Turco-Circassian elite (this same group also dominated the local economy and the government apparatus). ʿUrabi also took up the cause of other groups, even personally raising their demands before Khedive Tawfiq. Cole has accurately summarized the colonel's position:

> Ahmad 'Urabi demanded the reinstitution of the chamber of delegates and the drawing up of a constitution, complained of Ottoman ethnic dominance, and insisted on the restoration of the army to 18,000 men. In doing so, he created a platform upon which a variety of forces in civil society could agree.[27]

With the backing of the colonial powers, Tawfiq summarily rejected these demands. As a result, the confrontation snowballed into an open rebellion. Led by 'Urabi and his allies in the army, the insurrection merited the support of various sectors of Egyptian society. On the grounds that his policies were furthering Britain's interests and compromising those of Egypt, the rebels demanded that the khedive step down. Britain and France rushed to the aid of the viceroy, who had essentially lost the backing of wide swathes of the populace. The military campaign opened with a heavy bombardment of rebel positions in Alexandria. Thereafter, infantry troops parachuted down and secured the country's main transportation arteries. Britain's superior armed forces easily defeated 'Urabi's troops. Consequently, Tawfiq was able to solidify his rule. In addition, the rebellion paved the way for the British occupation of Egypt and its colonial regime.

Following the rebels' defeat, the powers that be vacillated over which juridical procedures would govern the trials against the insurgents and the punishments that would be assessed. The customary legal tradition in Egypt was radically different from how Britain's representatives wished to conduct the 'Urabi trial. Formally speaking, the decision was in the hands of Tawfiq. The khedive ultimately issued a decree that led to the establishment of four committees that were charged with investigating those suspected of collaborating with the rebellion, collecting evidence against the accused, and determining whether they should be tried before a military court or some other framework. Serving on these committees were a number of British assistants and two European judges. London's representatives exerted their influence on Tawfiq behind the scenes, and the final outcome was a compromise between the various stakeholders.[28]

'Urabi was convicted of leading a mutiny, but the Egyptian viceroy managed to lighten his punishment. Instead of carrying out the judges' death sentence, 'Urabi was stripped of his rank and property and exiled from Egypt. The British technocrats praised Tawfiq for not acting like a tyrant. Moreover, Lord Dufferin, the British Commissioner to Egypt, informed his superiors that "we got rid" of the rebels and Egypt is ready for "rebuilding."[29] The exceptional juridical procedures and firm punishments were to Britain's satisfaction. They also constituted an important legal and political precedent at the early stages of the British occupation of Egypt. It bears noting that the 'Urabi trial was conducted against the backdrop of a lively discourse on the possibility of adopting comprehensive judicial reform in the land of the Nile. Tawfiq and his cabinet, which was headed by Prime Minister Muhammad Sharif, were in favor of introducing a legal code that was based on French law. As per a khedival memorandum issued on December 7, 1883, the government's objective was to establish a liberal justice system that would suit Egypt's present needs.[30] In addition, the memorandum laid down some of the juridical principles that would undergird the new system.

Over the next few years, nationalist activists charged with assaulting Europeans and British army personnel as well as the khedival regime's rivals were tried in various frameworks. The former were, by and large, adjudicated in regular courts, pursuant to the country's penal code. However, a special decree issued by Khedive 'Abbas Hilmi II in 1895 was meant to standardize the court procedures for such offenses. It was within this framework that the special tribunals were institutionalized. Esmeir lucidly summarizes this decree:

> The special tribunal was composed of the judicial advisor, a British judge of the National Court of Appeal, the judicial advisor to the British forces of occupation in Cairo and Alexandria, and the chief justice of the court of either Alexandria or Cairo. The hearings were public, the arguments only presented orally, and defendants' lawyers admitted. The tribunal operated in accordance with the Code of Criminal Procedure, so long as it did not result in changing the summary and the swift nature of the proceedings, and the Penal Code; the tribunal could punish the offenders as it saw fit. . . . The jurisdiction of tribunals was confined to the cases put forward by the British consul-general through the Ministry of Foreign Affairs.[31]

The Egyptian justice system's resort to exceptional procedures was exemplified by the Dinshaway incident. This episode, which is ingrained in the Egyptian national memory as a traumatic event and a symbol of cruel colonialism, began with a pigeon hunt on the part of five British officers and a military physician in Dinshaway (a village in Menufiyya province). Much to the chagrin of local peasants who raised pigeons to augment their incomes, such hunts had become a popular hobby among British residing in Egypt.[32] Confrontations over these expeditions usually ended without casualties, but the events of June 13, 1906 proved to be an exception to this rule. In the British and Egyptian sources, the details of this incident read as a *Rashomon*, as there are wide discrepancies between how each of the sides recorded the facts and interpreted their ramifications.

Roger Owen, who predicated his account of this episode on a detailed British report, notes that the military personnel embarked on the hunt without receiving the customary approval of the head of the village. At some point, one of the officers fired a shot that lit up a pile of grain. A melee ensued between tens of incensed villagers and the hunting party, with both sides inflicting casualties. Major Pine-Coffin, the senior officer at the scene, ordered his men to hand over their weapons to the villagers, on the assumption that they would then be allowed to leave in peace. However, this gesture failed to mollify the residents, so the major ordered the doctor and a Captain Bull, who suffered multiple head wounds, to flee the scene and summon help. Upon reaching the nearby base, Bull collapsed due to his injuries and sun stroke and died shortly thereafter.[33]

At the initiative of Lord Cromer and the all-powerful British Agent and Consul-General and pursuant to ʿAbbas Hilmi's aforementioned decree, the government established a special court to bring the Egyptians involved in the Dinshaway incident to justice, even though the standard, national (*ahaliya*) courts had jurisdiction over such cases (including the authority to sentence to death those found guilty). It stands to reason that Cromer was afraid that a trial in the regular system would drag on for months. In any event, the diplomatic correspondence leaves no doubt that these proceedings were intended to fulfill a wide array of goals, which went far beyond securing convictions. In his riveting political biography on Lord Cromer, Owen maps out the ulterior motives that were at play:

> As he [Cromer] had written to the Foreign Secretary at that time, he wanted to have some machinery at hand that would deal "swiftly and summarily" with attacks on British soldiers and sailors with the power to inflict "severer punishment" than was possible in the national courts. Swift and summary it was.[34]

On June 24, 1906, fifty or so villagers were brought before the special tribunal. Presiding over the court was Butrus Ghali Pasha, the acting minister of justice; the future prime minister was joined on the bench by two British and two Egyptian jurists. The swift proceedings, which lasted only three days, ended with the main suspects being convicted of intentional murder. Notwithstanding the contradictory evidence surrounding the captain's demise, severe punishments were assessed without any recourse to appeal. The verdict was carried out the very next day in Dinshaway. Before hundreds of local residents, four villagers were hung to death. In addition, nine were literally whiplashed, and thirteen soon began prison sentences of varying lengths, including two life terms. It is worth noting that by virtue of ordinances that were passed several years earlier, flogging of this sort and execution by hanging were no longer practiced in Egypt. Prosecuting the villagers before a special court and the cruel punishments that were handed down were meant to shock Egyptian public opinion—to sow fear and terror and, above all, to demonstrate what awaited anyone who dared harm His Majesty's soldiers. In other words, these verdicts made it abundantly clear that the exceptional proceedings were a sanctioned means—albeit one that ran roughshod over the defendants' fundamental rights—for asserting control and achieving deterrence.

The harsh verdicts underscored the gap between the colonial regime's stated commitment to the rule of law and its conduct in practice. In fact, the Dinshaway incident made waves throughout Egypt as well as in Britain and France. Nationalist speakers and intellectuals, led by Mustafa Kamil (whose speeches and articles were published in Arabic and French), condemned the violent and arbitrary nature of British rule, especially the manner in which the regime exploited an ostensibly legitimate legal process and ignored the principles of justice and humanism. Moreover, these same observers exhorted the public to intensify the struggle for national liberation. A renowned poet, Sayyid Darwish, wrote poems about Dinshaway. The incident was interpreted as a watershed mark in the struggle for national liberation, as reflected in historical writing—including scholarly research, textbooks, and writings for general consumption—and popular literature.[35]

While later serving as prime minister, Judge Ghali was murdered in front of his office. In the subsequent trial, the assassin, Ibrahim Nasif al-Wardani, enumerated his reasons for killing the "traitor." Among the motives were the cruel punishments that the Ghali-led tribunal had imposed on the residents of Dinshaway. Al-Wardani actually merited the support of many segments of the Egyptian public, including members of the *Watani* (National) Party and senior politicians. Nevertheless, the assassin was eventually convicted of murder and sentenced to death by hanging. The court hearings netted a great deal of press coverage and triggered an extensive public discourse on a handful of burning national issues. In her meticulous research on the trial, the historian Malak Badrawi concludes, "The sentence was probably intended both as a precedent and as a deterrent, to show that the authorities would not tolerate the recurrence of similar acts."[36] In a letter to Foreign Secretary Edward Grey four months after the verdict, Lord Cromer remarked that he had heard from different sources that "Denshawi is forgotten,"[37] but this assessment was merely wishful thinking. Over a century later, the memory of this tragic event still weighs heavily on the Egyptian national memory.

The First World War scrambled the playing deck throughout the region. After the Ottoman Empire joined the Central Powers, Britain declared Egypt a protectorate and imposed martial law throughout the land. Put differently, the local populace was confronted with a new, less-forgiving system of justice. Esmeir writes,

> Martial law, then, became the mechanism used to deal with political dissent. Military courts tried Egyptians charged with attacking or killing Europeans. The summary nature of these courts was similar to that of the special tribunals, and defendants were often sentenced to capital punishment in the absence of evidence implicating them in the crimes with which they were charged.[38]

Following the war, anti-colonial sentiments and activities intensified. Under the leadership of Sa'd Zaghlul, the Wafd movement asserted itself as the main driving force behind the national struggle. Martial law, which remained intact, enabled the British administration to try nationalist leaders before special tribunals. In rapid proceedings, the judges sentenced defendants to stiff punishments for disturbing the peace and conspiracy. For instance, Zaghlul and his colleagues were exiled to Malta, but this measure only bolstered the party's status as the vanguard of the national movement. On February 28, 1922, Britain's unilateral declaration of Egyptian independence spawned a new ruling order. Egypt was declared a constitutional and parliamentarian monarchy, and Fu'ad I was crowned king. A year later, a new constitution was ratified. Besides defining the purview of the institutions of government, it legalized the establishment of martial law and the prosecution of citizens before special tribunals. Egyptian independence aside, the struggle against Britain's outsized presence did not wane. The monarchial regime continued to operate special courts, but only a small number of trials were conducted within this framework throughout the monarchial regime's three decades in power (1923–52). In contrast, approximately 1,000 citizens stood trial before special tribunals during the early stage of the July Revolution.

The 'Urabi and Dinshaway affairs have become milestones in the historiographical debate on modern Egypt. However, scholars have overlooked the legal aspects of these episodes. In fact, the attendant trials laid the foundation for the increased use of tribunals that are characterized by special procedures, violations of defendant's rights, and the pursuit of wider goals than mere prosecution. This tradition of political trials was designed not only to mete out harsh punishments to those found guilty but also to send a deterring message to the greater society, particularly those circles to which the accused belonged. In this respect, the 'Urabi and Dinshaway affairs constituted the legal and political basis for the establishment of *Mahkamat al-Thawra* and *Mahkamat al-Sha'b*.

Why the Dearth of Research on the Special Tribunals?

The special courts that were established by the RCC have garnered little attention in the scholarly and popular literature on the July Revolution. Elie Kedourie was the first scholar to address the work of the Revolution's Court. In an eight-page article he succinctly analyzes the formation of that court and the heavy punishments that it meted out to various defendants, including 'Abd al-Hadi. Kedourie criticizes the blatant violation of the accused's rights and justly claims that the court constantly ignored the political circumstances that prevailed in Egypt at the time the alleged crime took place.[39] Nonetheless, Kedourie does not discuss the trials themselves and merely calls them "a spectacular show."

Brown elaborates on the historical context of the establishment of the two special courts by the RCC and describes them as a continuation of the exceptional juridical frameworks that had operated in Egypt for approximately a hundred years. He asserts that the FO ran these courts for the purpose of conducting swift trials that would facilitate the efforts to crack down on their domestic rivals.[40] That said, Brown does not delve into the legal procedures and unique characteristics of these tribunals vis-à-vis their previously mentioned forerunners. Likewise, he ignores their significant role in shaping the contours of Egypt's new dispensation. The decrees establishing these special tribunals define their mission as defending the July Revolution's goals in the face of its adversaries. In so doing, the FO drew a firm and direct link between developments in the legal sphere and the struggles in the political arena. This definition of the court's purview was much broader than the stated mission of similar frameworks during the colonial era, whose mission was limited to contending with factors intent on "harming the security of the state" or fighting crime. As we shall see, the revolutionary courts had a substantial impact on the design of the authoritarian order.

Although the trials conducted in the Revolution's Court against the heads of the monarchial regime have garnered little attention in the historiography of the July Revolution, the discourse on the proceedings against the MB activists in the People's Court is more expansive. Those few studies that pertain to the People's Court and the Revolution's Court basically refer to their hearings as "show trials." For this reason, the authors of these works concluded that the tribunals were poor sources for understanding the political reality amid the July Revolution. A case in point is Gordon's disquisition on the first years of the FO's regime. Although he notes that the RCC prosecuted many of its opponents in special tribunals, he does not examine the reasons behind the launching of these institutions. Moreover, Gordon merely outlines the trials' proceedings and does not base his account on the courts' minutes. In this context, his stress is on the improper procedures that marred the MB activists' trials:

> Among other breaches of judicial process, the court attributed false testimony and confessions to comrades not present to refute them. Nonetheless, taking care to weigh the testimony itself, and taking into consideration the conditions under which it was delivered, much may be inferred about the Brotherhood's inner workings. The speed with which the tribunal was convened and witnesses brought forth—some within a day of their arrest—precluded the construction of an elaborate orchestrated show trial. If the court improvised freely as the hearings proceeded, it could do so because of the RCC's intimate knowledge of the Brotherhood.[41]

In his own work on the July Revolution, ʿAbd al-ʿAzim Ramadan, a distinguished Egyptian historian, generously intersperses excerpts from the court records of these show trials against the movement's activists and the Communists. However, he offers neither a textual analysis of the minutes nor insights on the trials' political ramifications.[42] Ramadan's negative view of both the FO's regime and the MB is quite evident throughout his book. These positions occasionally distort his accounts of the courts' proceedings and have led to unpersuasive conclusions with respect to the FO's intentions. Toward the end of his chapter on the People's Court, Ramadan extols the dignified comportment of the Communist defendants. They displayed "the courage and willingness to make sacrifices" for their cause and remained true to their worldview over the course of the trials. Moreover, the Communists took responsibility for their actions, which embodied their ideology. In contrast, Ramadan avers that the MB activists' performance at the People's Court exposed them as charlatans who merely traded in their movement's ideology. When push came to shove, they renounced their worldview as well as the actions that they took in its name. For instance, they washed their hands of the attempt on ʿAbd al-Nasser's life. "They were not ready," Ramadan scathingly concludes, "to die on behalf of this goal."[43]

As opposed to Ramadan, the historian Richard Mitchell is sympathetic to the MB. Published in 1969, his book *The Society of the Muslim Brothers* is considered the definitive work on the movement's first four decades of existence. Mitchell offers a general survey of the People's Court proceedings against the movement's leadership following the attempt on ʿAbd al-Nasser's life but devotes only a few sentences to the assassin's trial. He adroitly takes stock of and criticizes the Attorney General Office's efforts to demonstrate that the MB's top brass masterminded the assassination bid in an effort to bring down the government. In Mitchell's assessment, though, "the assassination attempt occurred . . . as the result of inaction rather than action by the leadership of the [MB]."[44] His succinct account, however, is not without its flaws. He serves up a few errant details on the planning in the run-up to the failed assassination. In addition, there is sparse coverage of the dramatic occurrences both inside and outside the courtroom throughout the trials in question. A possible reason for these shortcomings is Mitchell's reliance on press reports and interviews, rather than the court transcripts. Like most scholars who broached the topic, he considered the hearings to be mere show trials and completely missed their historiographical value. These trials were undoubtedly tools of oppression in the hands of the regime, as they blatantly violated the rights of the accused, and their indiscriminate use dealt a powerful blow to the Egyptian justice system. However, the problem lies with historians' tendency to emphasize these facts while missing the show trials' historiographical value.

Most of the works on these exceptional trials, whether academic or popular texts, embraces the narrative that recurs in the statements and memoirs of citizens who were prosecuted by the special tribunals. The RCC's opponents ran the entire gamut of the political spectrum, but every defendant described the proceedings against him as nothing more than a show trial. In his memoirs, former Prime Minister Ibrahim ʿAbd al-Hadi cynically described his trial as a performance "headed by a judge who was born a judge." Besides making a public mockery of him, ʿAbd al-Hadi claimed that the motive behind his prosecution was to appease the MB, which at the time was still the FO's closest ally. For this reason, the ex-premier decided to forgo the services of an attorney and remain silent throughout most of the hearing, even though as a trained lawyer he could have defended himself. In response to the judges' exhortations, ʿAbd al-Hadi declared that he is leaving the case to their discretion and that his fate would be on their conscience.[45] As we shall see in the third and fourth chapters, the picture is far more complex from the one that ʿAbd al-Hadi sought to paint in his autobiographical work.

Similar to the ex-premier, MB activists were inclined to dub the trials in the People's Court a "theatrical performance" (*tamthiliya*), which was meant, as the Arab proverb goes, "to harm two birds with one stone"—to neuter the MB and force out President Muhammad Naguib.[46] ʿUmar al-Tilmissani, who was convicted by the People's Court, yet would go on to become the MB's third General Guide, claimed that the performance in the trial was a sequel to the staged attempt on ʿAbd al-Nasser's life, as both were designed to eradicate the Islamic movement and purge the public sphere of all oppositional elements. He states in his memoirs:

> The court whose establishment was ordered by ʿAbd al-Nasser was not a court of law, but a means for taking control of the government by means of bloodshed and prisons. The lawyers were unable to fulfill their roles before this court. The defendants thought that they were facing a real court; [however, when] they were asked to revise their false confessions, which were taken from them under threats and torture, [Judge] Salem would stop the session and ask the prisoner to correct his confession. The accused would then be removed and beaten anew; and upon returning [to the stand], he would declare that his first confession was true.[47]

The RCC obviously used the special tribunals as a means of repression. Not only did the proceedings egregiously violate defendants' rights, but also the sweeping use of these exceptional frameworks constituted a severe blow to the Egyptian justice system. Nonetheless recent studies on political trials undermine the consensus view that, given their theatrical nature, such trials are not indicative of reality. Borrowing from recent theoretical and historical insights, I contend that there is much to be gained from evaluating the special courts in Egypt. Paradoxical as it may be, their transcripts are valuable sources precisely because the juridical dimension of the trials was ancillary. As Grunwald's pioneering study on political trials in the Weimar Republic of Germany shows, the oppositional parties from both the left- and rightwing used the hearings against them as a central platform for espousing their views. He principally claims, "The courtroom was a privileged site of ideological combat. Carefully stage-managed by party lawyers, political trials allowed Weimar parties to present riveting spectacles of idealism, implacable conviction and heroic sacrifice."[48] In fact, "sacrifice of the defendants underpinned the performance of ideology in court, and amplified the impact of the party comrades' practical solidarity."[49] Against this backdrop, Grunwald focuses more on the defense attorneys' arguments than that of the judges and the prosecution. Whereas other studies concentrate on verdicts and sentences, his work hones in on other stages of the legal proceedings and various occurrences inside the courtroom. Above all, he stresses the impact that the views expressed over the course of the trials had on the contemporaneous political discourse.

Grunwald's thought-provoking use of the concept of "performance" illuminates the practices, language, imagery, and symbols to which the Weimar regime's opponents availed themselves in an effort to articulate a coherent ideological narrative amid the trials and the attendant public discourse: "To speak of performance does not imply that trials were 'just' theatre. . . . Considering trials as performances of ideology highlights how they allowed nationalists and Communists to strike poses of fundamental ideological opposition."[50] He concludes:

> The extremist parties appear interested not in the legal outcome of proceedings so much as in the forceful representation of their ideology in court. . . . Weimar extremist parties turned judicial persecution from a legal liability into a propagandistic asset, and the courtroom, as a prominent Communist barrister claimed, into a "revolutionary stage."[51]

From the standpoint of the defense, the chief aim was not a favorable court ruling but to lose "with [a] splash. . . . The verdict was only one of many variables that political barristers sought to influence, and in many cases not the most important. In that sense, the 'echo' really was 'everything.'"[52] In sum, Grunwald's research places the spotlight on the efforts to "turn the courtroom into a revolutionary stage."

As opposed to the Weimar Republic, though, the revolution in Egypt was represented by the judges and the prosecution. While leaning on Grunwald's methodology, I argue that, in the trials under review, it was the state that turned the special tribunals "into a revolutionary stage." Likewise, there were appreciable differences between the German and Egyptian cases with respect to the composition and procedures of the courts. As we shall see, most of the Egyptian defense lawyers adopted a highly defensive strategy at the trials under review. Conversely, very few took an assertive approach toward the prosecution or attempted to cast doubt on the tribunals' authority.

As in other societies, Egypt's new regime claimed that the extraordinary measures it took, such as the establishment of special tribunals, were unavoidable given the "state of exception" that prevailed over the land following the overthrow of the corrupt regime and in light of the FO's efforts to construct a new dispensation. The reality that took root in Egypt during this transitional phase is consistent with the theoretical arguments put forth by Carl Schmitt concerning the mutual relations between systems of government and justice in the midst of national crises and states of emergency, such as military coups, revolutions, and civil wars. Drawing on Schmitt's insights, researchers have pointed to states of exception under a wide variety of regimes.[53] Most notably, Giorgione Agamben has elaborated on how these situations come to pass: "The state of exception is an anomic space in which what is at stake is a force of law without law." It constitutes "a point of imbalance between public law and political fact." Such crises shake the foundations of the legal system, to the point of suspending the juridical order itself. More specifically, the executive assumes unlimited authority, including the power "to issue decrees having the force of law."[54]

Building on these insights, I contend that the state of exception enables the ruling power to suspend the autonomy of the legislative and judiciary branches and subordinate them to its will. All this is achieved without the need to abrogate formally the existing legal system. In other words, the principle of checks and balances exists only in name, for all the authority rests in the hands of the executive. The hegemon reserves the right to promulgate decrees that are tantamount to laws and to revise or annul existing laws. As such, parliament is preempted by the executive branch or altogether dissolved. While the law is still valid, it is essentially suspended. The day-to-day administration of the law falls entirely into the hands of the government. Still, the regime attempts to preserve a semblance of obeisance to the law, as it is obliged to demonstrate its ability to "keep the peace" (in the broad and general sense of the word) and prevent society from deteriorating into anarchy. Safeguarding "the order" requires a certain attitude to the law. This state of affairs gives rise to what Agamben terms "a paradoxical articulation, for what must be inscribed within the law is something that is essentially exterior to it. That is, nothing less than the suspension of the juridical order itself." This "no-man's-land between public law and political fact" is severely compromised.[55]

In *The Concept of the Political,* Schmitt argues, "The specific political distinction to which political actions and motives can be reduced is that between friends and enemy. . . . [These] concepts are to be understood in their concrete and existential sense, not as metaphors or symbols."[56] States of exception afford the ruling echelon with the legal means to arbitrarily label individuals and groups as friend or foe. In practice, this involves arresting citizens or subjects and violating their constitutional rights. For example, members of the opposition are tried before special courts that have no compunctions against meting out severe punishments (the death penalty included). This sort of "labeling" was quite evident in the trials under review, as the RCC's judges and prosecutors frequently portrayed the accused as "enemies of the revolution or the people." By charging these same defendants with serious offenses, the scarlet letter "E" (for "enemy of the state") went well beyond the symbolic realm.

The unique characteristics of every society and regime notwithstanding, these theoretical insights strongly pertain to the dynamics that characterized the July Revolution. However, they fail to answer some crucial, overarching questions: How does a state of emergency or exception actually come to pass? What roles do jurists and courts play in this process? What are the public and political reactions to such circumstances? It is with these questions in mind that I have explored the instrumental role that the special tribunals played in the inception and perpetuation of the state of emergency during the first years of the July Revolution. The quasi-legal trials that were conducted within the framework of the Revolution's Court and the People's Court enabled the RCC not only to stymie its domestic rivals but also to extend the emergency atmosphere. Under the cover of this prolonged crisis, the regime managed to consolidate its power by dint of exceptional measures. An analysis of the establishment and conduct of these special tribunals offers us a propitious vantage point from which to plumb the inner syntax of the "state of emergency."

Conclusion

Since the introduction of special tribunals as part of Egypt's modern legal reform in the 1880s, the government has often availed itself of these institutions. Nevertheless, this topic has merited scant research attention. This is probably due to the widespread view that these courts are mere theaters for show trials and thus a dubious source for comprehending historical reality. Few would deny that their irregular legal process seriously compromised defendants' rights. However, this does not detract from the unique insights that may be gleaned from an in-depth study of these tribunals. Just as historians of the Catholic Church would never dream of ignoring the trials run by the Inquisition because confessions were obtained under duress and the accused could not receive a fair trial, researchers of the modern era should not turn their backs on special courts, especially the transcripts of their proceedings.

2

Whitewashing a Coup

On the morning of July 23, 1952, Egyptian radio informed citizens of the drama that had unfolded in the streets of Cairo during the night: army units had wrested control of command headquarters and the radio building, and military checkpoints had been set up all across the capital. After many long years of a corrupt regime and instability, First Lieutenant Anwar Sadat announced, "We will purify ourselves from the traitors and the depraved [*mustaḍʿafin*] on this historic day, and we will usher in a new period in the history of our land."[1] This military coup was spearheaded by Gamal ʿAbd al-Nasser and eight other officers who together formed the vanguard of the FO—an underground association that began to operate within the army's ranks in the late 1940s. In the immediate wake of the coup, the junta turned to General Muhammad Naguib, the fifty-one year-old chief of staff, who accepted its offer to stand at the head of the so-called Movement of the Army (*harakat al-jaysh*). A short while later, two other servicemen joined the revolution's leadership cadre. This forum of twelve officers assumed the power to run the affairs of state.

While the FO had managed to depose of King Faruq and wrest control of government with relative ease, their continued hold on the reins of power would be fraught with difficulties. Save for Naguib, the other leaders of the new regime were low-ranking officers in their thirties. None of them had experience administering large governmental organizations, and their knowledge of parliament, the constitution, and politics was cursory. Although the FO aspired to bring about far-reaching change, upon seizing the helm they lacked an in-depth plan that was grounded on a thought-out ideological outlook or even coherent goals. Above all, it was unclear if they planned to hold onto power for the foreseeable future or quickly pass the baton to an elected civilian government.

At first, the Movement of the Army garnered broad public support. Ambiguous as they were, the FO's statements concerning the urgency of adopting a set of values that suited the new reality and the populace's needs, along with their promises to root out corruption, were immensely popular.

In addition, the Movement of the Army netted the public backing of most politicians and educated Egyptians.[2] The junta placed much weight on the cooperation of the MB. For example, it informed the Islamic movement's leadership in advance of their plans for a military coup. With the ouster of the king, the MB publically threw in its lot in with "the blessed movement" (*al-haraka al-mubaraka*).[3]

A handful of the FO's early initiatives struck a resoundingly favorable chord with the average Egyptian, such as the discontinuation of the government's annual relocation from Cairo to Alexandria during the Summer months (July 24, 1952), the reintroduction of the old civilian titles (August 2), the opening of state parks to the general public (e.g., the spectacular grounds surrounding the Ras al-Tin and Montaza palaces in Alexandria), and the appropriation of the royal family's assets. Furthermore, many citizens applauded the naming of 'Ali Mahir, a seasoned politician, to head the government that was formed two days after the coup. That said, it was widely expected that the army would soon hand over the reins of government to elected officials and return to the barracks. In an article titled "The Philosophy of the Coup" (*falsafat al-inqilab*), Attorney Ibrahim Tal'at noted that this hope is based on the following premise: the military's intervention is not the beginning of "a dictatorship," which seized power with the barrel of a gun to force a military regime on the country, but a revolution in which "the people and the army" have formed an alliance to uproot corruption and restore "the honor of the constitution."[4]

It soon became obvious that King Faruq and his underlings were not the only targets in the FO's sights. The junta aspired to forge a new reality in Egypt by implementing dramatic political, economic, and social reforms. This realization prompted serious disagreements between the revolution's helmsmen and the traditional elites, which had long dominated the ruling apparatuses, politics, the business sector, and military circles. In seizing the helm, the so-called Revolution's Command viewed the Mahir government as a mere operational arm that was charged with executing the junta's decisions. Within days of the coup, the FO launched a far-reaching purge in the upper echelons of the military, the internal security apparatuses, and the police. In the process, hundreds of senior officers and bureaucrats with alleged ties to the monarchy were dismissed. Moreover, a special law was issued compelling hundreds of government workers into early retirement.[5]

Against the backdrop of "the purge" (*al-taṭhir*) campaign, violence reared its head on August 12–13, 1952 in Kafr al-Dawwar industrial zone, near Alexandria. A strike at the Misr Spinning and Weaving Company—a textile plant employing about ten thousand local residents—deteriorated into bloody encounters with security forces. This unrest, which would become a watershed mark in the FO's struggle against their rivals, erupted at the end of a long day of work. However, the causes behind this incident remain the subject of debate to this day. In the heat of a nasty dispute, machinery, vehicles, and management offices were set aflame. A police force was rushed to the scene, and a confrontation with incensed workers ensued. During the melee, a policeman was killed, five employees were injured, and dozens more were arrested. The next morning hundreds of workers tried to break into the sealed-off compound to free their detained colleagues. A military force that was dispatched to the plant also got caught up in a fracas with demonstrators. By the end of the day, there were dozens injured, six dead, and heavy damage to equipment. Fearing that the incident would spark similar outbursts, the revolution's top brass responded with a heavy hand. The RCC's reaction testified to its inexperience in running the affairs of state and to its members' willingness to adopt severe measures to quell what they viewed as a threat to their continued rule.

Even before the government launched its investigation, a decision was made to establish a tribunal—the Supreme Military Council (*majlis ʿaskari ʿal*)—to bring to justice those responsible for the Kafr al-Dawwar incident. The expeditious formation of this judicial body, which was accorded exceptional legal authority, exemplified the new regime's use of emergency powers. The FO exercised this authority on the grounds that these steps were inexorable given the combustible situation in Egypt. At the end of a swift trial, tens of workers were convicted of manslaughter, disturbing the peace, and property damage. Most of the guilty parties received harsh punishments. Two of the defendants who were found guilty of inciting the innocent workers to riot were condemned to the gallows. The judges ruled that, by means of violence and creating an atmosphere of insecurity and fear, the agitators sought to undercut the revolutionary process that was slated to lead Egyptian society to full independence and social justice.[6]

In the rhetoric of the FO's regime, these actions were considered a plot. More specifically, those allegedly pulling the strings behind the curtain were supporters of the monarchy who conspired to stymie the government's initiative to push through agrarian reform by sowing chaos in the countryside. According to Rafiʿi, "this cabal of lowly traitors assumed that Egypt's white revolution is but a small coup" incapable of preventing them from continuing to exploit the nation's resources for the benefit of themselves—a small yet exploitive group of people catering to imperial masters. They adopted various strategies, Rafiʿi continues, including the encouragement of violent acts, with the objective of preventing the execution of an agrarian reform that would put an end to their control over the majority of the agricultural land, from which they derived their economic and political power. The revolutionary command repeatedly declared that it would leave no stone unturned in its struggle against the owners of large estates, while championing the exploited peasant farmers who faced "conditions of slavery."[7]

One of the short-term consequences of the Kafr al-Dawwar incident was the FO's establishment of a security apparatus that was dedicated to contending with political crimes. In essence, the Movement of the Army was reviving the infamous Political Police, which had been abolished a few days after the coup. On August 22, 1952, the FO announced the formation of "the General Investigations" (*al-mabahith al-ʿammah*) unit. As per the government's statement, this body would take on the forces of "the counter-revolution" whose malicious intentions were recently exposed. The regime planned to have this apparatus fill a substantial role in the construction of the new order, as it was charged with waging an all-out war against the revolution's domestic adversaries. To this end, ample resources were placed at the unit's disposal. Among the founders of this potent apparatus was General (*liw'a*) Hasan Talʿat. In his memoirs, Talʿat described "the need for the establishment of a new force under the auspices of the police that would believe in the revolution and its principles." The unit's agents, he recalled, "would be dispatched throughout the country in order to take stock of the situation and control it."[8]

Over the next few months, the struggle between the junta and its domestic critics, primarily members of political parties, only intensified. Topping the agenda were perhaps the regime's two most controversial steps: the "purge" of the parties and the agrarian reform. The dozens of purge committees that were unleashed on the bureaucracy, the army, and the security forces encountered limited resistance. In fact, these committees were enthusiastically received by the general public.[9] *Ruz al-Yusuf*, a popular weekly, devoted the cover of its September 28, 1953 edition to this topic. The front page illustration portrayed run-of-the-mill Egyptians chasing the criminals of the old regime while brandishing the "sword of justice/the purge." Nevertheless, the regime's sweeping demand to cull the ranks of *all* parties, regardless of their place in the political spectrum, snowballed into an enormous crisis. The FO saw the parties as an integral part of the "old" order and a major culprit behind the political instability that characterized the parliamentary monarchy. In fact, the Movement of the Army held the parties and the palace equally accountable for the instability, the economic crisis, and the egregious social disparities within Egyptian society.

A mere eight days after the military coup, "the Commander of the Army," (General Naguib), signed a decree ordering the parties and several nongovernment organizations (excluding the MB) to purge their ranks.[10] More specifically, these groups were instructed to expel figures that held high-level positions before the coup and to revise their platforms in a manner befitting the new reality. In other words, the parties were being told in no uncertain terms to obey the new masters of the Nile and accept the new rules of the game. The ordered purge was not only meant to neutralize rivals that might call the army's rule into question; it was also intended to extract a sort of confession from the parties that they were part and parcel of the venal monarchy that had run roughshod over the country throughout the previous era. This dimension of the FO's demand was not lost on the parties' leaders, who described the purge as a serious blow to their standing as well as an act of unprecedented and unconstitutional meddling in party affairs. Moreover, the parties summarily rejected the claim that they bore any of the blame for the dire straits that Egypt had found itself in during the monarchial period.

As expected, the primary theater of this campaign pitted the new regime against the Wafd—the main protagonist in the Egyptian legislative arena for three consecutive decades. The new regime adamantly insisted on the dismissal of Mustafa al-Nahhas, the Wafd's distinguished and formidable chief. In response, the Wafdists coined a slogan that constituted the main headline of many of the next day's papers: "There's no Wafd without Nahhas."[11] This spirited counter-jab notwithstanding, the parties' reaction indicates that their top echelons had reached the conclusion that there was no choice but to at least partially comply with this demand. Nonetheless, they opposed a comprehensive purge of their top brass. In turn, the Revolution's Command issued another decree on August 10, 1952. Adopting a forceful tone, the document stated that in its present format the interparty rivalry is no less than a crime. Hence, a sine qua non for fixing parliament is a thorough purge of the parties' ranks. In addition, the government's speakers declared that if the parties acquiesced to this directive, parliamentary elections would be held within a number of months. However, should the parties continue to evade this duty, the army would simply execute the purge on its own.[12]

Agrarian Reform

The regime chose to advance an agrarian reform that set a ceiling on the amount of agricultural land any individual could own. This initiative quickly turned into another point of contention between the army and the traditional power bases. On the eve of the coup, approximately sixty-eight percent of the Egyptian population lived in rural communities, and agriculture was the largest sector in the country's economy. A small elite controlled an appreciable slice of the arable land. This monopoly fueled atrocious social and economic distortions that steadily worsened from the latter stages of the nineteenth century onward. The vast majority of peasant farmers (*fellahin*) worked the land of others in return for a meager salary that fated them to a life of hardship.[13] Baer showed that agrarian reform programs were only first broached in the 1940s, but these initiatives were rebuffed by traditional power bases, especially the palace, the owners of the large agricultural farms, and politicians of various stripes (members of the Wafd included). Whenever pressure was exerted for change, opponents claimed that a draconian ceiling on privately held plots and the reapportionment of nationalized land would produce neither social equality nor a significance rise in GDP. On the other hand, they claimed that higher taxes on the owners of sizeable estates would yield much greater economic benefits. In contrast, the new government perceived a ceiling on land ownership to be a major key to far-reaching economic and social transformation. An official report that was devoted to this topic reached the following conclusion:

> The object of the Agrarian Reform Law was not merely the liquidation of feudalist estates or the distribution of lands. It aims at something higher and more sublime, viz. the emancipation of the peasants. . . . Such will be the sound development which will help the achievement of higher social and economic levels for the whole nation.[14]

The FO, most of whose members rose from the lower-middle classes, was motivated to advance agrarian reform primarily out of a sense of "social justice" (*'adala ijtima'iya*)—a slogan that would fast become one of the more prominent rallying cries of the July Revolution.[15] Other important goals of this dramatic initiative were to paralyze the old economic and political elites and drum up greater public support. For decades, disagreements raged over the components of a viable agriculture policy. The FO's determination to push through this reform at an early stage in their tenure resulted in a head-on collision with the traditional elites. Given the "revolutionary spirit" in the air, the owners of large estates and their political allies had a hard time thwarting this initiative. Nevertheless, the bill's opponents managed to put up a fight. Even the MB, which was then the military regime's closest civilian supporters, took issue with the government's ownership threshold. While the Wafd objected to particular aspects of the reform, its leaders repeatedly stated that they were in favor of agrarian reform in principle.[16]

The revolution's helmsmen brought their full influence to bear in an effort to coax the Mahir government into passing their reform bill. The contentious terms of the legislation exposed the public to the appreciable limitations on the civilian government's autonomy and power under the military regime. Caught in the crossfire between the reform's patrons and naysayers, Mahir stepped down from the premiership on September 7, 1952—a mere six weeks after being invited to head the government. That same day the regime unveiled a new government, which was headed by General Naguib. Although the new prime minister continued to serve as "chief of staff of the Movement of the Army," most of the portfolio holders were still civilians.

Soon after its formation, the Naguib government issued two contentious laws. The first, Law No. 178, set a ceiling of 200 *feddan* (one *feddan* is roughly an acre) of agricultural land per person, while offering meager compensation to the owners of nationalized plots. Moreover, it directed the government to parcel out the appropriated land to *fellahin*. Finally, every peasant farmer was entitled to at least five *feddan* of land.[17] This agrarian reform was a foundational part of the FO's uncompromising struggle against the established parties, led by the Wafd. Many of the major landowners in fact supported the Wafd, and some of the party's own leaders were estate holders. According to the new regime's speakers, this explained why the venerable Wafd party refrained from advancing land reform throughout the decades in which it was in charge, for there was broad public support for such change. Thus, it is no coincidence that the RCC unveiled the Party Reorganization Law (No. 179) immediately following its roll out of the Agrarian Reform Law.

The Party Reorganization Law called for an appreciable makeover of the political parties. In essence, it ratcheted up the government's supervision of the parties' activity and their material holdings to an unprecedented level.[18] Along with the arrest of dozens of known political activists, this law stoked the fears that had begun to spread concerning the FO's intentions. Abu al-Fatah, the respected editor of the newspaper *al-Masri*, gave voice to the growing sense of dread on the eve of Mahir's resignation and the Naguib government's release of the party law in his column "Where To?" Many Egyptians, he asserted, are justifiably worried about the government's steps. The purge," (*al-taṭhir*) Abu al-Fatah wrote set the tone in the public debate:

> Everywhere we hear of nothing but the purge. The army utters "the purge," the clerks utter "the purge," the members of the parties utter "the purge," and the government utters "the purge"[—]everyone utters "the purge!!" [However,] this nice word has begun to cause serious blunders, for what are its boundaries, and what are its criteria, and how can it be achieved? [19]

The editor concluded that it behooves Prime Minister Mahir to publically clarify the scope and implications of the purge. The government's dispersal naturally freed Mahir from this "duty," but many Egyptians shared Abu al-Fatah's concerns; for instance, his troubling questions surfaced time and again in the opposition press. Moreover, opposition speakers cast doubt on the FO's claim that the establishment of the Naguib government stemmed from the need to improve the coordination between the military and civilian leaders.

The atmosphere of mistrust was exacerbated by a wave of arrests on the eve of the Mahir government's resignation. The arrests came as a shock to the general public, for among the detainees were scores of well-known politicians. For its part, the regime hoped to send an unmistakable message: the revolution is determined to advance its goals and will not hesitate to take other firm steps. At this early stage, though, most Egyptians believed that it was only a matter of time before the army stepped down. In fact, Naguib's memoirs demonstrate that he shared this view.[20] However, the precedent turned into a norm. For the next four years, the government was controlled by the RCC. Throughout this period, the government basically served as a facilitator of the FO's decisions. A legal opinion that was drafted by the Supreme Court justices Sanhuri and Hafiz sought to justify this state of affairs. Following the establishment of the Naguib government, the regime made more intensive use of legislation and juridical procedures in an effort to advance its goals. Correspondingly, the RCC availed itself of enforcement mechanisms to stamp out any and all resistance to its agenda. In so doing, the junta basically co-opted the powers of both the executive and legislative branches.

Jurists in the Service of the Revolution

Manifold segments of Egyptian society were in favor of the army's intervention and endorsed its plans for sweeping change. Besides the *fellahin* and the urban lower class, "the blessed movement" drew support from among the local clerisy and cultural vanguard. In addition, prominent jurists validated nearly all the revolution's steps with accommodating legal interpretations. Insofar as the heads of the revolution were concerned, it was crucial to display the trappings of a legitimate regime that was committed to enforcing law and order. Consequently, they went to great lengths to secure legal and constitutional legitimacy for their measures. In fact, it would be hard to exaggerate the importance of the role that senior jurists played at the height of the FO's struggle to outmaneuver their domestic rivals and consolidate its hold on power.

The ensuing discussion elaborates on this contribution by taking stock of the instrumental part that Sanhuri, the president of the Supreme Court (*majlis al-dawla*; literally, the State Council), and his deputy, Hafiz, filled in bolstering the new regime. Both men placed their professional services at the junta's disposal from the very outset of the revolution.[21] The historian ʿAbd al-ʿAzim Ramadan described Sanhuri as the revolution's "jurisprudence mentor" (*faqih al-thawra*). Others considered the Supreme Court president and the other jurists who supported the new dispensation to be the true rulers of Egypt.[22] Sanhuri and Hafiz's identification with the FO's aspirations for a major transformation must also be examined in the context of the struggle over the judiciary's standing. At around the time of the coup, the authority of the Supreme Court was severely curtailed by the palace and parliament. Sanhuri's critical view of the Wafd was common knowledge as was his attitude toward the entire legislature, where the party had been the dominant force for several decades. Like the FO, both Sanhuri and his deputy viewed the monarchial regime and the political order that was embodied by the Wafd as the main reasons behind the country's woes. Not all the members of the top legal echelons held such unwavering opinions. From this we may infer that it was no accident that the FO chose Sanhuri and Hafiz to be their legal advisors.

Three days after the coup, a military ceremony was held in Alexandria that epitomized the end of the monarchial age. To the accompaniment of a military salvo and the national anthem, King Faruq and his family members boarded the opulent royal yacht (*al-mahrusa*) and sailed off into exile. Beforehand, the monarch had signed a document agreeing to relinquish the throne to his six month-old son (Ahmad Fu'ad), to the establishment of a regency council, and to leave the country.[23] At the FO's request, this historic document was formulated by Sanhuri and Hafiz. After obtaining Naguib's approval, Hafiz presented the document to the king.

In the coming days, this pair of jurists delved into the ramifications of the sovereign's departure from a constitutional standpoint. Both of them operated on the assumption that the justice system possesses the tools to allow for efficient governance in the midst of a coup. Their opinion was premised on the argument that the Constitution of 1923 enables the government to issue laws if parliament is out of commission. Hafiz noted that "a revolution is not, as there are those who believe, destruction, slaughter, and ruin, but the abolishment of the corrupt [*fasid*] and erecting the worthy in its place" by leaning on exalted values and principles. "A revolution is also not, as there are those who understand it, anarchy and transgression of the law, but it is obeisance to the law and acceptance of its verdict." According to Hafiz, this outlook is what guided him and many of his colleagues to amend "laws and government orders that stood in contradistinction to the banners of the revolution and its goals." From the jurist's vantage point, these efforts were intended to reconcile the objectives of the revolution with the law. More specifically, they ensured that "the actions of the revolution in its first months would fall under the rubric of the legitimate [from a legal standpoint]. What worried us [the most] was finding the means that would allow for the abrogation or revision of whatever stands in contradiction to the laws. . . . I remained vigilant and placed" priority on guaranteeing "that the revolution . . . and all its actions would be commensurate with the law."[24]

The Constitution of 1923 does not explicitly refer to a situation in which the king surrenders the throne. Therefore, Sanhuri and Hafiz's point of departure was that the conditions are open to legal interpretation. It also bears noting that the army's intervention occurred several months after the legislature, the senate, and parliament had been dispersed. With this in mind, Sanhuri conceived of the idea of establishing a three-person regency council and transferring the lion's share of the king's powers to a provisional government until parliamentary elections and the swearing in of a new government. During the transition phase, the chief justice recommended, the government should lean on the legitimacy of the army and advance a new elections law.[25] At a lengthy meeting, the junta and their legal advisors agreed that *Majlis al-Dawla* would formulate a paper defining the constitutional situation that prevailed at the time and the means for contending with this state of affairs. Correspondingly, a serious internal dispute among the jurists in the Supreme Court's legislative department led to the dismissal of one of its most prominent members, Wahid Ra'fat. From this point forward, Ra'fat became a leading critic of the FO's regime, especially Sanhuri and Hafiz.

For the next twenty-four months, the two acclaimed jurists constituted the "legal minds" that sanctioned the regime's principal moves. One of their opinions concluded that Egypt now finds itself in an "exceptional situation." Hence, the army is legally entitled to exercise broad powers and take special measures throughout the transition phase.[26] In many instances, Sanhuri and Hafiz's position papers set the stage for constitutional declarations and orders that would have the force of law. For all intents and purposes, their work realigned the ruling, political, and social reality in Egypt. By dint of such decrees, governments were formed and dissolved; the Constitution of 1923 was suspended, and a committee was appointed to draft an alternative; parties were disbanded; the monarchial regime was abolished, and a presidential republic was declared; the MB was outlawed; and the two special tribunals that constitute the focal point of this book were established. In addition, Sanhuri and Hafiz authored several major bills that were put into effect soon after the coup, most importantly, the Agrarian Reform and the Party Reorganization Law.

At the same time, Hafiz and Sanhuri did not always see eye to eye. They belonged to different legal traditions and their political views diverged. Sanhuri started his legal studies at Cairo University's Faculty of Law but began to stand out while completing two doctoral theses at the University of Lyon. His extensive knowledge of both Islamic law (*fiqh*) and European traditions of jurisprudence are quite evident in his work which would eventually undergird the civil codex of Egypt and other Arab states. Furthermore, Sanhuri was the driving force behind the establishment of *Majlis al-Dawla* in 1946 and headed the court during the first years of its existence. Politically, he identified with the Sa'dist party.[27]

Sulayman Hafiz acquired his entire legal education at Cairo University. After working as an attorney for a number of years, he integrated himself into the country's legal establishment, serving as a legal advisor to the Court of Appeals. In parallel, Hafiz took an active part in Egypt's struggle against Britain. Suspected of involvement in the murder of Sir Lee Stack, the governor-general of Anglo-Egyptian Sudan, on November 19, 1924, he narrowly escaped the death sentence that was meted out to the rest of the accused. With respect to local politics, Hafiz was a severe critic of the Wafd.[28] In 1949, Hafiz accepted Sanhuri's offer to join *Majlis al-Dawla*. As the institution's deputy president, he ran the legislation department and formulated legal opinions. Early into the July Revolution, it was apparent that this senior jurist fully identified with the FO's goals.

Sanhuri immersed himself into the enterprise of legally bolstering the new regime's status. The legal reservations and occasional difficulties that he threw before the RCC culminated in a head-on collision between the regime and the Supreme Court.[29] During the March 1954 crisis, the chief justice sided with those demanding that the army return to the barracks. As the tension hit a crescendo, Sanhuri urged President Naguib to convene a national assembly tout de suite for the purpose of ratifying a draft constitution, which was prepared by an authorized committee. He also exhorted the general to declare the end of "the emergency phase" (*al-fatra al-istithna'iya*), which had begun on July 23, 1952. The next day an incensed mob charged toward his office, apparently at the directive of the General Intelligence Service (*mukhabarat*), and pummeled the esteemed scholar. Only a last ditch effort managed to save him from a lynching. Following his release from hospital, the Supreme Court president confined himself to his home, where he foreswore all legal and political endeavors.[30]

The first sign of differences between Sanhuri and Hafiz over the revolution's course surfaced during their work on the Party Reorganization Law. Siding with the FO, Hafiz asserted that the only way the parties can adopt themselves to the revolution's goals is by completely purging their ranks of figures that are identified with the old regime. Sanhuri initially objected to this demand but came around after the RCC accepted his position that disagreements over the law's implementation would be settled by an upper administrative court. The chief justice viewed this procedural step as a guarantee of effective supervision over the exercise of this law. While Sanhuri backed the decrees and laws that set in motion the parties' disbandment, it was Hafiz who embodied the legal-political symbiosis at this critical juncture in the revolution's struggle against its domestic rivals.

The RCC top brass was well aware of the considerable differences between their two senior advisors. It comes as no surprise, then, that the FO entrusted Hafiz with drafting the most sensitive and controversial pieces of legislation, including the party law and the Treason Law (*qanun al-ghadr*), which is examined later on in this chapter. Furthermore, he was charged with chairing a committee that was appointed to draft a provisional constitution (upon the repeal of the 1923 Constitution). With the formation of the Naguib government, Hafiz was named deputy premier and minister of the interior. As such, he became an indispensable part of the revolutionary government. In his ministerial capacity, Hafiz oversaw the implementation of "the purge" decree, which he formulated on his own.

A supporter of the National Party, Hafiz focused his efforts to uproot the old guard from the political landscape on the Wafd and its conspicuous leader Mustafa al-Nahhas, whom the jurist deemed to be his arch ideological enemy.[31] The steps that the Wafd took to adapt to the Party Reorganization Law, including its announcement that Nahhas would be made the party's "honorary president"—a position devoid of authority—were rejected by the jurist on the grounds that they do not adequately comply with the purge decree. Hafiz viewed the party's stance as not only a refusal to accede to the regime's legitimate demands but also, and most importantly, an expression of their inability to digest the fact that the final nail had already been driven into the coffin of the old order. Because the parties had refused to change their ways, the jurist concluded, "there was no choice but to legally force them to [carry out] what they refused to do at their own volition."[32] As minister of the interior, Hafiz petitioned the Supreme Court to punish the Wafd and the other parties for failing to abide by the new law. To strengthen his case, he pointed to the fact that Nahhas continued to serve as honorary president. The discourse surrounding the purge controversy was quite rancorous. On the legal front, the Wafd was represented by another one of Hafiz's aforementioned rivals, Attorney Wahid Ra'fat. The defense's main riposte came in the form of a lucid memorandum arguing that the Party Reorganization Law violated the constitution and must thus be annulled.[33] Ra'fat's argument gained considerable traction in public—a development that naturally roiled the FO.

In the first half of the twentieth century, the national parties cemented their status as the champions of the nation's will. While the junta's rhetoric obviously harmed these parties' reputation, many Egyptians continued to see them as a legitimate and extremely influential political force. It is against this backdrop that on November 13, 1952 the government issued a decree putting into effect the Party Reorganization Law. For the sake of "defending the revolution and the regime that is based on it," the document read, special powers were to be placed in the hands of "the chief of staff of the armed forces" for a period of six months (from the day of the coup). Pursuant to this law, it was henceforth prohibited to challenge the so-called sovereign actions of the regime in a court of law.[34] Needless to say, the right to press charges against the government in a court of law is a fundamental principle of modern jurisprudence, as it embodies the legislator's subordination to the law. By violating this fundamental pact with the governed, the Egyptian government transformed itself from a regime based on the rule of law to one that ruled by force of law.[35]

The Drafting of a New Constitution

Soon after the army seized power, questions arose regarding the status of the 1923 Constitution. At the advice of Sanhuri and Hafiz, it was decided to refrain from annulling the constitution for the time being. This decision was predicated on the jurists' interpretation of several articles therein. Foremost among them was article 41, which refers to a situation where an urgent need arises "to take measures that do not tolerate delay" when parliament is not assembled. Under these circumstances, the king has the right to promulgate "decrees that possess the force of law."[36] Because of Faruq's ouster and the legislature's dormancy, Sanhuri and Hafiz reasoned, the powers that this article confers upon the ruler should now be placed in the hands of the government, the regency council, and the military command. Furthermore, they opined that in light of the state of emergency, these bodies may take the necessary steps by issuing decrees and laws. Article 155 also states that any obligation whatsoever that is noted herein is irrevocable unless "it is done in a temporary fashion during times of war, or in the midst of martial law [*al-ahkam al-'urfiya*]." In essence, the coup triggered a vicious cycle, in which the regime's sanctioned resort to exceptional means fanned the flames of the emergency situation and vice versa. This dynamic was not lost on the FO and may explain why they were in no rush to bury the Constitution of 1923.

Needless to say, Sanhuri and Hafiz's interpretation was the object of heated debate. Opposition politicians and their legal counsel argued that the regime's treatment of its domestic adversaries violate the principles of the party-based system and the parliamentary regime, which are anchored in the constitution. On this basis, they challenged "the purge" policy and the incarceration of dozens of political figures (without a judge's order) in the courts. The purge policy and the party law undoubtedly set the stage for the imprisonment of dozens of political leaders and activists. After approximately two months behind bars, some of the detainees appealed to the courts. Their attorneys claimed that all the defendants were being held in prison without having seen either a judge or a bill of indictment. In their estimation, this measure violated article 5 of the 1923 Constitution: "It is prohibited to incarcerate any person or arrest him except in compliance with the provisions of the law." This appeal to the courts placed the regime in a political and legal bind. Hafiz described an argument that broke out at a meeting of the revolution's leadership following his request for suggestions as to how the government can fend off these petitions. At one point, an officer asserted, "We will not consent to [a situation] where the Supreme Court [*Majlis al-Dawla*] will control us."[37] It turns out that these arrests were not made in accordance with regular procedure but pursuant to an order issued by the minister of the interior. The latter justified these measures on the grounds that they were imperative to safeguarding the revolution.

Following this meeting, the regime decided to formulate a new law that would define "measures that the revolution's commander has the authority to take for the purpose of defending it [i.e., the revolution] and the regime that is based on it."[38] On account of this legal challenge, Hafiz came around to Sanhuri's view that, from a governing and legal standpoint, the most efficacious means for preventing the country from slipping into chaos was the ratification of a new constitution. Nevertheless, this and similar orders betrayed the regime's desire to couch extraordinary measures as "laws," through the good offices of the two distinguished jurists. In complying with these demands, Sanhuri and Hafiz were simply doing what was expected of them. Moreover, given their training and professional outlook, the two were guided by procedural rigor and legal positivism.[39]

Hafiz retroactively premised this step on "the holes" in the existing constitution that enabled the venal regime, which was headed by "a royal family that did not Egyptianize itself," to do whatever it pleased. In his memoirs, the jurist described how the FO was hesitant to take the dramatic step of repealing the Constitution of 1923. "In a series of meetings with the military colleagues," Hafiz wrote, "I convinced them of [the merits of] my position," and the decision was made to appoint a committee to draft a new constitution.[40] This account also indicates that some of the problems with the constitution came to light amid the struggle over the "purge" orders.

The RCC sought to expel figures that were identified with the monarchy from public service, but the existing law afforded immunity to elected officials. As a result, prosecutors would have been hard-pressed to convict the accused in criminal or administrative courts. In light of this situation, the FO issued special laws designating two types of "purge" committees: administrative committees for contending with bureaucrats accused of improprieties and legal committees that would concentrate on top officials from the previous regime (mostly ministers). However, at the outset of the legal committee's work, its members realized that the Constitution of 1923 also grants these senior figures immunity. For this reason, an initiative was put forth to legislate what turned out to be the Treason Law (*qanun al-ghadr*). Hafiz also drafted this law, with the help of a fellow Supreme Court judge, Muhsen ʿAbd al-Hafiz.[41]

The opposition parties were against the repeal of the 1923 Constitution. Instead, they proposed amending those sections that contravene the objectives and principles of the July Revolution. It is worth noting that a mere revision of the constitution was likely to shorten the transition period before general elections and the transfer of power to a civilian leadership. On the other side of the aisle, there were those who claimed that the overthrow of King Faruq had essentially terminated the old regime. Since the monarchy had predicated itself on the Constitution of 1923, it was incumbent on the Egyptian leadership to adopt a new constitution.[42] A dispute also reared up over the composition and nature of the committee that would be charged with either drafting a new constitution or amending the existing one. The RCC insisted that the government appoint all the committee's members, while the opposition favored an independent team. In an op-ed piece, Ra'fat reminded his fellow citizens that independent teams had formulated many of the constitutions that were adopted following the two world wars, including that of the French Third Republic (1875).[43]

At the height of this polemic, a constitutional declaration was issued by "the chief of staff of the armed forces and by dint of his position as head (*ra'is*) of the Movement of the Army" (December 10, 1952). This key document enumerated the far-reaching aims of the revolution. Most important, it reiterated the army's intention of pushing through comprehensive governmental and social change and ratifying a new constitution.[44] As evidenced by the declaration's opening lines, the junta believed that the parties had betrayed Egyptian society during the monarchial age and that they presently constitute an obstacle to the revolution's success. "The faulty political life," the text reads, "was expressed by the complete subordination of the legislative branch to the executive branch." Instead of the government being duty-bound to parliament, the latter was enslaved to the government. For its part, the government was under the yoke of the king and his allies. By exploiting loopholes in the constitution, among other means, the palace maintained a status quo in which the elite derived personal benefit at the expense of the nation's genuine interests. "The revolution's goal was not only to get rid of this king" but to attain broader objectives, such as guaranteeing a life of dignity, freedom, and justice for all Egyptians and repairing the institutions of government. During the "reconstruction phase," the regime planned to transform fundamentally the situation that prevailed in Egypt. To this end, a "new constitution . . . will allow the nation to achieve its goals," and the people will become "the true source of authority."

The constitutional declaration ended with the following announcement from General Naguib: "In the name of the people, I hereby proclaim the annulment of the Constitution of 1923" and the establishment of a committee to draft a new one. Upon its completion, the draft will be put to a public referendum. Throughout the ineluctable transition stage, "power will be held in the hands of the institutions [of government]." Put differently, no limits were placed on the military regime in all that concerned its authority to conduct the affairs of state or the duration of this interim period. However, one can infer from the declaration's vague language that the regime was drawing a correlation between the ratification of a constitution and a return to unadulterated civilian rule. In practice, this declaration freed the revolution's top brass from the constitutional constraints that had to this point kept it from neutralizing political rivals. As we shall see, the decree also allowed them to inaugurate legally the state of exception by defining it as an "interim period."

While politicians and public figures were mulling over the ramifications of the extraordinary powers that the RCC had assumed, the government promulgated Law No. 344, the Treason Law, on December 22, 1952.[45] In addition to drafting its content, Hafiz was the main proponent for the legislation's passage. This law enabled the regime to try monarchial-era officials, who were accused of misusing their power, before a special court. The justification for this draconian law was the purge committees' supposed revelations that the prior regime's abuses were on a large scale and entailed serious acts of subversion that threaten the public order and national security. However, there was also a more tangible reason behind the formulation of the Treason Law. Sanhuri and Hafiz had apprised the FO of the fact that the penal code makes no reference to the culpability of position holders for the past actions of the ruling apparatus. Consequently, they could not be brought to justice for their alleged role in the improprieties of the old regime. By filling this void, the new law was meant to root out corrupt officials, thereby laying the foundations for clean government.

As per clause 3 of the Treason Law, the accused were to be tried before a special court (*mahkama hasa*) comprised of a presiding judge from the Court of Cassation (*mahkamat al-naqd*), two judges from the Court of Appeal (*mahkamat isti'naf*), and four officers at the rank of major or higher. The judges were appointed by the justice minister, while the chief of staff chose the servicemen. Under "special circumstances," which this law did not specify, the tribunal was authorized to order investigations and incarcerations for indefinite periods. The Attorney General's Office was charged with formulating the bills of indictment and representing the state in court. On the other hand, defendants had the right to avail themselves of a single trial lawyer. Moreover, clause 6 specified that the court's judgements "shall not be subject to ordinary or extraordinary appeals."[46]

The Treason Law covered offenses that were allegedly committed by ministers, members of parliament, local councils, and "any person holding public office" after September 1, 1939. It also designated the actions that fall under the category of treason: (a) undertaking to corrupt the government and political life by harming the supreme interests of the state, or public servants that were derelict in their duty to protect these interests; (b) the exploitation of public office with the objective of deriving benefit for the offender or others; (c) misusing public office to secure public or political jobs for the offender or others; (d) abusing one's position to derive benefit for the public servant or others by directly or indirectly influencing the price of real estate, merchandise, and publically traded stocks; and (e) any attempt to sway judges and compromise the justice system. Clause 2 authorized the special tribunal to impose punishments that were not listed in the criminal code, including dismissal from public office, parliament, and local or rural councils; the suspension of the offender's right to participate in elections as either a voter or candidate for a position in one of the aforementioned bodies; barring an offender from public office, membership in a political party, or from managing companies and institutions that are under the government's authority; prohibiting an offender from working in fields that pertain to the shaping of public opinion, education, or the national economy; and even the partial or complete forfeiture of pension funds. All these restrictions remained in force for a minimum of five years. Furthermore, the special tribunal was authorized to revoke the Egyptian citizenship of anyone convicted of treason and to repossess any and all gains that were secured in this fashion.

According to clause 4, a file can be opened in the court by not only the Attorney General's Office but also any of the purge committees [*lijan al-taṭhir*].

This provision testified to the acceleration of the purge policy, which had already led to the removal of hundreds of clerks and officers from the governing apparatuses, the military, and domestic security forces. According to the Treason law, these committees who were directly controlled by the RCC, were imparted with special powers that were ordinarily the sole preserve of the Attorney General's Office and investigative judges. Clause 4 also instructs the presiding judge to set the opening day of the trial within no more than fifteen days from the submittal of the case. Moreover, the defendant was to receive a notification that he must appear before the court at least eight full days before the hearing on his case, and he was permitted to avail himself of a single lawyer. The hearing could not be postponed more than twice, each time for no longer than a week. As per clause 5, if the defendant or his counsel failed to make the court date, the hearing would be held in absentia. The final paragraph of the Treason Law obligated the government to publish the text of the law in the state's public record and in two newspapers with wide circulations within a week of its release. Furthermore, every minister would implement this law in the office under his purview.

Much importance should be attributed to a special appendix to the Treason Law (signed by the prime minister). According to this codicil, the objective of this law was to cleanse public life and all public activity in this "new age" from those "lacking a conscience and [a sense of] national duty, who seek to continue taking advantage of their positions of power to derive personal benefit for themselves and their cronies." These offenders must be removed from office lest they continued to "constitute a stumbling block on the road to progress."[47] In addition, the appendix stresses that the establishment of the treason court is a lawful act. It also notes that the modern Egyptian justice system was inspired by French criminal law, which allows for the establishment of special tribunals in emergency situations. The French code, in fact, refers to a situation in which an offense was committed during a period when the act was not illegal.

Within the codicil is a legal interpretation that compares Law No. 344 to a bill that was passed in France toward the end of the Second World War. The latter governs actions that undermined French nationalism (*indignite nationale*) during the Nazi occupation. Pursuant to this law, a French citizen suspected of directly or indirectly assisting Germany and its allies or of harming national unity, civil liberties, or the equality between citizens can be brought to trial and severely punished. The Egyptian supplement points out that the legal procedures established in the law itself are more lenient than its French counterpart. In contrast to the latter, the Egyptian law entitles defendants to legal counsel. All the property and funds of a defendant found guilty of sedition may be expropriated under the French law, whereas the Egyptian version sets a ceiling of 2,000 Egyptian pounds. Unlike its French antecedent, the law in question sets no restrictions on the defendant's continued residence in Egypt. Lastly, the French law allows the judges to prohibit a citizen convicted of treason from voting or running for public office in perpetuity. The appendix's conclusion states that the Egyptian Treason Law "is commensurate with the French law with respect to the goal of eradicating corruption and expelling corrupt figures from the sphere of public life, but the Egyptian law is more moderate" in all that concerns the special tribunal's authority and the punishments that can be handed down.[48]

Amid the tempestuous public debate over the Treason Law, yet another blow was leveled at the opposition camp. In an unprecedented move, the RCC issued a decree on January 16, 1953 calling for the parties' disbandment. Prime Minister Naguib, "the revolution's commander," informed the general public of this step in a dramatic radio announcement the next day. To begin, he mentioned that a plot to sabotage the Movement of the Army's efforts at forging a new reality in Egypt was recently exposed. "Destructive forces" have conspired with a foreign country, and their actions threaten to reignite the governing corruption and anarchy. Conveying an air of resolve, Naguib proclaimed that the government authorities have been instructed "to take tough steps against every deviant [*mariq*] or traitor that attempts to sow division within the ranks of this nation." Thereafter, he announced:

> [The immediate] dispersal of all the parties . . . and the confiscation of all their funds for the good of the people. In order to achieve stability, I hereby declare a transition period . . . of three years during which we will be able to establish a bona fide democratic and constitutional regime. From this day forth, I will not allow any attack against the homeland's interests and will hit with full force the hands of anyone who stands in the way [of] our goals.[49]

The parties' dissolution and the launching of a treason court epitomized the RCC's determination to abolish the political order that had existed for three decades. At the top echelons of government, there were nascent signs of discord over the revolution's next steps, but at this stage the FO put on a public display of unity. For instance, ʿAbd al-Nasser, the RCC's strongman, insisted that the order disbanding the parties bear but one signature—that of General Naguib. Moreover, all the revolution's leaders emphasized that this measure was imperative due to a plot involving hostile factors in Egypt along with the representatives of an unnamed foreign country. Ignoring the history and diversity of the Egyptian parliament, the decree whitewashed the distinctions between the various parties, portraying all of them as a monolithic, reactionary force. This measure, Bishri accurately observes, indiscriminately harmed those parties that were open to change and untainted by corruption. Instead of grappling in a lawful manner with those same parties suspected of collaborating with foreign agents to undermine the state's interests, the RCC resorted to an oppressive campaign that was intended to eliminate all its political adversaries.[50]

Against the backdrop of the heightening political crisis, ʿAbd al-Nasser asked Hafiz to formulate a document that "would define the government's authority . . . so that the public will know that it is not being ruled by means of despotism [*tughyan*]." As the jurist proceeded, it became clear that this was a text of profound legal and political importance. On February 10, 1953, the so-called provisional constitution (*al-dustur al-muʾqat*) was issued by the "chief of staff of the armed forces and the commander of the revolution of the military."[51] This title beneath Naguib's signature bore witness to a marked change in the way the new regime perceived itself. From this point on, the FO defined the reality in Egypt as a "revolution." In this context, the provisional constitution designated that the powers of government, including the authority to shape policy, would be placed exclusively in the hands of the RCC and the revolution's commander until the end of the transition phase. As stated in the preamble, the document establishes the principles that would guide the government throughout this interim period and defines the rights and duties of all the country's citizens.

The first section of the provisional constitution ("General Principles") declares that "the nation is the source of all the authority" (*jamiʿa al-sultat*). Adopting an unequivocally legal style, Hafiz laid forth the following principles: the equality of all citizens before the law as well as the universal protection of individual rights, freedom of expression, religion, and worship. Clause 7 affirms the independence of judges and the judicial branch. The crux of this document, though, is its second part: "the Branches of Government" (*niẓam al-hukm*). Both the regime and its opponents placed great weight on clause 8 of this section whereby "the commander of the revolution in the Revolution Command Council" possesses the ruling authority. As such, he may take whatever steps he deems necessary to safeguard the revolution, its government included, and achieve the goals of the "blessed movement." Likewise, the commander will have "the right to appoint the ministers and dismiss them." The powers of legislation and the executive branch were placed in the hands of the regime. By giving the "commander" carte blanche, the junta now had unlimited room to maneuver against its rivals along with the legal legitimacy to take exceptional measures. In fact, Sanhuri and Hafiz opined that this document pulled the ground out from beneath the regime's adversaries. For their part, the opposition ardently claimed that its provisions are unconstitutional.

The unbridled authority that clause 8 conferred upon the new regime also offers a fleeting glimpse at the behind-the-scenes power struggle between Lieutenant Colonel ʿAbd al-Nasser, who enjoyed the support of the majority of the RCC, and General Naguib, who was far and away the most popular figure among the wider public. The declaration's wording betrays a belabored attempt to avoid the formation of a clear hierarchy between the RCC and "the revolution's commander." The opening sentence of clause 8 clumsily patches together the irreconcilable positions of the two camps. Listing the panoply of military and civilian titles that Naguib currently held, the document's closing paragraph declares "our absolute faith in the need to establish a fully constitutional democratic regime at the end of the transition period." This general statement harbors a compromise that was reached to settle a dispute between the Naguib and ʿAbd al-Nasser camps over the amount of time needed to lay the foundations for a democratic regime. The general favored a quick transition of several months. His supporters, including Hafiz, emphasized that the declaration speaks of a transition to a "full-fledged" democracy. From this provision, they deduced that strides must be taken in this direction throughout the interim phase. However, this interpretation was quite a logical stretch; in other words, it essentially constituted nothing more than the personal hopes of the Naguib camp. In practice, the wording of this clause reflected the uneven distribution of power at the summit of the RCC, for it was wholly consistent with the outlook of ʿAbd al-Nasser and his backers. To wit, after having dispersed the parties less than a month earlier, the regime now issued a provisional constitution that established a transition period of three years. Furthermore, it was devoid of any specific guarantee that steps would be taken during this phase toward the realization of a democratic regime.

Needlessly to say, the order to disband the parties stirred the wrath of the country's political circles. While many Egyptians were critical of the parties' functioning during the monarchial era, these organizations had spearheaded the struggle for national liberation from the early twentieth century until the late 1940s. Moreover, the Egyptian legislature had simultaneously cemented its status as a powerful governing institution.[52] For their part, the MB was pleased with the incapacitation of the parties, especially those of its rivals from the liberal wing. However, even at this early stage, cracks began to form in the partnership between the MB's leaders and the FO.[53] As a result, six months after seizing power, the revolution's helmsmen essentially found themselves bereft of outlets for shoring up their legitimacy among the general public. In an effort to replace the parties and prevent a vacuum from forming in the political sphere, the RCC oversaw the establishment of the Liberation Rally (*hayat al-tahrir*)—a grassroots political organization that was unaffiliated with any party. Designed as an umbrella group for all sectors of Egyptian society that supported the July Revolution, the FO touted the Liberation Rally as a manifestation of the "nation's unity."[54]

Propelled by its thirst for legitimacy, the regime toiled feverishly to enlist the backing of the unions. Millions of workers belonged to these organizations, some of which had already been quite active for decades in both professional and national arenas. Consequently, the unions quickly turned into a political battleground in the power struggle between the military regime and its opponents. Through the years, the parties frequently ran candidates in union elections, most notably those of the formidable lawyers, engineers, and teachers groups. For decades, these associations were headed by members of the Wafd. Unlike the parties, the unions were not disbanded in the aftermath of the coup. Instead, the RCC co-opted them by dint of its purge policy. A case in point is the engineers union, which had previously been under the Wafd's control. Until January 1953, its ranks were comprised solely of civil engineers. At the behest of the RCC and its supporters, though, the union's guidelines were revised to allow for the inclusion of military engineers, who were guaranteed a twenty percent stake in the federation's management.[55]

Exceedingly truculent campaigns were waged over the lawyers and journalists unions, which exerted quite an influence over the public and political discourse. The heads of these groups reproved the draconian steps that were taken by the RCC. Moreover, the lawyers union demanded that its members who were rounded up during the wave of arrests in October 1952 be released at once. Pari passu to its co-option of the existing associations, the regime set up new professional unions for sectors that were sympathetic to its cause. At the government's initiative and with the passionate support of its president, Muhammad Abu al-Hadid (who backed the revolution from its inception), the Teachers Association was converted into a professional union. As the crisis between the RCC and the opposition parties boiled over, Abu al-Hadid published a heartfelt op-ed piece describing what the coup meant to him: "I discovered my homeland . . . just as a person finds his relatives after a long time."[56] It also bears noting that the regime destined a major role for the teachers union in its plan to transform the education system. Following its unionization, the association was placed under the aegis of the Education Ministry and its minister, Husayn Kamal al-Din.[57]

The Road to a Republic

To some extent, revolutions are informed by contradictions. A fine example of this is the RCC's initiative to draft a new constitution. On January 13, 1953, the government issued a decree appointing a fifty-member committee to draft a new constitution "that is at one with the aims of the revolution." Despite the brutal campaign that the FO was then waging against the parties, the committee included distinguished politicians, intellectuals (Ahmad Lutfi al-Sayyid and Taha Husayn), and jurists (Sanhuri and ʿAbd al-Rahman al-Rafiʿi). In addition, it consisted of representatives from various sectors of Egyptian society. Among its members were eight delegates who were affiliated with the liberal wing (including four members of the Wafd) as well as three from the MB. The army and police were represented by three generals in toto. Accordingly, there was a fair share of delegates who were known for their criticism of the RCC and who saw the ratification of a new constitution as a potential means for expediting the departure of the military regime. As its chairperson, the committee selected the ʿAli Mahir.[58] The integration of figures from across the political and socio-economic spectrum was meant to symbolize the FO's inclusive vision of governance. All told, the quality of the committee's composition, hearings, and its eventual recommendations were outstanding.

General Naguib delivered the opening remarks at the committee's festive inaugural session on February 21, 1953. Thereafter, the representatives formed a number of subcommittees. The central subcommittee, which was dubbed "the committee of five," focused on the critical issue of defining the type of regime that best suited the country: Should Egypt stick with the monarchial system or institute a republic? And if a change is deemed preferable, should the country adopt a presidential or parliamentary system? After a couple of sessions, it was evident that the delegates were leaning toward a synthesis between the French Third Republic's ruling method and the bicameral legislature of the United States. 'Abd al-Rahman al-Rafi'i, a member of this subcommittee, recalled that he and his fellow delegates had stressed the faults of the monarchial regime, particularly hereditary succession.[59] As reported on the front page of the next day's papers, the committee of five unanimously recommended abrogating the monarchial regime and setting up a presidential-parliamentary republic in its stead. The Naguib government's deliberations over the committee's decision were extremely tense. While some of the civilian ministers categorically objected to this system of rule, the RCC welcomed the proposal and sought to implement it at the government's earliest convenience without any effort to reconcile between the two sides. As a result, the "anti-republic" ministers stepped down and their positions were filled by members of the armed forces.[60]

With the type of government in place, the subcommittees charged with formulating the rest of the constitution's articles could proceed with their work. On May 19, 1953, the committee of five reached the conclusion that the executive branch should be headed by a president. Directly elected by the people, the president would be limited to a maximum of two five-year terms in office and have the authority to both appoint and dissolve the government. The committee over which Sanhuri presided recommended a handful of checks and balances on the powers of the executive and legislative branches—a decision that was subsequently passed by a large majority in the committee of fifty.[61]

The recommendation for a presidential republic merited wide support in the public discourse and among the ranks of the FO. However, the regime was also interested in significantly curtailing the legislative's authority and establishing a prototypical presidential regime. To this end, the 'Abd al-Nasser camp endeavored to water down the committee of fifty's proposals.[62] By virtue of the provisional constitution, the FO was basically free to do as it pleased. Accordingly, they chose a model in which the legislative powers were merged with those of the executive. The government itself was to be appointed by the revolution's commander and the senior portfolios were assigned to officers, most of whom had seats on the RCC. In so doing, the FO tore down the barriers separating the legislative from the executive branch, thereby precluding any meaningful public supervision of the government's actions.

In the beginning of the summer, the FO convened a series of meetings on the new system of government and Egypt's constitutional state of affairs. Leaks from these gatherings soon found their way into the press. Among the news items were rumors of a major change on the horizon. On June 18, *al-Ahram's* headline read: "The Republic is on the Way but the Date of its Announcement has yet to be Set." Following marathon discussions that very same day, the RCC made a dramatic, if anticipated, late-evening announcement replacing the monarchial regime with a presidential republic. In parallel, the government issued the following decree: "In the name of the people," it proclaimed "the annulment of the monarchial regime and the rule of the Muhammad ʿAli dynasty" as well as the establishment of a republican-presidential regime. Signed by "the commander of the army's revolution, General Naguib" and all the members of the RCC, the pronouncement reflected a new narrative for the era that had begun with the reign of Khedive Ismaʿil and came to a sudden close with King Faruq's exile. Henceforth, the revolutionaries described this period as "a series of betrayals." More specifically, the monarchy had collaborated with the forces of imperialism and was thus responsible for the protracted British occupation. In contrast, the revolution identified with and advanced the "true needs of the people" (*al-shaʿb*). This incipient hegemonic narrative clearly distinguished between the revolution ("us") and its enemies ("them"). Within this framework, the latter were portrayed as reactionaries who are in league with foreign agents and continuing to undermine the people's liberties.[63]

According to the second clause of this decree, General Naguib would serve as the republic's president while holding onto the powers afforded to him by the provisional constitution. This appointment was an expression of Naguib's immense popularity vis-à-vis his colleagues in the upper echelons of government, ʿAbd al-Nasser included. It also demonstrated that the vacillation over the ruling system had yet to run its course. Pursuant to the third clause, "the regime would stay in place throughout the length of the transition period" and "grant the people the last word in determining the model of the republic and the election of the president upon the ratification of the new constitution."[64] As could be expected, the next day's headlines were "The Fall [*suqut*] of the Muhammad ʿAli Family"; "The Proclamation of the Republic"; "Muhammad Naguib is President of the Republic and Prime Minister"; "Gamal ʿAbd al-Nasser is Deputy Premier and Minister of the Interior"; and the like. Naguib's acceptance speech opened with sharp barbs at the Muhammad ʿAli dynasty's legacy, whereupon the president turned to the ramifications of this historic decree: "In the name of the people, today we are hereby declaring the abrogation of the monarchial regime and the rule of the Muhammad 'Ali family, including the removal of the titles that the members of this family bore." The general also informed his listeners of the new official name of the state—the Republic of Egypt (*jumhuriyat misr*).[65]

This turn of events only exacerbated the power struggle between Naguib and 'Abd al-Nasser. In an effort to alleviate the tension between the two camps, 'Abd al-Hakim 'Amr, 'Abd al-Nasser's closest ally, was appointed chief of staff of the armed forces (pursuant to Presidential Order No. 1). In other words, Naguib was forced to relinquish direct command over the military. According to his confidantes, the president was deeply hurt by this step, which also upset his relations with the rest of the RCC top brass. Nonetheless, *al-Ahram* reported the next day that these "important developments" would lead to the establishment of a unified and efficient ruling apparatus. In turn, a strong regime would help restore stability and allow the country to get through the transition stage in one piece.[66] Finally, these measures signified the RCC's assumption of both the civilian and the military reins of power.

The republic was officially declared on Friday, June 18, 1953. National and religious motifs were intermingled in the wide array of ceremonies that were held to mark this occasion. The newspapers provided extensive coverage (along with photos) of the official ceremonies (e.g., the president and other RCC members attending Friday prayers, the swearing in of ministers, and various speeches to the nation) as well as spontaneous expressions of joy. In his account of the jubilant throngs packing the streets from al-Azhar Mosque to 'Abdin Palace, an *al-Ahram* reporter noted, "I have no idea how the people knew that their esteemed president would be coming to 'Abdin Palace in the evening." During this same event, it was announced that the names of the palace and the large adjacent square would be changed to "the official residence of the republic's presidency" and Republic Square, respectively.[67]

Many private firms and businesses ran congratulatory newspaper advertisements in honor of the monarchy's abolishment and the declaration of the republic. The text and illustrations in these ads complemented the headlines, photographs, and text of the news reports and commentary. Likewise, the subtext was in sync with the rhetoric of the RCC and its supporters: under the army's leadership, the people and the regime are forming "one hand." A case in point is the advertisements of a local tea manufacturer and a trading company that appeared on *al-Ahram*'s front page the day after the republic was proclaimed: the space that was allotted to the festivities was greater and more detailed than the commercial information. Moreover, both ads extolled the revolution's leaders, especially President Naguib, for their historic achievements on behalf of the people: the disposal of the tyrannical monarchy, the declaration of the republic, and the promise of liberty.

In the hegemonic discourse, strong emphasis was placed on the regime's commitment to the "six goals" of the July Revolution, which were first unveiled in early 1953. The first three revolved around the "elimination" of what was described as the faults of the old order: imperialism and its traitorous allies, feudalism, and the monopolies. The remaining objectives were meant to reflect the new dispensation: a strong national army, social justice, and a democratic system of government.[68] The public dissemination of these goals left no doubt as to the aspirations of the "blessed movement." It is not by chance, then, that from this stage onward the term "revolution" steadily became a popular synonym for the new order. The leaders' declarations and actions were evidence of their desire to bring a "new" and "revolutionary" order to the ruins of the "old" and "reactionary" monarchy—the symbols of which the FO toiled to erase from the public sphere. The RCC's slogans—such as "Unity, Order, Work" (*al-itihad, al-nizam, al-'aml*)—were highlighted in the pro-government newspapers. In fact, "unity" was increasingly the order of the day, as it was viewed as a prudent alternative to the discord and strife that had informed Egypt's political parties for years on end.[69]

The previously noted expressions of support indicate that a substantial proportion of Egyptian society identified with the military's revolutionary regime. However, this impressive display was not enough to conceal the piercing criticism from other segments of the population regarding the FO's continued hold on power a year after the coup, its dispersal of the parties, and the silencing of parliamentary life. Among the naysayers were many who backed the toppling of the monarchy and some of the RCC's goals but were disappointed by the army's refusal to transfer power to civilian representatives. This position was espoused by distinguished intellectuals including Taha Husayn, Tawfiq al-Hakim, and Naguib Mahfouz. *Al-Hilal*—the venerable monthly that constituted a platform for a vibrant intellectual discourse—dedicated a special edition to these topics on the first anniversary of the coup. Under the heading "The White Revolution" (*al-thawra al-bayda'*), prominent writers opined on whether the revolution had attained its goals. The introduction by *al-Hilal*'s editorial board noted that some of the contributors were split on this question. Those who believed that these objectives had yet to come to fruition argued that "one year is not enough for a large-scale revolution" of this sort. Without exception, all the participants expressed their unconditional support for the dismantling of King Faruq's corrupt government. That said, they were at loggerheads over the issue of the RCC's lengthening occupation of the halls of government.

The junta's position was faithfully represented by Fathi Radwan. In an article titled "Has the Revolution Completed Its Mission?" the new minister of culture asserted that the July Revolution has not completed its mission and has yet to achieve its aims "because these are much greater" than assumed, even by the coup's "fomenters." An analysis of the other pieces in this edition of *al-Hilal* points to a sophisticated use of the claim that the revolution had already fulfilled its goals. For example, there were several iterations of the following persuasive argument: if the revolution had, in fact, succeeded, then it is legitimate to demand that the reins of government be transferred back to a civilian leadership. Fikri Abaza, the well-known publicist and former member of parliament for the National Party, championed this argument in "The Revolution Has Succeeded." At the outset of the article, he commended the army for disposing of the king. This was followed by the observation that "the revolution has a logic of its own, and this is a logic that has a rationale."

Nevertheless, Abaza subsequently lashed out at a number of the FO's major policy initiatives. For instance, he agreed that the agricultural sector begs fixing, "but I was not among the devotees of capping ownership" of arable land to such an unwarranted extent. Similarly, he noted, "I was adamantly opposed" to the Party Reorganization Law and am not a "devotee" of a single-party system. Moreover, he cast doubt on the chances that the "Liberation Rally" will attain its objectives. Ahmad Amin, the editor of the respected magazine *al-Thaqafa*, wrote an illuminating piece titled "Reflections on the Modern Coup." In the beginning of this article, Faruq's ouster is said to signal a transition from life under "a regime of subjugation" to a government that may very well blaze a path to liberty and an equable political order. However, Amin alluded to the fact that the revolution's first anniversary also gives cause for concern. According to the editor, the coup stemmed from exceptional circumstances.

> That said, our great hope is that reality will return to its natural state in which Egypt will be ruled by a just constitution and a free and clean parliament. . . . There is no doubt that placing matters in the hands of professional politicians and a parliament whose members were chosen in a free and impartial manner is a more equitable model for running the country.[70]

In contrast to the mild criticism in the press of the FO's extended hold on power, there were increasingly strident expressions of opposition to the new ruling order, the detention of political activists, and the dissolution of the parties. Correspondingly, signs of the feud between the ʿAbd al-Nasser and Naguib camps were already quite evident as they were for the crisis between the RCC and the MB, which had intensified over the course of the year. To begin, the movement had turned down the government's requests to participate in events marking the revolution's first anniversary, and the absence of the MB leaders from the official ceremonies of state was indeed glaring. In addition, the manifestoes that the MB was now circulating took issue with the government's policies. Members of the dispersed parties, among others, contentedly watched the emerging fallout between the RCC and the MB.

It is against this backdrop that one must view Mustafa al-Nahhas' diatribe against the FO at a ceremony commemorating the twenty-sixth anniversary of Sa'd Zaghlul's passing on August 23, 1953. The occasion on which Nahhas chose to upbraid the RCC was no coincidence nor was the presence of many Egyptian and foreign journalists. Shunning the Ministry of the Interior's instructions, the veteran party chief, along with a coterie of senior-level Wafdists, arrived at the mausoleum housing the remains of the venerated "leader of the nation." Following the wreath-laying ceremony, Nahhas delivered a plucky speech condemning the military government's infringement of liberties and parliamentary life, violations of the constitution, and other undemocratic measures. For example, he clamored for the immediate release of all political detainees. In addition, the ex-prime minister lambasted the government's positions in talks with London and its concessions regarding the future of the Sudan. A short while later, a manifesto containing Nahhas's speech was handed out at major urban squares.[71] In the days ahead, public criticism of the FO's handling of the negotiations with Britain swelled. 'Abd al-Nasser and his RCC colleagues unveiled their response to this "intransigence" some three weeks later, at a mass rally at the Square of the Republic. Despite being a symbol of the national struggle, Nahhas was placed under house arrest, and several months later the Revolution's Court indicted the distinguished politician on charges of treason along with his wife, Zainab al-Wakil.

Conclusion

As part of its efforts to advance the "goals of the revolution," the RCC repeatedly availed itself of legal means to solidify its rule and curb the opposition. Drawing on an analysis of the FO's steps, we found that constitutional declarations and legal decrees—in particular, the Party Reorganization Law and Treason Law—assisted the junta in gaining control of the public sphere. The deep involvement of two leading Supreme Court judges in formulating these decrees helped legitimize many of the critical steps that the regime took, including the heavy obstacles that it threw in the opposition's path. Despite Sanhuri's reputation as the Arab embodiment of the "rule of law," he contributed immensely to the FO's "rule-by-law" strategy. This turn of events was exemplified by the formation of the two special courts under review.

PART II

Judges As Historians

3

The Revolution's Court

On Tuesday, September 15, 1953, thousands of citizens, many of them bureaucrats working in the vicinity, assembled in the Square of the Republic (*midan al-jumhuriya*), the new name given by the Naguib's government to the square in front of 'Abdin Palace that formerly housed the offices of the monarchy. Egypt's new flag hung from adjacent buildings and nationalist songs were blasting from huge speakers. Moreover, the VIP stand was filled with the country's political elite (the president, government ministers, and the members of the RCC) and representatives of the religious communities, including Shaykh al-Azhar, the heads of the Coptic Church, and even Egypt's chief rabbi.[1] Dubbed "the popular council," this impressive rally was called to announce the establishment of the Revolution's Court (*Mahkamat al-Thawra*)—a special tribunal that would adjudicate citizens accused of seriously compromising state security and corrupting the heads of the previous regime. The hearings were not only intended to try those charged with attempting to sabotage the FO's efforts to institute a new order but primarily to document the folly of the "old" order and present the revolutionary regime and its policies as an exceedingly better alternative.

The justifications that the new helmsmen provided for launching this special tribunal were indicative of the FO's broad objectives for this body. President Naguib and the chairperson of the RCC, 'Abd al-Nasser, described the current struggle over the reins of government as no less than a fight for survival and vowed that the revolution would wield an "iron fist" against both its domestic and foreign enemies. This attitude revealed the manner in which the revolutionaries linked the events of the past to the present. In fact, this massive rally was the genesis of not only this exceptional court but also of a new hegemonic narrative for modern Egyptian history.

The first of the speakers at this rally was President Naguib. He emphasized that "the goal of the revolution was and remains the struggle against imperialism." Moreover, he asserted that the deeds of a "particular group of citizens," in conjunction with hostile foreign elements, are akin to a war against the nation. Time and again, the president distinguished between the nation and its domestic enemies, whom he broadly categorized as "them." These same factors, in his estimation, are endeavoring to overthrow the present government, and their actions constitute a serious blow to national interests.

> They know, as the nation knows, that they are errant and causing others to err, and they are liars and hypocrites [*munafiqun*]. These subversives, as well as all Egyptians, should know that we are about to lay down principles that will guarantee victory in this campaign—this campaign over life and death.

He then stressed that there is no escaping this confrontation, which will no doubt be arduous and protracted. The speech ended with a most significant statement: "The change in our policy and our adoption of a tougher policy" stems from the special circumstances that Egypt faces. It is a "compulsory step" that was decided upon after contemplating the measures that must be taken at this stage in the revolution. "We will not be able to contend with and triumph in the war against imperialism before we contend with those forces in our midst that are undermining the [national] interest and the greater good." Lastly, this struggle is a "sanctified duty" of all the country's citizens. According to *al-Ahram*, Naguib's words merited applause that sounded like "a barrage of shots fired from a thousand cannons all at once." The ovation was accompanied by chants of "death to the traitors."[2]

At this point, ʿAbd al-Nasser took the floor and gave a fiery speech. Time and again, he referred to a group of "traitors" who continue to think according to the pre-July 23 logic. These people, he claimed, are disseminating lies and rumors for the purpose of harming the nation's interests and the greater good. In an act of desperation, this "fifth column" is attempting to "drive a wedge" between the army and the people and to split the military's ranks.

> The wagon of the revolution will continue to make progress and run over every traitor in its path; and from this day on, the revolution will only know resolve and power versus anyone that is determined to stand in its path. . . . Against them, all of us—army and people, a single and united . . . force—will fight on behalf of a single cause . . . to purge the homeland of imperialism and the traitors that are helping it."

Furthermore, ʿAbd al-Nasser claimed that these reactionaries were shrewd enough to control Egypt for a quarter of a century by dint of the constitution, which, in fact, safeguarded their own interests. The democratic and parliamentarian regime that they set up was fundamentally flawed, as it only bestowed liberties and rights upon a thin sliver of the population. In parallel, the vast majority was left without protection, and the country's interests were sacrificed for the good of this exploitive minority. "Everybody knows that what allowed for the consolidation of imperialism in our land are these traitors . . . and if we examine the past, we will find that all the nationalist movements were harmed by the actions of these Egyptian traitors." Our revolution is confronting these elements, he concluded, and is determined to fight them until the bitter end.[3]

The myriad references to "traitors" in these two orations set the stage for the declaration unveiling the special tribunal. The actual reasons behind this mass rally were not revealed until the final speech of the day, which was given by Salah Salem. In his capacity as minister of national guidance, Salem had earned a reputation as the new regime's speaker. Over the course of numerous public appearances, Salem demonstrated that he had no compunctions against resorting to demagoguery. Featuring an aggressive oratory style, he tended to belittle the RCC's adversaries. The speech that he delivered on this occasion lasted some forty minutes, and the recurring theme was "we shall not forget." According to Salem, the monarchial leadership was cut off from most of Egyptian society and its needs. In the name of parliament and democracy, "the [ousted] representatives of the people" had stood and applauded the raising of the Union Jack in Tahrir Square. For the most part, the heads of the old regime labored to advance their own narrow interests.[4] "Imperialism dominated Egypt not by virtue of its soldiers and weapons," but in part due to "treasonous Egyptians." Consequently, a major goal of the July Revolution, from the standpoint of the FO, is to destroy the link between "imperialism and the domestic reactionaries."

> We mustn't forget that back in the day some of those people who ruled us in the name of the constitution, parliament, freedom, and democracy stood in the name of the people as they reviewed the soldiers of occupying England in Isma'iliya [presently] Tahrir Square, and they did not forget to salute the flags of Britain as they blew over their heads.

As Salem proceeded, it became evident that the traitors are party heads who "peddle in nationalism."[5] While often presenting themselves as a "dam" that protects the nation from the palace, they were actually the "king's closest allies." Time and again, these politicians declared their commitment to attaining freedom for Egypt and its citizens, but their actions served the interests of a negligible minority. Moreover, Salem asserted that this traitorous leadership had not only abandoned civil society, but the Egyptian military as well. "Did you know that your army, which was sent to war on May 15, 1948 to fight in Palestine, lacked vehicles to ferry the soldiers' food, ammunition, weapons, and drinking water?"[6] This statement was no coincidence, as the military's shortcomings were destined to become the focus of the Revolution's Court. "There are those who ask 'Is it not preferable to look ahead and eschew settling the scores of yesteryear?' We hoped that this was indeed the case, for we aspired to continue in the way of the 'white revolution' [*al-thawra al-bayda'*] that we had launched." Due to their "exaggerated optimism" that the previous leadership would leave the public sphere, the FO did not take any punitive measures against it. However, this approach turned out to be "the biggest mistake that . . . the revolution made." While the RCC opened "the prison doors and granted full freedom to all," the traitors "returned to dream their dreams." They have misconstrued the new regime's lenient policy toward them as an expression of weakness and are seeking to drive a wedge between the army and the people by disseminating "rumors and lies."[7]

Drawing on a top secret document obtained by the Egyptian intelligence services (*al-mukhabarat*), Salem argued that the collaboration between domestic and foreign elements, namely the intelligence services of a foreign, non-Arab country, whose name he did not wish to reveal, had become a real threat to the security of both the people and the revolution. This document exposed the close relations between the "imperialist forces and the reactionary traitors in our land." Operating out of its embassy in Egypt, the former was endeavoring to build an "internal front" aimed at disposing of the regime. It hoped to achieve this goal by fomenting hostility and anger between the nation and its leadership and by impairing the Egyptian economy. These conspiratorial activities were meant to pave the way for the monarchy's return or, at the very least, to topple the revolutionary regime by stirring up resistance to the RCC in the army's ranks and souring the atmosphere in the civil service. According to Salem, the main targets of this agitation were college students and the working class. These measures were designed to whittle away at the population's confidence in the present government and the army.

Thereafter, he expanded on the role of the local and foreign press. As per that same intelligence document, Salem insisted, the press was heavily involved in a campaign to erode the government's legitimacy by spreading false rumors in foreign media outlets with Arabic programs, such as the BBC, that the new government was incompetent. He then excoriated Egyptian journalists for advancing subversive agendas of multiple hostile factors. As minister of national guidance, Salem professed to have made every effort to "guarantee the freedom of the press" and reduce the censure's mandate. However, in light of this plot, "I steadfastly declare that the censure . . . in Egypt will continue to be strong and will raise its sword over every head that undertakes to sow destruction," confuse innocent citizens, "and spread discord and deterioration among the ranks of the Egyptian nation."[8]

The final part of Salem's speech centered on the dramatic announcement unveiling *Mahkamat al-Thawra*. He explained the rationale behind the RCC's decision to create a special tribunal that would examine those accused of undermining the new regime. "Having described" the predicament in which the revolution finds itself, he continued by saying that he "would like to respond to" those who believe that these allegations should be handled by "our regular judges and courts." To begin, he heaped praise on the judicial system. For example, he noted that the present leadership holds it in high esteem. That said, from a historical standpoint, the fortunes of not one revolution have been "deliberated in an ordinary trial."

> The regular laws have constraints and limitations that its judges cannot breach, and the reason for this is that these [checks] were legislated for the circumstances of natural life. . . . For this reason, I hereby declare in the name of the Revolution [Command] Council the establishment of *Mahkamat al-Thawra*, which shall be composed of a number of members of the RCC and will adjudicate forthwith the matter of those accused of actions against the interest of the state and against the principles of the revolution [*kiyan al-thawra*].

Moreover, he announced that the RCC would submit the names of the accused to the tribunal's secretariat and that the verdicts will be declared by the special court. "We took this step" of founding this court "for your protection and to preserve the unity that abides amongst you at this sad phase in which the fate of the country is going to be determined." Unlike the revolution of 1919, we will not allow "any traitor or heretic [*mariq*] to harm your revolution."[9]

Whereas these particular reasons were directed at the general public, other declarations made by the keynote speakers at this same rally attest to three wider considerations behind the decision to establish the Revolution's Court. First, the RCC perceived the special tribunal as an emergency measure for coping with the severe threat that the regime's domestic opposition posed. Second, they reached the conclusion that Egypt's standard court procedures were inappropriate for the exceptional circumstances that prevailed in the wake of the military coup. Lastly, the trials of the regime's adversaries would revolve around the slogan "we shall not forget," thereby forging a new narrative of past and present. It soon became abundantly clear that the official speeches given at the "popular council" were but one in a series of moves aimed at ensuring that the special tribunal would be established without delays and operate in an efficient manner.

The day after the rally (September 16, 1953), a special meeting was held in the defense minister's office. Among those present were the RCC top brass, and representatives of the Attorney General's Office and the Military Prosecutor's Office. The participants composed guidelines for the special tribunal's work, divided the labor between the various factors involved, and determined how they would interact. The brunt of the meeting, though, was dedicated to writing the decree establishing the Revolution's Court. Several hours later, a special session of the RCC was convened. By the end of the day, the final draft of the order was approved and signed by all the Council's members. The lengthy, nine-section document went into force that same evening.[10]

As stated in its preamble, the decree is based on article 8 of the provisional constitution. Like many of the other steps taken by the RCC, the special tribunal was a direct outcome of the extraordinary politico-legal situation that had prevailed in Egypt since the military coup. The first article consists of the special tribunal's constitutive declaration and lists the names of its three judges. The next article defines the crimes that the court will hear: "Actions deemed to constitute an act of treason against the homeland [*khiyanat al-watan*], or against its well-being, from within or abroad; and actions directed against the present government, or against the foundation upon which the revolution was instituted." In addition, the tribunal will adjudicate defendants accused of aiding and abetting the corruption of the government and enabling the penetration of colonialism into the country, "and all that has caused the rotting of the political life, or the exploitation of influence without taking into account the good of the homeland."

Deviating from judicial norms, the court is endowed with the power to hear any and all cases that the RCC will refer to it, "even if they have already been [tried] before regular courts or before other judicial authorities, so long as a verdict has not been handed down in the matter." Moreover, the regular courts will cease to deliberate over cases that are brought before the special tribunal. This clause ostensibly preserves the legal principle whereby individuals are not to be judged for crimes for which they have already been convicted. In practice, though, transferring a proceeding that was being heard in a regular court to a revolutionary one is an exceptional power that heavily compromised the defendants' rights.

Article 3 grants the Revolution's Court the authority to impose any punishment that it deems fit, such as heavy fines, life in prison with hard labor, and the death penalty. The judges can even order "to confiscate [*musadara*] all or part of the defendants' assets" if they derive from illicit gain. Pursuant to article 4, an attendant office for investigations and prosecution is to be set up at RCC headquarters. The staff will consist of representatives from the army and the Attorney General's Office. These departments will conduct the investigations and prepare statements of indictment and present the cases before the special tribunal. The Investigations Bureau is conferred with the unassailable and unobjectionable "authority to detain the defendants and hold them in custody for designated periods."

Article 5 is also informed by a dearth of legal procedures and by infringements on defendant rights. To wit, it stipulates that an individual is to receive advance warning of at least twenty-four hours before being stood trial. The accused or his attorney may ask for only one postponement "for a period of no more than 72 hours." Should a defendant fail to appear before the court, he or she may be subject to arrest and incarceration. It also states that the accused can either defend themselves against all the charges brought against them or appoint a lawyer to do so. The next article sets the order of the hearings and the progression of the trial. Furthermore, the judges reserve the right to take additional steps at their discretion "and objections to the court's stuff or [to] one of its members will not be allowed." In other words, the RCC essentially ruled out the possibility of appealing to another body with regard to the special tribunal's legal procedures or the composite of its judicial panel.

According to article 7, the trials "will be conducted in a public manner [*bi-tariqa 'alaniya*], unless the Court decides to hold a secret hearings [*jalsa sirriya*] for reasons that it sees fit." In practice, the majority of the trials were open to the public, thereby enabling the court to interact with and shape the public discourse. This section also stipulates that the verdicts "will be handed down in an open session and this after its approval [*tasdiq*] by the RCC, that reserves the right to commute the punishment to a level that it sees fit." In other words, the judges did not have the last word over the sentences. Likewise, article 8 reads that the special tribunal's verdicts are "final and no appeal will be accepted in any way or before any authority whatsoever, and appeals will not be permitted on court procedures or their implementation." The final article tersely states that the order will take effect forthwith. Immediately beneath these words, the RCC members approved the document with their signatures.

Housed in a separate wing of RCC headquarters, the Prosecutor's Bureau for State Security Affairs and the affiliated Investigations Bureau were the lynchpin of the special tribunal. Overall responsibility for these bodies was assigned to Zakariya Muhyi al-Din, a member of the RCC. Around the time of the court's establishment, he was appointed interior minister and head of military intelligence (*al-mukhabarat al-'askariya*).[11] The daily operations were managed by six men, half of them lieutenant colonels in the army. These three jurists spearheaded the interrogation of witnesses and the preparation of the indictments. In addition, they headed the prosecution team throughout the trials. There were significant professional differences between these officers and the judges. Most important, the former had strong legal credentials. Upon completing law school, they enlisted in the army and served as military prosecutors in various corps. The most senior member of the three was Muhammad al-Tab'i (a native of Mansoura, b. 1914). In official government documents, he comes across as a sophisticated jurist who carefully weighed every word he uttered. The other half of the sextant was comprised of senior jurists from the Attorney General's Office, the most prominent of whom was Mustafa al-Hilbawi.[12] Attached to the Prosecutor's Bureau were four veteran army sergeants along with two secretaries from the Appeals Court in Cairo. 'Abd al-Rahman Salah, the deputy attorney general, oversaw a substantial portion of the civilian group's workload.[13]

Over the next few months, both departments tended to dozens of lawsuits against citizens suspected of a multitude of offenses. The files were divided among work teams that were usually comprised of a military prosecutor, a civilian prosecutor, and an auxiliary clerk. While most of the indictments were prepared within a few days, special teams toiled over the more complex cases for around a week. As per the RCC's instructions, the Ministry of the Interior, Military Intelligence, and the *Mukhabarat* made every effort to comply with the prosecution's demands for information. Lastly, the general secretariat of the Revolution's Court was staffed with six clerks, four of them military officers.

The conduct of the trials themselves was placed in the hands of three officers who, like their fellow members of the RCC, were in their mid-thirties: ʿAbd al-Latif al-Baghdadi (1917–99) was named chief judge.[14] Some three months before launching the Revolution's Court, Baghdadi was appointed defense minister in the Naguib government, so that his involvement with the special tribunal spoke volumes of its importance to the new regime. To his right on the judge's dais sat Anwar Sadat. At the time, he was serving as the general manager of *Dar al-Tahrir*—an organization that administered various publications on behalf of the regime. Among the titles was the newspaper *al-Jumhuriya* (the Republic), the mouthpiece of the RCC.[15] During the period preceding King Faruq's expulsion, Sadat was one of the officer corps' most prominent nationalist activists. In this context, he was arrested and tried on charges of involvement in the assassination of Minister Amin ʿUthman. On the morning after the coup, it was Sadat who read the army's first statement on national radio. The third judge was Hasan Ibrahim, who was entrusted with managing the Liberation Rally.[16]

The Trial

On the day before the special tribunal's opening session, the names of the defendants were published in the newspapers. Although the list included three ministers and two army officers, most of the public's attention was drawn to the case against Ibrahim ʿAbd al-Hadi, the former prime minister and ex-chief of the Royal Divan. The bill of indictment against this prominent figure entailed a number of serious counts, including treason against the homeland, breach of trust, corruption, preparing the atmosphere for the murder of Hasan al-Banna, and indirect culpability for the Egyptian army's defeat in the Palestine War.

ʿAbd al-Hadi was born in al-Zarqa, a town near the northern city of Damietta, in 1899. As a law student, he joined the national struggle, which was then led by the Wafd movement and its venerated chief, Saʿd Zaghlul. Like many of the activists behind the Revolution of 1919, ʿAbd al-Hadi spent time (four years) behind bars. The unflinching national struggle ultimately led to Britain's unilateral declaration of Egyptian independence on February 28, 1922. Within a year, a government was formed under the Wafd's leadership, a constitution was instituted, and most of the political prisoners, ʿAbd al-Hadi included, were released. Disagreements within the liberal camp over what to do next splintered the ranks of the Wafd movement. ʿAbd al-Hadi joined the Saʿdist party (1937/8), where he rapidly ascended to the top of its hierarchy.

By this stage, he was already married and the father of three children. He held a number of senior posts from the late 1930s onward, including that of minister in several governments.

In late 1946, Faruq enjoined ʿAbd al-Hadi to become chief of the Royal Divan. Fellow Saʿdists, who thought that it would be inappropriate for a member of their movement to serve in this capacity, tried to persuade him to decline the offer. However, to the surprise of many, he accepted the position on the grounds that it would strengthen the party vis-à-vis its political rivals, especially the Wafd.[17] Following the assassination of Prime Minister Mahmud Fahmi al-Nuqrashi (December 28, 1948) ʿAbd al-Hadi was appointed in his stead, but his tenure was short-lived. These two senior-level roles indeed constituted the high point in the defendant's political career and stood in the spotlight of his trial in the Revolution's Court.

When the monarchy was dismantled, ʿAbd al-Hadi was the leader of the Saʿdist party. Given his high standing therein, the FO basically asked him to purge the Saʿdists' ranks—a demand that was made of all the country's political parties. Sayyid Marʿi, who was then a member of the Saʿdist party's young leadership and subsequently became a fast-rising star in the Nasserite regime, provided an illuminating account of the military coup's impact on Egyptian politics. In this context, he expanded on the meetings that the Saʿdist chiefs held with the FO, most of which he personally attended. According to Marʿi, ʿAbd al-Hadi asked his interlocutors to clarify what they meant by "purging" the party's ranks. However, he only merited a vague answer. "I don't understand exactly what the officers want," he reportedly told Marʿi. The latter estimated that the new regime was not interested in the continuation of party activity "neither in our party nor in any other party."[18]

At 10:00 in the morning of Saturday, September 26, 1953, a military jeep stopped by the entrance to RCC headquarters. Accompanied by military police, Ibrahim ʿAbd al-Hadi got out of the vehicle (in a scene that was immortalized by press photographers) and proceeded to the opening of his trial. The location of the special tribunal, a royal palace on the southern tip of Zamalek Island, along the banks of the Nile, was chosen with much care. Dedicated as a marina for royal yachts a year before his removal from the throne, Faruq barely used this site. The location was indeed one of Cairo's most scenic lookouts, as it offered an unobstructed view of the iconic sites across the river: the exclusive Garden City quarter, the British embassy, and the Shepheard's Hotel. Moreover, the adjacent Nile bridge connects Zamalek to the modern center of the Egyptian capital, at the heart of which sits Tahrir Square. From the standpoint of its dimensions and architectural style, the headquarters was modest in comparison to other former residences of the Muhammad ʿAli dynasty. It could very well be that this is why the heads of the revolution chose to launch their enterprise from this spot. The part of the compound that was allocated to the tribunal consisted of nine rooms, most of which served the prosecution.

At the entrance to the courtroom was one of Egypt's new tri-color flags bearing the inscription *Mahkamat al-Thawra*. On one end of the chamber was the judges' dais, with the prosecution's and secretariat's table to its right and left, respectively. The benches were arrayed in the middle of the hall. Most of the front-row seats were reserved for the defense. The media occupied the next two rows, and another fifty seats were set aside for the general public. Attending the opening session were twenty-eight journalists and ten photographers from both the Arab and the foreign press. Microphones were placed by the judges' stand, the prosecution's table, and the witness area. The Egyptian Broadcasting Authority, which offered extensive coverage of the trials, was charged with recording and broadcasting the proceedings. Citizens wishing to attend the spectacle were admitted to no more than a single hearing, after obtaining approval from the press office and undergoing a security check at the entrance. Lastly, the Military Police was charged with securing the judicial wing.[19]

Several days before his trial, ʿAbd al-Hadi was arrested and detained in Cairo's al-Ajanib Prison.[20] A few minutes after his arrival, Warrant Officer ʿAbd al-Rahman Hefnawi, the special tribunal's announcer, signaled to the crowd in the hall to rise in honor of the judges by shouting the word "*Mahkama!*" (Court!). Donning military uniforms decorated with officer ranks, the three judges took their seats. "In the name of Allah and in the name of the revolution, we open the inaugural session of *Mahkamat al-Thawra*. Is the defendant present?" With these words, Judge Baghdadi commenced the deliberations on prosecution file no. 1. "Yes, your honor, I am present," replied ʿAbd al-Hadi, who was wearing a suit, tie, and a fashionable red tarbush on his head. To begin, Mustafa Marʿi, the defendant's lawyer, sought to push off the trial by seventy-two hours. However, the chief judge answered that a decision would only be made once the bill of indictment has been read, which was the next step.[21] While ʿAbd al-Hadi sought to take issue with each charge, the judges insisted that he suffice with either "guilty" (*mudhnib*) or "not guilty." In temporarily rebuffing both the accused and his counsel on technicalities, Baghdadi showed that he had every intention of adhering closely to the rules laid forth in the constitutive decree.

The first count imputed to ʿAbd al-Hadi "activities that are considered treason against the homeland, against its well-being, and the foundation upon which the revolution was instituted." Over the course of 1953, the indictment read, the accused "was in contact with foreign elements whose objective was to harm the present government and the supreme interests of the state."[22] To the question of whether he admitted to the charge, the defendant swore "to Allah that all this is untrue." Baghdadi read the next count:

> Actions that are considered treason against the homeland and against its wellbeing in the internal and external [theaters], and which helped

> the colonialism acquire a firm position in the land, and this because over the course of 1948 at the time he was serving as the head of the previous King Faruq's bureau, he undertook to carry out his wishes in embroiling Egypt's army in the Palestine campaign.

ʿAbd al-Hadi then pleaded "not guilty" to this allegation as well. The third count imputed to the defendant activities that corrupted the government during his tenure as premier and interior minister (December 28, 1948–July 25, 1949). In these roles, the indictment stated, he imposed a "reign of terror" (*hukm al-irhab*) that compromised the population's basic liberties. For instance, he presided over the arrest of thousands of citizens and instructed his adjuncts to torture many of the detainees. "These steps," according to the text, "were unnecessary from the standpoint of the state's security and its well-being."

As per the fourth count, the defendant was accused of corrupting the foundations of government. In 1949, he "provided his assistants the justifications" for assassinating Hasan al-Banna and subsequently obstructed the investigation of the shaykh's murder. "Not guilty," the former prime minister replied. "I am indeed absolutely innocent of all this." The last two counts charged him with both ministerial and personal acts of corruption. More specifically, he was accused of facilitating the ostentatious renovation of the "grand royal yacht" (*al-mahrusa*) with public funds and of exploiting his standing to have a road paved next to his place of residence. All told, the bill of indictment dovetailed neatly with the crimes enumerated in the decree establishing the special tribunal. Likewise, betrayal of the homeland and corruption were building blocks of the revolutionary narrative according to which the *ancien régime* was responsible for the dire straits in which Egypt now found itself.

Procedural Faults

After the bill of indictment was read, the judge allowed ʿAbd al-Hadi to respond briefly to the allegations. To begin, he denied all the charges that were leveled against him. The defendant then claimed that the bill of indictment should be invalidated on the grounds that he was presumably not informed of the counts against him before the trial. Consequently, he was unable to respond to the charges, gather evidence, or summon the appropriate witnesses in advance, which are violations of both his citizen rights and the guidelines of the constitutive decree.[23]

ʿAbd al-Hadi benefited from impressive legal counsel during the initial stages of his trial. At the beginning of the preliminary hearing, he was joined by two lawyers. However, the attorney general, Lieutenant Colonel Muhammad al-Tabʿi, pointed out that article 5 of the decree expressly states that the accused has the right to appoint no more than a single attorney. In response, the defendant stated that his counsel is Mustafa Mar'i, but he would be grateful if the court were to allow Attorney 'Ali Ayub to provide legal assistance. "It is in your hands, judges," 'Abd al-Hadi intoned, "to determine . . . the number of lawyers." Mar'i stressed that, in light of the case's complexity, he would be hard-pressed to bear the burden on his own. However, the motion was denied on the grounds that it contravenes the wording of the decree.

Over the course of his truncated appearance before the special tribunal, Mar'i excoriated the legal procedures that were in force and exposed several flaws in the prosecution's work, especially the wording of the bill of indictment. Though the odds were stacked against him, he attempted to create the impression that the interests of the defense and the judges were basically the same: the search for truth and the provision of a fair trial. To this end, the counselor motioned to postpone the hearings, arguing that he had not been given enough time to study the file, collect documents, and go over the investigative material (on the assumption, he cynically added, that an investigation was even conducted). Furthermore, the counselor asked to have fifteen witnesses summoned on behalf of the defense, whereupon Baghdadi announced that he would refer to this motion only after all the requests were presented.

At this point, Attorney Mar'i touched upon each of the counts against his client. He noted that it is impossible to refer to the first charge with the seriousness it deserves because the prosecution has not submitted any evidence. Consequently, there is no documented basis for the charges.[24] With respect to the second count, he motioned the court to order the prosecution to release the records of a secret meeting of the Representative Council (*majlis al-nu'ab*, the Egyptian Parliament) that preceded Egypt's declaration to enter the 1948 War. The prosecutor interjected that the minutes exist and will be added to the evidence. Thereafter, Mar'i requested the records of another meeting and asked the court to subpoena a few senior army officers who were involved in the decision to invade Palestine, among them Major General Ahmad Muhammad 'Ali al-Muawi, Major General Ahmad Fu'ad Sadiq, and the chief of staff, Lieutenant General 'Uthman al-Mahdi.[25] The prosecutor responded that Muawi was asked to testify but is unable to do so due to illness. 'Abd al-Hadi remarked that the defense can make do without him, but Mar'i told his client to "shut up and don't talk." He then suggested that the officer be interrogated at home and that the resultant affidavit serve as testimony. The court should not suffice with a mere deposition, Mar'i added, because the circumstances warrant an in-depth interrogation as to how Egypt entered the war. "Let's assume that Muawi has passed away," Baghdadi cynically replied, for the fact remains that the witness is unable to appear today. The court can make do, the judge said, with a report that Muawi will formulate on his own. Mar'i vehemently objected to this solution, arguing that an interrogation is essential because the witness must be apprised of the precise issues under review. Counsel's insistence paid dividends, as the judges assented to this demand.

Mar'i then listed the names of other men that he wished to summon, among them ministers in the Nuqrashi government, including 'Abd al-Razzaq al-Sanhuri and Naguib Iskandar, under whose watch Egypt joined the fray. "These figures know how the war was declared," the defense attorney reasoned. "Likewise, they know that Ibrahim 'Abd al-Hadi had no hand in embroiling the Egyptian army in the Palestine War."[26] The manner in which Mar'i phrased this request indeed betrayed his intention of painting the decision to embark on war as a preordained failure, one in which the accused had little part. Henceforward, the issue of responsibility for the army's drubbing in the 1948 War was a focal point of the 'Abd al-Hadi trial.

Another freighted issue on the bill of indictment was the continuous violation of civil liberties during the period leading up to the July Revolution. This count was alluding to the previous regime's treatment of the opposition, first and foremost the MB. The disagreements between the movement and the RCC were already common knowledge. However, both sides had an interest in sullying the image of the monarchial regime. Mar'i also requested that the prosecution forward it a number of documents that pertained to this topic, such as the order dismantling the MB, the verdict in the Nuqrashi murder trial, the government report on the Banna assassination (February 12, 1949), and a certain memo on the torture of interrogees.[27] After the prosecutor confirmed that there was nothing to prevent the transfer of most of these documents, the counselor asked to summons two witnesses with knowledge of the yacht renovation and the road work in 'Abd al-Hadi's area of residence.

The defense attorney then raised an interesting point concerning the trial's duration and the prospects for a fair hearing. He turned the judges' attention to the fact that, as per the constitutive decree, the start of a trial can only be delayed for a short while; that said, there is no limit concerning "the date of the trial's conclusion, regardless of whether it lasts . . . a month, two months, or ten days." In other words, the court can take as long as it needs to complete its deliberations, so that "this matter is subject to the dictates of your [i.e., the judges'] conscience."[28] Following a twenty-five minute break, Baghdadi announced that some of the defense's summons requests were approved and that Muawi would be interrogated. Finally, the prosecution was told to subpoena the witnesses for the next hearing, which was scheduled for the day after tomorrow.

On the morning of Tuesday, September 29, the second hearing got underway. The first order of business was a motion put forward by the prosecutors to relieve Mar'i of his duties. They predicated this request on the shaky grounds that, due to the counselor's long relationship with Hasan al-Banna, he was privy to confidential information. More specifically, the state submitted an opinion that was signed by the general prosecutor, Captain 'Abd al-Bassat al-Banna. As per this document, in light of Mar'i's involvement in the Banna assassination trial (file no. 1071 for the year 1952), it is legally and ethically inappropriate for him to represent the accused.[29] The defense attorney countered that he is surprised by the prosecutors' motion and their unfounded reasoning. Mar'i also noted that he became acquainted with the MB founder when the latter asked him to mediate between the movement and the 'Abd al-Hadi government. The counselor then informed the court of a phone call he received the day before from the head of the Egyptian Bar Association. The latter told him that some members of the organization do not believe he should represent the accused given the fact that Mar'i was a minister during 'Abd al-Hadi's stint as premier. However, at an emergency board meeting later that day, the Bar Association decided that there is no legal impediment to his taking on the case.

Following a short consultation, the presiding judge announced that Mar'i would continue representing the accused. Counsel subsequently lambasted the state attorney for not inviting him to participate in the questioning of Muawi. Not only would he have to contend with a fait accompli, but "I regret to inform you that I have read the affidavit and have learnt that the questions that were essential to be raised before him were not raised." In light of this, it is abundantly clear, Mar'i asserted, that the prosecution is intentionally throwing obstacles in the way of the defense.[30]

At this point, the judges, the attorney general, and the defense counselor engaged in a tempestuous discussion. On the face of things, the disagreements were mostly over procedural issues. Mar'i contended that the judges are interpreting the decree establishing the court—a document that, as it is, severely limits defendant rights—in an overly literal fashion. The judges and the prosecution retorted that Mar'i is turning a blind eye to the fact that his client is standing trial before a special tribunal, which is bound by a unique procedure. The issue that triggered this dispute was the state's request to hear the first two counts, which imputed to 'Abd al-Hadi "actions deemed to be treason against the homeland and against its well-being and the foundation on which the revolution was instituted," behind closed doors. The prosecutor announced that this was necessary because "the sources from which I drew the information are confidential."[31] Mar'i vehemently objected and urged the judges to overrule this motion on the grounds that it constitutes a major infringement of the trial's publicness, a foundational principle of Egyptian law.

"It seems like it has escaped our wisdom," the presiding judge chided the defense attorney, "that we are talking about a court of the revolution." The new leadership, he argued, could have acted like other revolutionary regimes, but instead it graciously offered "the accused the opportunity to defend himself in an independent fashion or by means of a lawyer of his own choosing . . . this points to the generosity of the revolution and its nobility."[32] If the court indeed wishes to be magnanimous, Mar'i replied, "It behooves you to declare a public hearing." However, the lawyer's attempt to expand on the trial's publicness was cut off by Baghdadi, who implored him to keep things short, focus on the essence, and refrain from delaying the proceedings. Once more, the judge stressed that this is a revolutionary court whose judges possess the exclusive authority to determine whether a hearing is open or closed to the public. Moreover, he noted that, save for the constitutive decree, the judges are not bound to any legal code. The attorney answered that he has no intention whatsoever of delaying the hearing and is well aware of the court's revolutionary nature; he merely insists on being allowed to carry out his duties as defense counsel in an appropriate fashion. Yet Baghdadi cut him off again: "There is no getting around the fact that we have to understand that this trial will be conducted swiftly."[33]

Marʿi reprised his promise to assist the court in this regard but demanded permission to clarify his positions on the following issues: the openness of the next session; the absence of a pre-trial meeting between himself and the client; the fact that he was not previously informed of the charges against ʿAbd al-Hadi; and the prosecution's failure to make so much as a single document available to the defense before the trial. These deficiencies, in Marʿi's valuation, clearly violate the constitutive decree of the Revolution's Court. It is quite possible, the attorney claimed, that he would have accepted the motion for a secret hearing if the prosecution had presented him a document showing why the security and well-being of the state warrant such an extreme measure. The charge of treason, he concluded, is not sufficient cause for a close-door hearing. However, it was obvious that the judges were not moved by these words, and Baghdadi once again demanded that Marʿi cut to the chase. Chafed by what he perceived to be the judges' antagonism toward his case, the attorney resorted to the last trick up his sleeve: "I regret to say that it appears as though I will not be able to fulfill my duty." Marʿi then vented his professional frustration and reached the following conclusion:

> I am only asking to explain my point of view. . . . You are working in a court over which the flag of the revolution hangs—the flag of integrity. [Yet,] I am not permitted to express my view. What's more, I declare before you that there is absolutely no chance of carrying out my work and [fulfilling my] duty. It is with an open heart and sorrow that I say to this man [ʿAbd al-Hadi] that I am unable to fulfill my obligation toward him; and with your permission, I will resign from my position as his counsel. I am overcome with regret.[34]

A mere fifty or so minutes after the opening of the second session, the revolutionary court stood before its first decision that was directly linked to its standing as a special tribunal. Given the large contingency of local and foreign journalists in the room, the judges probably realized that the acclaimed lawyer's resignation would command extensive media coverage that was likely to trigger a public discourse on the very ability of the revolutionary court to provide its defendants a fair trial. Baghdadi exchanged a couple of words with his colleagues, and, following a brief consultation with the litigators, he announced that the court has accepted Marʿi's resignation. Therefore, "the accused must choose who he sees fit to defend him or take the defense upon himself."[35] At this juncture, a fifteen-minute break was called to allow ʿAbd al-Hadi to ponder his next move.

When the hearing resumed, the defendant was asked whether he had selected a new counsel, but he refrained from directly answering the question. In any event, from this stage onward, the ex-prime minister ran his own defense. Throughout the trial, he occasionally regurgitated the arguments that Attorney Marʿi had raised with respect to the court's problematic legal framework. For the most part, though, he sufficed with laconic responses to the serious charges brought against him. While utterly rejecting all the accusations, he repeatedly placed himself at the mercy of the judges' consciences.

For the next hour or so, ʿAbd al-Hadi was allowed to discuss the bill of indictment. During this extemporaneous peroration, he stressed, "I am convinced of my innocence. At the age of 56, after dedicating my best years to working on behalf of the homeland, there is no basis for accusing me of treason nor have they [i.e., the state's lawyers] presented any evidence to this effect." The accused then described how he had been involved in the national struggle ever since he was a teen. As an adult, ʿAbd al-Hadi held posts in which he helped to "lay the foundations for Egyptian independence." Moreover, he noted that many of his relatives "are military officers and others were active in the struggle for national liberation." The defendant then urged the court not to be fooled by the protracted, slanderous campaign that is being waged against him in the press, which "is distorting" his life's work. With respect to his performance in senior government posts, ʿAbd al-Hadi claimed, "I operated within the framework of the law and the constitution and conducted myself as any person with authority was obliged to act by dint of his position." The ex-premier then vehemently denied that he was among Faruq's closest confidants.

By this point, many of ʿAbd al-Hadi's thoughts were being left unfinished, thereby attesting to the tumultuous state that he was in. Likewise, the defendant raised a slew of questions—"Why am I here? And what do they expect of me?" "Did I corrupt the government?" "Was I the one who facilitated the king's wishes to enter the Palestine War so that he could sacrifice the sons of his nation?"—none of which he bothered to answer. Instead, he put forth a number of arguments that were similar to those raised earlier by Attorney Marʿi, such as the issue of the closed-door hearing, the lack of time to prepare, and the withholding of documents. "I am unable to defend myself like a lawyer," he professed.

> Therefore, I am stating my case even if they [sic] are not organized as is required by law. After dedicating my entire life to the service of the country, I am hereby accused of treason, and this without any proof.

> . . . I was and remain an Egyptian like you, and it is my right to ask the revolutionaries and the court to provide me with the means to defend myself; and you [the judges] are under no constraints, except for your consciences. Act as you wish. I stand before you and my fate is in your hands. . . . I place my trust in the justice that you will render, and I place my trust in Allah.[36]

With the completion of ʿAbd al-Hadi's quasi-opening statements, the prosecutor once again requested that the hearing on the first two counts be conducted behind closed doors. He stressed that the evidence includes "sources from which the intelligence [*al-mukhabarat*] directorate drew its information," and their exposure would harm the supreme interests of the state's security. Immediately thereafter, a half-hour recess was called to enable the court to decide how to proceed in the absence of a defense counsel. Upon returning to the court hall, Baghdadi announced that the accused would defend himself in accordance with article 5 of the decree and that the hearing on the charge of treason would be held in secret, to the exclusion of the press and even the Attorney General.[37]

It was soon apparent that ʿAbd al-Hadi intended neither to appoint a lawyer nor to defend himself in earnest. Over the course of the trial, he frequently pointed to the absence of a defense counsel. As could be expected, Baghdadi offered several variations of the following riposte: "We indeed recommended that you take a lawyer. Why aren't you doing so?" On one occasion, the defendant rhetorically asked whether "we are indeed dealing with the issue of a lawyer?" In so doing, he succinctly underscored the special tribunal's dubious procedures. This biting criticism was not left unanswered, as the court once again dwelled on the general circumstances behind its establishment and its modus operandi. "We already made it clear," the judge said, "that the Revolution's Court will not grant a defendant all the rights." On the other hand, the court could have "summoned him and reached a verdict five minutes later. However, the revolution displayed its generosity and granted you the right to appoint a lawyer . . ., and you said that you would defend yourself. Does not all this [attest to the revolution's] generosity?" "Far be it from me," ʿAbd al-Hadi countered, to deny that the revolution has this right.

> All I'm saying is that the revolution was intended for the entire public and you are representing everyone, so you must take into account my right. . . . And as I have said, in order for me to fulfill my obligation to assist the court in its work, it is incumbent upon you to afford me with my right. Give me my right and listen to a report and evidence. Give me the chance.

This exchange ended with an illuminating observation by Judge Baghdadi: "The meaning [of your request] is that we will implement procedures like the procedures of *regular* courts and try Ibrahim ʿAbd al-Hadi for the course of a year and *halt* the revolution for an entire year!"[38] In essence, this statement reveals the correlation that the regime's helmsmen (the judges were, as noted, members of the RCC) drew between the establishment of the special tribunal and the continued path of the July Revolution. Most important, this exchange sheds light on the flawed procedures of this judicial body.

Henceforth, the accused barely reacted to the claims raised by the prosecution, and, when he did, his explanations were rather terse. That said, the chief judge often sought out his opinion following statements by witnesses or the state attorneys. It is evident that the court aspired to entrench the idea in the public mind that ʿAbd al-Hadi was given an opportunity to present his case but declined to do so. For example, at the end of the third session, the defendant once again refused to give his take on the events under review. Instead, he sufficed with a brief statement negating the prosecution's case in its entirety and arguing that he was being deprived of the necessary means to prove his innocence. "In other words," Baghdadi cautioned, "you still insist on not helping the court?" ʿAbd al-Hadi answered that he has no desire to impede on the court's work. In fact, "I am eager" to respond, but to do so the appropriate tools must be placed at my disposal.[39]

At the latter stages of this hearing, the attorney general returned to the matter of the court's procedures, in an effort to forestall the possibility that the judges or the public would infer that ʿAbd al-Hadi lost the case for this reason. To this end, Tabʿi regurgitated Judge Baghdadi's argument whereby the special tribunal "is not circumscribed by the accepted limitations of regular courts or military tribunals." He also claimed that the prosecution had given the defense "all the documents that it requested. The accused kept silent," Tabʿi added, "for he was unable to refute the witnesses' words; and every time it appeared as though there was a hole in their case, he [i.e., ʿAbd al-Hadi] indeed wasted no time making himself heard."[40] What is more, the attorney general insisted that Mustafa Marʿi decided to step down once he realized that the arguments in the bill of indictment are solid and well-founded. However, these assertions were far-fetched. In fact, the court's transcripts show that at the outset of the proceedings, a fair share of the defense's requests for investigative material were overruled, including documents that underpinned the case against the accused.

The matter of poor procedures surfaced in other trials that were conducted in the Revolution's Court. On October 4, 1953, two lieutenant colonels, Saʿd al-Din al-Sunbati and Ismaʿil al-Maligi, were tried before the special tribunal. The first count imputed to the officers "actions that are considered treason against the homeland and against its well-being and the foundation on which the revolution was instituted, and this because over the course of 1953 [the defendants] covered up for the efforts of others who stood in contact with foreign elements for the purpose of harming the present government and the supreme interests of the state."[41] This marked the first time that the prosecution sought a treason conviction for aiding and abetting "the efforts of others" (who were not even tried), rather than a direct action. Like the 'Abd al-Hadi trial, the prosecutor requested a closed-door hearing on the grounds that the source enjoyed immunity from the law. Maligi's counsel, Wahid Ra'fat, predicated his objection to this motion on the very wording of the special tribunal's constitutive decree. In fact, Ra'fat's performance justified his reputation as one of Egypt's most gifted lawyers. He cast doubt on the very legitimacy of the special tribunal. The court's establishment, he argued, was supposed to take effect only after the decree was filed in the state's records. However, the government never went through the motions, as it only published the order in the press.[42]

At this point, Ra'fat unfurled his principal argument, which he chose to present in a sophisticated and roundabout way: "As the Court of the Revolution, you are not obliged to act in accordance to the regular laws, such as the criminal code or the penal code." It is no coincidence, though, that the decree unmistakably "anchored the defendant's right to legal counsel," albeit limiting each of the accused to a single lawyer (article 5). Furthermore, the next article refers to the "means" (*ijra'at*) that are placed at the judges' disposal. Ra'fat wondered "what is the meaning" of the clause stipulating that the judges may take "means beyond" those stated in the decree "should they see fit?" Put differently, the judges had indeed been granted ample room for maneuver, as they "are not compelled to act solely on the basis of those steps explicitly noted in this decree."[43] With this shrewd step, Ra'fat basically took one of the document's most problematic clauses and turned it on its head by dint of an original interpretation. He then drew a correlation between his analysis of articles 5 and 6 and the prosecution's request to conduct the hearing on the charge of treason in secret by raising the following three points: the defense is not opposed in principle to a closed session; likewise, it accepts the prosecution's argument that the greater good occasionally necessitate these sort of measures, even at the price of compromising the defendant's rights; and acknowledging these principles does not obviate the need to preserve the defendant's right to counsel, even behind closed doors.

If this were not enough, Ra'fat placed this argument in the universal context of other revolutions. The principle of safeguarding a defendant's right to counsel is accepted throughout the world, to the point where "it is obligatory" for the state to provide the accused a lawyer. The epitome of this right dates back to "the great French Revolution, over the course of which Louis XVI was tried." The deposed king's trial was held in public, and he merited the counsel of three former ministers and three lawyers. Since the French Revolution, "the presence of a lawyer has become a foundation of the foundations of the principle of the defense of the accused." In his summation, the defense counsel reiterated that it is within the judges' purview to decide on whether to hold a session behind closed doors but entreated them to allow the defense to accompany the accused to this hearing. Moreover, he assured the judges that nothing will leak from these deliberations. "The objective of the revolution was to attain one goal—the protection of individual rights"—foremost, "the right to counsel." This notion has become, in Ra'fat's estimation, a universal right. In fact, all the monotheistic faiths command their judges to conduct a fair trial, and the right to counsel is an unequivocal expression of this precept.[44] At any rate, this brilliant analysis failed to persuade the judges, who ruled that the hearing in question would be conducted without the representatives of the defense and prosecution. In both these cases, the closed-door session lasted about an hour, and the court ultimately acquitted the defendants of treason.

Conclusion

The FO's perception of *Mahkamat al-Thawra*'s objectives is latent in the manner in which the court was publically unveiled, the choice of its name and venue, the design of its courtroom, and, most important, the decree specifying its authority and modus operandi. The us-versus-them rhetoric that inhered the tribunal's formation was ratcheted up during the hearings, as terms such as "subversion," "traitor," and "enemies of the people" come up time and again. Insofar as the FO was concerned, the offenses perpetrated by the accused and the danger they posed to the revolution and society rendered the special court the only suitable institution for bringing them to justice. Furthermore, the RCC's speakers argued that the steps taken by *Mahkamat al-Thawra* were typical of revolutions throughout the world.

The opening two sessions of the Ibrahim ʿAbd al-Hadi trial concentrated on procedural issues. Its first major controversy revolved around the prosecution's demand to hold a closed-door session on the counts of treason against the former prime minister, lest the identities of *al-mukhabarat*'s confidential informants become public knowledge. In upholding this motion, the judges predicated themselves on the decree establishing the court, which gave them full discretion to run the proceedings as they saw fit. Under the dire circumstances in which Egypt found itself, the panel ruled, this was the sole way to ensure due process and a fair trial. The defense also referred to this decree and the emergency atmosphere, albeit in a markedly different fashion. More specifically, Attorney Marʿi enumerated substantial legal flaws in the tribunal's procedures, which severely infringed upon his client's rights. While the judges admitted that some of Marʿi's points were not without merit, they argued that this is, after all, a revolutionary court and that a lawful decree has granted them unlimited powers.

In sum, the procedural aspects of this trial are reflective of the general situation in Egypt at the time. Be that as it may, these facets of *Mahkamat al-Thawra* are not even alluded to in the handful of other topical studies dealing with this special court. This absence is all the more glaring with respect to the court's sessions on distinctly historical topics. The judges who presided over the 'Abd al-Hadi trial essentially conducted themselves as historians upon deliberating over Egypt's entry into the 1948 War.

4

Who Was Responsible for the 1948 Debacle?

A substantial portion of the ʿAbd al-Hadi trial was dedicated to clarifying the role of the accused in Egypt's decision to enter the Palestine War. More specifically, the hearings focused on three topics: the monarchial regime's decisions in the run-up to the invasion, especially that of the various decision-making bodies; the Egyptian army's combat readiness in all that concerned ordnance, training, and logistical support; and the leadership's conduct during and in the aftermath of the campaign. Accordingly, the prosecution focused on the question of why an "unprepared army" was sent into battle.[1]

Waging War

The court's rhetoric portrayed the regime's flawed decision-making process as a direct expression of the government's unscrupulousness, which led to the stinging military defeat. From a legal standpoint, the prosecution and judges put an emphasis on determining ʿAbd al-Hadi's involvement in the war effort at two critical junctures: on the eve of Egypt's invasion, when the defendant was chief of the Royal Divan, and toward the end of 1948 when he secured ceasefire and armistice agreements in his capacity as prime minister. The evidence submitted before the court was intended to paint the accused not only as one of the government's top officials but also as a central player in the decision-making apparatus at various stages of the campaign. For instance, the chief of the Royal Divan was described as a critical link in the two-way flow of information between the palace and the military and political establishments.

ʿAbd al-Hadi adamantly denied any responsibility for the invasion and stated that he was completely cut off from the king's inner circle. He also claimed that the position of the Royal Divan chief and its purview were not defined in any regulation or law. In making his case, the accused sought to distance himself from any formal responsibility for the decisions that culminated in the 1948 War. However, his words failed to convince the court, as Baghdadi aired his doubts out loud: "Does it stand to reason that the king's political advisor did not have a say in and knowledge of the decision" to enter the campaign? In response, the defendant maintained that the prime minister was the king's leading advisor. As head of the Divan, he merely forwarded to his supervisors "what was brought to my attention on the military's lack of readiness." Moreover, ʿAbd al-Hadi claimed that he had only learned of the army's dismal state, including the acute shortage of weapons, after the war had already broken out.[2]

From this point on, the court adopted a strategy of ascertaining facts that would demonstrate how illogical it is for an official of ʿAbd al-Hadi's stature to have been left out of the loop. A case in point is the following exchange: "What is the position that you held in the governing apparatus," the chief judge asked, "during the Palestine War?" "I was the head of the king's Divan," the defendant replied. However, he denied that this title exposed him ipso facto to confidential information on the Egyptian military.[3] In addition, he repeated the claim that the chief of the Royal Divan lacked the authority to participate in the decision-making process.

Whereas the prosecution and judges wanted to focus on the domestic sphere and, above all, the fields in which ʿAbd al-Hadi was involved, the defendant's answers shed light on the broader context in which the key decisions were made. In this respect, his testimony constitutes an important historical source on the 1948 War. Time and again, the ex-prime minister stressed that the basic decision to take up arms should a Jewish state be declared was made on the pan-Arab level. More specifically, this political decision was made by the Arab heads of state. As chief of the Royal Divan, he did not participate in the relevant discussions, which King Faruq attended on behalf of Egypt. Moreover, pursuant to the 1923 Constitution, the monarch was the supreme commander of the Egyptian armed forces. In this capacity, the king frequently consulted with Minister of War Lieutenant General (*fariq*) Muhammad Haidar. The latter presided over various forums that weighed the pros and cons of launching an invasion. In ʿAbd al-Hadi's view, the war minister's reports in these frameworks on the army's preparedness turned out to be misleading and unsubstantiated.[4]

According to the hegemonic narrative of the Palestine War that was crafted by the RCC, the king and much of the political elite were portrayed as being driven by ulterior motives: the king aspired to consolidate his status as the leader of the Arab world, while the premier and his ministers simply bowed to Faruq's whims. Because the cabinet members well knew, the FO claimed, that the army was ill-prepared for war; they were derelict in their duty as publically elected officials.[5] Against the backdrop of these allegations, a discursive dialogue took form in the Revolution's Court on the matter of those who stood behind Egypt's decision to go to war. In this context, ʿAbd al-Hadi repeatedly stressed the role of local public opinion and the Arab media: public support for entering the campaign stretched from wall to wall; sizeable demonstrations in favor of liberating Palestine were held in town squares and university campuses; and the press was rife with commentary offering moral and civic justifications for thwarting the establishment of a Jewish state.[6] Furthermore, there was extensive media coverage of the mentioned pan-Arab summits. These reports created the impression that the Arab world was uniting its ranks and mobilizing its resources behind this shared goal. Naguib Iskandar, the former minister of health, offered a similar account in his testimony: While the king may have given the order to set out for war, the entire populace "pushed" in this direction. As a politician and senior member of the Nuqrashi government, it was impossible to withstand this "heavy public pressure."[7]

ʿAbd al-Hadi's claims as to his minor role as chief of the Royal Divan in the run-up to the invasion were accurate. However, his contention that he had nothing to do with the war preparations was soon debunked. According to the defendant, he had no information on the state of the army's readiness, so that he was unable to report on this matter to the king. He even testified that "I only heard [about the attack] when the general public was informed about it." Over the course of his trial, a great deal of evidence was submitted that contradicted these statements. It turns out that ʿAbd al-Hadi took part in a number of senior government and military meetings on a wide range of issues that pertained to the eventuality of joining the campaign. In this context, the presiding judge employed a clever gambit that was intended to tie ʿAbd al-Hadi directly to the malfeasance of the governing echelon during the final phases of the 1948 War: "While serving as prime minister," Baghdadi asked, "did you order the mobilization of all the state's resources and manpower in light of the state of the war?" The defendant answered that he was preoccupied with "stopping the fighting" and "stopping the catastrophe [*karitha*]." By this juncture, he had already realized that the other Arab armies were not pulling their weight, and the "pressure was thrust entirely on the Egyptian military." According to ʿAbd al-Hadi, despite the awful situation on the front, Minister of War Haidar averred that "the Egyptian army was capable of handling the campaign on its own. . . . I was not the minister of war and the responsibility on the matter of the army's readiness and the shortage of weapons [is] not on" my shoulders.[8] Under these difficult circumstances, he toiled without respite to obtain a ceasefire and armistice agreement.

Unmoved by the defendant's explanations, the chief judge demanded an answer to the following question:

> What is the reason that a country [i.e., Egypt] with a population of 22 million and resources that are greater than the other state [Israel], which numbers one million [people], was unable to come out on top? There is a fundamental reason that the army was unable to fulfill the

> mission, and you, prime minister, are supposed to know what it is. What is the reason for this tragedy?[9]

Once again, ʿAbd al-Hadi failed to muster a persuasive answer. All he managed to say was that, according to the reports he had received, the army was seeking "an immediate political solution [*hal siyasi fawran*]" aimed at rescuing the troops from the dire straits which in they found themselves. Baghdadi countered that if he were prime minister and such troubling information came to his attention, he would have conducted an in-depth investigation of why the army failed "to meet" the challenges of the campaign. "At the same time," the accused replied, "we did not deal with this. . . . All that we worked toward was saving the army."[10]

According to ʿAbd al-Hadi's testimony, three options were examined at this juncture of the war: fighting on, at the risk that the situation would deteriorate even further; an American-backed ceasefire; and a truce (*hudna*) between Israel and the Arab states. ʿAbd al-Hadi then described how he had contacted the political advisor of the United States Embassy in Cairo for the sake of inquiring about the possibility of a cessation of hostilities. He discovered that Israel was uninterested in a ceasefire. Instead, the enemy was leaning toward a *hudna*, a truce within the framework of far-reaching understandings with the Arab states. The diplomat then asked ʿAbd al-Hadi whether Egypt was open to an American ceasefire proposal. The latter told him that the government would accept a serious offer on the condition that the United States guarantee that Israel keeps its hand off the trigger. By this point in the hearing, it was obvious that the accused was under tremendous stress: "I'm sorry," he told the judges with a broken voice, "but I am unable to continue in this fashion without the [counsel] of a lawyer."[11]

With ʿAbd al-Hadi at a loss for words, the court called to the stand the prosecution's central witness—Lieutenant General Haidar. The ex-minister of war was viewed as one of King Faruq's closest confidantes. Much to the chagrin of many veteran army officers, the palace had "parachuted" Haidar into this plum post straight from his job as director of the Prison Authority. That said, the witness presented himself as the speaker of the military command and attempted, albeit with limited success, to distance himself from Faruq. The minister's description of his part in the military's disastrous performance in the 1948 War could not have been further from the revolutionary narrative. Even before the military coup, the FO placed most of the blame on the army's top brass, Haidar included. In one of the revolutionaries' first manifestos, the military rout was described as a failure of the high command. For this reason, "it is incumbent upon Egypt" to remake the army and replace the top officers. Another manifesto, titled "A Warning and a Promise," reprised the demand to carry out a sweeping reform of the armed forces. Moreover, the document urged "loyal officers and soldiers" to see to it that the military is rebuilt, so that it can confront "the forces of imperialism that are parked in Egypt" and serve the people, rather than oppress them (as they believed it had done until now). In proclamations circulated in the weeks before the coup, the FO clamored for a purge that would rid the army of collaborators and described the majority of officers in the high command as "unsuitable appointments."[12]

Soon after taking the oath, Haidar came under a barrage of sharp questions. "You were the war minister when the war was declared and Egypt went into Palestine," the presiding judge started things off. "How did Egypt enter the war?" According to the witness, public pressure to jump to the aid of "Palestine's Arabs in their just struggle against Zionist aggression" began months before the outbreak of hostilities. Young Egyptians, including military officers, wanted to go out to the front, and the military command decided to support them. To this end, Ahmad 'Abd al-'Aziz was named the chief commander of a volunteer force. The army provided the volunteers with the "clothing of Palestine's Arabs; we equipped them with arms, and we changed the color of the artillery pieces."[13]

Baghdadi then asked the witness "from whom did you learn that the army would enter the war on May 15." "It was mentioned in the papers," he replied, "that the [Arab] armies would enter the war. Afterwards, the officers of the general staff convened for a meeting."[14] Judge Baghdadi, who was a major general and an air force pilot in his own right, refused to let the ex-minister off the hook: "The general staff assembled on the basis of a notice in the press?" Instead of answering this provocative question, Haidar described how he had ordered his staff officers to investigate the situation thoroughly, and they found "that the army's ordnance is inadequate and the deficiencies are vast." This information was immediately conveyed to Prime Minister Nuqrashi.

To the best of the witness' knowledge, though, the decision to have the Arab armies invade Palestine was reached by "the king of Egypt and the Arab heads of state in a meeting that was hosted at Inshas by Faruq" in May 1946.[15] He also claimed that this critical decision was made before the military command was even asked to present its view on the topic. In so doing, the witness sought to divert the lion's share of the blame for the misguided invasion onto the political echelon. The main culprits in his view were Prime Minister Nuqrashi and King Faruq, whom he repeatedly called "the supreme commander of the armed forces." He also asserted that the king had turned a blind eye to the military's reports that its troops were ill-prepared for war and lacking in crucial areas.

The Army's Preparedness

In practice, high-level discussions on the army's state of readiness did not begin until a week before Egypt entered the war. Apart from a session of the House of Representatives on May 12, 1948, major studies on the Palestine War surprisingly do not refer to these hearings, including the major doubts as to the wisdom of launching an attack that were broached therein.[16] Nevertheless, the ʿAbd al-Hadi trial indicates that a pivotal discussion was held in the war minister's office between Haidar, Prime Minister Nuqrashi, and senior members of the army command two days before the offensive. Although the defendant did not attend this meeting, most of the participants testified that he was waiting in an adjacent room and was subsequently briefed by the premier. Haidar dedicated a few minutes to this important discussion in his own testimony. As opposed to other accounts, he claimed that ʿAbd al-Hadi was present, but "listened to what was said and did not speak." According to his testimony a number of senior officers surveyed the army's state of readiness at this meeting, each of whom underscored the acute shortage in armament. Haidar then reiterated that Nuqrashi was told in no uncertain terms that the army was unprepared for the campaign and that "the condition of the munitions is terrible." Despite this professional assessment, the prime minister "said that there is no choice but to enter the war," and the participants understood that the die was cast. To the question of whether the military asked for an extension to prepare for combat, the ex-minister answered no.[17]

When it became clear that Haidar had no intention of discussing this particular meeting any further, the prosecutor turned to the manner in which information on the army's readiness was presented at an emergency session of the House of Dignitaries (*majlis al-shuyukh*), Egypt's Senate. This meeting, which was categorized as secret by the speaker, was held three days before Egypt joined the fray. At the outset, the ex-war minister had a difficult time answering the question of whether he was present at the meeting.[18] Consequently, ʿAbd al-Hadi cut in and scornfully suggested the obvious: "Check the documents and see if he took part." The transcripts note that "the prosecutor is turning the papers before him," whereupon the chief judge posed the following question: "Is it noted in the minutes [of the senate hearing] that the army's condition is awful?" The state attorney submitted a copy of the document to the judges and stressed that "it was made perfectly clear that the army is ready!" In fact, the prime minister "noted that . . . the Arab forces, all of them, are capable of eradicating [*sahq*] the Zionist forces. It did not say that the army is unprepared." To bolster his argument, the prosecutor read Nuqrashi's closing statements from the transcript: "The Egyptian army is ready, and its weaponry is sufficient [*wafiya*] and [so is] the ammunition at its disposal."[19] In other words, the prime minister intentionally withheld information as to the army's weaknesses from the Senate.

ʿAbd al-Hadi then entreated the judges to go through all the exchanges in that session, not just random segments. In addition, he suggested that the court examine the records of the military commission that investigated this topic, but his words did not merit a response. Which commission Haidar had in mind is unclear from the available sources as a handful of committees were established to investigate this matter in the aftermath of the war. The attorney general also referred to several unidentifiable texts. For example, he alluded to a document titled "The Position of the Egyptian Forces in al-ʿArish" that was forwarded to the chief of the general staff. Despite this passing reference, the report was neither exhibited before the court nor did the prosecutor survey its content.

During Haidar's testimony, Baghdadi sought to clarify with whom the power to declare war rested, and the ex-war minister outlined the standard procedure for making this decision: The military command was supposed to have held discussions and formulated estimates within internal forums. Thereafter, it should have presented its professional opinion to the senior political echelon. The next step was for the premier to convoke a governmental hearing with the objective of articulating a position that would then be brought before the House of Representatives. The Supreme Defense Council (*majlis al-difāʿ al-aʿalā*) was also supposed to have convened, but in practice this body did not function. Once again, the witness stressed that, according to the constitution, the king had the final say on this matter. He also noted that Faruq's leading advisors were, in descending order, the prime minister and the chief of the Royal Divan. These two officials sat atop an apparatus that was designed to furnish the palace with trustworthy information and express its opinion on crucial issues.[20] In light of this, the witness posited, Nuqrashi and ʿAbd al-Hadi played a key role in the decision-making process (with regard to entering the war) and thus bore responsibility for the debacle.

In reality, Haidar contended, the decision-making in the run-up to the campaign was fundamentally flawed. Although the military command informed the prime minister of the abysmal state of the armed forces, Nuqrashi had already declared—before an official government hearing was even held on the topic—that there was no choice but to enter the fray. A forum was subsequently convened, and it approved of the decision post factum. According to the witness, the top generals inferred from Nuqrashi's words that the king and the premier were on the same page. The order for the army to enter the Palestine War, he concluded, was given by King Faruq. However, Baghdadi did not suffice with this general description and prodded the ex-war minister to furnish a specific answer to the question of "Who are the individuals that are responsible for the entry into the war?" "The supreme commander," Haidar replied, "namely the king." After a short pause, he added, "the prime minister had no choice but to defer to the king's decision."[21]

The next topic on the court's agenda was ʿAbd al-Hadi's role in the decision to unleash the troops. To begin, he declared "that I have sworn to tell the truth, and the truth is that I did not discuss this topic with him [the accused]." Several minutes later, he noted that Nuqrashi passed on information to the king regarding the army's condition both before and during the war, such as news from the front, via Chief of the Royal Divan ʿAbd al-Hadi. The witness then remarked that some of this information was based on discussions that he had held with Nuqrashi in his own capacity as war minister. In so doing, he contradicted the defendant's expressed denial that he had served as a conduit for the king.

This testimony also suggests that Haidar never directly presented the army's own view of its battle readiness to Faruq. Moreover, the minister insisted that he did not even meet with the king in the run-up to the momentous decision. This claim sharply differed from other accounts that were given in the course of the trial that the monarch's door was open to Haidar. Furthermore, he claimed that "everyone knows that the Palace was in the habit of keeping in touch with officers in the army," and it intervened in the administration of the war "behind my back."[22] In other words, the witness was implying that not only did Faruq meddle in the army's affairs, but so did his assistants and advisors, ʿAbd al-Hadi included. Despite being asked to do so, the minister refused to mention the names of those same individuals in the "palace."

On this note, the ex-war minister's testimony came to a close. Baghdadi then sought to compare the versions of the witness and the defendant, but the latter would not respond to Haidar's words. Instead, ʿAbd al-Hadi once again declared that the court has already heard all that he has to say. Now, he concluded, the burden is on the judges to establish the truth and to act according to their conscience.

An hour later, Naguib Iskandar took to the stand. His testimony was considerably more detailed and persuasive than that of Lieutenant General Haidar. The former had served as a health minister in Nuqrashi's government and was considered among the premier's closest advisors. He was originally summoned as a defense witness, but ʿAbd al-Hadi chose to abjure. Nevertheless, Iskandar was allowed to give his testimony and, in fact, shed light on the shift in Nuqrashi's position on the merits of entering the 1948 War. According to the witness, heavy public and political pressure was exerted on the government both from within Egypt and throughout the Arab world to support the entry into the war at once. At the outset, the prime minister had reservations about joining the fray under the existing circumstances. Above all, he was reluctant to dispatch the troops into Palestine so long as there were British forces on Egyptian soil. In general, Iskandar said, "we [i.e., the government's ministers] agreed with the prime minister's view." However, "sometime later, the king, by dint of his position as supreme commander, ordered the army to move for the purpose of teaching a lesson to those Jewish gangs." It was, in fact, Faruq who made the pivotal decision to enter the war, and "the topic was not subject to debate." The ministers and parliament were presented with a fait accompli and had no choice but to approve the king's announcement. As politicians, the witness admitted, the members of government were attentive to the sentiments of the general public, which was almost unanimously in favor of launching an invasion. In addition, he claimed that the ministers' position was influenced by a declaration on the part Lieutenant General Haidar that the army was good and ready.[23]

While Baghdadi wanted Iskandar to focus on the decision-making in the run-up to the war, the latter touched on some other dimensions of the affair. For instance, he described how the enemy was perceived by Egypt's helmsmen: "In our eyes, Israel was not a state that was worthy of declaring war on, but a group of gangs." As such, "certain units of the army were instructed to take action in order to teach a lesson to those ruffians." In response, the stunned chief judge asked the following question: "It turns out that we entered the Palestine War without declaring war?" Iskandar confirmed his suspicions and added that "at the time, anyone who would have tried to speak out against entering the fray would have been considered a traitor." Even at this stage, according to the witness, Nuqrashi had second thoughts about the decision to enter Palestine. That said, had the prime minister resigned at that moment, he would have exposed the Egyptian army's weakness to the other Arab states.[24]

A similar account was given by Muhammad Husayn Haykal, the president of the Senate (*Majlis al-Shuyukh*, 1945–50). According to the distinguished intellectual, Nuqrashi changed his position concerning the war on May 11. Until then, he was jittery about sending the army to Palestine with British forces stationed along the Suez Canal. His unexpected change of heart was voiced in the mentioned secret meeting of the Senate. Haykal attributed the sudden volte-face to the sway of Arab public opinion and the Egyptian senior command, both of which assumed that the army would "throw the Jews into the sea . . . and . . . torpedo the UN's decision [to partition Palestine] on the day of its implementation." Owing to the propaganda broadcast in the Arab media, it was widely believed that "Tel-Aviv, the capital (of imaginary Israel), would fall into the hands of the Egyptian army within days."[25] Finally, in blatant violation of the rules laid forth in the constitution, Haidar received a direct order from the king to send the army toward the border, "without the knowledge of the prime minister and without waiting for the decision of parliament or . . . the government."[26]

The subject of the military's combat readiness was further accentuated in the hearing on the affidavit of Major General Ahmad al-Muawi, who was named general commander of the Egyptian forces in Palestine on the eve of the war. As noted, the bed-ridden officer was questioned exclusively by representatives of the Attorney General's Office and without the participation of the defense. Dated September 25, 1953 and signed by the witness, the document submitted to the court was roughly four pages long.[27] Although Muawi was not a Free Officer, his testimony dovetailed neatly with the prosecution's case. Lacking so much as a thin layer of varnish, this unique report expounds upon the abysmal state of the Egyptian army before the campaign.

On May 10, 1948, Muawi was rushed to staff headquarters in Cairo from his command post in al-ʿArish to share his views on the looming invasion with the senior brass. Summaries of the discussions in which he took part over the next few days constitute the lion's share of the affidavit. To begin, the officer debriefed Chief of Staff ʿUthman al-Mahdi on the situation along the front lines. Before long, Haidar stepped into the room. In response to the war minister's question, Muawi explained that "in all honesty, the army is absolutely unqualified to enter any campaign whatsoever." He reminded Haidar that, during the war minister's visit to the bases in al-ʿArish, he had personally witnessed the shortage in combat-worthy arms, and officers informed him of "the tough situation that the army is in."[28]

That afternoon, another meeting was held in Haidar's office, which was attended by Prime Minister Nuqrashi and a number of high-ranking officers. This discussion makes up the brunt of Muawi's testimony. He was asked by the premier to give his opinion "on the state of the army and the prospects for its entering the war in Palestine." After surveying various aspects of the military's operational strength, the officer concluded "that the army is in no way qualified to enter any campaign whatsoever, without any connection to what has been said about the weakness of the Jews. Our army is smitten by shortages in all the [necessary] means, foremost among them the weapons that stand at the combat soldiers' disposal." Those in stock are in poor condition, beginning with rifles and ending with artillery pieces and tanks. Furthermore, Muawi bluntly stated that the troops are unskilled in warfare due to a lack of proper drills and training. For example, during exercises, every soldier is allotted "ten rifle bullets instead of" the "two hundred" or so that are needed to adequately prepare them for battle. Thereafter, he elaborated on the awful state of the field corps, especially the auxiliary forces that provide logistical support to the combat units including the transport vehicles that shuttle, supply, and provide logistics for the front-line troops. In his estimation, a large share of the trucks was unfit for driving in the conditions that prevailed in the theater of operations. Consequently, the fleet was only capable of ferrying small amounts of personnel at a time. Similar deficiencies characterized the water carriers and the medical units, whose serviceable ambulances he estimated at a mere ten to fifteen percent of capacity.[29]

Muawi pinned the subpar combat readiness on insufficient training for combat missions. For many years, he explained, the army's training regimen was geared toward internal security. "There is no [program of] exercises in the sense of training and readiness for entering a war" because the unit that is charged with exercises "set a clear goal for its operations" according to which "the army is designated for internal security [missions] and not war." In other words, the troops were used for preserving the order within Egypt. For example, it secured voting booths during elections, quashed demonstrations, assisted in disaster recovery, and fulfilled an array of other police missions.

In essence, the Egyptian leadership had tacitly agreed that the British forces stationed in the country would deter outside threats. As a result, hardly any major annual war exercises were held. Muawi concluded this profound survey by welcoming "the chief of staff or the minister of war to take issue" with any of his arguments, but not a word was uttered by either man.[30]

According to Muawi, Nuqrashi's reaction to the estimates of the military officers signaled that the invasion was nonetheless a fait accompli. It also turns out from the affidavit that the prime minister offered the commanders an historical explanation for his position: On the eve of the Second World War, the English troops were not fully prepared, but this did not stop them from entering and ultimately beating the Germans. In wrapping up the discussion, Nuqrashi asked to visit the operations room. Upon his arrival, the premier was given a map of the Jewish settlements and a run-down of the forces along the border. However, the information that he received was plagued by false assumptions concerning the state of the Egyptian army. Moreover, the enemy was described as "a band of divided gangs" lacking in offensive initiative and incapable of persevering against the Arab forces.[31]

At this point in the court hearing, ʿAbd al-Hadi raised a question aimed at buttressing his contention that he was uninvolved in the decision-making process: Is Muawi claiming "that I was present at the meeting?" Attorney General Tabʿi confirmed that the affidavit implies that the defendant was waiting in a nearby room. The prosecutor then repeated his claim that ʿAbd al-Hadi bore responsibility for the army's entanglement in the 1948 War, which had "grave consequences for Egypt."[32] The chief of the Royal Divan, Tabʿi argued, held one of the most influential positions in the monarchical order, serving as King Faruq's "senior advisor on . . . law, policy, and other general issues." Moreover, the defendant "connected between the king and the government" and between the palace and the army. Given this position, the attorney postulated, ʿAbd al-Hadi was involved in the decisions that led to the offensive as well as the palace's role in the administration of the war. Instead of making the interests of the nation his top priority, the accused endeavored to "find favor with the king." For this reason, he failed to properly handle the information that had come to his attention with respect to the army's myriad shortcomings. The defendant well knew that the weapon systems and ammunition were unsatisfactory both in quantity and quality for launching a full-fledged campaign. The decisions that culminated in a war that the army was ill-prepared for were, in Tabʿi's estimation, fundamentally flawed. The government ignored standard procedures, the Supreme Defense Council never convened, and King Faruq drew on "horrific advice" from his senior advisors, including ʿAbd al-Hadi. As a result, "the country had thousands of casualties from the flowers of its youth—the most daring of its sons—and tens of millions of its funds. . . . Tremendous harm was caused, and its good name and national honor were badly damaged."[33]

Insofar as the prosecution was concerned, ʿAbd al-Hadi could have taken a different course. Even if he had failed to keep the country out of the war, the accused could have demonstrated his "good intentions" and lived up to the standards of his lofty position. The accused had direct access to the king, so that it was within his power to alert Faruq as to the gravity of the situation. Furthermore, he could have exposed the public to the imminent dangers by stepping down from his post. The prosecutor also reminded the court that ʿAbd al-Hadi and Nuqrashi headed the Saʿdist party, which at the time enjoyed a majority in parliament. By virtue of their standing, these two leaders were well aware that the military was unprepared for war but did not take advantage of the means that were available to them. During the critical hearings on the eve of the war, they gave a false impression of Egypt's combat readiness. This course of action, Tabʿi insisted, was not the lone option on the table. By threatening to resign, Nuqrashi and ʿAbd al-Hadi could have exerted pressure on the king and set off the alarm bells. In shunning this path, the two were directly responsible for the ignominious defeat.

In summation, the prosecutor claimed that "Ibrahim ʿAbd al-Hadi betrayed the trust and was part of the corrupt" circle—he did not confront the king with the truth, "despite knowing about the state of the army."

> On the contrary, he sided with the king and prime minister in compelling the army to fight. . . . The campaign in Palestine was an illuminating example of governmental corruption. . . . Is it logical for a country to enter a war when it is not ready, and this in order to mollify public opinion and for fear of losing the helm? Is there any greater corruption than this?"[34]

"Judges of the people," Tabʿi concluded, "this was the situation before May 10 [1948]: shortage [in munitions], a dearth of preparation, and a determined stance on the part of the military staff regarding the need to wait. Despite this, the army received an order to enter the fray. . . . Is it reasonable [to expect] the army" to enter a war footing overnight? In this same context, the attorney pinned the king's motivation to launch an attack to "his desire to lead the Arab states, break the military's strength, and appease his imperial masters."[35] Tabʿi then remarked that "the motivation [for entering] the war was not the defense of humanism, the prevention of" a massacre, "or the safeguarding of Arab rights, but satisfying the urges of the king who has no interest in his country's rights or its constitution."[36]

At this point, Judge Baghdadi offered the defendant an opportunity to respond to Muawi's report and the second count against him. However, ʿAbd al-Hadi countered "that there is no sense in" saying anything beyond what has already been submitted to the court. Nevertheless, the testimonies that were submitted throughout this long day in court shed light on a number of significant facts: the view that the armed forces were unprepared for war was prevalent among the military top brass; the latter provided a detailed estimate on the army's condition to Prime Minister Nuqrashi and War Minister Haidar; updated information and appraisals were in fact passed on to ʿAbd al-Hadi in his capacity as chief of the Royal Divan; Nuqrashi, Haidar, and the accused provided Faruq data and estimates on the army's state; and by virtue of his authority as supreme commander of the military, the king gave the order to enter the Palestine War.

Conclusion

The prosecution and judges in the ʿAbd al-Hadi trial offered a resolute answer to the question "Who was responsible for the 1948 debacle?" In their estimation, the military's loss was the inevitable result of misguided decisions made by Egypt's corrupt parliamentary-cum-monarchical government. To wit, the responsibility lies with the king, the prime minister, his cabinet, and legislators. While the literature portrays a united Egyptian front in the run-up to and throughout the duration of the Palestine War, the court transcripts point to tensions within the upper echelons of the government and the military along with inconsistencies in the positions held by an array of key players on the eve of hostilities. Moreover, this rare documentation shows that, in contrast to the prevailing scholarly view, the FO did not fully absolve the army of Egypt's defeat. For example, most of the high command are imputed with direct responsibility for the defeat. More specifically, they were accused of presenting the decision makers with false information on the capabilities of both the Egyptian military and the enemy, which was usually portrayed as a motley crew of "Zionist gangs." On the other hand, the combat forces, including many in the FO, were described as having been sent into battle devoid of sufficient preparation. In other words, the soldiers were the victims of blunders committed in the Cairene halls of power.

That said, the transcripts of *Mahkamat al-Thawra* abound with the resounding "silence" of testimony discarded by judges that was incommensurate with the narrative that the junta endeavored to lodge into the public consciousness. For instance, the panel ignored statements by the accused and key witnesses concerning the general atmosphere in Egypt and within the army's ranks and the sway of this mood on the powers that be amid the run-up to war. This negation of accurate observations is perhaps tied to the FO's relentless efforts to pin the defeat on the monarchial elites. Nonetheless, the transcripts of the ʿAbd al-Hadi hearings show that the popular mood in Egypt and other Arab countries had a major impact on the leadership. For example, Naguib Iskandar, the deposed minister of health, testified, "At the time, anyone who would have tried to speak out against entering the fray would have been considered a traitor." This sort of documentation indicates that, despite their propensity for show trials, special courts are, in fact, valuable historical sources.

The judges' line of questioning and approach to documentary evidence seems to indicate that they took it upon themselves to rewrite the historical narrative of Egypt's entry into the 1948 War. This quasi-legal assessment of the pre-war decision-making process was aimed not only at highlighting the colossal failure of government officials but also at justifying the FO's coup four years later. Assuming the mantle of historian, the judges formulated a new hegemonic narrative. While focusing on the past, this storyline had clear implications on the present. The revolutionary regime was determined to do everything in its power to launch a new socio-political order in Egypt. The rhetoric of *Mahkamat al-Thawra* would play a major role in this enterprise.

5

Rhetoric and Historical Polemics

During its sessions, the Revolution's Court drew a sharp distinction between the flaws of the ancien régime and the "new" dispensation's commitment to a just, social-minded, and democratic order. The historical debate over the image of Egypt's past was not limited to the courtroom. A case in point is the lively dispute that erupted between prominent historians regarding the legacy of the Muhammad 'Ali dynasty's 150-year reign.

Reign of Terror

Quite a few of the bills of indictment that were submitted to *Mahkamat al-Thawra* charged the defendants with embezzlement and other violations of the Egyptian people's constitutionally guaranteed rights. These accusations dovetailed neatly with the FO's narrative according to which governmental, political, and economic corruption was rampant during the monarchical era. In the third count against 'Abd al-Hadi, the ex-premier was charged with "corrupting the government apparatus" as part of "a reign of terror that harmed the general liberties." More specifically, he was accused of, among other crimes, "a wide-scale campaign of detentions" over the course of which "he ordered his assistants to torture a large group" and personally supervised "the implementation of" these tactics. Torture was "absolutely unnecessary" to keep the peace, the document read, "but [stemmed] from the need to avenge" the MB for the murder of Prime Minister Nuqrashi.[1]

Although the special tribunal did not contend that 'Abd al-Hadi bore direct responsibility for the assassination of Hasan al-Banna, it did implicate him with creating an atmosphere that led "others" to plan the assassination of the movement's founder, who the defendant considered an enemy of and danger to the regime. In another trial that was conducted by the same court, the identity of those so-called others was revealed as the Political Police (*al-bulis al-siyasi*). This apparatus, which ʿAbd al-Hadi oversaw as interior minister, was dissolved with the establishment of the revolutionary regime.[2]

Attorney General Mustafa al-Hilbawi repeatedly claimed that during his tenure as premier and minister of the interior, the accused conducted himself like a tyrant. For instance, he habitually resorted to unconstitutional means of suppression against innocent citizens, thereby helping to produce a reign of terror. The prosecutor enumerated the crimes of the defendant that fell under this rubric. As part of the previously mentioned wave of detentions, many victims were placed under solitary confinement, tortured, and completely cut off from the outside world. According to state evidence, ʿAbd al-Hadi instructed his subordinates to ratchet up the pressure on those suspects who refused to collaborate. Some of the interrogees even died under these conditions. The sole reason for these crimes was to sate "the defendant's lust for revenge" against the government's reputed adversaries, especially those responsible for the murder of Nuqrashi. This campaign was also driven by ʿAbd al-Hadi's desire "to find favor in the eyes of the former king [i.e., Faruq] and the colonialists."[3]

At this point, the chief judge urged ʿthe accused to respond to these claims. "My defense leaves much to be desired," the latter said, "and therefore I have left this matter to you." Once again, Baghdadi noted that it was the defendant who decided to forgo the services of an attorney after Mustafa Marʿi's resignation. "Is this indeed a question of a lawyer?" ʿAbd al-Hadi scoffed. The judge then sealed this exchange with the following rejoinder: "The court decided and granted you an opportunity and you refused."[4]

On the heels of this tussle, the first witness, al-Sayyid Rajib, was called to the stand to take his oath: "In the name of Allah the almighty, I will say the truth [the preceding passage was repeated twice more], and nothing that is not true. And Allah is my witness for what I will say." This version differed from the others taken during this trial.[5] For example, the next witness was asked to repeat the following words: "In the name of Allah the almighty, I will tell the truth."[6] Perhaps this discrepancy was tied to the fact that Rajib was a high-ranking member of the MB. At any rate, the witness was subsequently asked to describe the torture that he had endured following his arrest on May 16, 1949. Rajib opened with a preamble ("In the name of Allah . . ., the honorable president") but was immediately cutoff: "We are not interested in a sermon," the judge scowled, "but facts. Details."

The witness then described how five or six police officers had banged on his door in the middle of the night while he was asleep. They pointed their weapons at him and began to search his room. Soon after, the police ordered him to get out of bed and come with them. At this point, the MB official was interrupted yet again: "We are not interested in stories," Baghdadi reprimanded him. "Explain the facts in spoken language. Speak exactly as you speak with one of your friends."[7] Picking up where he had left off, Rajib described how he was taken to a police station and interrogated by one Isma'il al-Maligi, the sibling of the accused (Maligi would also stand trial before the Revolution's Court) on the suspicion of activity on behalf of the movement. According to the witness, 'Abd al-Hadi was at some of these sessions. Whenever Rajib claimed ignorance on a certain topic, he was moved to a different room and cruelly tortured.

The interrogation continued even after he was transferred to another police station. In the presence of several officers and soldiers, he was disrobed and thrashed with a whip (*kurbaj*). The beating was so severe that he lost consciousness. At some stage, the witness was placed in a room with 'Abd al-Hadi, who vulgarly demanded that he fork over information about a certain person. When Rajib insisted that he was unfamiliar with anyone by that name, the ex-premier gave the order to continue roughing him up. After a couple more days of interrogation, he was transferred to a prison. The witness spent about five difficult months in this facility without meriting his day in court. On this note, Rajib's testimony had run its course.

Ahmad al-Malat, a medical doctor and the head of the Cairo chapter of the Red Crescent, was then called to the witness stand. A third version of the oath was heard within a number of days at the special tribunal—yet another manifestation of its unusual legal procedures. He expounded on his own arrest (May 12, 1949), which also entailed harsh torture and humiliation.[8] The interrogators sought to coax information on a few MB activists out of him. However, the prisoner denied that he was acquainted with any of them, which only exacerbated the torture to which he was subjected. Like Rajib, Malat claimed that the defendant had attended some of the interrogation sessions. More specifically, the Red Crescent official was questioned on a number of occasions in 'Abd al-Hadi's office and denigrated. During his testimony, Malat submitted the names of other MB activists who were tortured at the same prison where he was detained.

With this testimony, the discussion on the third count against 'Abd al-Hadi basically came to a close. Throughout this stage of the proceedings, the questioning of the witnesses was conducted intermittently by the prosecutor and the chief judge. The accused remained in his seat and did not actively participate in the exchanges. Even after this particular trial, the Revolution's Court continued to scrutinize the alleged reign of terror on 'Abd al-Hadi's watch. For example, the topic came up in the trial against Lieutenant Colonel Sa'd al-Din al-Sunbati (October 4, 1953), among the heads of the Political Police and its commander in the Gharbiya region, who was charged with sowing terror and savagely torturing many citizens. Moreover, Sunbati was described as one of the senior officials that did 'Abd al-Hadi's bidding. During his trial, the prosecutor emphasized that the Political Police frequently tormented ordinary citizens by means of unlawful arrests and harsh torture. The prosecuting attorney also listed thirteen forms of torture that were employed by this organization.[9]

The Assassination of Hasan al-Banna

The next topic on the agenda of the ʿAbd al-Hadi trial was one of the episodes that roiled Egyptian society during the late 1940s—the assassination of Hasan al-Banna. As per the fourth count, the defendant had steered a policy that created the atmosphere for this murder. In the second half of that decade, the struggle between the MB and the monarchial regime steadily intensified, as the Nuqrashi government embarked on a no-holds-barred campaign against the movement.[10] For its part, the MB leadership pinned the loss in the 1948 War on the political elite and ratcheted up the public criticism against its heads. Furthermore, the Secret Apparatus carried out numerous acts of sabotage, including the assassination of Judge Ahmad al-Khazindar on March 22, 1948. In turn, the government had the security forces clamp down on the movement's activists—many of whom were sent to jail—and subsequently outlawed its activity. Twenty days later, a student member of the MB killed Prime Minister Nuqrashi.[11]

The attorney general placed the General Guide's assassination in the broader context of the political reality in Egypt. According to his analysis, the party that was most interested in eliminating Banna was the British, who were alarmed by his vitriol against their policies. For example, the shaykh deemed the royal army's continued presence in Egypt to be the "source of [all] corruption." To this end, London convinced the palace that Banna's views constituted a threat to Faruq's life and the continuation of his rule. Consequently, Britain and the monarchy were on the same page in all that concerned their view of the Islamic movement and its founder. The prosecution's basic argument was that even if it is impossible to prove that the defendant was a party to the assassination plot, there is evidence that he stirred up considerable animosity toward and was involved in the decision to outlaw the MB. Thereafter, as prime minister and minister of the interior, he led a vicious campaign against the MB that saw 2,659 of its members put behind bars. The state's representatives also claimed that the defendant's assistants subsequently concealed evidence in an effort to stymie the murder investigation.[12]

The regime endeavored to convict the accused by means of testimony and documents. It was in this context that ʿAbd al-Karim Mansur, a senior MB activist who was married to a member of the General Guide's family, took the stand. Mansur was among Banna's closest confidantes. During his testimony, the witness aired some of the most prevalent claims that were making the rounds among the Brothers about their leader's demise. For example, he drew a correlation between the assassination and the crackdown against the movement's activists. In other words, the prime minister's decision to keep Banna out of prison was intended to isolate the latter from his adherents and thus prevent a violent backlash against the murder. The removal of the tight security that had hitherto been provided to the shaykh and the confiscation of his licensed pistol were also part of this same conspiracy.[13]

At this juncture, Baghdadi intervened and demanded that the witness focus on relevant details, rather than mere commentary. The MB activist then offered a first-hand account of the final moments of Banna's life: At 8:30 pm, the General Guide left the MB Youth building, along with Mansur. The two got into a cab, and the driver began to pull away slowly. Within a few seconds, a burst of gunfire rattled the street. Instead of stepping on the gas and fleeing the scene, the cabby hit the brakes and allowed the assassins to finish off their target. Mansur tried to stop one of the perpetrators, only to be shot in the chest. The witness then expounded on the security forces' lack of respect for the deceased. For instance, he noted that the authorities prevented the shaykh's legion of admirers from attending the funeral.[14]

The court sought to corroborate Mansur's account by summoning Major General Ahmad ʿAbd al-Hadi to the witness stand. At the time of the General Guide's assassination, the witness was governor of the capital Cairo (*hikmadar misr*) and, for all intentions, its chief of police. The major general testified that, upon assuming this job in late 1948, he was preoccupied with the campaign against the MB. At the urging of the presiding judge, the witness explained that the wholesale arrests came in response to a wave of terror and violence that was put in motion by the movement. Among the most blatant acts that were attributed to the Brothers were the murders of Khazindar and Salim Zaki, Ahmad ʿAbd al-Hadi's predecessor as governor.[15]

Baghdadi then sought to verify a number of the specific contentions that arose in Mansur's testimony. To the question of "Who was responsible for the surveillance of Banna?" the witness responded, "After I entered the post, a dispersal order was issued against the MB." Thereafter, he described a few of the meetings that were held to formulate a strategy against the movement. The participants, including Nuqrashi, weighed the possibility of arresting the shaykh. In the end, though, the participants reached the conclusion that it was best to eschew this option, lest it "spark a revolution." Moreover, Banna's freedom enabled "us to reach understandings with him."[16] The police chief added that the security forces decided to plant agents (*mukhbirin*) in the vicinity of the shaykh's home, with the objective of keeping track of his associates. However, the vigil was removed due to the complaints that were lodged by the beneficiary himself. The witness's testimony also reveals that the authorities charged him with handling the arrangements for the shaykh's funeral.

According to the police chief, the detention of MB activists and leaders in the wake of the movement's outlawing was carried out by members of "the political department in security." The witness confirmed that the accused "was occasionally present" during interrogations. However, he stressed that he had no knowledge of suspects being tortured and not in the presence of the premier. At the end of this session, the accused was asked if he had any questions for the witness, to which he curtly responded "No." Baghdadi then sought to entice the defendant into reacting to the police chief's account, but ʿAbd al-Hadi once again refused to take the bait.[17]

Corruption

The court immediately turned to the last two counts, which imputed to ʿAbd al-Hadi acts of corruption and abuse of power for personal gain. Over the last decade of Faruq's reign, there was more and more talk about improprieties at the palace as well as the highest levels of the government and army. The FO released official statements accusing all of these factors with a wide range of venal acts. In his memoirs, Muhammad Husayn Haykal brought up the topic of Faruq's salacious nightlife—going to trendy nightclubs and high-stake gambling in casinos—during the final years of his reign.[18] At the end of June 1950, when the rumors became too much to countenance, a group of senators from the opposition, including Haykal, decided to take matters into their own hands; they crafted a lengthy epistle and had it sent directly to the king. In this extraordinary document, the teetering situation in Egypt was linked to the personal and ministerial corruption sweeping through the land. The authors also noted that the king's behavior had become the object of ridicule throughout the Nile valley and beyond. Consequently, Faruq was beseeched to change his lifestyle. This letter piqued the king's anger at the opposition. In response, Prime Minister Mustafa al-Nahhas excoriated the signatories and labeled them "criminals" slandering the country.[19]

The fact that ʿAbd al-Hadi was among the signatories of this letter did not even come up over the course of his trial. On the contrary, the prosecution argued that he was in cahoots with the king in the matter of these indiscretions and took advantage of his own standing for personal gain. The fifth count, in fact, focused on the defendant's involvement in the renovation of the royal yacht while serving as chief of the Royal Divan. As per the indictment, the enormous sums that were allocated to this project epitomized the unscrupulousness of "the ruling system." The accused had exerted all of his considerable influence to advance the renovation, with the objective of ingratiating himself to "the former king."[20] Furthermore, the prosecution harped on the fact that this ostentatious expenditure coincided with the war in Palestine, which the army fought despite being strapped for the most elementary means.

During the hearings on this matter, Hilbawi presented a document showing that the initial request for the renovations was put forth by the palace on May 13, 1948. Over the next few minutes, the attorney general underscored the fact that the requisition was submitted at the height of the discussions on the army's preparedness. The negligence of Faruq and his confidantes thus reached the point of jeopardizing the nation's interests. Moreover, Hilbawi claimed that ʿAbd al-Hadi pushed the project forward in the face of the treasury officials' firm demands for austerity and the strong reservations voiced in the House of Representatives. To substantiate these claims, the state called ʿAbdallah Jirjis, the general comptroller of the Egyptian Finance Ministry's Budget Department during the period in question, to the witness stand. The witness stated that the original estimate for the yacht's renovation was 350,000 Egyptian pounds but also noted that the final price had skyrocketed to 1,450,000—an enormous sum that was in fact deducted from the state budget. To Baghdadi's question of "Did you have a budgetary surplus" at the time, the witness answered that "the total deficit stood at around 16 million Egyptian pounds."[21]

It also turns out from the official's testimony that when the government first received this requisition, a document was prepared at Nuqrashi's behest warning that it was an inappropriate time for such a steep outlay. The topic was subsequently placed on the backburner; however, the palace renewed its request in December 1949, adding that the contractors were willing to spread out the bill over three years. By this stage, ʿAbd al-Hadi was already prime minister. Following an exchange on the matter with the finance minister, he ordered the latter to initiate the transaction. Nevertheless, the renovation was postponed for about a half year due to the invective it drew from the Senate Finance Committee.[22]

At the end of Jirjis's testimony, the presiding judge asked for ʿAbd al-Hadi's response to these allegations. The latter repeated his claim that he had been rendered defenseless. To contend with these accusations, the ex-premier added, many documents would be needed that are currently unattainable owing to the circumstances in which the trial is being held. In response, Judge Hasan Ibrahim, who had until now remained silent during this hearing, quipped, "Your lawyer who resigned said that he is drowning in documents." Thereafter, the prosecutor chimed in with the following offer: "Are you interested in having me submit the documents to you?" ʿAbd Al-Hadi countered that the witness had insidiously cherry-picked from the numerous discussions on this subject. For this reason, he added, the court would be best advised to predicate its ruling on an examination of the full dossier. Once more, the presiding judge reprimanded the accused; by refusing to participate in the proceedings, Baghdadi argued, he was basically shooting himself in the foot.[23]

Following a short break, the session resumed and the court turned its attention to the sixth count against the accused: the unlawful pavement of several roads near his place of residence between 1945 and 1949. Besides failing to take into account the general good, the indictment read, ʿAbd al-Hadi did not go through the proper channels in initiating the work.[24] According to the prosecution, this charge was based on memoranda from the Egyptian Roads and Bridges Authority, which were included in the dossier submitted to the revolutionary tribunal. "What is the defendant's view [on this count]? " the presiding judged asked. "All these allegations" of abuse of power "are incorrect," he responded, "and I don't believe that any responsible clerk should take the responsibility upon his shoulders to prove this." Baghdadi cut off the defendant with the words "Good, good," whereupon he announced that the court would now call the "defense witnesses" to the stand. At this point, though, the accused spoke up, declaring that he did not wish to have "any of them" testify on his behalf. The scheduled witnesses were part of a long list of people that Attorney Marʿi requested to summon at the outset of the trial, when he was still representing the client. In practice, only three of these figures were eventually subpoenaed, and their testimony was given when ʿAbd al-Hadi was already bereft of counsel. Although the prosecutors and the judges constantly referred to them as "defense witnesses," they were enlisted to help the state secure a conviction.[25]

The Verdict

Throughout the trials at the Revolution's Court, the state representatives drew a correlation between the personal corruption of the monarchy's leaders (first among them King Faruq) and the corrosive internal and foreign policies that they steered. More specifically, top members of the regime were accused of unabashedly dipping into public funds for their own pleasure. According to the judges and prosecution, bribery and lining up jobs for family and friends by manipulating laws and even the constitution became norm among the elite. In this manner, three forces that were linked in an intricate web of mutual interests—the palace, the politicians, and the colonial powers—exploited Egypt and its resources to the max. "It is not surprising," the prosecution's representative lamented, "to find that corruption, for all its manifestations and shades, has spread to every part of the state and has permeated every sphere of life," thereby miring the country in a protracted "dark period."

Focusing the criticism on the king alone, the prosecutor added, ignores the substantial role that was played by most facets of the political system in the evolution of this failed regime. The senior echelons of government ruled without constraints and were, in fact, legally exempt from accounting for their deeds. Similarly, the law and constitution were cynically exploited by the palace and party heads, on route to an unprecedented level of moral depravity.[26] In essence, the prosecuting attorney depicted a self-perpetuating cycle of power and corruption wherein senior officials ignored the greater good and shirked their duties. In addition, the unmitigated deference to the king's authority on the part of members of parliament and government had disastrous ramifications on the nation, most importantly, the ignominious defeat in the Palestine War.

At precisely ten o'clock on the morning of October 1, 1953, the final session of the ex-premier's trial got underway. "In the name of Allah and in the name of the revolution . . .," Judge Baghdadi intoned, "the court sentences the defendant, Ibrahim 'Abd al-Hadi, for the charges against him as follows: 1. Execution by hanging. 2. Confiscation of all that remains of his property and funds to the good of the people." In reaching this verdict, the judges basically accepted the state's primary argument that it had been proven beyond the shadow of a doubt that the accused was involved in serious offenses, including, most severely, "treason against the homeland." The marathon sessions, the irregular legal procedures, and the heavy punishments that were imposed on the accused fit the decree establishing the special tribunal like a glove. Pursuant to that same order, though, the RCC commuted the death sentence to life in prison with hard labor.[27]

With the reading of the verdict, the opening chapter of the Revolution's Court came to a close. The next trial began in that same auditorium twenty minutes later. Like 'Abd al-Hadi, the second defendant, Ahmad Muhammad 'Awad, was charged with "acts that are considered treason against the homeland and against its well-being from within and abroad."[28]

In the months that followed, dozens of senior Wafd politicians were tried before the Revolution's Court. The most time-consuming trial was that of Fu'ad Siraj al-Din. As per his indictment, this powerful figure was accused of embezzlement, breach of trust, and malfeasance (including the "Cairo Fire" episode) while serving as minister of the interior in the last Nahhas government (1950–2). The military judges sentenced Siraj al-Din to fifteen years behind bars.[29] Among the highlights of this special tribunal were its proceedings against the two most dominant figures on the Egyptian political scene during the first half of the twentieth century: Mustafa al-Nahhas, the famous leader of the Wafd party, and his well-heeled wife, Zainab al-Wakil. The two were convicted of, among other felonies, corruption, profiteering, and embezzlement, which were committed during his tenure as prime minister. Pursuant to the Treason Law, the judges stripped them of their political and civil rights for five years and had most of their assets confiscated. Both husband and wife would remain under house arrest for the rest of their lives. The trials that were conducted in this framework betrayed the RCC's determination to take exceptional measures against domestic political adversaries, especially senior members of the Wafd.

The Republic versus the Ancien Régime

The rhetoric that was employed by the judges and the prosecution in the 'Abd al-Hadi trial was meant to draw a contrast between the inept governance of the monarchial era and the FO's incipient republican order. The bill of indictment, testimonies, evidence, and questioning of the defendant pointed to a direct link between the previous regime's turpitude and its responsibility for the severe damage that was caused to the nation's interests and to citizen rights. The state representatives put an emphasis on the relations and mutual interests between the monarchial regime and the colonial powers, especially Great Britain. Echoing the myriad public statements of President Naguib and members of the RCC, they repeatedly claimed during this and other trials that, from the day of Faruq's ouster, the fomenters of the June Revolution considered its main objective to be ridding the country of the imperialists and purifying the state from every manifestation of corruption that had vexed the populace for years on end. "The revolution undertook to cleanse the state and society from this despotic and unscrupulous regime," the prosecutor asserted, "that collaborates with the imperialism and doesn't do a thing for the greater good. Instead, the old order was exclusively concerned with "the welfare of the hedonists that ruled Egypt." While Faruq and his inner circle were the lead perpetrators of governmental and personal corruption, the political elite were also guilty of this crime. ʿAbd al-Hadi was described as a "foundation of the foundations" of the monarchial regime. The venal acts that were committed by this ruling echelon were presented as both serious infractions of the law and insightful examples of the regime's skewed moral and religious norms.

In this context, the state's rhetoric included demagogic use of the Quran. On a few occasions, the previous leadership was even accused of being despotic and heretical. "How similar Faruq is to Pharaoh," the attorney general posited, "and how similar ʿAbd al-Hadi is to Hamān." Conversely, "How similar the revolution is to the mission [*risala*] of Moses, peace be upon him."[30] The prosecutor argued that as chief of the Royal Divan, the defendant played a crucial role in King Faruq's brain trust in all that concerned the decision to enter the 1948 War. As the monarch's senior advisor, he added, the defendant could have apprised him of the dangers and suggested alternatives. ʿAbd al-Hadi also "could have resigned," which would have sent a message to Faruq and the general public as to the severity of the situation. However, the accused chose to continue facilitating the misguided decisions that culminated in the military debacle.[31]

Egyptian society in general and the army in particular were depicted by the state's representatives as victims of a corrupt regime. The revolution that the FO spearheaded "in the name of the people and on its behalf" was intended and indeed managed to put an end to the old political and economic order. Whereas the monarchy catered to a tiny segment of the population, attorney al-Tabʿi stressed during the summations that the July Revolution serves the interests of the entire Egyptian public. Accordingly, "the army and the people work hand in hand." The FO "carried out the revolution and the people were with you [the FO]. The revolution essentially stemmed from the nation and [was carried out] for its sake."[32] On the basis of the evidence presented over the course of the ʿAbd al-Hadi trial, the court found that there are still subversive elements seeking to depose the new regime and reinstate the old ruling order. In the prosecution's estimation, the struggle that is being waged against the defendants in the special tribunal is nothing less than a struggle over the revolution's prospects.

Another emphasis of the court's rhetoric was the decency of the present regime. Its government was deemed to be a continuation of the FO's bloodless "white revolution." For over a year, the presiding judge stressed, the RCC made every effort to institute a new governing order while diligently refraining from settling scores with the heads of the deposed monarchy. According to the prosecutor, the remnants of the old order viewed this reconciliatory approach as an opportunity to leave their holes and "disseminate their sick views." Consequently, the revolutionaries were forced to modify their approach toward these subversive and hostile elements. The Revolution's Court was established under these trying circumstances to adjudicate and "*document* in historic trials" the crimes that "the traitors" committed against the people.[33]

By mobilizing its extraordinary powers, the RCC took other steps that were aimed at buoying the transition to a new order. For example, it shut down the Political Police—an organization that was portrayed in the special tribunals as one of the monarchial regime's preferred and most sinister tools of oppression. In so doing, the prosecutor opined, the revolution destroyed one of the pillars of the monarchy and the colonial powers. "Egypt and its citizens will not forget the crimes of these policemen" or the damage they exacted on citizen rights.[34]

During the ʿAbd al-Hadi trial, the judges and prosecutors frequently broached the issue of responsibility for the defeat in the Palestine War. They repeatedly stressed that there was a close link between the rout and the unscrupulousness of the monarchial order. Their principal claim, which surfaced time and again, was that the army was free of blame and that the responsibility rested entirely on the heads of government, particularly the king, his senior advisors, and Prime Minister Nuqrashi. Despite the fact that some high-ranking military officers forewarned that the troops were unprepared for major combat, all the top political leaders were in favor of entering the fray. In making this case, the court essentially provided legal backing for the FO's argument that the decision-making with respect to the war and its administration were fundamentally flawed. Put differently, the leadership's personal corruption and malfeasance augured the defeat on the battlefield.

A related point was that the political leaders and military officers who did not bother to train the army for combat duties (there were no full-fledged maneuvers) were the same ones who sent it on an impossible mission. In addition, ulterior motives and criminal negligence underpinned the decision to launch the war. From a military standpoint, there was clearly a severe shortage in armaments, transportation means, and logistical equipment.

To make matters worse, the intelligence reports on the enemy were unsubstantiated and grounded on flimsy assumptions. On the diplomatic and political front, there were egregious oversights in the decision-making process. The king was primarily motivated by the desire to prevent his fellow Arab heads of state from gaining the ascendancy in pan-Arab rivalries. The political echelon was derelict in its duty; instead of reaching decisions on the basis of thoughtful consideration, it deferred to the caprices of Faruq and pandered to the saber-rattling that informed Arab public opinion in Egypt and throughout the world.

The Defective Weapons and Ammunition Affair

"The defective weapons and ammunition" affair was a central topic in the discourse on the army's defeat. In this context, the special tribunal fulfilled a unique role in documenting those who were involved in this scandal.[35] The court's hearings and verdicts bolstered the arguments that would soon undergird the revolutionary narrative of the 1948 War. The weapons affair—details of which were already the subject of debate back when Faruq was still on the throne—was presented as cutting proof of the monarchy's dereliction of duty and its breach of public trust. The genesis of the current discourse was a session of the Egyptian Senate on May 29, 1950 on suspicions of impropriety in a handful of cases. During this hearing, Senator Mustafa Mar'i posed a question on the faulty weapons affair to the prime minister.

Facing down pressure to shelve this topic, Muhammad Husayn Haykal, president of the Senate, proceeded to hold a hearing on this ostensible scandal. During this session, Interior Minister Fu'ad Siraj al-Din testified on the government's behalf. It turns out from his lengthy answers that on the eve of the campaign, the military command was notified that all the budget limitations on arms procurement had been lifted. Moreover, he noted that the war minister, Muhammad Haidar, had formed a special committee to determine what was lacking and obtain these items at once.[36] In light of the heated discussion in the Senate, the novelist and journalist Ihsan 'Abd al-Quddous published a number of stories in *Ruz al-Yusuf*, a popular weekly, between May and October 1950. His principal argument was that the Egyptian army was bested by domestic enemies, not the Zionist forces. Brandishing a razor sharp pen, 'Abd al-Quddous implicated senior government officials and a number of middlemen in fishy weapon deals. According to the writer, most of the munitions that reached the army were unusable.[37]

Public interest in this affair skyrocketed following the attorney general's decision to open an investigation on the topic and to thus charge thirteen suspects, including senior defense ministry officials, military officers, and arms dealers. The trial, which opened in January 1951, lasted for about two and a half years. Dozens of witnesses testified, and the hearings dragged on and on. After a stoppage brought on by the July Revolution, the following verdict was released on June 10, 1953: "It was proven to the court that nothing of the topic of the defective weapons and ammunition, the charge that is imputed to the defendants, was a cause of any harm to anyone from the security forces over the length of the combat operations in Palestine or another place."[38] Though stunned by this ruling, the FO desisted from openly venting their frustration, lest they exacerbate the mounting criticism of their refusal to return to the barracks.

Since the end of the Palestine War, the FO had trumpeted this affair as a significant factor behind the army's poor showing. In proclamations that were regularly distributed to military units and in city squares, the authors contended that the deals signed on the eve of and during the campaign yielded subpar weapons, which harmed many soldiers on the front and influenced the outcome of the campaign.[39] A better known example of this narrative is the historic letter that Muhammad Naguib dispatched to Faruq demanding that the king relinquish the throne immediately (July 26, 1952). Justifying his demand, the general wrote that, among other mischiefs, the Palestine War and "the damaged-weapons scandal" exemplified the regime's depravity.[40]

Against this backdrop, it stands to reason that the acquittal of the defendants in the "defective weapons and ammunition" affair was among the primary catalysts behind the RCC's decision to establish and try their adversaries from the old regime before a special tribunal (i.e., the Revolution's Court). The choice of ʿAbd al-Hadi as the first defendant suited the RCC's needs for a quick conviction. The revolutionaries estimated that conducting this trial in a civil court would drag on for too long. Moreover, this sort of venue would obligate the prosecution to adhere to the statutes of Egyptian criminal law and the rules of evidence, which would decrease the odds of attaining a conviction. For this reason, they decided to operate within a legal framework that was grounded on procedures that differ from those of ordinary courts. I contend that the principal reason for establishing the Revolution's Court was not legal, but rather the RCC's desire to forge a new narrative that would validate the military coup and explain why it was incumbent upon the FO to remain at the helm until the revolution achieved its goals.

The documents and testimony on "the defective weapons and ammunition" affair that were presented in the Revolution's Court attracted a great deal of press coverage and revived the public discourse on this topic. During the pertinent hearings, the state representatives argued that this scandal attests to the immoral character of the old order. While the troops were contending admirably with insurmountable obstacles on the front, the palace and political elite continued with their cossetted daily routines. In parallel, the cronies of senior officials lined their pockets with handsome broker fees from dubious arms transactions. This affair was also tied to the ostentatious lifestyle of the king and his henchmen. In the ʿAbd al-Hadi trial, the prosecution contended that Faruq demanded exorbitant sums for upgrading the royal yacht while the army was still engaged in heavy combat.

The quasi-legal hearings of the Revolution's Court thrust the "defective weapons and ammunition" affair to the forefront of the new hegemonic narrative on the 1948 War. According to the revolutionaries, the manner in which the Egyptian leadership conducted itself during this episode well reflected the entrenched corruption of the monarchial order. Given this turpitude, the army's termination of the Muhammad ʿAli dynasty was appropriate from a civil, political, religious, and ethical standpoint. In fact, the very emphasis on the weapons scandal in the 1948 War was critical to the FO's legitimacy. Strange as it may seem, the military defeat was portrayed not as a failure that exposed the army's weaknesses but as an incident that buttressed the revolutionaries' narrative according to which the senior political and military echelons were to blame for the rout.

After an honorable showing in the ill-fated war, the troops reached the same conclusion that every ordinary Egyptian felt in his or her heart: the debacle stemmed from a litany of treasonous, corrupt, and negligent acts on the part of the ruling elite—especially King Faruq, his assistants, the premier, and the rest of the government ministers. The popularity of this narrative was evidenced by the wide support for the coup. Likewise, Egyptian society by and large backed the RCC's vigorous attempt to purge every last remnant of the old order from the institutions of government and the political parties; even the cleansing of the army and police drew extensive support. It was not enough to dethrone and exile the king: the circumstances warranted a comprehensive reform of the entire governing system.

Starting with civics and history textbooks and ending with academic and semi-academic works, this narrative was replicated in countless ways in Egypt's official historiography.[41] The weapons affair commanded center stage even though a government investigation and a civil court ruling found that there is no basis for the claim that the army was defeated as a result of faulty munitions. More up-to-date and in-depth studies have reached similar conclusions. The Egyptian historian ʿAbd al-Munʿim al-Jumayʿi contends that this narrative penetrated the public consciousness. However, in the introduction to *The Defective Weapons and Their Role in the Palestine War of 1948*, he poses the following questions: "Were the damaged weapons indeed in the use of the Egyptian army during the Palestine War . . . and did these arms have a crucial impact on the course of the war? Or was this affair perhaps meant to vilify the monarchy and an excuse for the Egyptian army's rout in 1948?" Al-Jumayʿi claims that a study has yet to "come out that proves that the 'damaged weapons' affair was the reason for the rout."

Drawing on written sources,[42] al-Jumayʿi concludes that "no use whatsoever was made of defective arms, so that it did not have an influence on the battlefield." According to the historian, there were in fact cases in which faulty armaments were discovered, but they remained in the boxes and were not sent to the front. For instance, there is nothing to suggest that soldiers were injured in battle due to defective hand grenades. While there were mishaps with some of the procured weapons, these derived from a failure to properly follow the manufacturer's instructions. He agrees that the purchase of defective armaments was part of the rampant corruption in Egypt during that same period. Moreover, the inept leadership bore considerable responsibility for the lack of appropriate training exercises, which loomed large in the army's difficulties on the battle pitch. In light of these considerations, the questions that beg asking are: Why did Egypt enter the war under these circumstances, and who compelled the army to join the fray?[43]

Reassembling the Puzzle of Modern Egyptian History

The Revolution's Court also delved into the topic of the July Revolution's standing in Egyptian history. In so doing, the tribunal constituted another platform for the debate between the proponents of two contradictory narratives on the monarchial era, particularly Egypt's involvement in the 1948 War. The manner in which the chief judge and prosecutors questioned those who took the stand indicates that the objective was to justify the revolutionary narrative, which gradually penetrated the national consciousness in the immediate aftermath of the coup. From the group's very inception, the FO viewed the previous epoch as a low point in Egyptian governance and society. "Let us go back a bit to the past—to the period before July 23, 1952—and see how this land was ruled," the military prosecutor, Lieutenant Colonel Muhammad al-Tab'i, suggested in the closing arguments of the 'Abd al-Hadi trial. This statement is redolent of the dramatic radio announcement that the FO broadcast on the morning of the coup. The opening and closing lines of "announcement no. 1," which was read by Anwar Sadat (who was currently serving as a judge on the special tribunal), included two ideas that soon became pillars of the revolutionary narrative: "In its recent history, Egypt went through a sad period as a result of corruption and instability," and "On this historic day, we will purify ourselves from the traitors and the reprobates [*al-mustaḍ'afin*], and we will begin a new era in the history of our land."[44]

As demonstrated by a panoply of sources, the arguments that were raised before the Revolution's Court were building blocks for a new hegemonic narrative on the annals of modern Egypt. This revised picture of the past was disseminated to the greater public by various means, including official proclamations and documents, text books, the names of streets and squares, an overhaul of the state's symbols, and a wide array of cultural and artistic enterprises, such as works of literature, cinema, theater, and music. An article in the October 1953 issue of *Majalat al-Katiba al-Thamina*, a journal published by the army, keenly noted that the changes to the main symbols of the state were necessary because those of the monarchical epoch "were not in line with our present."[45]

The events of July 23, 1952 were presented as a watershed mark in the annals of modern Egypt. "The blessed movement," the popular epithet of the military coup at around the time of its execution, was described as a true expression of the Egyptian people's aspirations for liberty and dignity. Moreover, it was deemed to be the final curtain of the Muhammad ʿAli dynasty, which exacted an unbearable toll on society. In contrast to the shortcomings of the old order, the July Revolution was hailed as the historic "rebirth" of the Egyptian nation—the first step in removing the fetters that were placed on the nation by both foreign rulers and local moguls for hundreds of years. This narrative accentuated the contrast between the monarchial regime, which was out of touch with most of the populace and whose policies doomed the country to stagnation, and the FO, which was shepherding country through a legitimate and widely backed historic process and was on the threshold of ushering in modernization and progress. After generations in which the country was ruled by elites who were detached from society and unaware of its needs, the reins of government were now held by true representatives of Egyptian society. The "white revolution" (*thawra bayda'*)—namely, the bloodless succession—redounded to the credit of the RCC.

Given that the military coup of July 1952 brought about its demise after 150 years in power, the Muhammad ʿAli dynasty merited a vibrant public discourse during the initial stages of the revolution. The FO castigated this ruling house, especially the successors of its founding father. Nonetheless, Muhammad ʿAli's reign (1805–48) continued to be viewed as a historical turning point. During his years in power, the stage was set for the establishment of modern Egypt, and the country began to shake off the chronic torpor of the Ottoman period.[46] That said, the administrative, military (e.g., native Egyptians were enlisted into its ranks for the first time), educational, and agricultural reforms of the early nineteenth century were attributed to Egyptian society and not necessarily the wisdom and skills of the dynasty's architect.[47]

A similar reading of these years informs the work of post-monarchial Egyptian historians who contributed significantly to the content and inculcation of the revolutionary narrative, especially ʿAbd al-Rahman al-Rafiʿi, Muhammad Anis, and Amin Saʿid.[48] A recurrent theme in their scholarship was that it is less than accurate to represent Muhammad ʿAli as the undisputed progenitor of modern Egypt, the special conditions that prevailed in the country, and, most important, the efforts of its people as what fueled this sea change. "It was Egypt that created Muhammad ʿAli, and not Muhammad ʿAli who created modern Egypt," Rafiʿi claimed in an article that was published on the first anniversary of the coup. According to the renowned historian, Egypt knew prosperity and independence during the period in question, but the main impetus behind these achievements was the masses.[49]

Muhammad 'Ali's successors, especially Isma'il Pasha (r. 1863–79), Fu'ad I (sultan 1917–23, king 1923–36), and Faruq (r. 1937–52), were cast in an unambiguously poor light. More specifically, they were depicted as reactionaries and corrupt despots who were preoccupied with enhancing their political and economic power, even when this was clearly detrimental to the interests of government and society. By dint of a feudal-like agrarian policy and a suppressive ruling apparatus, the palace monopolized the country's limited fertile area, where most of the population was concentrated. As a result, millions of *fellahin* (peasant farmers) and salaried workers were, for all intentions, vassals. In other words, they were deprived of elementary rights and barely eked out a living.[50]

Although the elite class constituted a minute segment of the population, thanks to their economic prowess and social connections, its members had the ear of the institutions of government, especially parliament. For example, the regime's legally sanctioned monetary policy enabled them to strengthen their political and economic power to the point of dominating Egypt's financial, industrial, and trade sectors. In other words, a distorted social, economic, and political order subjected the majority of the populace to the authority and good graces of a numerically diminutive clique, which was socially and culturally alienated from the rest of the country. As per this teleological and overgeneralized narrative, Muhammad 'Ali paved the way for the corrupt "old order" and not necessarily a modern and enlightened country. This view was prevalent among the revolutionary top brass. A quintessential example of this outlook can be found in an article that was published by 'Abd al-Nasser in the American journal *Foreign Affairs* in 1954:

> The system of foreign rule was built on the corrupt monarch and the feudal system that had been instituted under Mohammad 'Ali. . . . He had taken for himself an absolute monopoly of land and resources, treated farmers as slaves, and created a new feudal class formed by his own family. . . . Hence the cleavage between the ruling family and the enslaved masses, and the seeds of hatred that germinated and flowered throughout the reigns of his successors, Ibrahim, Isma'il and Tewfik.[51]

A substantial portion of the revolutionary narrative was dedicated to the final ten years of the Muhammad 'Ali dynasty. Faruq's reign was described as the nadir of a lowly period, which began in the second half of the 19th century. According to this outlook, the king's policies seriously hampered Egypt's independence and autonomy, subordinating its foreign and defense policies and the economy to the interests of the colonial powers. On June 18, 1953, the RCC officially proclaimed the abolition of the monarchy and the establishment of the Egyptian republic:

> The revolution demanded of King Faruq to relinquish his throne because he symbolizes the cornerstone upon which imperialism rests. . . .

> The history of the Muhammad ʿAli family was a series of acts of betrayal against the people's rights. . . . The crown had become like a curtain, on the other side of which imperialism toiled to sap the energy of the nation and [stifle] its capacities, to obliterate its essence, its morale, and its liberties. Faruq out did all his predecessors in the dynasty in the many properties [that he accumulated], in that he threw off all restraints, behaved imperiously, and denied what was most important. He sealed his end and fate.[52]

Similar historical representations abounded in op-ed pages, popular histories, and books on current affairs. A case in point is *King versus People* (*malik ḍid shaʿb*), which came out in the new serial "Books for All" (*kutub lil-jamiʿa*) in the summer of 1953—roughly the same time as the establishment of the Revolution's Court. Befitting its title, the colorful illustration adorning the work's cover features King Faruq and Muhammad Naguib exchanging nasty stares. The illustration also depicts Egyptian society, in the form of women and men, youth and adults, clergy and effendis, and rural folk and urbanites. Over the length of the book's 130 pages, Faruq is presented as a wanton leader whose awful decisions flung Egypt over the precipice. Led by General Naguib, the army is described in the concluding chapter as toiling in the name of the people to save Egypt from this venal monarch. Similarly, the rout in the 1948 War is portrayed as a manifestation of the king's misguided policies, the implementation of which was left to senior officials, such as Prime Minister ʿAbd al-Hadi. The chapter on Faruq's role in the military defeat is titled "The Merchant of Death." In this context, the book claims that as supreme commander of the Egyptian army, the king failed to prepare his country for the campaign, so that the loss was essentially preordained. Against this backdrop, it was only natural that the military was the institution to rid the country of this "treasonous commander."[53]

In contrast to these unflattering representations, the new hegemonic narrative raised the banner of several figures that were presented as distinguished national leaders. For example, the government decided a few months after the coup to transfer the remains of the "first leader," Mustafa Kamil (1874–1908), to a mausoleum in Salah al-Din Square, right bellow Cairo's medieval citadel.[54] The second funeral procession was held on the anniversary of his passing (February 12, 1953). Members of the top brass spoke of the profound impact that the first leader's nationalist views had on their own convictions. The reinternment was presented as a metaphor of the connection between Kamil, a man who was ahead of his time, and the fomenters of the July Revolution. His famous statements calling for the full national rights of the Nile Valley's residents and their struggle to end the British occupation were showcased as an identical message to that of the RCC. "We are not transferring the bones of Mustafa Kamil from tomb to tomb," Minister of National Guidance Fathi Radwan declared. "We are commemorating a new victory for the spirit of Egypt. Once again, the spirit [of the words] of Mustafa Kamil have triumphed, an hour in which it has touched the words of the land whose goal is the evacuation [of British troops] from . . . the Nile Valley."[55] Hundreds of thousands of citizens took part in the funeral procession, which merited extensive coverage in the press. The procession was headed by President Naguib and other leaders of the new regime; behind them marched a long line of representatives from various sectors of Egyptian society (e.g., workers, students, police, and soldiers).

A few months later, the remains of Muhammad Farid (1868–1919), a national leader who followed in Kamil's footsteps, were transferred to the same mausoleum. The ceremony was held on the thirty-fourth anniversary of his death (November 15, 1953) and was widely covered by the local media. The statements made by senior officials accentuated the current revolutionaries' determination to implement the nationalist ideas of prominent figures such as Kamil and Farid. In a speech delivered at the end of the reburial ceremony, Naguib dwelled on the importance of commemorating those who stood up against the monarchy's oppression and against foreign invaders. The president declared,

> The transfer of Farid's bones from the small and neglected grave to this elevated and spacious spot is akin to the Egyptian people's transition in history from the bedrock of the oppression and the dark in which they were [trapped] to a place that is glittering in the light and sun.[56]

The most exalted figure in the revolutionary pantheon was Ahmad 'Urabi (1841–1911). The army officer was lionized time and again by the regime's speakers and in textbooks. He was also commemorated on stamps, the names of streets and squares, and various national enterprises. The man and his deeds were considered an expression of the powerful forces inherent to Egyptian society. Referred to as "the popular leader" (*al-za'im al-sha'bi*), 'Urabi was extolled for demanding Khedive Tawfiq "to grant liberty to the people."[57] In a book for educators on teaching modern Arab history, entire pages were dedicated to this encounter between the officer and the despot. It was depicted as "a glorious day in which the words of the nation and the army met." The book even provided a quasi-transcript of their conversation: "We have come to present before you the requests of the army and the nation," 'Urabi opened the dialogue. Tawfiq responded, "You have no right to present these requests; I inherited the rule over this land from my forefathers, and you are nothing but servants that are subject to our graces." The officer countered, "Allah is the one who begat us as freemen [*ahraran*]."[58] This exchange affirmed how vital the military's intervention can be in trying times.

Many textbooks placed an emphasis on the nationalists' origins: "The 'Urabian Revolution" was led by a native son from a small village in the delta. Upon completing his studies at al-Azhar, he enlisted in the army where he distinguished himself as a superb officer and a born leader. The revolutionary narrative also stressed the affinity between the social backgrounds of those who fomented the ʿUrabian and July Revolutions. According to the historian Rafiʿi, all of these impressive men rose from the less privileged classes of Egyptian society. In addition, the raison d'être of both undertakings reflected the yearning of the people for an end to the dictatorial regime.[59]

Historians and pseudo-historians played an instrumental role in articulating and disseminating the revolutionary narrative. The vast majority of works that were published by these researchers during the first years of the republic painted an idyllic portrait of the measures taken by the FO. However, like the proceedings of the Revolution's Court, their writing spawned a discursive process. The arguments that were put forth by the RCC's supporters triggered a counter-narrative on the part of its critics. The opposing camps were led by two prominent historians: ʿAbd al-Rahman al-Rafiʿi and Shafiq Ghurbal. As the new regime consolidated its position, though, its naysayers were gradually excluded from the public sphere.

When the FO seized power, Rafiʿi (1889–1966) was nearing the completion of a book series (in Arabic) titled *The History of the National Movement*. The acclaimed historian's identification with the fomenters of the military coup soon came to expression in his writing. In newspaper and journal pieces, he glorified the dramatic events that were transpiring in Egypt. He also sealed the series with two books on the July Revolution. The first, *Introduction to the Revolution of July 23, 1952*, fully exhibits the FO's narrative of the difficult circumstances in which Egypt was mired during the monarchial era. In the process, Faruq's reign was described as corrupt, detached from society, and undemocratic. As suggested by its title, *The Revolution of July 23, 1952: Our National History in Seven Years*, Rafiʿi's second book is a paean to "the blessed movement." Although the July Revolution was still in its nascent stages, he averred that it will undoubtedly go down as "the most successful of the revolutions in the modern history of Egypt."[60]

Unlike Rafiʿi, Shafiq Ghurbal was a prominent critic of the revolutionary narrative. In the eyes of many of his contemporaries, he was also the leading Egyptian historian of that generation. On the anniversary of the military coup, Ghurbal penned an article that summarizes the views of the oppositional school of thought: "Every revolution wishes to anchor its enterprise in the past, and our revolution is no different at an hour in which it seeks to view ʿUrabi's revolt as its father [-cum-] begetter. However, ʿUrabi did not engender the revolution of 1952." Given the differences between the periods in question, Ghurbal argued that there is no connection between the two events. "The historical fatherhood"—the outlook according to which the July Revolution is a product and continuation of the ʿUrabi one—is a misrepresentation, for it is predicated on a hypothesis that ignores the historical processes that played out during the seventy-three-year interim between these two momentous events. "In history," he concluded, "there are no vacuums."[61]

Conclusion

The rhetoric of *Mahkamat al-Thawra* was the central venue of the junta's efforts to rewrite the country's hegemonic narrative. Besides investigating charges against its defendant, the ʿAbd al-Hadi trial was a prime venue for the quasi-authoritative documentation of the monarchical regime's failures, such as the corruption of the ruling system, the gross civil rights violations, and the army's implosion in the 1948 War. Many of the hearings concentrated on historical issues. In fact, the indictment and questioning phases were designed to revise and spread the hegemonic narrative of modern Egyptian history. This version was not only meant to convince the populace that the FO was compelled to intervene and overthrow the monarchical regime but also to explain why the army should continue running the state. Put differently, the tribunal's rhetoric sought to debunk the monarchical era's hegemonic narrative and replace it with one that would strengthen the credentials of the RCC.

In this context, the rhetoric of the judges and the general prosecutor categorically distinguished between the constitutional and political order existing during the monarchical era and the dispensation that the RCC sought to establish. This dichotomy between past and present is also evident in the court's "us-versus-them" mentality. Whereas "us"—namely, the revolution's supporters—represent the "will of the people," the vaguely defined "them" object to "the principles of the revolution" and the establishment of a new order. The serious charges brought against ʿAbd al-Hadi were actually directed at the monarchial order in its entirety. In keeping with the RCC's historical narrative, figures and organizations whose contribution to Egyptian independence was previously beyond reproach, were portrayed as accomplices of the old dynasty, especially the Wafd and the Saʿdist parties. As per the court's rhetoric, the army and the people were presented as "one hand." However, this statement begs qualification. In his book *The Philosophy of the Revolution*, ʿAbd al-Nasser admits that he was extremely disappointed with the tepid support that the FO garnered from the public during the nascent stages of the revolutionary transition period.

Nevertheless, ʿAbd al-Hadi was convicted of treason and of abusing his senior position for illicit personal gain. Though sentenced to death, his punishment was ultimately commuted to life imprisonment. The Revolution's Court ceased operations in April 1954. However, six months later, the RCC issued a decree calling for the establishment of another special tribunal—*Mahkamat al-Shaʿb*—for the purpose of bringing members of the MB to justice. Although the movement had been allied with the FO on the eve of the coup, it had subsequently become the "enemy of the people and the revolution."

PART III

Turning Friends into Foes

6

The Advent of the People's Court

At 10:00 am on Tuesday, November 9, 1954, the trial of Mahmud ʿAbd al-Latif opened at the headquarters of the RCC in al-Jazira. The defendant was shuttled to the court directly from a military prison, where he had been confined since his attempt on the life of Prime Minister ʿAbd al-Nasser two weeks earlier. In plain language bereft of judicial pomp, Major Gamal Mustafa Salem, the presiding judge, called "prosecution [case] number 1 for the 1954 year" into session. After the accused was identified by his full name, the most serious charges on the bill of indictment were read aloud, including the following:

> Actions against the present regime and against the well-being of the homeland from within and abroad, and this because on October 26, 1954 and beforehand in Cairo and Alexandria: 1) [He] collaborated with others in planning a conspiracy to carry out a criminal offense that was intended to cause a blood-drenched civil war [*fitna damiya*] aimed at toppling the regime; and this by establishing a special and armed secret organization to commit acts of murder on a wide scale and most severe acts of sabotage, and to sow destruction throughout the country, in preparation of a hostile takeover of the government on the part of the organization to which he belonged. 2) He intended [*sharʿa fi*] to murder the prime minister, Major [*bakbashi*] Gamal ʿAbd al-Nasser.[1]

As ʿAbd al-Latif was asked if he understood and admitted to the charges against him, the dozens of people in the hall stared at the accused—a skinny young man of average height wearing a white cloth shirt and gray striped pants. Though seemingly in a daze, he tepidly answered in the affirmative. At this point, the defendant was asked whether he was "guilty or not guilty." Much to the surprise of the judges, ʿAbd al-Latif answered "Guilty" (*mudhnib*). In turn, they requested that he list the name of lawyers who might be prepared to represent him, whereupon the accused mentioned three names. Judge Salem then adjourned the hearing, which had lasted all of a few minutes.

While the proceedings of ʿAbd al-Latif's trial were open to the general public, most of those who had squeezed their way into the undersized hall were journalists. The trial was a twelve-day marathon, over the course of which senior figures from the MB, including the General Guide and heads of both the Guidance Office (*maktab al-irshad*) and the Special Apparatus (*al-jihaz al-khas*; SA), were called to the witness stand. While the Egyptian populace was quite familiar with ʿAbd al-Hadi, the same could not be said for the would-be assassin, ʿAbd al-Latif, who was virtually unknown. The social background and political affiliations of the two men could not have been further apart. Although both defendants were residents of Cairo, ʿAbd al-Latif lived in the poverty-stricken neighborhood of Imbaba, while the former prime minister made his home in one of the capital's modern districts and had substantial financial assets and real-estate holdings. Their worldviews were utterly different too. ʿAbd al-Hadi was a member of the liberal-secular elite, whereas the gunman belonged to the militant wing of the MB.

The ʿAbd al-Latif trial was merely the beginning of a juridical torrent. In the months that ensued, state attorneys submitted over eight hundred bills of indictment against MB activists who were subsequently tried before *Mahkamat al-Shaʿb* (the People's Court). This special tribunal was established by power of a governmental decree on November 1, 1954, four days after the failed attempt on the life of ʿAbd al-Nasser.[2] This order clearly attests to the exceptional powers of this tribunal, which severely violated the defendants and witnesses' rights. Some of its sections are identical to those in the edict that established the Revolution's Court a year earlier. Both documents state that these special tribunals have been set up pursuant to section 8 of the constitutional declaration of February 10, 1953, stipulating that "the commander of the revolution" possesses the ultimate authority to take "the measures that he will find to be critical to the defense of the revolution and the government."[3]

The decree's nine sections include details on the tribunal's composition, its jurisdiction, and modus operandi. For example, article 2 stipulates that the court will adjudicate "actions that are deemed to constitute treason against the homeland [*khiyana lil-watan*] or are detrimental to its well-being both from within and abroad as well as actions directed against the governing order [*niẓam al-hukm*] or the foundations [*usus*] upon which the revolution was instituted." The court has also been granted the authority to try alleged offenses that were carried out before the decree's promulgation and cases of indirect assistance to "anyone that abets" the previously mentioned offenses "in any way." Furthermore, the court is authorized to take up any case that the RCC submits before its judges, even if it is currently being heard in ordinary courts, so long as a verdict has yet to be released. The next section states that *Mahkamat al-Shaʿb* can mete out the death penalty, life imprisonment with forced labor, "or any other penalties" that the judges find appropriate.

As per the edict, the proceedings will be conducted at the RCC headquarters in a public manner [*bi-tariqa ʿalaniya*]. However, the judges have the authority to hold a session behind closed doors. Defendants will receive a warning of at least twenty-four hours before the start of their trial. Hearings can be deferred for up to forty-eight hours but only once per trial (article 5). Lest there be any doubt as to the court's power, the decree stipulates that the judges reserve the right to take any steps they find necessary (article 6). This authority is neither subject to appeal nor may litigants request the removal of any judge from their case. In addition, the RCC is authorized to confirm the rulings, which are to be announced by the judges in open sessions. Yet another manifestation of the tribunal's draconian power is the formally and unambiguously phrased section 8 according to which the court's rulings are absolutely irrevocable.

For all purposes, the decree establishing *Mahkamat al-Shaʿb* compromised the Egyptian judiciary's autonomy, which the RCC had promised to uphold upon seizing control.[4] Perhaps the most salient expressions of this change was the regime's assumption of the right to transfer cases that are already underway in the regular court system to the special tribunal and to impose "any other penalties," even those that are not on the existing books. These sweeping powers are commensurate with the exceptional state of affairs that characterizes revolutionary transition phase.

Within days of the decree's release, the compound at the RCC headquarters was placed at the disposal of the People's Court. This wing was once again bustling with dozens of investigators, jurists, clerks, and officers working under the watchful eye of the regime's top brass. The tribunal's physical expanse and the symbolic design of the courtroom duly represented the "new" hegemonic order, as it conspicuously displayed the central symbols of the revolution: the recently unveiled flag of the republic (bearing an eagle on its red, white, and black background), which had replaced that of the deposed monarchy, and slogans of the revolution.[5] The venue was also teeming with army officers fully attired in dress uniforms sporting their ranks and decorations. These same symbols were consistently in sync with the judges' and prosecution's rhetoric as well as the phrasing of the charge sheet.

The newspapers featured photos of the court's three judges, most often seated on a raised dais. This platform was dominated by a wooden table laden with documents and files. An armed soldier was positioned to the side of the judges' perch. Unlike other courts in Egypt, the hall of *Mahkamat al-Shaʿb* lacked both a special witness stand and defendant's booth. Instead, the witnesses occupied the benches in the first few rows and the accused was seated on a wooden bench just to the right of the judges. When called upon to give testimony, the witnesses stood opposite the judges' stage. Between the latter and the front row were microphones via which the trial was broadcast on public radio. The attire embodied the unique reality of the proceedings. While the judges donned military uniforms, the defendant, the witnesses, and most of the other attendees sported the garb of men belonging to the new *effendiya* middle strata: cloth pants and shirts along with a jacket; the elderly were even spruced up in tarbushes and ties.[6]

The three judges—Gamal Mustafa Salem, Muhammad Anwar al-Sadat, and Husayn al-Shafi'i—were senior members of the military regime. This particular composition, especially the appointment of Salem to head the court, had a substantial impact on the trials' character. At this stage in the revolution, Salem ardently favored extending the FO's rule, rather than transferring the reins of government to civilians. During RCC meetings and in his public statements, Salem espoused hawkish views that he articulated using harsh language. Some of his colleagues described him as a short-tempered man of strong words. These traits would, in fact, come to expression over the course of the tribunal's proceedings. Sadat's appointment to the bench symbolized the reversal in the FO's relations with the MB—a topic that would merit a substantial portion of the court's attention. Sadat was known for his hardline views on national issues and his unflinching support of 'Abd al-Nasser's policies. Soon after the July Revolution, the future president took part in several conciliatory meetings with the MB leadership, whereas now he was helping run a juridical body that endeavored to paralyze the movement by delivering a knockout blow to its leadership and institutions. Rounding out the judge's panel was Shafi'i. Endowed with a pleasant disposition, he played the role of the forgiving and compromising mediator.[7]

Among the "judges of the people" (one of the popular nicknames for the court's triumvirate in the Egyptian press), Salem was the one who clearly called the shots, to the point where his peers' voices were seldom heard throughout the dozens of sessions. The questions that he frequently directed at the witnesses occasionally resembled an outright grilling. In addition, he repeatedly denigrated them and expressed hostile views of the MB. On several occasions, he labeled its activists "liars," "a stain on the forehead of Muslims," and "cancer cells" in the body of the nation. He even went so far as to equate Ibrahim al-Tayyib, among the heads of the SA, with "Hitler, Hess, and Göring." Hindawi Duwayr, 'Abd al-Latif's direct commander, was dubbed "an enemy of Islam." Similarly, the presiding judge called an MB activist from the Giza area, who worked as a high school teacher, "a liar and a hypocrite—a teacher who teaches small children lies and hypocrisy in the name of Islam." After one of the witnesses stated that he earns a modest "12 Egyptian pounds a month," Salem once again spewed his venom: "You aren't worth 12 milliemes" (the equivalent of a few pennies).[8]

He also often turned to the spectators in the courtroom with the clear objective of ridiculing the defendants. Following General Guide Hasan al-Hudaybi's statement that the movement's acts are consistent with Islamic law, the judge posed a rhetorical question to the crowd: "Did you see my Muslim brothers how [the MB] interpret our religion? Did you see how they laugh at the peasants [*fellahin*], and how within seconds they mislead your children?" Thereafter, one of the attendees chimed in that the MB "indeed led [people] astray in the rural area." At one point, Salem even declared that "it was a stupid move on the part of the revolution to pardon you [i.e., MB activists] and release you from jail."[9]

The tribunal's investigation and prosecution offices were headed by three military officers and three civilians, all of whom were appointed by the RCC. The attorney general put together a special team of jurists, which was headed by the same officials who had run *Mahkamat al-Thawra*'s litigation team a year earlier: Mustafa al-Hilbawi, the head of the Public Prosecutor's Bureau for State Security Affairs; 'Abd al-Rahman Salah, the deputy attorney general; and Muhammad al-Tab'i, the military prosecutor. The three jurists closely accompanied the work of the Investigations Bureau and drafted the bills of indictment. Pursuant to the special tribunal's broad jurisdiction, the staff had the power to arrest citizens, conduct searches, and take any other steps that they felt would bolster the government's case—all this "without the constraints of regular laws and procedures." Major (*bakbashi*) Muhammad Kuni al-Badawi was responsible for security arrangements, maintaining order during the hearings, and media relations. Two clerks from the Attorney General's Office served as the court's secretaries.[10] The general administration and coordination between the prosecution and investigation teams was entrusted to Interior Minister Zakariya Muhyi al-Din. Assigning this task to such a high-ranking member of the RCC was indicative of just how important these trials were to the revolution's top brass.

The Defense

The second session of the 'Abd al-Latif trial was convened on November 11 at 10:20 am. Once again, the audience in the courtroom consisted mostly of journalists, whose reports filled the next day's papers. At the behest of the presiding judge, the accused reconfirmed that the indictments against him were clear and that he admitted to committing the offenses in question. At the defendant's side was his attorney, Hamada al-Nahil. Judge Salem heaped praise upon the latter for agreeing to take on this sensitive task. In turn, Nahil obsequiously thanked the special tribunal for showing trust in him. This exchange hints to the minor drama that transpired behind the scenes in all that concerned the state's efforts to find suitable counsel for the accused. Following the opening session, the Attorney General's Office turned to the Bar Association for help recruiting a defense attorney. After a number of candidates turned down the job, the association's directorate called an emergency meeting to discuss its members' professional and ethical duty to provide worthy counsel for the defendant and to recommend a qualified candidate. There was a short piece about this meeting in the press, but no details were provided regarding its results.[11]

The three lawyers who 'Abd al-Latif mentioned during the first hearing turned down the request due to national and personal considerations. One of the prospects, Fathi Salamah, said, "I decline to serve as this criminal's counsel for two reasons. First of all, I am an attorney of law with national feelings; secondly, since I despise this criminal, how am I to defend him? I am unable to take this case because we are talking about an attack on the country's savior and the leader of Egypt's awakening [i.e., 'Abd al-Nasser]." Salamah also noted that, were he to participate in this trial, he would side with those clamoring for the death penalty.[12] 'Abd al-'Azim Ramadan, a renowned Egyptian historian, characterized their behavior as "disrespectful and defeatist." In his view, their refusal to represent the accused was akin to turning their backs on the principle of defendants' rights. Moreover, they were passing up an opportunity to help reinforce Egyptian democracy. "If these three lawyers had displayed [some] courage," Ramadan concluded, "it would have been possible to turn the trials of the Brothers into trials against the dictatorship [i.e., the RCC] and to thus mend the way of the revolution."[13]

'Abd al-Latif neither chose Nahil to be his lawyer nor cooperated with him. From the information in the transcripts, it is doubtful that the two even conferred outside the courtroom. That said, upon being asked at the outset of the second session if he wanted to respond to the charges against him or have his counsel do so, 'Abd al-Latif deferred to his attorney. Soon after, Nahil asked to call witnesses on behalf of the defense. This request offered a spark of hope that the accused would merit competent advocacy. However, the lawyer's words were cut off by the prosecutor who argued that there was no need for this step because the defendant had already confessed to all the charges against him. At this critical juncture in the trial, the judges approved the prosecutor's request. Throughout the examination phase, the defense attorney's participation in this quasi-legal process steadily tapered off. The judges and prosecution ignored his presence, directed their words to the accused, and demanded that 'Abd al-Latif personally answer their questions. Nahil's primary line of defense was to present his client as an innocent victim that had fallen into the clutches of a criminal outfit run by the heads of the MB.[14]

The counsel's narrative stood in stark contradistinction to his client's own statements; for throughout the proceedings his client fully identified with the movement's positions. While on the witness stand, the defendant expounded on his activity in the MB. Among the main topics that he discussed was the cell members' justification for killing the prime minster.[15] According to 'Abd al-Latif's testimony, he joined the movement in 1942. The reasons behind this move were his sympathy for the Brothers's religio-conservative agenda and their positions on national issues, such as the movement's armed struggle against Britain's continued military presence in Egypt and its opposition to the establishment of a Jewish state. In fact, 'Abd al-Latif considered the activists who participated in these campaigns to be paragons of self-sacrifice. Like many of the organization's members, he believed that these struggles epitomized the MB's deep commitment to the nation and Islam. Accordingly, the defendant considered his decision to join the MB a national and religious act in equal measure. Due to his affiliation with the movement, 'Abd al-Latif was briefly incarcerated in 1949. It also bears noting that he joined the National Guard (*al-haras al-watani*) shortly after its establishment in 1954 and, like many other MB members, frequently took part in its activities.[16]

According to the defendant's testimony, he joined an SA cell about four months before the attempt on 'Abd al-Nasser's life. His enlistment in the paramilitary wing constituted a show of support for its leaders' assertive and uncompromising approach to the RCC. As a low-ranking activist, 'Abd al-Latif had scant knowledge of the movement's institutions and was only acquainted with a handful of fellow members. Compartmentalization, secrecy, and deference to orders were rigidly enforced within the SA's ranks, so that it was quite common for activists to be unfamiliar with their peers. This was particularly true of 'Abd al-Latif, who had only recently joined this covert undertaking. Hindawi Duwayr, who recruited the would-be assassin into the SA, was its point man in Imbaba, a primarily lower class neighborhood of the Egyptian capital in which the defendant lived. As his direct commander, Duwayr placed the new recruit in a cell that operated in the district. Due to the SA's extensive support in Imbaba, it was quite active within its borders. In fact, most of the people involved in the assassination attempt lived and worked in this area. However, it bears noting that the defendants and witnesses' biographies attest to the MB's wide base of support. Aside from the poor, members of the urban *effendiya* strata also made a significant contribution to the movement.

The would-be assassin was married and the father of three children. According to the court minutes, he possessed a junior high education and was a tinsmith (*samkari*) by trade. Like many of the neighborhood's disadvantaged residents, 'Abd al-Latif lived with his family on part of an apartment building's roof. Over the course of the trial, he described the intimate and intensive relationship that quickly developed between the three members of his cell. Held in private homes, most of their meetings were dedicated to memorizing Quran verses, studying religious commandments, and pouring over the Prophet's biography. These discussions served as an interpretive framework for evaluating current events. In this context, the members of the cell formed a highly critical view of the revolutionary regime, especially its domestic and foreign policies. According to 'Abd al-Latif, they were particularly upset over the evacuation treaty that the RCC had signed with Britain on October 19, 1954, which they considered an act of treason (*khiyana*) that severely hurt Egypt's national interests.[17]

The Botched Assassination

It is unclear from ʿAbd al-Latif's testimony when the idea of expressing opposition to the withdrawal treaty by harming Gamal ʿAbd al-Nasser—the head of the Egyptian negotiation team and the official who signed the accord on behalf of the state—was first broached. In fact, the prosecution and judges did not invest much of an effort in clarifying this particular matter. This, then, would appear to strengthen my argument that convicting ʿAbd al-Latif soon became a secondary goal of the People's Court. The accused and other witnesses dwelled on the planning of the assassination. According to the defendant, following a number of meetings on this subject, the cell members unanimously agreed that killing the prime minister was appropriate from a religious and national standpoint. Moreover, all of them expressed a desire to take part in the operation.[18]

According to the signed confession of the accused and his testimony in court, ʿAbd al-Latif chose the date of the assassination in a random fashion. After reading in one of the papers that the prime minister was scheduled to deliver a speech in Alexandria on the evacuation treaty with Britain, he simply decided to assassinate him at this event. It could very well be that ʿAbd al-Latif fabricated this account to take full responsibility for the crime and thus save his colleagues from harsh punishment. His testimony contradicts the details that were given by his accomplices, especially those of his direct commander.

Duwayr, a lawyer by trade, was a member of the MB's hardline camp and one of the masterminds behind the assassination plot. Like most of the witnesses, he also linked the decision to kill the prime minister to the agreement with Britain.[19] However, in contrast to others, he claimed that the assassination was meant to ignite a "popular revolution" (*thawra shaʿbiya*) aimed at deposing the military regime and transferring power to Muhammad Naguib, whose critical views of ʿAbd al-Nasser and the RCC were already common knowledge. According to Duwayr, the MB had no intention of seizing the reins of government because "the country is not ready to accept a full-fledged Islamic government."[20]

With respect to the actual plan, Duwayr stated that he personally chose ʿAbd al-Latif to carry out the assassination. He also noted that several leading figures in the SA were involved in the planning, to the extent that they determined that the mission would be assigned to the Imbaba cell. Likewise, Duwayr claimed to have learned about the plot from his own direct commander, Ibrahim al-Tayyib, who headed the SA's Cairo operations. In addition, Tayyib intimated to him that the General Guide had approved of the plan and had given the military wing the green light.[21] Duwayr's testimony dovetails neatly with the regime's contention that the MB's leadership conspired to overthrow the government. However, it stands in contradistinction to the version that was submitted by ʿAbd al-Latif and the majority of witnesses at his trial, including the General Guide himself. The purported involvement of the movement's leadership, especially Hasan al-Hudaybi, in the conspiracy would become one of the major issues in this case. This question notwithstanding, the following discussion is dedicated to a comprehensive description of the assassination attempt itself.

On the morning of Tuesday, October 26, Mahmud ʿAbd al-Latif left his home in Imbaba for what would be the last time in his life. Following a short meeting with his colleagues from the SA, he got on a tram that took him to Cairo's central train station. The operative was already set for the mission, as the night before he parted ways with Duwayr who deposited a German-made Mauser gun and fifteen bullets in his hands.[22] ʿAbd al-Latif's train reached Alexandria at approximately 1:00 pm. The would-be assassin then passed the next few hours wandering about the center of town, where he had lunch at a cheap restaurant.

During those same hours, the city held a number of events in honor of the visiting prime minister and his entourage, which included a handful of other RCC chiefs including Salah Salem, ʿAbd al-Hakim ʿAmr, and Sadat. Daily news programs, which were screened at movie theaters, previewed the mass reception that awaited Egypt's leaders in the main streets of Alexandria. Thousands of citizens gathered along the delegation's route. Riding in open convertibles, the helmsmen of the revolution waved to the cheering crowd. In the week since the signing of the *jalāʾ* (the evacuation) agreement, the heads of government had launched an intensive campaign to market it to various sectors of Egyptian society. This, then, was the backdrop for the RCC's visit to the country's second largest city.[23] The trip's schedule was brimming with events. At most of the stops the prime minister and his colleagues delivered short speeches trumpeting the pact as a historic achievement that would put an end to decades of occupation and exploitation.

While the prime minister was attending a closed reception at the local Chamber of Commerce, the assassin made his way to Manshiya Square where tens of thousands of citizens had already gathered for the night's main event. The time and place that ʿAbd al-Nasser chose to deliver the keynote speech of his visit were draped in national and political symbolism. Besides the controversial accord with Britain a week earlier, exactly fifteen months had passed since the ousted King Faruq and his family left the country via the city's famed port.

The prime minister delivered his grand oration from the balcony of the Chamber of Commerce, which was located in the heart of Manshiya Square. It was nearly eight in the evening when ʿAbd al-Nasser approached the podium. ʿAbd al-Nasser drew a correlation between the end of the monarchy and the evacuation treaty, which he presented as the most prominent achievements of the July Revolution. As a native of Alexandria, the setting reminded the leader of experiences that he had as a local high school student in the beginning of the 1930s. In this very plaza, he was arrested by the police after stumbling into a demonstration against the policies of the Isma'il Sidqi government (1930–3). In an interview with the *Sunday Times* reporter, the prime minister reminisced that it was only during his incarceration that he had learned who had organized the rally—the Young Egypt party. As in some of his earlier speeches, he shared these experiences with the sea of Egyptians assembled before him: "I began my [national] struggle as a young teen in this very square . . .. Today I celebrate here with you the Evacuation holiday [*'id al-jalā'*], a day of freedom, pride, and honor."[24]

As the masses responded to these words with an ovation and cries of support for the revolution, 'Abd al-Latif was standing two hundred feet from his target. Twilight was descending on the Mediterranean coast as the assailant brandished his pistol and fired eight shots. The bullets missed their mark, but severed 'Abd al-Nasser's symbolic link between the course of his life and the annals of his country. Amid the panic, the prime minister was hastily escorted out of harm's way. Two eye-witnesses—Salah al-Desuqi and 'Abd al-Karim Darwish, who served in the army unit that was responsible for securing the rally itself—offered similar accounts of the drama that unfolded in the immediate aftermath of the failed assassination, both inside the building and down in the square. Upon hearing the gunfire, guards rushed the prime minister inside the Chamber of Commerce. Within minutes, the other members of the entourage reached the room along with the prime minister's father, Husayn 'Abd al-Nasser, who had difficulty concealing his worry.[25]

At the same time, a soldier, Ibrahim Hasan al-Halati, who happened to be standing near 'Abd al-Latif, set himself upon the perpetrator, knocked him to the ground, and seized his weapon. The two were instantly surrounded by hordes of onlookers. Security forces ran to the scene, arrested 'Abd al-Latif, and took him to the nearby police station.[26] Pandemonium erupted in Manshiya Square, as some of the crowd began to flee the area. Word soon spread that the prime minister was unscathed but that several bystanders had been hit by the stray bullets.

Moments later, the Egyptian leader adamantly demanded to return to the balcony and address the people. Following a short consultation, the agitated voice of the prime minister made itself heard over the din. 'Abd al-Nasser turned to the crowd and urged them to stay in their place, whereupon he tremulously repeated the following phrase three times: "My blood is a sacrifice on your behalf; my life is a sacrifice for you" [*dami fidā lakum; hayati fidā lakum*]. The people who had remained in the square received these words with applause. "This is Gamal 'Abd al-Nasser speaking to you," he continued in an agitated tone. The traitors and those collaborating with imperialism are the ones that tried to harm me. However, I will continue "to struggle and labor on your behalf until my death, for the sake of your freedom and honor." One of the prime minister's colleagues urged him to wrap things up, but he continued to speak for a few more minutes: "You are all Gamal ʿAbd al-Nasser," he iterated. "If ʿAbd al-Nasser was to die today or tomorrow, you are all Gamal. My blood is like yours, my spirit is like your spirit, and my sensation is like your sensation."[27]

Following his improvised monologue, the prime minister was driven to the nearby promenade, which runs the length of Alexandria's breathtaking coast. He then entered the Cecil Hotel, where the Egyptian Bar Association was throwing a reception in honor of the high-ranking guests. The representatives of state went ahead with their planned speeches emphasizing the advantages of the treaty with Britain, but the signs of stress are quite evident in the news footage of this event. While the entourage's arrival merited an ovation from the audience, the camera also documented the crestfallen faces of Egypt's young helmsmen. Smoking one cigarette after another, ʿAbd al-Nasser, Salem, and ʿAmr seemed to be immersed in themselves. The hosts tried to alleviate the tension by expressing their trust in the revolution and applauding their guests' remarks.

After Salem's patriotic talk about sacrifice and struggle, the prime minister assayed the tragic and treasonous circumstances behind the attempt on his life here in Manshiya Square of all places. Even had the plot succeeded, he was certain that many of his fellow Egyptians would "meet the call of duty and continue the fight to advance these just causes." This is not the "struggle of a single man," but the "yearning for freedom on the part of generations of Egyptians." When the event was over, the delegates continued to the nearby hospital to visit the injured. Meanwhile, the preliminary interrogation of ʿAbd al-Latif was well underway at the police station.[28]

The next day ʿAbd al-Nasser and his entourage headed back to Cairo via train. Hundreds of thousands of citizens stood along the tracks and cheered for their leaders. What was a warm welcome upon reaching the capital quickly turned into a mass show of support. A few hours before their arrival, the MB's headquarters in the Cairene neighborhood of al-Hilmiya was set on fire.[29] A new and harrowing round in the ongoing struggle between the regime and the Islamic movement was underway. The public sphere, especially the capital's squares, was transformed into a grand stage on which the RCC brass—most importantly, the prime minister—repeatedly espoused their views on the continuation of the July Revolution. At these mass rallies, the regime's senior officials described "the nation and army as one hand."

Three days after the Manshiya incident, an enormous pro-Nasser rally was held at Republic Square (*midan al-jumhuriya*) in downtown Cairo. Over one hundred thousand citizens crammed into the plaza and the adjacent streets, where they cheered for the members of the RCC. Their rhetoric at this demonstration redrew the battle lines between the revolution and its supporters on the one hand and the accomplices of the corrupt monarchy on the other. At this gathering, ʿAbd al-Nasser delivered his most comprehensive speech since the failed attempt on his life. He presented the signing of "the evacuation" (*al-jalā'*) treaty as a "small Jihad"—a modest step in the construction of a new society that is grounded on "true social justice." Attaining this goal, he said, will allow the country to embark on a "big Jihad," in which the revolution's supporters will contend with "the deviation from the honest path and the surrender" to the forces of imperialism and the treason.

Most of the thirty-six-minute oration, though, was dedicated to excoriating the MB, particularly the General Guide. In this context, 'Abd al-Nasser revealed traces of the conflict between the regime and the MB that was waged behind the scenes on the eve of the evacuation treaty. According to the prime minister, the RCC had discovered that trained operatives were dispatched, with the blessings of General Guide Hudaybi and his underlings, "to carry out personal operations and assassinations" for the purpose of thwarting the agreement that would finally put an end to the seventy-year presence of British troops on Egyptian soil. 'Abd al-Nasser's rhetoric left no room for doubt as to the dramatic turnaround in the FO's attitude toward the Islamic organization. From here on, it would display little tolerance toward the movement:

> We will no longer allow an association of this sort or any other to base itself on a secret apparatus, and we will not allow the establishment of a state within a state. . . . We will overcome the terror and subversion, and we will institute a real democracy just as we promised.

In a personal message to 'Abd al-Latif, 'Abd al-Nasser declared, "I hereby swear to God that I bear no grudge against him." The "accusatory finger" must be pointed at those who exploited and misled citizens like the assassin in the name of Islam. "Whereas the revolution has set a goal of eradicating poverty," the MB and its leaders have sought to take advantage of the indigent under the facade of religious enterprise.[30]

The day after the pro-Naaser demonstration at Republic Square, Salah Salem, a member of the RCC and now the minister of National Guidance (*al-irshad al-qawmi*), held a news conference in which he disclosed details of a conspiracy that ostensibly came to light during the interrogation of 'Abd al-Latif.[31] According to the minister, the objective behind the attempt on 'Abd al-Nasser's life was to instigate "a total change of the regime in Egypt by means of a large series of assassinations that a secret apparatus of the Brothers planned down to the [final] details over the past few months."[32] However, this account runs counter to the testimony that 'Abd al-Latif gave at his trial.

Over the next few days, senior members of the RCC put in numerous high-profile appearances. Cairo University hosted an event in which the presidents of this institution and Alexandria University expressed their support for the evacuation agreement and strongly condemned the attempt on 'Abd al-Nasser's life. In addition, the prime minister received a delegation of residents from the Imbaba district, whose members chastised their former neighbor

'Abd al-Latif. This unusual meeting attracted extensive media coverage. The prime minister thanked the Imbaba residents for their support and declared that he did not consider the assassin a representative of their community. Instead, 'Abd al-Latif merely stood for the MB movement and the "lowly goals that they deviously conspire to advance in the name of the Islamic faith." The shots that he fired were directed against the revolution, even though the RCC pursued this course "for the sake of attaining a good and dignified life for Mahmud 'Abd al-Latif and citizens like him."[33]

The "Special" or the "Secret" Apparatus?

Throughout the 'Abd al-Latif trial, it was obvious that the court was attempting to substantiate the claim that the MB's leaders had plotted to overthrow the government and that they had placed this mission in the hands of the "Secret" Apparatus.[34] Hasan al-Banna originally established this wing for the express purpose of recruiting and training volunteers for the armed struggle against the British presence in Egypt. In subsequent years, the SA supported the pan-Arab effort to prevent the establishment of a Jewish state in Palestine, which Banna classified as a religious and national duty. Following a nuanced study Brynjar Lia concluded, "There are many uncertainties surrounding the founding of the Special Apparatus," and he convincingly claimed that it was formed "sometime in 1940" and that "with a few exceptions the Special Apparatus remained quiet during the war years."[35] It is worth noting that not one litigant denied the existence of this body throughout the hearings at the People's Court, and the movement's senior officials even confirmed having received a request from the FO to shut the armed wing down. That said, a dispute erupted over whether the MB's current leadership, particularly the General Guide, controlled the SA's operations.

Another complex issue that surfaced in this context was the long-standing cooperation between the movement's activists and the FO. The judges and prosecution focused their arguments on the formal legal sphere. In their opinion, government officials had repeatedly demanded that the SA be terminated, but the MB heads continued to maintain this "militia" for the purpose of ousting the regime. They also contended that the movement's leaders ignored the government's orders because this illegal outfit served the Brothers' agenda. In other words, the movement and the SA were one and the same; namely, both the parent and the subsidiary bodies held the same radical views and pursued various schemes to advance them.

Over the course of the proceedings, the judges and prosecutors referred to the wing as the Secret Apparatus, whereas the MB representatives insisted on calling it the Special Apparatus. Far from a matter of nuance or semantics, this difference reflected the significant gap between their positions on the armed wing's goals and intentions. The regime's obdurate insistence on using the name "Secret Apparatus" constituted a legal and public act that was intended to label the MB a subversive group that not only violated the law but shunned the values of the Islamic faith. While the movement trumpets the slogan "Islam is the solution," the RCC argued that its treasonous and reprehensible actions demonstrated that religion was merely a pretense for drumming up support. These claims, which were frequently voiced at *Mahkamat al-Sha'b's* hearings, echoed the declarations of the ruling elite both before and during the 'Abd al-Latif trial and were also prevalent in the Egyptian media—all of whom employed the appellation Secret Apparatus.[36]

Alternatively, the court transcripts remain the only extant source that records the MB members' unflagging use of the name "Special Apparatus." This, then, is a compelling example of the court's records importance as a source that documented voices of resistance. The MB leaders contended that the SA can hardly be considered a clandestine operation, as its existence was common knowledge. Furthermore, they noted that in the not-so-distant past the FO had actually trained the wing's members and supplied it with arms.[37]

In a similar vein, most of the movement's senior brass vehemently denied the tribunal's claim that the Brothers' activities (the SA included) were unlawful. This argument was duly expressed in the testimony of Hindawi Duwayr. Sporting a brown jacket and fashionable shirt, Duwayr appeared to be relaxed. He greeted the judges with the blessing of "*al-salam 'alikum*" (Peace be upon you), to which Judge Salem responded in kind. Countering the judge's characterization of the wing as an "illegal" undertaking, the witness stated "that this is naturally the vantage point of the state." With respect to a government decree from January 14, 1954 ordering the entire movement to disperse, he noted that this is "an un-Islamic act that no Muslim can support." Duwayr even predicted that this demand would transform "everyone" into "a secret apparatus."[38] He also added that the movement's top echelons had analyzed this edict and reached the following conclusions: the RCC intends on waging a public struggle against the MB, and it will attempt to split the organization's ranks by dispensing jobs to those activists willing to cooperate with the regime.[39]

In building its case, the prosecution highlighted a request that the RCC forwarded to the MB leadership in May 1953 calling for the movement to sever all its ties with the security forces immediately, shut down the SA, and hand over all its weapons to the authorities. These demands were among the many points of contention that arose during the testimony of Ibrahim al-Tayyib, the SA's Cairo chief. Tayyib stated that he was unaware of this communication. On the contrary, his commander, Yusuf Tal'at, informed him that the regime was encouraging the operations of the MB-led *fidā'in* (fighters) against British forces in the Suez Canal zone. In fact, he asserted that senior government officials, among them Husayn Kamal al-Din, passed on a message to the organization that these efforts were serving the government's interests. At this point, Salem cut off the witness and gave his own take on the events in question: It was the MB, the judge insisted, that turned to Kamal al-Din and offered to provide manpower for the *mukhabarat*, but their proposition was summarily rejected. In a characteristic fit of anger, Salem reminded the witness that it was the FO who carried out the revolution, "while you were asleep in your home," for the purpose of "liberating you from the oppression and corruption that was rife in this land . . . We [the FO] exiled Faruq," he added, whereas "you [the MB] dubbed him 'the gracious king' [*al-malik al-karim*]." Lastly, "we came to save you from governments that were treating you like merchandise in the name of the constitution, the parliament, and elections."[40]

At this juncture, the prosecutor cynically surveyed the MB's repeated violations of decrees that were promulgated by the ruling authorities. For instance, it failed to comply with an order issued by the Nuqrashi government (December 8, 1948) to close down the movement. The state's representatives also noted that the movement's activists carried out a series of terrorist acts against Egyptian citizens and bodies, including Jewish businesses and institutions.[41] For this reason, according to the prosecution, the security and intelligence agencies continued to keep track of the SA after the coup.

Neither the prosecution nor the judges were prepared to explain why the regime did not take any practical steps to disband the SA and sufficed with asking the MB leadership to do so on its own. As members of the RCC, it stands to reason that the judges were well aware of the extensive support that the FO, especially its members in the security forces and police, gave the movement. In light of this relationship, the regime may have feared that its heated disagreements with the movement, which reared up from 1953 onward, or a crackdown on the SA would trigger a hostile response from the MB. They were also concerned that its continued attacks against the British would disrupt the RCC's efforts to hammer out a withdrawal agreement with London.[42]

Throughout the trial, it was also apparent that the People's Court was turning a blind eye to the intensive cooperation between the wing's activists and the FO in the three years that preceded Faruq's ouster. For example, numerous operations that the SA conducted against British soldiers and installations (primarily in the Suez Canal zone) garnered the support of many Free Officers, some of whom even took part in these assaults. ʿAbd al-Munʿim ʿAbd al-Raʾuf, a high-ranking member of the FO with considerable military experience, described how he helped train MB activists at several camps that he ran.[43]

One of the more dramatic hearings in the ʿAbd al-Latif trial got underway on November 18, 1954, when General Guide Hasan al-Hudaybi was summoned to testify on behalf of the defense. The prosecution, which had planned on calling him to the witness stand at some stage in the proceedings, sought to build the case that Hudaybi was directly responsible for all the operations that were carried out within the framework of the MB, including the SA. The extensive press coverage that the General Guide's testimony attracted, which included detailed reports on his interactions with the court's representatives, betrayed the enormous public interest in this compelling figure. These news pieces were accompanied by photos showing a clean shaven Hudaybi in a three-piece suit and tarbush testifying before the judges. It is quite evident that the regime sought to deliver a message to the public that, despite Hudaybi's involvement in the movement's despicable deeds, he was treated fairly by the authorities. This policy may have been an attempt to refute the rumors concerning the heavy-handed treatment that MB activists faced in prison and during interrogations.

As can be gleaned from contemporaneous media reports, Hudaybi was the target of harsh criticism from the RCC leadership in the four months that preceded the assassination attempt. Similarly, this hostile attitude was evident during his testimony at the ʿAbd al-Latif trial. However, it would intensify sevenfold during Hudaybi's own trial, which opened several days later. At one point, Hudaybi testified that the MB-organized demonstrations against the regime in the summer of 1954 concentrated on the following topics: the reinstatement of constitutionally guaranteed civil liberties, the resumption of parliamentary life, and the release of political prisoners.

Judge Salem countered that these statements are nothing but attempts to avoid giving direct and pertinent answers to the court's questions. The General Guide asserted that he was not being evasive, but he may not recall every last detail because his memory was not in top form and his overall health was poor. "I ask for your testimony," Salem responded. "You have the freedom to remember what you feel like [remembering] and to forget what doesn't suit you. . . ." "What if I don't recall?" Hudaybi protested. "And I say that I don't remember." After the judge repeated the same accusations, the witness reminded the court, "I suffered a stroke that impaired my memory and ability to speak. When I say that I don't remember, it means that I don't remember."[44]

The prosecution also sought to exploit Hudaybi's dignified reputation as a judge. The witness was one of the first graduates of the Egyptian University's Faculty of Law (1915). Although he worked as an attorney for several years, the brunt of his career was spent as a judge in the Criminal Court system (1924–51).[45] On several occasions, Hudaybi was requested to present his legal outlook with the objective of extracting a statement proving that he had always put more weight on the Islamic law (*Shariʿa*) than codified law. However, the General Guide invariably responded that the two traditions are consistent with one another. Oddly enough, this issue culminated with a question that was raised by the defense: "Which law did you implement in the period that you served as a judge?" The General Guide replied that he was charged with adjudicating in accordance to the civil and criminal codes. Thereafter, Nahil asked whether he was morally satisfied with the state's laws. Hudaybi reiterated that, "to exclude the matter of interest," the civil code is in accord (*mutafaq*) with Islamic law and enables jurists to lean on *Shari'a* principles. He also noted that the Quran and the *Sunna* specify the punishments for only seven infractions, whereas the government has the power to determine the punitive measures for all other criminal offenses. The ruler also "has the prerogative" to refrain from meting out the *Shari'a*-prescribed punishment (*hudud*).[46]

The General Guide's detailed testimony entailed responses to a long list of questions on the SA. According to Hudaybi, this wing was primarily intended to train believers who are capable of protecting their land. Moreover, he claimed that the true scope and nature of the armed wing's activities only came to his attention once he had entered office. On realizing that some of its operations were illegal, he ordered the SA to desist from such acts.[47] At his behest, the MB's institutions decided that the armed wing would thereafter operate exclusively in accordance with the Guidance Office's directives. Hudaybi also managed to replace its senior command. The new chief, Yusuf Tal'at, agreed to implement the General Guide's moratorium on unlawful activity.[48] From reports he subsequently received, Hudaybi was under the impression that the SA was no longer involved in violence and that it was focusing exclusively on training activists to defend the country.

The General Guide also rejected the use of terrorist means for any purpose whatsoever. In the past, "I declared that terrorism hurt the movement, hurt Islam, and hurt Egypt. And I warned of this on more than one occasion and disseminated my thoughts among the Brothers."[49] Likewise, Hudaybi testified that, in a personal meeting with Tal'at, he reemphasized that any criminal activity and "any assassination" will only damage the Brothers' interests. Therefore, "I will not permit them to carry out" these sort of acts. In addition, he let his subordinates know that this matter is not open for discussion. Later on in the trial, the prosecutor returned to this statement, presenting it as evidence that the General Guide was aware of the plot to kill 'Abd al-Nasser. The witness countered that he was not referring to a specific plan but was merely stating his principled objection to any criminal offenses, including the assassination of political rivals.[50]

According to Hudaybi, in his capacity as General Guide, he was not directly involved in the operations of the SA. Moreover, he was only loosely acquainted with its senior personnel and even less so with its activists. Hudaybi swore in the name of Allah that he did not give an order to harm the regime's senior figures including the prime minister. By prompting such comments, Judge Salem managed to get MB chiefs to label each other liars. "Will you swear on this to Allah, may he be praised that you were not involved in the conspiracy," Salem then asked. "Yes," Hudaybi replied. "Swear into the microphone," the judge demanded. "I swear to Allah, may he be praised, that I did not give the order." "No," Salem insisted, "swear that Hindawi Duwayr is a liar and that Ibrahim al-Tayyib is a liar." Hudaybi sought to qualify his response, but Salem cut him off: "Your honor [i.e., Hudaybi], you are standing here as a witness that responds to questions that are directed at you and not as a lawyer." The General Guide then declared that Duwayr and Tayyib indeed lied if they said that "I ordered them to assassinate ʿAbd al-Nasser."[51]

According to Hudaybi's testimony, upon assuming the top post he got the feeling that some of the SA's leaders "have no faith in me. . . . These people think that they are somewhat greater warriors [*mujahidin*] [than I am], while I am an elderly person."[52] This statement clearly alludes to his poisoned relations with the armed wing's chiefs. However, the court chose to ignore the dissension within the movement's ranks, despite its relevance to clarifying who was responsible for the decision to assassinate the prime minister. With these words, the defense's questioning of the General Guide came to a close and the prosecution began to cross-examine the witness.

The prosecution immediately embarked on an offensive aimed at impugning Hudaybi's description of the MB's chain of command. The prosecutors' aggressiveness notwithstanding, the General Guide continued to be treated with respect by virtue of his standing in Egyptian society. The attorney's opening question was whether as an esteemed jurist Hudaybi felt that it was lawful for the MB to be holding arms. "It is illegal," he answered, "but the entire country is teeming with weapons."[53] In an effort to clarify the necessity of maintaining the armed wing following the July Revolution, the prosecution allowed Hudaybi to present his view regarding the current state of affairs in Egypt and the logic behind the Brothers's modus operandi. He averred that the SA's operations are essential so long as British forces are parked on Egyptian land, the Jews are striving to establish a state in Palestine, and other Muslim nations are struggling to extricate themselves from the yoke of foreign occupation. The General Guide added that the movement had received communications from the FO in the aftermath of the coup but was not required to dismantle the armed wing.[54] At this juncture, the court president announced a fifteen-minute break "in order to allow the witness to rest a little."

Forty-five minutes later, the hearing resumed and, with it, the prosecutor's efforts to demonstrate that the "Secret" Apparatus was superfluous. His argument centered on the National Guard (*al-haras al-watani*)—one of the new regime's flagship projects. Established in the wake of the revolution, the National Guard was intended to attain the same objectives that Hudaybi ascribed to the SA. Like many of the other witnesses who contended with this argument, the General Guide insisted that the continued existence of the SA did not detract from the training camps that the regime had set up. He also noted that numerous MB activists had joined the ranks of the National Guard. Their association with this government-sponsored organization bolsters the movement's case that there is no contradiction between national and religious causes. For example, Mahmud al-Huwatki, a twenty-three-year-old chemistry teacher in an elementary school testified how he had joined the MB during the third year of his studies at Cairo University. The witness stated that he had joined the SA for the sake of contributing to the Jihad in Palestine and the Suez Canal. Later on, he joined the National Guard out of a desire to share the combat experience that he had acquired as a member of the SA in the 1948 War against Israel. In devoting himself to these causes, Huwatki believed that he was fulfilling his duty to be a "good citizen" (*muwatin salih*). Echoing the view of some of his colleagues, he asserted that the MB members stood out from the other volunteers in the National Guard from the standpoint of training, education, and values: "In the Brothers, they educate the individual in every respect. . . . They steel his character and his behavior from a religious and spiritual perspective."[55]

Such accounts challenged the view that there is an irreconcilable gap between commitment to religious values and the national agenda. While the judges and prosecution frequently made this case, the witnesses repeatedly claimed that it is impossible to divide the two. A riveting expression of this is found in the following exchange between the presiding judge and Huwatki. "What takes preference in your eyes—the national side or the religious side?" the former inquired. "The two complement each other," the witness replied. "And what if a dispute should arise between the religious and national sides?" the judge questioned. "Disagreement between them is impossible," Huwatki answered. "Islamic enterprise" supplies a framework for all fields of endeavor, he contended, so that it is "wrong" to distinguish between religion and state, religion and politics, and the like.[56] In his own testimony, Tayyib opined that one would be hard-pressed to draw such a distinction in a political context because the Muslim faith encompasses the totality of life. Likewise, Hudaybi declared that Islam stands above all else, and the homeland is merged within this framework. When the General Guide was asked to rate the importance of religion and the state, he insisted that there is no need for such a hierarchy, but if compelled to do so, the order is "Islam, then the homeland, then the association [i.e., the MB]; and the homeland is integrated into Islam."[57]

Who Controls the Muslim Brothers?

The hours of testimony on the SA undergirded the court's decision to convict the MB's leadership as accomplices in a conspiratorial plot to overthrow a legitimate regime. First, the judges and prosecutors endeavored to prove that the MB was a hierarchic organization whose members unwaveringly abided by their superiors' instructions, especially those of the Guidance Office and the General Guide. In other words, it is unfeasible that the plan to assassinate ʿAbd al-Nasser did not involve the input and consent of the movement's top brass. Although the discussion on the Brothers' chain of command may have seemed to be a side issue, the hearings on this topic constituted the basis for *Mahkamat al-Sha'b*'s ruling.

From the judges' perspective, the evidence demonstrated that the MB was a structured organization in which the executive level fully controls all the movement's departments, including the SA. Put differently, there is a direct (and not just circumstantial) link between the movement's formal decision makers and its operations in the field. As a result, the MB leadership's culpability for the offenses that were perpetrated in the organization's name is no less than that of the would-be assassin. Another of the special tribunal's primary goals was to inflict serious damage to the MB's public reputation. In this context, the movement was portrayed as a manipulative body that induced naïve citizens to take part in their evil plot to seize the reins of government under the false pretenses of religious enterprise.[58]

The exceptional powers that were conferred on the People's Court allowed it to easily attain convictions against the vast majority of defendants. Nonetheless, its hearings provided witnesses ample opportunity to present a completely different and much more nuanced picture of the MB than the state's version and to raise arguments that cast doubt on the hegemonic narrative of the prosecution and judges. The transcripts show that the MB's senior and low-level activists crafted an informative mosaic of the organization's institutions and its officials' bailiwick. For example, Hudaybi provided an illuminating description of the movement's hardships at the beginning of 1953. Although four years had passed since the killing of Hasan al-Banna, the position of General Guide had yet to be filled and the organization was in a state of disarray. A short while earlier, Hudaybi had retired following a long, distinctive career as a judge. He agreed to assume the Brothers' helm only after repeated entreaties on the part of its senior officials. The movement was seeking a figure with a track record in public service and who was uninvolved in the internal power struggles that had splintered the organization's ranks.[59]

Upon entering the post, Hudaybi quickly realized that the MB's activities covered a wide range of fields but was paralyzed by severe flaws in its chain of command. For instance, its key departments were operating without any supervision or direction from the top brass.[60] Correspondingly, Hudaybi discovered that some of the SA's operations were illegal. Consequently, he attempted to rehabilitate the movement's hierarchical integrity and put an end to any activity that was in violation of Egyptian law. The new leader placed great importance on manning key posts, especially within the Guidance Office—a body that he viewed as a sort of directorate that formulated the movement's policy and supervised all its activities.

Many of the MB's activists took issue with Hudaybi's makeover. The SA's inner circle, which had opposed his appointment to begin, expressed their opposition—both in words and deeds—to the general direction in which he attempted to steer the movement. After nine months of relentless struggle between the two sides, Hudaybi managed to remove the armed wing's old vanguard and insert his confidant, Yusuf Tal'at, at the head of the pyramid.[61] However, it quickly became obvious that these steps had only exacerbated the disputes between the General Guide's conservative camp and its militant counterpart, which was strongly identified with the SA. To Hudaybi's chagrin, several high-ranking members of the Apparatus continued to pull the strings and ignored the wishes of Tal'at, who had a difficult time gaining traction. Against the backdrop of the MB–RCC crisis in the spring of 1954, a handful of activists, led by Duwayr and Tayyib, pursued a course that was intended to advance their radical agenda. Without so much as seeking the approval of the movement's leadership, they began recruiting new activists for the SA, making sure to select men who would answer exclusively to them.[62]

A recurring pattern throughout the trials of *Mahkamat al-Sha'b* sheds light on this unauthorized campaign. All the defendants and witnesses were asked to submit personal details, including the dates they joined the MB and its armed wing and the code of behavior that was expected of them. Not only was each member of the Imbaba cell a veteran of the MB, but they were also all recruited into the wing by Tayyib in mid-1954, that is, a few months before the attempt on 'Abd al-Nasser's life. Furthermore, they were required to adhere strictly to their handler's orders, and the cell itself was tightly compartmentalized and disciplined. These traits ensured that not even a hint of the assassination plot would leak outside the cell. Against this backdrop, it stands to reason that the conspirators could have proceeded with their plan without the knowledge of the movement's leadership.

The hopes that the new General Guide would put an end to the MB's internal struggles quickly evaporated. The rivalries within the movement's top echelons also continued to hinder its activity. Burdened by a sense of personal failure, Hudaybi asked to step down and demanded that the Guidance Office find a replacement for him. As he remarked in his testimony, "I bear witness that I am unfit to lead this movement, and I have remained at the helm against my desire." Only his "sense of duty" compelled Hudaybi to stay on, but his involvement in the affairs of the movement steadily waned.[63] From the court's records, it is evident that at least some of the SA's senior figures were aware of the damage that these feuds had exacted.

Taking the witness stand at the opening of the eighth session, Muhammad Khamis Humayda, the Deputy General Guide (*na'ib al-murshid al-'amm*), elaborated on the creation of autonomous power bases within the movement. Humayda, a pharmacist from the city of Mansoura, was a member of Hasan al-Banna's inner circle. Since joining the MB in 1939, he filled a raft of positions within the movement. Following Hudaybi's appointment, he was promoted to the Deputy General Guide job. Although the position did not previously exist, he was vested with substantial authority.[64] Humayda convincingly described the infighting that the movement endured throughout the Hudaybi era. Of special interest is his testimony on the dynamics that enabled the SA to operate under the radar of the Guidance Office, such as the creation of independent fiefs between the assassination of Banna and his successor's appointment. Consequently, it was possible for members of the armed wing to operate without the knowledge or approval of the movement's leadership.[65] In an effort to refute the circumstantial evidence Humayda provided, Salem interrupted his testimony and demanded that he answer the following questions in a simple and concise manner: Was there an SA? Who formally headed this outfit? And who was the direct superior of the latter? Humayda confirmed the existence of the Apparatus and noted that it was led by Yusuf Tal'at, who answered to the General Guide.[66]

This pattern of questioning, which was quite prevalent throughout the hearings, created a semblance of matter-of-fact inquiry. In practice, though, it prevented the witnesses from responding to questions in a comprehensive and thoughtful manner. For instance, Salem thwarted Humayda's attempt to expand on the matter of who wields the true power over the SA. From the judges and prosecutors' standpoint, the obvious conclusion was that, given his standing as General Guide, Hudaybi was accountable for all the movement's activities. This approach enabled the court to substantiate ostensibly its argument that the Brothers possesses an orderly chain of command, so that its top official bore full responsibility for the assassination plot and plan to murder ʿAbd al-Nasser and overthrow the regime.

The transcripts of the trial clearly show how *Mahkamat al-Shaʿb* repeatedly chose to ignore the implications of the acrimonious disagreements within the movement's ranks. The prosecution summarily rejected the arguments and explanations that the General Guide and his deputy put forth with respect to the pervasive chaos within the movement's ranks. According to the prosecutor, the MB conspired "to bring the [General] Guide and his henchmen to the seat of power in the name of the [Islamic] faith, which is untainted by all their deeds, namely their turn to bullets and terror."[67]

The verbal jousting between the prosecutors and the witnesses practically always ended with the intervention of Judge Salem who, inter alia, thwarted a comprehensive discussion on the stages leading up to the assassination attempt. Nevertheless, the court transcripts preserved snippets of information on this phase that were supplied by MB representatives. Their statements enable us to piece together a completely different narrative than the one that the regime sought to lodge in the public consciousness. Moreover, the court records are among the only known sources that capture the substantive disputes between the MB's conservative and militant camps over a multitude of issues such as, for example, the Call to Islam (*daʿwa*). Hudaybi and his colleagues in the Guidance Office interpreted the Call to Islam as an ongoing enterprise in the fields of education, welfare, and social outreach. In contrast, the militants wanted to exploit this commandment for their aggressive campaign against the regime. For example, since "the revolution has turned to a non-Islamic direction," Duwayr stated that the Call to Islam should be geared toward action, rather than sufficing with a definition according to which it is merely a framework for disseminating the precepts of the faith.[68]

A more detailed characterization can be found in the testimony of Tayyib, a lawyer by profession who was among the leaders of the movement's hawks. During his first years in the movement, Tayyib worked in the legal department. Thereafter, he joined the ranks of the SA and quickly became one of its stalwarts, heading its operations in Cairo. By virtue of this position, he was a member of the movement's General Council, which was headed by the General Guide. During his testimony, the senior activist opined that the SA was established to defend the *da'wa* both within one's society and against external enemies. This is the reason, he continued, that the SA trains and dispatches skilled warriors to fight alongside their brethren in Tunisia, Algeria, or "wherever it is needed."[69]

However, the court turned its back on the evidence as to a fundamental disagreement within the MB over the Call to Islam. In fact, the attorney general repeatedly stressed that the movement's leaders exploited this directive as a cover for advancing criminal objectives that have nothing in common with the imperative to cling to the values of this exalted religion. Instead of fulfilling these lofty principles, the prosecutor argued, the MB advanced plans to commit murder and spread mayhem while riding roughshod over the state's laws. The movement's senior figures "cynically portray themselves as people toiling in the name of Islam," but in practice they have violated a wide range of explicit religious prohibitions. Above all, its "opportunistic leadership" has undertaken to oust violently a legitimate regime and, in the process, has led many citizens astray.

"The political corruption" that the movement's senior figures were involved in is a direct continuation of their distortion of the *da'wa*.[70] Judge Salem attempted to extract statements out of witnesses that would corroborate this argument. For several long minutes, he tried to convince Shaykh Muhammad al-Farghali, a long-standing MB activist in Isma'iliya, to admit that the movement had strayed from the path of the Prophet and the Righteous Caliphs. In his response, this member of the Guidance Office explained that "this entails no distortion." Even when "mistakes occur," this does not mean that "the entire enterprise" is misguided. In turn, Salem warned "Muslims, the residents of Egypt, and the residents of the Arab states" to take heed of the fact that the MB is "leading you astray" in the name of Islam.[71]

Similar claims as to the exploitation of believers surfaced in the court's rhetoric concerning the MB's allegedly dissolute chiefs. For example, in a discussion on the movement's income, Salem drew a correlation between the donations that it raised and the extravagant lifestyle of its officials. At the time, the witness stand was occupied by al-Sayyid Hassanein Abu Salem, an educated thirty-year old senior clerk at the Revenue Tax Office in Mansoura and one of the heads of the SA. In his testimony, Abu Salem estimated that the organization's membership rolls numbered around two hundred thousand people, the majority of whom paid an average of about ten piasters (roughly twenty-five cents) in annual dues. The judge responded that this money was used to fund the MB leaders' debauchery "on the backs of" unsuspecting, low-income citizens.[72]

Time and again, *Mahkamat al-Sha'b* emphasized that Islam constitutes a paragon of tolerance and its tenets are as distant from the MB leaders' radical interpretation of the Quran and the Prophet's biography as the East is from the West. The implementation of this exegesis, according to the judges, was liable to push Egyptian society to the brink of civil war (*fitna*), which Muslims historically view as one of the most pernicious threats to the nation of believers. On several occasions, the court compared this ostensible misreading of the *da'wa* to the iniquities of the Kharijites (*al-khawarij*)—a sect of several thousand Muslims that mutinied against and killed the fourth caliph, 'Ali Ibn Abi Talib (656–61). The Prophet Muhammad is attributed with remarks that explicitly warn against religious zealots who deviate from the true path of Islam. Due to the sect's exceedingly negative reputation in the annals of Islam, the word "Kharijites" has become a derogatory term for various groups that were accused of heretic inclinations and of unjustifiably resorting to violence. "In your activity to disseminate the revelation of Islam," Judge Salem asked Humayda, "have you gone in the way of Muhammad and the Righteous Caliphs, or have you gone in the way of the Kharijites?" The Deputy General Guide was stunned by the very notion that someone could identify the Brothers with this ignominious sect. Before Humayda could even regain his bearings, Attorney Nahil lashed out at him: "What is the difference between you and *al-Khawarij*?" This time, however, Salem interceded on the witness's behalf, declaring that the court has no interest in scrutinizing this comparison any further and announced a fifteen-minute break "so that you [the participants] can smoke a cigarette."[73]

When the hearing resumed, the court continued to examine the movement's interpretation of religious issues, including the call to holy war (*jihad fi sabil Allah*). The prosecution claimed that the MB's radical exegesis of this commandment sowed the seeds for the plan to kill the prime minister and violently overthrow "a legitimate government." Here, too, the transcripts attest to the gap between the regime and the MB's outlook on the events under review. For instance, at Salem's behest, 'Abd al-Latif reiterated that a considerable portion of his cell's meetings was dedicated to the subject of Jihad, that is, memorizing pertinent Quran verses and discussing this precept in an effort to understand its meaning.[74]

Such statements were presented as incontrovertible evidence that the members of the SA held extreme views and had no compunctions about using any means possible to achieve their goals. On the other hand, the court's preoccupation with the subject of Jihad enables us to take stock of the differences in the way each side interpreted this commandment. At the opening of the second session, the prosecutor asked ʿAbd al-Latif to explain how he understood this precept. The defendant replied that Jihad is "a battle [*muharaba*] against the enemies of Islam and freedom." However, much to the lawyer's dismay, he added that in our own time "Islam's enemies" are the English, the Jews, and anybody that stands in the way of the *daʿwa*. Before the prosecution could react, ʿAbd al-Latif remarked on the immediate national political context of this perspective: The cell members had reached the conclusion that the evacuation treaty with Britain was a serious act of treason (*khiyana*). Because combating treason is essentially the commandment of Jihad, "I understood that the president [sic] is an enemy of Islam."

He also noted that they had looked into the possibility of assassinating Anwar al-Sadat, who was now sitting a few feet away on the judge's dais. ʿAbd al-Latif and his comrades had studied articles by Sadat in the newspaper *al-Jumhuriya* and reached the conclusion that his writing is an affront to Islamic values. For example, they inferred from one of these pieces that the future president believed that when there is a contradiction between religion and progress, one must give priority to the latter. Thereafter, the prosecutor sought to turn ʿAbd al-Latif's argument against him: "You said that you frequently read from the Quran—does the Quran permit the killing of a Muslim?" ʿAbd al-Latif naturally answered no. "If so, why did you want to kill President [sic] Gamal ʿAbd al-Nasser and the Colonel [*qaimaqam*] Anwar Sadat—Are they not Muslims?" The defendant answered that they are "indeed Muslims," but he understood from Duwayr, his commander, "that they are deviating from Islam." ʿAbd al-Latif added that, following the assassination attempt, he began to feel as though he had made a mistake, that his deed "contradicts Islam."[75]

This expression of remorse on the part of the first defendant of the People's Court was important to the regime's rhetoric. In the public discourse on the trials against MB activists, the government's speakers and supporters used ʿAbd al-Latif's misgivings to bolster their case that the MB is a manipulative organization that took advantage of innocent people. Nahil argued that his client's regret was proof that he was "insane." Accordingly, the defense attorney petitioned the court to have the accused institutionalized for the purpose of running tests and getting a professional opinion as to his fitness to stand trial. In turn, the prosecutor objected to this motion on the grounds that the defendant is a normal person who is cognizant of his actions. Following a short exchange, Nahil's request was overruled. Salem predicated the judges' decision on ʿAbd al-Latif's own declaration that at the time of the Manshiya incident he was not driven by personal motive but consciously executed the instructions of his handlers.[76]

Conclusion

The stated objective of the People's Court was to bring MB members that were allegedly complicit in the attempt on 'Abd al-Nasser's life to swift justice, but the RCC also saw it as a means for advancing much broader goals. From a purely legal standpoint, it would have been possible to adjudicate those involved in this crime before an ordinary court of law and to mete out severe punishments in accordance with the standard Egyptian penal code. The circumstances behind the tribunal's establishment and its far-reaching powers leads us to the conclusion that its underlying aim was to strike a fatal blow against the MB. At the time, the movement enjoyed the support of wide swathes of the Egyptian public, and its leadership was highly and openly critical of the RCC.

The transcript of the 'Abd al-Latif trial indicates that hardly any juridical resources were allotted to plumbing the depths of the assassination plot itself. Instead, the questioning focused on broader issues, such as the goals of the MB, its interpretation of Islam, and the national and civil commitment of the movement's activists. The judges and the prosecution sought to demonstrate that the MB was cynically exploiting the religious beliefs of innocent civilians to promote a radical agenda that threatened to plunge Egypt into civil war.

The questioning phase also gave oppositional figures a chance to voice narratives that the regime otherwise toiled to suppress. For instance, both senior and junior MB activists emphasized that from their standpoint there is no difference between religious and national affairs because the *Shari'a* explicitly rejects such a distinction. This outlook was elucidated by testimony of MB members who joined the National Guard—the flagship project of the RCC—while continuing to serve in the SA.

The judges and the prosecutor tried to present the MB as a highly organized movement with a clear hierarchy in which lower level members defer to the leadership's discretion, but the transcript of the 'Abd al-Latif trial tell a different story. According to the defendants and witnesses, including the General Guide, in the wake of Hasan Banna's murder, there was a power struggle within the MB's ranks over the future direction of the movement. Furthermore, they submitted a completely different and much more nuanced version of the attempt on 'Abd al-Nasser's life. For instance, the organization's leaders utterly rejected the state's central argument that they were involved in the plot. To the contrary, the MB leaders claimed that the perpetrators of the assassination bid were loose cannons who acted at their own volition. Much to the judges' chagrin, these figures also discussed their organization's intimate and prolonged cooperation with the FO. In addition, the crisis with the regime was stoked by the protraction of military rule and the controversial Evacuation Agreement with Britain. Put differently, the strife revolved around distinctly political and national issues. However, the line of questioning shows that the state's representatives had practically no interest in these matters.

In setting up this judicial framework, the regime sought to prove that the MB was a hierarchical organization in which orders, particularly from the Guidance Office and the General Guide, were strictly obeyed. For this reason, the judges and prosecutors contended, the assassination bid would not have materialized without the approval of the movement's leadership. The court ruled that the MB top brass was no less responsible for the crime at hand than 'Abd al-Latif, for it was the former that had dispatched this low-level activist in the movement's name. However, there are serious doubts as to the accuracy of the RCC's depiction of the ideological agenda, chain of command, and activities of the MB.

7

Officers–Brothers Relations: What Went Wrong?

In his study *The Concept of the Political*, Carl Schmitt raised the following claim with respect to political relations: "The specific political distinction to which political actions and motives can be reduced is that between friends and enemy. . . . The friend and enemy concepts are to be understood in their concrete and existential sense, not as metaphors or symbols."[1] However, Schmitt did not show how relationships change from alliances to rivalries. The ensuing deconstruction of the special tribunal elucidates the MB's transformation from the closest friend and partner of the revolutionary regime to its principal adversary. This dramatic shift was triggered by far-reaching changes in the political sphere that steadily took root in the aftermath of the FO's coup.

The transcripts of the special tribunal provide a rare look at the peaks and valleys that informed the intensive, decades-long relationship between the movement—particularly its top brass—and the Egyptian security forces. The cooperation and amity between the two bodies in the decade that preceded the July Revolution of 1952 gradually waned in the first two years of the revolutionary government. Each party's interests were fundamentally altered, and political feuds spawned a cavernous chasm between the former allies. The RCC's us-versus-them rhetoric was already quite evident in the year before the ʿAbd al-Latif trial. Moreover, the establishment of the special tribunal and the rhetoric that was generated by its judges and the prosecution constituted a seal of approval for the categorical reversal in the government's ties with the movement. The fact that nearly all the court's sessions were open to the public helped thrust this rhetoric into the spotlight.

Gradually Evolving Relations

ʿAbd al-Latif's membership in the MB, beginning with his decision to join the movement at the height of the Second World War and ending with the minor activist's attempt on the prime minister's life, essentially embodies the turnabout in RCC–MB relations. During his testimony on the circumstances behind the decision to join the Brothers, a riveting discussion took shape on the genesis of the ties between the MB leadership, especially Hasan al-Banna, and officers from the Egyptian army and police. As per the court transcripts, the two sides warmed up to each other as a result of the "crises of February 1942." Despite the passing of six decades since Britain had conquered Egypt and Sudan and despite the unilateral declaration of Egyptian independence in 1922, which ostensibly ended the state of occupation, London continued to exert its clout. In fact, Britain's deep involvement in the affairs of the Nile region encompassed most government dealings. While London's primary emphasis was on security and geopolitical issues, it also made its presence felt in local politics and the economy. As this intervention heightened, so did local resistance—a development that slowly assumed the contours of a national liberation struggle involving various sectors of the Egyptian populace.

Whereas the Anglo-Egyptian Treaty of 1936 putatively expanded Egyptian sovereignty, developments during the Second World War attest to the limits of Cairo's political independence. At the height of the war, the Churchill government feared that General Erwin Rommel's advance through the Sahara Desert would ultimately repel Britain from the continent. Adding fuel to the fire were expressions of support for the German army at all levels of Egyptian society. For example, Sir Miles Lampson (Lord Killearn), the British ambassador to Egypt, dispatched reports to London of anti-British positions that were voiced by no less than Prime Minister ʿAli Mahir and King Faruq. Consequently, Lampson and Foreign Minister Anthony Eden attempted to coerce the monarch into forming a Wafd-led government under the premiership of Mustafa al-Nahhas. Faruq initially refused to accept this dictate but relented on February 4, 1942 following an ultimatum from London to either comply or be ousted from the throne. This message was personally delivered to the sovereign by the ambassador, who arrived in a convoy of armored vehicles that menacingly surrounded ʿAbdin Palace.[2]

Many Egyptians considered this episode to be a national humiliation and a worrisome reminder of the government's weaknesses and the fragility of the country's independence. Various groups—both established organizations and grass-root initiatives—looked for ways to resist. After enjoying widespread support during his first years at the helm, Faruq's popularity sunk to an all-time low. Similarly, the decision by the Wafd, which had once headed the nationalist camp, to accept the ultimatum and anchor a new coalition seriously damaged its public reputation. This turn of events also seeded partnerships between the MB and a bevy of officers and soldiers in various security forces. Moreover, ʿAbd al-Nasser wrote that the events of 1942 sparked a change in the mindset of his generation of officers:

> In the Army, the event wrought a radical change, in both the spirit and disposition of the officers. They formerly talked of nothing else but enjoyment and pleasure. They now spoke of sacrifice and devotion to duty—of readiness to give up their lives for the dignity and integrity of the Mother-country. They were grieved they did not intervene, despite their manifest inability, to retrieve and wash with their blood the country's dignity.[3]

By this stage, the MB had already consolidated its position as a reform movement whose chief objective was to establish a society and regime that would revolve around a progressive and pragmatic interpretation of Islamic law (*Shari'a*) as well as a compatible ideological platform, which was crafted by its founder, Hasan al-Banna. Under the inspiration of Banna's leadership, the MB expanded its purview in social, cultural, and political spheres. A considerable portion of its resources were allocated to projects in the fields of education, welfare, and *da'wa*.[4] Filling the vacuum left by Egypt's shoddy infrastructure and the perpetual dearth of services, the movement buttressed its standing as the country's largest nongovernmental organization. As a champion of the idea that religion and state must not be separated, the organization raised the banner of intensive public outreach, which included taking positions on national and political issues.

In 1942, the movement established a quasi-military wing—the SA, and from that point on, its activists carried out numerous attacks against British troops and installations (primarily in the Suez Canal Zone). The MB adamantly opposed the UN's plan to divide Mandatory Palestine into two states, on both religious and national grounds: religiously speaking, Palestine constitutes Muslim endowment (*waqf*) land, which cannot be partitioned. From a national or pan-Arab standpoint, the establishment of a Jewish state would constitute a grave injustice and mortal blow to the Palestinian people and their aspirations for political independence. In 1948, the movement even sent armed volunteers north of the border to help thwart the founding of a Jewish state.[5]

In those years, the MB's platform was based on views that Banna had promulgated in sermons and missives. However, these normative texts (the movement subsequently published others) did not constitute the lone source of its policies. The MB leadership's declarations and publications over the years betray a shift in its views on various issues. Drawing on Althusser's insights, MB's ideology examined here not merely through the prism of its normative texts but also through its actions.[6] Although the movement's commitment to the principles of its founder's gospel survived his passing, it is equally important to take stock of how these tenets were adjusted to suit the changing political, economic, and social map. Put differently, the organization's position and modus operandi are indicative of its unflagging dedication to the values of Islamic fundamentalism, but they are also clearly swayed by the major issues and challenges standing before contemporary society. As such, the heads of the MB have consistently argued that there is no contradiction between Islamic values and the institution of a modern state. In his deft analysis on this dynamic, Sami Zubaida suggested that the movement should be viewed as "a modern political party, with a systematic organization and recruitment, and a political programme imbued with the assumptions of the modern national political field. . . . The desirable future order is postulated in terms of an . . . Islamic form of the nation state."[7]

The extent of the MB's involvement in the political arena has been a controversial issue since the group's establishment in 1928. While its senior officials recognized the Islamic principle whereby no differentiation should be made between the affairs of state and religion, there were extensive internal debates as to whether the organization should accentuate the *da'wa* at the expense of both its political enterprise (on both the municipal and parliamentarian levels) and outreach among professional unions and college students. Throughout the 1940s, the movement played a key role in the policy struggles between nationalist parties (most important, the Wafd) and the monarchy. The historic rivalry between the Wafd and the MB paved the way for some collaboration between the latter and the palace. By this juncture, the movement had already earned the support of broad swathes of the Egyptian public. Following the FO's coup, the movement ratcheted up its involvement in government affairs to what was then an unprecedented level by throwing itself into the efforts to revamp the Egyptian government. The transcripts of the People's Court document the intensive dialogue between senior officials from the RCC and the MB on the character of the new regime.

These same discussions also point to the increasing support that the movement garnered from within the ranks of the security forces, especially the army, in the years leading up to the coup.[8] The MB's indignation over the situation in Egypt and Palestine was shared by many Egyptians. Whereas the majority of the state's political parties were mired in internal bickering and thus unable to put forth feasible solutions to the country's problems, Hasan al-Banna offered a lucid ideological framework, according to which fundamental change would be attained in both Egypt and Palestine by means of arms, which drew many young men into the movement's ranks.

In addition, according to the testimony given by MB members before *Mahkamat al-Sha'b*, the movement merited extensive support from within the army and the police. Over the years, soldiers and officers provided its activists with, among other things, weapons and combat training. In several instances, joint operations were carried out by civilians, MB members included, and security personnel. For the most part, such collaboration occurred on a personal basis, but there were also a few cases of quasi-institutional cooperation. While a fair share of the security associates that supported the Brothers' pugnacious approach limited themselves to identifying with its enterprise, some elected to join the movement. Needless to say, the official historiography of the July Revolution obfuscated the involvement of army officers, including ʿAbd al-Nasser and Sadat, in the movement's activities. However, in his seminal study on this chapter of modern Egyptian history, Gordon takes stock of what was, in fact, a close relationship:

> In the early 1940s the Muslim Brotherhood began recruiting junior officers into its secret organization. . . . Hasan al-Banna charged Salah Shadi, a young police officer, with supervising the police cell. The army he delegated to Mahmud Labib, a retired major. . . . In one of these cells [ʿAbd al-]Nasser, Khalid Muhyi al-Din, Kamal al-Din Husayn, ʿAbd al-Munʿim ʿAbd al-Raʾuf, and several other officers met in one another's homes on a weekly basis from 1945 to 1948. They discussed politics and their role on the national liberation struggle far more than religion. They also circulated pamphlets.[9]

Among the FO members with close ties to the movement's top brass was ʿAbd al-Munʿim ʿAbd al-Raʾuf. In his memoirs, ʿAbd al-Raʾuf wrote that immediately after joining the MB in May 1942, he and Mahmud Labib organized "the Brotherhood Officers" (*al-ḍubat al-ikhwan*)—a framework in which the organization's leadership provided guidance to army commanders. He also claimed to have personally enlisted ʿAbd al-Nasser into this group and that it ultimately served as the basis for the establishment of the FO.[10] However, in the surfeit of research on the July Revolution and the MB, there is no evidence that the charismatic leader ever belonged to the Islamic movement. Barbara Zollner, whose study on this question is based on the testimony of MB activists and FO members, concludes that this matter "cannot be answered with clarity."[11]

In all likelihood, Sadat never formally joined the movement either but was in constant touch with its senior officials. Like many Egyptians, he commended the MB's resistance against the British. Sadat's autobiography also mentions the enormous respect that he had acquired for Hasan al-Banna ("My admiration was unbounded") and the MB's organizational capacity ("I was struck by the perfect organization of the Muslim Brotherhood, and by the respect, even extraordinary reverence, which the General Guide commanded"). Sadat recalled telling the movement's founder about the group of army officers that was planning to overthrow the regime. At the end of the conversation, the interlocutors agreed that their respective groups would cooperate with one another. The autobiography also notes that while Sadat was in prison Banna notified his family that the MB had decided to support them financially ("Sheikh Hasan's offer of help was invaluable").[12] Sadat was incarcerated for a year and a half during the trial of Amin ʿUthman's assassins. During ʿUthman's tenure as minister of financial affairs, nationalist groups accused him of collaborating with Britain in a manner that was highly detrimental to Egypt's national interests. Sadat, who was then a low-ranking officer in the Communication Corps, noted that he was a member of a group that decided to kill the minister for making the following statement: "the relationships between Egypt and Great Britain was in affect a Catholic marriage, so that even if Britain chose to dissociate herself, Egypt could never do the same. That declaration was tantamount to a self-imposed death sentence. On January 6, 1946, the sentence was carried out."[13]

In his nuanced study on the formation of the FO, Eliezer Be'eri points out that the ties between several officers, who would play a key role in the 1952 coup, and the MB "grew in importance parallel to the steady rise of the Brethren's influence during the 1940's. The dialogue between the parties intensified with and after the establishment of the Free Officers group in late 1949."[14]

In the run-up to the military coup on July 23, 1952, the magnitude of the contacts between the two groups' leadership ranks steadily increased. According to in-depth testimonies given during the ʿAbd al-Latif trial, this interaction reached the level of formal ties and substantial coordination. Senior MB members described how on the eve of the military coup, ʿAbd al-Nasser and other officers personally gave the movement's top brass a general overview, timetables included, of their plan to seize control of government.[15] However, the prosecution and judges sought to muffle statements concerning the amity and cooperation between the MB and the regime. Nonetheless, to the RCC's chagrin, direct and indirect expressions of the intensiveness of these relations surfaced time and again over the course of the trial.

Free Fall

"If extreme distance leads to indifference, extreme closeness can lead either to pity or to destructive rivalry," argues Ginzburg in his thought-provoking piece on the moral implications of distance.[16] The regime's ties with the MB bolster this argument. With the launching of the revolution, the movement's cadres saw themselves as the closest allies of the FO. Consequently, they viewed the military coup as an historic opportunity to institute a new ruling order in which the Brothers would merit significant representation.[17] With this in mind, the MB presented its sizable constituency as a strong base of public support for the revolution. Likewise, the new regime deemed the movement to be a crucial ally.

In reality, though, the dramatic change in the political sphere upended the MB's relations with the RCC. At the same time, the FO swiftly transformed itself from a band of conspirators to the face of government. Hereafter, the dialogue between the two bodies was more specific, and topics were aired out within the framework of negotiations, which exposed significant disagreements.[18] In other words, the dialogue was more intimate than ever before, but signs of dissension began to rise to the surface. Within two years, these tensions deteriorated into a serious crisis that redefined the rules of government–opposition relations for decades to come. The first disagreements centered on the incorporation of MB representatives in the new cabinet, the scope of agrarian reform, and the wording of the new constitution.[19] This friction was exacerbated by the regime's demand that the MB wind down the SA. An even more serious breach of trust from the FO's vantage point was the fact that the MB had joined the chorus of those pressing the RCC to transfer the reins of power to a civilian leadership as well as the movement's piercing criticism of the evacuation treaty with Britain. There were also disputes over the last two issues within the revolutionary leadership, so that the positions taken by MB leaders heightened their organization's involvement in the all-out struggle between the ʿAbd al-Nasser and Naguib camps.

A week after the military coup, General Naguib (whom the media now dubbed "the commander-in-chief") met with the General Guide, Hasan al-Hudaybi, in Cairo. The mass-circulation newspaper *al-Masri* reported that the two held a lengthy and important conversation but did not provide any details regarding its content. The newspaper did observe "rather extensive activity" within the movement since the exile of King Faruq. In the aftermath of his talk with Naguib, the General Guide convened a meeting with approximately one hundred of the movement's senior members. Hudaybi declared that the objective of this gathering was to scrutinize the new reality in Egypt. At the end of the meeting, he enjoined the attendees "to be on the alert *mutahabyin*] for any eventuality." A journalist remarked that, under the circumstances, there were very specific connotations for the word "alert," but the General Guide did not deign a response.[20] Thereafter, Hudaybi convened the MB's two highest forums—the Guidance Office and the Founding Authority (*al-hayah al-ta'sisiya*)—for a series of urgent meetings. According to official MB speakers, the movement's leadership was formulating proposals for "ineluctable reform."

These discussions yielded a thirteen-page document that was composed by the members of the Guidance Office and signed by the General Guide on August 2, 1952.[21] This detailed missive included the MB's recommendations for post-monarchical Egypt. Moreover, it contained the seeds of a dispute that gradually transformed the alliance between the regime and the MB into a bitter rivalry. We may infer from this document that the movement viewed Faruq's ouster as a unique opportunity to change the priorities of the Egyptian government and to advance the goals that the movement had championed since its inception. The missive regards the coup as "the blessed movement" (*al-haraka al-mubaraka*) and a window of hope for the Egyptian nation's revival.[22] Its smattering of citations from the Quran aside, the memorandum was couched in practical language. For instance, it asserts that "the time has come to set our eyes forward." The overarching objective was defined as "activity to advance a comprehensive reform [*al-islah al-shamil*]."

In this context, the movement felt obliged to let both the new regime and general public know that it believed the state should be governed on the basis of Quranic exegesis (*tafsir*).

The memorandum is divided into a number of subchapters, the most prominent of which are "The General Purge," "The Moral and Educational Reform," "The Constitution," and "Social Justice." As per the introduction, the "first issue on the agenda is to locate and settle the score with every person that was part of the corrupt and tyrannical regime headed by King Faruq." Most important, the monarchy's senior figures and police officers who persecuted innocent citizens must be dismissed from their posts and, without exception, prohibited from ever serving in the public or political arena. In addition, anyone who exploited their power to compromise liberties, harm the innocent, or torture oppositional activists is to be "tried without any hesitation or partiality," including those who "had a known role in the assassinations of public figures" such as Hasan al-Banna.

The army's takeover of government was also presented as an opportunity to repair society from an ethical standpoint. Among the key factors in this reform would be the education system. According to the missive, religious education constitutes "the best path" to prosperity for a new generation whose hearts will pulsate with the spirit of Islam and nationalism and that will adhere to high moral standards "in private and public life." Therefore, it is incumbent upon the government "to prohibit that which Allah prohibited and outlaw phenomena that stand in contradistinction to this [Islam,] such as gambling, alcohol, venues for leisure [activities] and dancing, movies, and publications that stimulate earthly urges."

In the chapter on the constitution, the authors note, "Successful revolutions abrogated constitutions from the age that preceded them." Consistent with its long-standing opposition to the Constitution of 1923, the MB now portrayed that text as contravening the new reality in Egypt and devoid of a legal basis. Against this backdrop, the memorandum called for the establishment of a committee to draft a new constitution that would accurately express the principles and values of the Egyptian people and protect the national interests. "The foundations of the constitution will be based on the principles [*mabadi*] of Islam." This would apply to "all fields of life," including the government's commitment and respect for the principle "that all are equal before the law." In addition, it behooves the drafters to learn from "past constitutional attempts, so that our progress toward reform will be grounded on realistic and tangible foundations."

The missive also put forth a number of steps that the government should immediately take. At the top of the list was industrialization and agrarian reform. Although the latter had been on the public agenda for decades, a heated debate erupted between the various interest groups over the maximum amount of agricultural land that any individual can own. It is safe to assume that the call for the government to prioritize land reclamation and generously subsidize public services merited widespread support. The document also reflected the prevalent view in Egyptian society concerning the full realization of the country's sovereignty: "the English will exit Egypt and Sudan and the colonialists will exit the lands of Islam."

Similarly, in tune with the public consensus, the drafters urged the government to release the political prisoners and dismantle "the political police [*al-bulis al-siyasi*]," which had encroached on all fields of life. In contrast, the MB's recommendation to outlaw interest-bearing debt and basically shut down the stock market—both of which the movement deemed to be violations of the *Shari'a*—prompted a fierce debate. The Guidance Office's missive also gave expression to its members' aspirations to play a vital role in the formulation of the new regime's value system. With this objective in mind, the document called upon the FO to integrate the movement's officials into the legislative and executive branches.

Over the next year, the movement's leaders became regulars in the halls of government and their involvement in political and government matters steadily rose.[23] In parallel, the FO was working on the composition of the new government, and it, in fact, made overtures to the MB. However, it refrained from issuing a public response to the memorandum, even though it aroused their suspicion that the MB was planning to exploit the military coup by forcing its religio-political platform on the state. The RCC ultimately decided to limit the MB's representation to two ministers—an offer that the movement rejected. These negotiations were indicative of the festering mutual suspicions on both sides of the fence.

However, at this stage, the two bodies refrained from burning bridges.[24] For example, on January 17, 1953, the regime issued an edict dispersing the country's political parties, but it stipulated that associations involved in "social, cultural, or religious activity shall not be considered a political party," thereby enabling the MB to proceed as usual. On the eve of the decree's release, the movement dispatched a communication to the Interior Ministry stating that it is not a party from either a legal or an organizational standpoint. The memorandum also noted that, pursuant to the goals laid forth in its charter, the MB worked to advance Islam and its values. It also stated that "Islam does not differentiate between matters of religion and state."[25]

A ceremony on February 12, 1953 marking the fourth anniversary of Hasan al-Banna's passing demonstrates that the regime was still on close terms with the MB. The visit on the part of top government officials, including Naguib and 'Abd al-Nasser, to the fallen imam's tomb merited extensive coverage in the press and was broadcast live on Egyptian radio. A photograph that was run in most newspapers showed President Naguib wiping a tear at the ceremony. In his graveside speech, the general recalled Banna's lofty virtues and the special way in which he tethered the national campaign in both Egypt and Palestine to the struggle against moral and political corruption. In addition, he declared that the MB founder was an exemplary figure who worked on behalf of the greater good and was guided by the belief that religion guarantees national edification and empowerment. While this outlook, Naguib stressed, has led many Egyptian youth to sacrifice themselves on the altar "of national honor, liberty, and justice," it also motivated the "criminals" and "traitors" who were responsible for the imam's murder.[26]

During this period, the MB was allowed to operate freely on campuses and to run training camps for university students. *Al-Daʿwa*, the movement's organ, ran a story about an international camp that was held in the summer of 1953 for collegiate members of the movement. Alongside the Egyptian participants were activists from Nigeria, the Sudan, Libya, Syria, Lebanon, India, Yemen, Bahrain, and Palestine. The program's director stated that its primary goal was to enable the participants to discuss all the problems with which the movement was concerned and hammer out a uniform stance with respect to each issue on the agenda. The ideological point of departure for all the camp's discussions was that Islam constitutes an all-encompassing system for both the private and the communal lives of the faithful. Likewise, all the attendees who were interviewed for this piece stressed that no differentiation should be made between the affairs of religion and state, ethics and politics, or the education of the individual and public norms.[27]

The regime also warmed up to Sayyid Qutb, who had already built a reputation as a prominent Islamist thinker. He was invited to lecture at official government events and attended a number of meetings that the RCC held on the matter of reforming the education system. According to Calvert, Qutb was excited about this attention. In the first months of the FO regime, he spent most of his time working on behalf of the revolution.[28]

The movement's proximity to the centers of government entangled its senior figures in the power struggles between the ʿAbd al-Nasser and Naguib camps. ʿAbd al-Nasser was the unrivalled leader of the cabal of, by and large, junior-ranking officers that had pulled off the military coup. With the establishment of the RCC, he consolidated his position as the head of this body. Upon seizing the helm, the junta asked General Naguib to assume the reins. Correspondingly, they appointed ʿAli Mahir—a seasoned politician who had already presided over three governments—to form the first coalition of the revolutionary era. However, due to the Mahir government's opposition to the RCC's agrarian reform, it lasted for only six weeks, and Naguib subsequently formed a new government. Upon the monarchy's official termination, Naguib was declared the first president of the Egyptian republic.[29]

Despite the general's position atop the executive branch, the RCC constituted the government's main decision-making forum. Needless to say, this system wrought innumerable conflicts over power and prestige at the upper echelons of government. While the top brass put up a façade of unity for public consumption, numerous Egyptians were well aware of the strong disagreements over the future direction of the revolution. During the first eighteen months of the military regime, the ʿAbd al-Nasser and Naguib camps engaged in a bitter feud over the division of power between the various players in the revolutionary constellation. However, the most contentious issue was the transfer of government to an elected civilian leadership.

Like the majority of political factors (including the MB), President Naguib was in favor of returning the military to the barracks. At the time, the general was immensely popular, as many considered him to be the leader of the revolution and believed that his calls for a civilian government were sincere. However, ʿAbd al-Nasser and most of his colleagues on the RCC argued that there was no escaping a multiyear transitional phase. More specifically, they claimed that the government needed time to neutralize the power bases from the monarchical era and establish a new ruling culture, lest the old elites reassert themselves. Rushing to the ballots, the ʿAbd al-Nasser camp posited, would nip the political, economic, and social reforms in the bud.

Although President Naguib did not endorse the MB's platform and could hardly be counted among its staunchest supporters, the deep-seated differences between the MB and RCC inevitably led the former into the general's arms. Similarly, the movement's backing of Naguib's views—especially his call to transfer the government to an elected civilian leadership—also stemmed from pragmatic considerations. The MB considered elections an opportunity to translate its wellspring of public support into political power, which would enable the movement to advance its vision. Against this backdrop, the ʿAbd al-Nasser camp kept a nervous eye on the intensive dialogue between the MB and President Naguib and began accusing the MB's leaders of conspiring to undermine the stability in Egypt by spreading lies and baseless rumors about the RCC. Soon after, on January 13, 1954, a government decree was issued calling for the dismantlement of the MB and the confiscation of its assets. Furthermore, the Interior Ministry, which was now headed by ʿAbd al-Nasser, ordered the arrest of hundreds of the movement's activists and leaders including the General Guide on the grounds that, despite the toppling of the regime, the MB was continuing to operate as an underground outfit.[30]

Within a few weeks, the struggles at the upper ranks of government reached unprecedented heights. On February 23, Naguib announced that he was stepping down as president. Three days later, the RCC issued a dramatic statement accepting his resignation. Moreover, the Council declared that it would assume the executive powers and appointed ʿAbd al-Nasser prime minister.[31] This dramatic turn of events triggered public protest, which merited the backing of several army units. At a rally in ʿAbdin Square, the following chants could be heard: "Muhammad Naguib or the revolution;" "Gamal [ʿAbd al-Nasser] to jail;" and "Salah [Salem] to prison."[32] Consequently, the heads of the RCC entreated Naguib to return to office. The general agreed but consented to the demand (on March 1) that ʿAbd al-Nasser remain prime minister and assume the post of RCC chairperson. Despite his reinstatement, the FO subsequently excluded Naguib from the decision-making process, rarely let him participate in administrative matters, and even limited his public appearances.

At the same time, the tension between ʿAbd al-Nasser and the MB steadily increased. The transcripts of *Mahkamat al-Shaʿb* offer unambiguous documentation of the substantive disagreements between the movement and the RCC over a host of central issues. Furthermore, they show how the MB's senior members got caught up in a clash of titans between the Naguib and ʿAbd al-Nasser factions. The prosecution and judges prodded the witnesses into offering their take on these issues. According to their accounts, the first signs of discord between the MB and the military junta arose shortly after the coup. At this stage, the thorniest issues were the Guidance Office's memorandum and the question of the movement's representation in the cabinet. According to Deputy General Guide Muhammad Khamis Humayda, in the aftermath of Faruq's disposal, "we submitted to the heads of the revolution an official memorandum containing a special chapter dealing with the government." It expressed our "hope that the new constitution will be grounded on Islamic foundations." To Judge Salem's question of what those "foundations" were, he replied that the movement was calling for the establishment of a "consultative council" (*shurā*).[33]

Toward the end of October 1952, the movement's senior members met with ʿAbd al-Nasser in his bureau for the purpose of clearing the air between them. Shaykh Muhammad Farghali, who attended the meeting on behalf of the MB, noted that he intended to put all the cards on the table, so that each side knew where the other stood According to Farghali, the MB's chief complaint was that the revolution lacked what the movement deemed to be the obligatory Islamic dimension. The witness was then asked to be more specific, but he claimed that only members of the Guidance Office were privy to the exact details of the movement's requests.[34] Another participant, Khamis Humayda, came away with the impression that the main points of contention were national and political issues, especially the RCC refusal to restore parliament. The deputy General Guide claimed that ʿAbd al-Nasser justified this measure on the premise that "it is impossible to fathom significant parliamentarian life in a country with a separate authority possessing a Secret Apparatus."[35]

These accounts soon served as raw material for *Mahkamat al-Shaʿb*'s rhetoric concerning the extreme objectives that the MB leadership was allegedly pursuing. The judges and prosecutors sketched out a dichotomous picture: on one side was the regime, which sought to institute a system of government predicated on democratic values, and on the other side was the MB, which endeavored to commandeer the revolution and institute a fanatical theocracy. According to the FO's narrative, the RCC was sincerely interested in integrating the movement into the new ruling order. However, during coalition bargaining, the MBs true positions—including its goal of setting up a theocracy in Egypt—came to light, many of which the government summarily rejected.[36]

Another central theme in *Mahkamat al-Sha'b*'s rhetoric was that the MB constituted a conspiratorial movement. At first, it planned to exploit the military coup for the purpose of establishing a regime that is committed to its extreme platform. When this failed to pan out, the organization's leaders planned a "popular coup" in which the reins of government would be transferred to General Naguib. In fact, the prosecution claimed that it had documents showing that the insurrection was supposed to begin with a string of attempts on the lives of senior government officials, which would be carried out by the Secret Apparatus. In the wake of these assassinations, President Naguib would deliver an address over the radio aimed at calming the nation. According to the prosecution, it had even demonstrated that there is a connection between the attempt on 'Abd al-Nasser's life and President Naguib's supposed involvement in the MB's plan to foment a second revolution.

1954—The Year of Resolution

In the historiography of the July Revolution, much has been said about the "crisis of March 1954." At the height of this imbroglio, the RCC was bracing itself against a broad front of civilian forces that were demanding an immediate transfer of power to an elected government. In essence, that entire year was rife with showdowns between the revolutionary government and its adversaries (especially the MB) and between the 'Abd al-Nasser and Naguib camps—all of which reached an endgame by the end of November. In light of this situation, I have chosen to dub this period "the year of resolution."

The immediate catalyst behind this crisis was President Naguib's resignation on February 23, 1954, which triggered three days of large-scale demonstrations against the RCC. The principal demands of the opposition were the immediate transfer of government to an elected civilian leadership, the army's return to the barracks, and the resumption of party and parliamentarian life.[37] Certain army units sided with the protestors, while other units supported the RCC. Nonetheless, it was only after Naguib's reinstatement that the tension between the RCC and the opposition boiled over (March 25–31). This direct confrontation quickly became a watershed mark in the annals of the July Revolution. As a result of this strife, 'Abd al-Nasser called a press conference in which he vowed to implement the following measures by the second anniversary of the revolution: lift the moratorium against party activity, establish a committee to draft a new constitution, hold parliamentary elections, and wind down the RCC.[38] Several days later, the promises were retracted on the grounds that the demonstrations flooding the boulevards threatened to unhinge the entire country. Moreover, the revolution's speakers couched the protest as an attempt by the "old" regime to wrest back control of the public sphere and return to the helm.

The understandings that were reached between ʿAbd al-Nasser and Hudaybi are indicative of the FO's dramatic about-face. At the height of the crisis, they essentially agreed to turn over a new leaf in RCC–MB relations. Within the framework of these understandings, the movement would be allowed to resume its operations and hundreds of its activists would be released from jail.[39] Under the March 27 headline of "The Muslim Brothers Renewed Their Activity Yesterday," the daily newspaper *al-Masri* surveyed a handful of meetings that the General Guide initiated on the emergent situation in Egypt. Moreover, the paper covered a handful of MB-sponsored events, including the main ceremony marking the rapprochement with the government at the organization's headquarters in Hilmiya. Until that morning, the offices were bolted shut and surrounded by police. However, the watch had been lifted, and an MB rally was held in the adjacent square. This event, particularly the speeches delivered by the movement's luminaries, merited a great deal of attention from the press.

In the ceremony's opening remarks, Deputy General Guide Humayda stressed that those jailed activists who had just been set free are now "much stronger and more determined" to persist in the struggle. He then called upon the attendees to unite behind the Brothers' leadership and explained how its commitment to social outreach accorded with the Islamic principle of the "greater good" (*al-maslaha al-ʿammah*). As a show of good faith, Humayda added, "It is incumbent upon us" to put the regime's past mistreatment behind us and set our sights on rectifying the situation. The keynote speaker was none other than the General Guide. Hudaybi remarked that since his release from prison, he has noticed a deep rift in the upper reaches of government but has no intention of publicly commenting on this sensitive issue. At the end of the rally, a journalist asked the General Guide whether there is any basis to the reports that the MB favors a certain side in the power struggle between the ʿAbd al-Nasser and Naguib camps. Hudaybi's answer was noncommittal and vague: "As is their custom, the Brothers always have their special policy of siding with justice [*al-haq*]."[40] Immediately after the ceremony, the Guidance Office convened for a lengthy discussion on recent developments and the movement's future course of action.

On the face of things, the standoff ended with a compromise. From ʿAbd al-Nasser's perspective, though, the agreement that he had worked out with the General Guide was a cold and calculated move. His primary goal was to neutralize the MB at the height of a crisis that threatened to incapacitate the RCC government. Hudaybi's public exhortation to eschew settling "past accounts" with the regime ensured that most members of his organization's large and disciplined base would remove themselves from the public square and return to their daily routine. Besides sanctioning the MB's activities, the

'Abd al-Nasser camp acquiesced with the demand that Naguib resume his presidential duties. In return, the general's supporters countenanced 'Abd al-Nasser's appointment to both the premiership and the RCC chair.

In practice, though, the imbroglio ended with a crushing defeat for President Naguib and the forces of civil society. The former was essentially pinioned at the critical stages of the March crisis. By the time the smoke had cleared, Naguib was so fatigued that he had to be hospitalized for several weeks. Conversely, his spry adversaries reasserted their control over Egypt. What was hitherto a see-saw battle ended with the 'Abd al-Nasser camp firmly in the ascendancy. The forces of civil society, which had demanded that the army return to the barracks, were utterly defeated and expelled from the public sphere. Intellectuals, including dozens of university professors, who had signed manifestos clamoring for a liberal constitution and the restoration of parliament, were dismissed from their jobs.[41] Opposition elements within the security forces were detained, and some were forced into early retirement. In contrast, RCC loyalists grabbed the command posts in both the army and police.

Before their second honeymoon was over, the MB–FO marriage was back on the rocks. Government speakers intensified their rhetoric against the movement, and the verbal understandings that were reached between the leaders of the two sides were only partially implemented at best. In a letter to the prime minister dated May 4, 1954, the General Guide noted that "you certainly remember our agreement to end the aberrant situation, and that we would once again cooperate with the objective of ensuring 'the greater good.'" The regime, Hudaybi asserted, did not stand by its commitment, as it prohibited the movement from fully resuming its activities and some of its members were still behind bars. In this missive, the General Guide also raised several demands. Besides restoring parliament, which is the "basis for every modern-day government," he urged 'Abd al-Nasser to respect the citizens' right to free speech and to release political prisoners, to include a portion of those "convicted within the framework of the special tribunals. . . . Even if the extraordinary measures have contributed to a temporary respite and stability, they are indeed allowing the situation to reach a boiling point [*ghulyan*] and are stoking the fire. . . . And they lack the wherewithal to guarantee the future of the homeland."[42]

As is to be expected, the hearings of *Mahkamat al-Sha'b* delved into the tumultuous developments that informed "the year of resolution." We may deduce from the court transcripts that as the crisis deteriorated, the MB leadership reassessed its relationship with the military government. More specifically, the witnesses provided illuminating details on the acerbic debate between the MB's "conservative" and "militant" wings on this very issue. Both of these factions described the March crisis as a turning point in the movement's relationship with the RCC.

An extraordinary account of this conflict was provided by Hindawi Duwayr who was surprisingly allowed to speak at length. In his estimation, the March

1954 crisis sharpened the disagreements not only between the movement and the regime but also within the ranks of the former. "As you know," the SA operative noted at the beginning of his testimony, "the Muslim Brothers generally supported the revolution, namely they went in the way of the revolution, until the onset of the March [crisis]." At this juncture, though, the MB "stumbled into a dispute with the revolution." Against this backdrop, Duwayr averred that three approaches to the regime emerged within the movement's top brass. On one end of the spectrum were the revolution's supporters who felt that the MB should back the FO in their brutal confrontation with nearly the entire opposition. The middle-of-the-road approach, which was spearheaded by Deputy General Guide Humayda, called upon the organization to maintain its neutrality, lest it become embroiled in a destructive conflict with the authorities. The third group averred that the RCC's policies were anathema to the MB's core beliefs. Within this camp, especially among the SA, the circle of those pressing the movement to take action against the regime steadily expanded.

At this point in Duwayr's testimony, the prosecutor asked him to go into further detail on the armed wing. In response, he opined that, from the hawks' perspective, "the revolution is turning in a non-Islamic direction and that this situation is harming the Islamic *da'wa*."[43] However, given the People Court's desire to inflict a mortal blow on the organization and its leadership, it is no coincidence that the court simply ignored the evidence pertaining to these internal debates and continued to refer to the MB as a united and monolithic movement.

The positions that the movement adopted during the March crisis resembled those of other oppositional groups. For instance, there was basically a consensus throughout the entire opposition that the government must take the following steps: uphold the liberties that were promised to the citizens at the outset of the revolution, restore party and parliamentarian life, and suspend the extraordinary measures that it was wielding against domestic rivals. However, the prosecution claimed that the movement's demands were part of a radical plan to overthrow the regime and advance its leaders' personal and sectorial interests. In contrast, Tayyib testified that "the Brothers did not have any secret demands [*talabat*]; and in an message that they [the MB leadership] sent to the prime minister, they requested that liberties" be conferred upon the entire populace.[44]

Likewise, in his testimony on an aborted demonstration the movement had organized, the General Guide asserted that the focus of this effort was on the government's undemocratic measures, such as the shutdown of parliament and the detention of activists for taking part in protests. He also stated that the RCC's use of force to prevent citizens from pursuing their right to free expression was a mistake that only served to aggravate the crisis. In Hudaybi's estimation, if the regime had permitted the citizens to demonstrate, the protest would have been conducted in a peaceful manner, and everyone would have then returned to their daily affairs. Thereafter, the prosecutor asked the witness if he was cognizant of the fact that demonstrations are illegal. The latter confirmed that he was aware of this law but noted that in practice rallies continued to be held and were attended by people from various sectors of Egyptian society.[45]

In building their case as to what they felt was the considerable gap between the MB senior figures' demands for freedom and democracy on the one hand and the autocratic, centralized, and hierarchical manner in which the movement is run on the other, the judges and prosecution availed themselves of instances from the March crisis. Put differently, the regime claimed that the Brothers' comportment during this period was another example of how the movement failed to practice what it preached. Likewise, they claimed that MB officials appointed themselves and their cronies to posts in which they enjoyed profligate salaries and benefits. During his cross-examination, the General Guide was asked to demonstrate how his movement adheres to the Islamic principle of consultation (*shurā*), which it was now demanding of the government. Hudaybi replied that he had conferred with the movement's Founding Authority on the agreement with Britain and his talks with the senior British diplomat (Trefor Evans).[46]

The prosecution attempted to refute this claim by drawing on the testimony of Deputy General Guide Humayda. The witness came under a barrage of ostensibly technical questions that were designed to cast the MB in an undemocratic light. The attorney asked Humayda to describe the movement's structure and the manner in which senior positions are filled. From his response, we may infer that the MB's principal leadership forum was the Founding Authority. Comprised of 148 members, ten of whom were replaced each year, the Founding Authority, according to Hudaybi, elected twelve members of the Guidance Office; in turn, the latter selected another three members on their own. The Guidance Office was and remains the movement's highest decision-making body. Its chief function is to advise the official who presides over this forum—the General Guide. After Hudaybi completed his survey, the presiding judge quipped, "Is there a greater dictatorship than this?" He then turned to the audience and said, "Look at the deception in the name of the religion [of Islam]."[47]

The Evacuation Agreement

For decades, the attainment of a full withdrawal of British troops from Egypt and the annulment of all restrictions on Egyptian sovereignty were among the major topics on the country's agenda. The prolonged British occupation had a significant impact on the contours of the Egyptian government, the constitution, and political order.[48] For over a generation, an assortment of parties and organizations (including the MB) toiled to end colonial dominance and intervention in Egypt. While some of these groups advocated a nonviolent civilian struggle, others took up arms and even carried out terrorist operations against the foreign occupier. Regardless of the contrasting means to achieving this end, the goal of ridding the land of the British was shared by all the political and nationalist parties in Egypt.

There were also pronounced differences over the terms of any potential withdrawal agreement with London. On July 27, 1954, the RCC and British representatives wrapped up their negotiations by initializing a heads of agreement. All that remained was to set a date for the signing of the final draft. The critical phase of these negotiations had been conducted against the backdrop of the March crisis. 'Abd al-Nasser, the lead Egyptian negotiator, did not take the trouble to update the leaders of the political parties or civil society as to the details of the work in progress.

In their public statements, the regime's senior officials frequently touted the advantages of the historic accord, but these words failed to dampen the increasingly outspoken criticism of the manner in which the talks were conducted and, more important, the terms of the deal. The day after the signing ceremony, Hudaybi granted an interview to *al-Manar*, a Damascus-based newspaper. He told the reporter that the agreement "harms the interests of Egypt and the Arab states" because it allows Britain "to return and capture the canal" if one of its regional allies (Turkey and several Arab countries) is attacked. Besides excoriating specific clauses of the treaty, the General Guide lambasted the process in which the document was ratified. His overall stance garnered wide support from his colleagues in the Guidance Office. Moreover, the MB leadership declared:

> [A]ny agreement whatsoever between the Egyptian government and any foreign government will not be finalized before it is submitted to a parliament that was chosen in free and clean elections and fairly represents the desire of the Egyptian people. Similarly, the censorship of newspapers must be terminated, so that every citizen may express his view of this accord.[49]

The RCC, which viewed this criticism as an affront to its policy, reacted with characteristic anger. In speeches given over the months of August and September, 'Abd al-Nasser castigated the naysayers, especially those who "practice deception in the name of Islam." Furthermore, the prime minister said that the Brothers, "who did not attempt to overthrow Faruq, are [now] trying to ruin the revolution that freed them from prison and was a source of national pride."[50] Upon returning from a lengthy trip to Syria on September 9, 1954, Hudaybi published a missive to his constituents that encapsulated his recent experiences: from his release from jail and his meeting with 'Abd al-Nasser and Salah Salem on through his arrival back in Egypt. In addition, the letter stated that not only had the RCC failed to honor its commitments, but it had also waged a nasty media campaign over the summer accusing the movement's leaders of launching a plot to overthrow the FO. The regime's machinations hit a nadir with "the prevention of the holiday prayer, the arrest of preachers in mosques, searches in the Brothers' homes, and the arrest of some of them."[51] Fearing imprisonment, if not worse, the General Guide and many of his colleagues went into hiding. However, it was only a matter of time before the FO and the MB would lock horns.

For its part, the ruling elite viewed the agreement with Britain to be a historic achievement for Egypt and a critical step toward consolidating its own position at the head of the revolutionary government. On October 19, 1954, a short yet festive signing ceremony was held in the Egyptian Senate's Hall of Pharaohs. The Egyptian and British delegations were led by ʿAbd al-Nasser and Anthony Nutting (the minister of state for foreign affairs), respectively, both of whom duly signed the historic document on behalf of their countries.[52] Appendixes were added to the treaty's thirteen sections.

As per the preamble, the treaty was intended "to establish Anglo-Egyptian relations on a new basis of mutual understanding and firm friendship." The first section stipulated that the United Kingdom would completely withdraw its troops from Egypt within twenty months. Sections 3 and 4, which drew the most fire from the regime's domestic critics, stated that a number of bases along the Suez Canal "shall be kept in efficient working order capable of immediate use." Moreover, as noted earlier, these bases would be placed at Britain's disposal "on a war footing" in the event of an attack against one of its Arab allies or Turkey. According to the fifth section, British forces shall withdraw as soon as hostilities come to a close. Barring any agreement to extend the treaty, it will expire after seven years.

Although disputes over the terms of the withdrawal were evident throughout the entire negotiation process, the transcripts of the ʿAbd al-Latif trial indicate that the signing of the Anglo-Egyptian Treaty was the straw that broke the camel's back in all that concerned MB-RCC relations. Against the backdrop of the enormous tension that was building up in the public arena following the March crisis, a torrent of rumors about the terms that were being discussed by the negotiators inundated the country. Within the ranks of the MB, the prevailing view was that the emergent treaty severely compromised the Egyptian national interest, as it allowed Britain to reoccupy its positions in the event of an emergency.

That said, the movement failed to reach a consensus on its response to the signing. Instead, the MB splintered off into competing factions, as different activists pushed their own initiatives. As in other instances, senior and low-level members acted in an independent fashion without consulting or receiving the approval of the Guidance Office or the General Guide. It bears noting that this internal dissension further weakens the regime's case that the MB was a hierarchical organization. In any event, the majority of the organization's leaders, including Hudaybi, concentrated on publicly voicing their criticism and transmitting their outlook on the accord to the regime's helmsmen. A few of the SA's leaders focused on the public sphere. Besides organizing demonstrations, they circulated manifestos bearing titles such as "The Agreement Won't Pass" or "The Conspiracy." Not surprisingly, these missives described the Anglo-Egyptian Treaty as "a detrimental contract."[53] Some of the former heads of the SA began to consider ideas on how to prevent the agreement from being carried out. Among the options that were considered was the plot to kill the living embodiment of the treaty—'Abd al-Nasser. The members of the Guidance Office, including the General Guide, were not privy to this plan and only learned of "the Manshiya incident" after the fact.

Over the course of his testimony, 'Abd al-Latif claimed that the cell members had poured over the text of the accord in addition to related newspaper articles. Responding to Judge's Salem's question of "What else bothered you about this agreement," the would-be assassin said, "There was no need for a treaty because the [British] presence in Egypt would have become illegal after 1956, and they would have left on their own."[54] Moreover, he claimed that London had only contemplated a full evacuation thanks to the armed Jihad that was waged against them in the Suez Canal Zone. 'Abd al-Latif's response attests that he was, in fact, well-versed in the relevant details. It is also worth noting that this level of knowledge contradicts the image that the judges and prosecution sought to paint of him: an illiterate and ignorant simpleton who fell victim to devious recruiters and carried out the assassination attempt without truly understanding the consequences of his actions. Tayyib, one of the chiefs of the SA, was also asked to list the faults of the Anglo-Egyptian agreement. He answered that its weaknesses were outlined in a letter that the General Guide had sent to 'Abd al-Nasser. In his estimation, the MB's chief reservation was that the treaty allowed Britain to violate Egyptian sovereignty in the event of an attack on one of its regional allies.[55]

The missive that Tayyib referred to warrants a closer look. At Hudaybi's behest, the Guidance Office held a prolonged discussion on the Anglo-Egyptian Treaty. The attendees knew that the RCC was aware of the disagreements over the accord within the movement's top brass. For this reason, a decision was made at the end of this meeting to forward the RCC a letter explaining the movement's lone official position. Later on, parts of this text were integrated into communiqués that MB activists circulated and its speakers' public statements. Despite the frequent references to this letter in the court deliberations, the text was not attached to the minutes. Two decades later, the full version was published in the movement's organ.[56]

Another dispute between the MB and the regime centered on the movement's contacts with British representatives. The RCC argued that these talks were carried out behind the government's back, undermined the delicate negotiations with London, and were part of the MB's grand design to seize power. Over the course of the trial, the judges and prosecutors played up Hudaybi's meeting with Trefor Evans, the oriental counselor of the British Embassy in Egypt.[57] From the Deputy General Guide's testimony, their meeting was held in his boss's residence on February 9, 1953. According to Humayda, Muhammad Salem informed Salah Abu Rafiq that the British advisor wished to talk with the MB leader, and a meeting was subsequently arranged. In preparation, the General Guide had these two senior MB activists put together a report.[58]

Several days after the conversation, high-level government and MB officials met at RCC headquarters to scrutinize the Hudaybi–Evans meeting. The regime was represented by ʿAbd al-Nasser, Kamal al-Din Husayn, Salah Salem, and Anwar al-Sadat, while the General Guide and other senior members of the Guidance Office, including Khamis Humayda, attended on behalf of the MB. After Hudaybi debriefed the participants as to the content of the meeting, the conversation turned to the positions of Britain and Egypt, the prospects for reaching an agreement, and how different versions of the treaty would affect the country.

The next section of the trial's transcripts exposes some of the irregularities that characterized the tribunal's functioning. Humayda was explaining the complaints with regards to the Anglo–Egyptian Treaty that senior MB members brought to the RCC's attention when an irate Judge Salem demonstratively cut him off. At this point, the latter turned to a couple of spectators and asked for their impressions of the deputy General Guide's testimony: "The brother sitting behind the man wearing glasses, do you accept these words of Khamis as an explanation for this topic?" He answered, "I neither accept nor understand them." Apparently satisfied with this response, Salem addressed another person in the crowd: "My lady, do you accept these words?" After she also expressed her doubts, the judge reached a sort of interim conclusion. The meetings between the regime and the movement's leaders were not of any particular importance, he averred, for the government regularly holds such talks with figures from across the social spectrum, "so that they may explain to us their point of view." For example, the judge continued, the RCC has met with "some of the representatives of the old parties, business people, professional associations, teachers, university professors, and journalists."[59]

According to Salem, the message that ʿAbd al-Nasser delivered to the MB leadership was short and to the point: the sort of meetings that they held with the British diplomat compromise the Egyptian national interest. More specifically, they weaken the position of the state's official negotiators, as British representatives take advantage of the estimates that come in from back channels. Salem added that the MB's opposition to this historic treaty, which the government had labored to close as well as its unlawful, surreptitious contacts with British officials attest to its helmsmen's desire to close a secret deal with London. This unfounded claim elicited an unusual reaction from Humayda who interrupted the judge's words with the following remark: "On this matter, I object." When he realized that Salem was letting him speak his mind, the witness added: "When the treaty was initialed, we said that as a popular authority we will present our view on the agreement to the leadership. I swear to you on my honor that our intention was to strengthen the Egyptian negotiator; therefore, we quickly dispatched copies of the popular declaration," which was formulated by the members of the Founding Authority and the Guidance Office, "to the president."[60]

Instead of confronting the deputy General Guide's arguments head on, Judge Salem once again turned to a member of the audience: "Sir, are you satisfied with these words?" This question set off a bizarre episode: "The citizen—looked confused and embarrassed [*muḍtarib wa-mutarjih*]," according to the transcripts. "What is your name?" the presiding judge asked. "Mustafa al-Wazan," came the reply. Assuming a censorious tone, Salem scolded him for failing to come up with a decisive answer: "Have we come here to have fun?"

The judge then resumed his assault on Humayda. Not only does the MB's secret dialogue allow the British to recapture the country in the event that the United Nations defines an emergency situation as a state of war, but "you agreed to" leave an unlimited number of English experts on Egyptian soil.[61] Over the next few minutes, the presiding judge sought to force Humayda into admitting that the terms the government secured were far superior to those that the MB would have attained. However, the deputy General Guide refused to budge, as he reiterated his claim that the movement's positions and actions were designed to improve the leverage of the state's negotiators.

When it became obvious that the witness was sticking to his guns, Salem reverted to his earlier antics, soliciting the opinions of five spectators on the plausibility of the witness' descriptions. The answers that he fielded labeled the MB's actions as treason, hypocrisy, harmful to the state, a criminal act, and chicanery. Salem's histrionics, which he displayed intermittently throughout the course of the proceedings, is reminiscent of the public admissions that were wrenched out of defendants in well-known show trials.

In sum, the testimony of three particular MB activists can be said to reflect the outlooks of the movement's mainstream with respect to the Anglo–Egyptian Treaty: ʿAbd al-Latif represents the rank-and-file activist, Tayyib represents the militant wing, and Humayda represents the viewpoint of the organization's senior leadership. All told, their accounts betray a narrative that was held by the majority of the MB members, namely, that certain elements of the accord seriously damaged Egypt's national interests. This picture stands in sharp contradistinction to the official position whereby the accord fulfilled a national goal that a generation of Egyptians had longed for.[62]

Whereas the RCC claimed that the nation unanimously backed the treaty, the defendants and witnesses who appeared before *Mahkamat al-Shaʿb* revealed the document's Achilles's heel. In addition, they described the multiple ways in which they voiced their displeasure at the agreement's ratification, including demonstrations, public manifestos, and private letters to the regime's top brass. According to the evidence recorded in the court transcripts, the MB's opposition to the Anglo–Egyptian Treaty was couched in national, rather than religious, terms. For instance, they did not present the accord as anti-Islamic. Hence, there is little reason to suggest that the organization mounted a religious discourse of resistance. In fact, the criticism that it leveled against the accord was identical in substance to that of other political and nationalist forces. What is more, the similarities between the views of the MB, the liberals, and the communists were greater than their differences.

The Closure

Saturday, November 20, 1954 was devoted to the closing arguments of both the prosecution and the defense.[63] "Honorable judges, judges of the people," Mustafa al-Helbawi, the head of the Public Prosecutor's Bureau for State Security (*niyabat 'amn al-dawla*), opened, for the past few days the court has heard about "the corruption of political life" and the manipulation of innocent citizens in the name of religion on the part of the MB. Over the next hour and a half, the attorney unfurled the prosecution's case. However, throughout his presentation, he barely referred to the primary defendant, Mahmud ʿAbd al-Latif, as the lion's share of his closing arguments was devoted to the alleged crimes of the entire movement. From Helbawi's perspective, the movement not only harmed the legitimate government but also the Islamic faith. In addition, he portrayed the MB as a conspiratorial organization. Under the guise of religious enterprise, the MB top brass had constructed a secret apparatus, which planned and carried out murderous and destructive acts. The objective behind these machinations was to "bring the [General] Guide and his henchmen to the seat of government. Despite the movement's turn to bullets and terror" in the name of Islam, Helbawi reassured the crowd, the Muslim faith remains unblemished.

Thereafter, he claimed that Sayyid Qutb, a senior MB ideologue, provided his interrogators with details of the movement's plot to launch a coup once the General Guide had returned from Syria. Upon toppling the regime, the lawyer continued, the reins of government would be transferred to General Naguib. He then accused the movement's senior figures of disseminating slogans that were designed to lure naïve citizens, some of whom were indigent people desperate for aid, into their web.

According to Helbawi, the MB ignored the authorities' demand to wind down the SA and turn in their arms. "The government will not allow a group or party to constitute a state within a state," the prosecutor asserted, or "for a militia to operate alongside the state's official army." He then labeled the meetings between MB officials and Evans, the British advisor, "a secret negotiation that was conducted behind the [government's] back." During these talks, Helbawi said, the movement agreed to terms that were inferior to those that were ultimately obtained by the RCC. At this point, the attorney leveled his most serious accusation at the MB: their actions were liable to drive Egypt into a civil war (*fitna*). In this context, he evoked the following Quranic verse "*al-fitna* is worse than killing" (*al-Baqara*, 191).

Judge Salem then announced a short recess, and the hearing resumed an hour later. The deputy prosecutor, ʿAbd al-Rahman Salih, picked up where his superior had left off. Toward the end of the state's arguments, he asserted that, "in the name of the people" and in light of all the evidence, "this corrupt band of traitors," which under the façade of disseminating the faith (*daʿwa*) threatened to crush the ruling order and plunge society into civil war, deserves the maximum sentences available under law.

The court then adjourned for another break and reconvened at 4:00 pm to hear the defense's closing arguments.[64] To begin, Attorney Hamada al-Nahil spoke about his decision to serve as ʿAbd al-Latif's counsel. He was not only motivated by the opportunity to defend the accused but also sought to protect the thousands of citizens who were led astray by the "repugnant leadership" of the MB. These people were deceived by a group that warrants the appellation "the terrorist Brothers association or more precisely the terrorist Brothers gang [*ʿisbat al-ikhwan al-irhabiyun*]."[65] Echoing the prosecution's claims, Nahil said that the movement's actions were liable to sow anarchy throughout the country and divide the nation rather than unite it. In essence, his line of defense was predicated on the argument that the MB leadership habitually exploited innocent citizens. Their recruitment and deployment of the accused was his case in point. Taking advantage of his hardships, ʿAbd al-Latif's operators goaded him into carrying out a heinous crime that would advance their devious plans to seize power by means of an armed insurrection. According to Nahil, his client was unaware of the broader context of his enlistment or the attempt on ʿAbd al-Nasser's life.

In accusing the MB of misusing the Islamic faith, the defense counselor availed himself of even harsher language than the prosecution. For instance, he claimed that ʿAbd al-Latif's handlers conspired to assassinate not only the leader of the revolution (ʿAbd al-Nasser) but Islam and "the homeland" too. At the end of his closing arguments, Nahil petitioned the court to refrain from issuing a verdict against his client until a more comprehensive investigation was conducted of the SA and its operations. However, this motion was summarily denied, and the hearing was adjourned.

Conclusion

The transcripts of *Mahkamat al-Shaʿb* provide a compelling record of the dramatic swing in the relations between the FO and the MB. Although completely ignored by the state's representatives, the ʿAbd al-Latif trial included detailed testimony of the intimate dialogue between the leaders of the junta and the MB prior to and in the aftermath of the coup. As opposed to the prosecution and the judges' simplistic description of the MB as a hierarchical organization whose members blindly obey the top brass, the witnesses revealed that the movement was in the midst of a serious leadership crisis after the killing of Hasan al-Banna, which persisted even after Hasan al-Hudaybi's election as General Guide. For instance, there were internal disagreements over whether and to what extent the MB should cooperate with the junta. The accounts of this internal dialogue weakened the RCC's claim that the movement's leaders were firmly in control of their organization and that the General Guide was thus fully responsible for the attempt on 'Abd al-Nasser's life.

The tribunal's transcripts also constitute a rich source for reconstructing Egypt's tenuous state of affairs in 1954, including the FO's rift with the MB. In the court's estimation, this fallout was a direct result of the movement's fanatical views, which also threatened to plunge Egyptian society into civil war (*fitna*). On the other hand, the accused and most of the witnesses made it abundantly clear that their aversion to the RCC's positions largely stemmed from their political and national convictions, which cannot be separated from their religious beliefs. Both the movement's helmsmen and rank-and-file members had come to the conclusion that, in practice, the RCC's policy was negating the resumption of parliamentary life. Similar to other opposition groups—the MB demanded that general elections be held at once, followed by a transfer of power to the elected civilian government, the granting of freedom of expression to all citizens, and the release of political prisoners. In response to these exhortations, the junta heightened its rhetoric against the MB.

Whereas the opposition excoriated its terms, the RCC considered the evacuation treaty with Britain its most significant policy achievement to date. As recorded in the transcripts of the 'Abd al-Latif trial, the MB top brass conveyed its main problems with the accord to the FO and publically disseminated these views in leaflet form. Consequently, government spokesmen launched a media blitz aimed at demonizing the movement. In parallel, a small group of SA activists hatched a closely guarded plan to assassinate the prime minister. 'Abd al-Latif and his accomplices testified that the decision to eliminate 'Abd al-Nasser was made after they had studied the details of the withdrawal agreement and had come to the conclusion that it harms Arab and Egyptian interests. At the court's behest, the conspirators listed the clauses in the pact that they took issue with, whereupon the judges contemptuously dismissed their apprehensions.

Without thoroughly investigating the cell's objectives, the panel determined that the assassination was intended to violently overthrow a legitimate government. Moreover, it found that the MB leadership shared the same degree of responsibility for this crime as the perpetrators themselves. The prosecution's closing arguments betray the sizable gap between the evidence that emerged from the testimony and the accusations that were leveled at the MB. Among the serious charges brought against the organization's leaders were the following: corruption of political life in Egypt, distorting religion for the sake of increasing the movement's ranks and recruiting some of these "conscripts" for terrorist activities, and plotting to seize power and establish a theocracy in Egypt by dint of sabotage, murder, and the like.

The proceedings against the gunman's handlers and MB luminaries, foremost among them General Guide Hasan al-Hudaybi, got underway immediately after the prosecution's closing arguments in the ʿAbd al-Latif trial as the court did not even wait for the sentencing of the guilty parties. Given the general public's fascination with the Hudaybi trial, it was the highpoint of the court's activity. During the trial's sessions, issues were raised that did not come up in any of the other hearings before *Mahkamat al-Shaʿb*. For this reason, the trial against the General Guide constitutes the focal point of the next chapter.

8

The Trial of the *Murshid*

At precisely 10:30 am on Monday, November 22, 1954, the shrill call of "*Mahkama*" (Court!) pierced through the courtroom, signaling the entrance of the three judges and the start of what would be another riveting event—the trial of General Guide Hasan Hudaybi. Several days before completing his second year at the movement's helm and nearly a month since his arrest and detention in a military prison, Hudaybi, a retired judge, found himself on the other side of the aisle in a courtroom packed with journalists.[1] The hearing opened with the reading of the bill of indictment:

> The perpetration of actions against the present regime and against the well-being of the homeland from within and abroad in the period leading up to October 26, 1954 in the cities of Cairo and Alexandria. 1. The accused devised along with others a criminal plot that was intended to sow a bloody civil war [*fitna*] and execute a violent coup against the government, and this by means of a meticulous plan to carry out a large number of murders, serious acts of sabotage, and large-scale destruction throughout the country, and this in preparation for the seizing of the government by force on the part of the association that he headed. 2. He organized an armed secret apparatus [*jihaz sirri*] that was subordinate to him and ordered [the execution] of deeds that contravene the state's laws. In addition, he assigned the apparatus to carry out the coup that he planned.[2]

There were fundamental differences between these charges and the ones brought against 'Abd al-Latif. The General Guide was essentially accused of masterminding a plot to launch an armed insurrection, which was liable to plunge Egypt into a civil war. After pleading not guilty to the presiding judge's query, the defense counselor, Sami Mazen, sought to postpone the trial on the grounds that he was not given sufficient time to prepare the case or even study the material from the investigation. At the end of a brief consultation between the judges, his motion was denied. In the process, Judge Salem cynically advised him to go over the file while the court listened to the witnesses' testimony. Over the next two days, a long row of senior MB figures appeared before the court, including the Deputy General Guide, members of the Guidance Office, heads of the SA, and Sayyid Qutb (the editor-in-chief of the movement's publications). Most of the questions and answers during the hearings were akin to those in the previous trial. In addition, the majority of these same witnesses soon found themselves in the defendants' bench, where the accounts that they had given in the ʿAbd al-Latif and Hudaybi trials were directed against them.[3]

On the third day of the proceedings, the closing arguments were already delivered by both the prosecution and the defense. While the state's case was a veritable replay of its performance during the ʿAbd al-Latif trial, the defense's closing arguments provided some real drama. The nub of the prosecution's closing arguments was an attempt to depict the MB as an organization that misappropriated religion and acted in complete contradistinction of the spirit and principles of Islam.[4] To this end, ʿAli Nur al-Din, the deputy attorney general, peppered his peroration with a bevy of citations from the Quran, with the intention of underscoring the MB's putative deviation from the right path and demonstrating that the movement's actions were liable to have disastrous consequences for honest and innocent believers. At the very start of his closing arguments, he even averred "that it was the will of Allah," who looks out for the well-being of Egypt, for the attempt on ʿAbd al-Nasser's life to fail.

According to the prosecutor, the Brothers' goal was to seize power in an armed insurrection. Contrived to wreak havoc throughout the land, the coup would entail acts of terror, such as the liquidation of senior government officials. In his estimation, though, the movement's top echelons lacked the requisite skills for running a government, as evidenced by the undemocratic fashion in which the organization was run. Although MB leaders clamored for the revolutionary government to conduct the affairs of state in accordance with the principles of consultation (*shurā*), the attorney claimed that the General Guide and his henchmen did whatever they pleased within their own movement.

If this were not enough, they resorted to chicanery and even conspired to sabotage the government's efforts to defend the state's interests. For example, "they stockpiled weapons and received assistance from the army" but did not use it "in the campaign [against Britain] in the Canal." Instead, they planned to use these assets and know-how to oust the regime. "The Secret Apparatus," the prosecutor argued, was a full-fledged militia whose operatives sought, with the knowledge of the movement's top brass, "to destroy the homeland. . . . Honorable judges, we are not laying false blame on or discriminating against [the MB] at the hour in which we accuse this group of veering off the path of virtue—a deviation that is intended to lead the homeland to loss and destruction." Instead, we have proven that the movement amassed weapons and trained its men, "to carry out their planned coup . . . part of which was the attempt on the prime minister's life."

At this point, the focus shifted to the direct responsibility of the accused. The prosecutor contended that in his capacity as General Guide, Hudaybi was accountable for the movement's conduct, including the operations of "the secret and armed apparatus—the terrorist apparatus." Hudaybi, Nur al-Din continued, did not heed the government's request to dismantle the SA and turn in its arms, even though he had the power to do so. The machinations of the MB and its armed wing are liable to foment "a civil war [*harb ahliya*] against the government and against the Muslim sons of the homeland. . . . In the name of the nation, which pines for the revival of the homeland, and in the name of the millions who wish to live in fraternity and quietude, we ask the people's judges to sentence the accused to death"—an entreaty that was predicated on the following legal rationale:

> The Egyptian penal code and all the penal laws in the world expressly state that the death sentence will be imposed on anyone convicted of membership in an armed gang [*'isbah musallaha*] that contrived to overthrow the existing government, or planned to launch a coup against the government. Section 87 of the Egyptian Penal Code [stipulates] that the death penalty will be imposed on anyone that organized an armed gang for [the purpose of] executing this crime, and this will be the verdict against anyone who ran [this sort of outfit] or took part in its leadership.[5]

In summation, the prosecutor cited verse 33 from the Table Sura of the Quran that calls for the most severe punishment for those guilty of harming Islam or corrupting the land:

> Indeed, the penalty for those who wage war against Allah and His Messenger and strive upon earth [to cause] corruption is none but that they be killed or crucified or that their hands and feet be cut off from opposite sides or that they be exiled from the land. That is for them a disgrace in this world; and for them in the Hereafter is a great punishment.[6]

On this note, the prosecution rested its case, and Judge Salem announced a fifteen-minute break.

The impressive performance of attorney Sami Mazen during the previous stages of the expedited trial raised expectations for the defense counselor's closing arguments, and the gifted trial lawyer did not disappoint. According to the court transcripts, Mazen's closing arguments were put off until the end of a long day of hearings.[7] By the time the counselor took the floor, it was nearly nine o'clock in the evening. However, this did not stop him from continuing to expose the weak points in the prosecution's case or from indirectly criticizing the rhetoric of the special tribunal. To begin, Mazen showcased his primary arguments. He asserted that Hudaybi is completely innocent, for he had tried to curb the SA from the moment he assumed the post. More specifically, Mazen noted that the General Guide dismissed the SA's commander and appointed a close associate (Yusuf Tal'at) in his place. Furthermore, he ordered all the movement's personnel to cease and desist from all the illegal activities in which they were previously involved and expressed his opposition to violence as a means for advancing the organization's goals.

At this juncture, the lawyer unveiled a point that would recur throughout his closing arguments; namely, the crimes that were committed by members of the MB must be adjudicated as individual, rather than collective, acts. Egyptian criminal law, he explained, requires that all indictments and punishments be directed against individuals. Consequently, it is unlawful to punish the General Guide for the crimes of others. While Hudaybi oversaw the movement, he obviously could not have known what every last subordinate was up to. In addition, the prosecution has not shown that, in Mazen's legal opinion, the defendant had approved of unlawful acts. The counselor then turned his attention to the General Guide's decision not to wind down the SA. As leader of the MB, he claimed, Hudaybi felt that the wing must continue to exist so long as the British occupied the Suez Canal zone, for Egypt needed a framework for training volunteers seeking to rid the country of the foreign presence.

At this point, Mazen chided the government attorneys for exhibiting a lack of professionalism throughout the trial: "I attentively followed the prosecutor's words, and I would like to know what are the laws . . . that the defendant has violated. I naively expected the prosecutor to declare that the accused 'had broken law number so and so.'" In the absence of a specific charge, Mazen vociferously contended, a person cannot be accused of violating the law, even before a special tribunal.

> This is a new legal procedure [*taklif*]. It is true that [this is] a special tribunal, and it is true that the situation is exceptional, but come what may, it is unconscionable that in this situation we will deviate from the required prerequisites on this matter: the court, the prosecution, the defendant, the defense, and the bill of indictment. These are principles without which a trial is inconceivable, regardless of whether it is extraordinary or not.[8]

If, for example, the government contends that the accused was in possession of an unlicensed weapon, then this should have been explicitly stated. In this sort of case, Mazen argued, the law refers to individuals suspected of bearing a weapon, and only the person who actually possesses such contraband can be held responsible. In addition, the allegation that his client "established a secret and armed organization from scratch" does not hold water because the SA was in existence long before he became General Guide. He also noted that the RCC's edict dispersing all the parties except the MB strengthens his argument that the movement had no intention of seizing power. Given the absence of "any proof for this far-reaching claim," how can the defendant be tied to "a criminal conspiracy" to "precipitate a violent civil war [*fitna damiya*]" aimed at overthrowing the government?[9]

Once again, Mazen urged the judges to abide by the principle of personal criminal responsibility, especially considering the immense size of the MB. He also mildly rebuked the court for preventing the defense from questioning Ibrahim al-Tayyib. "Even if the procedures [in *Mahkamat al-Sha'b*] are exceptional, it was my right to hear the words of this witness," for we could have learned that the General Guide was not directly involved in the assassination or the supposed coup attempt.[10] Adopting a scornful tone, he lashed out at the prosecution for inferring from circumstantial evidence—including his client's meetings with MB activists—that he had conspired to overthrow the government and was abreast of the plot to kill 'Abd al-Nasser. This serious accusation, in Mazen's view, was based "on neither proof nor the coattails of proof."[11]

The prosecution, he recalled, had expanded on Hudaybi's alleged role in the planning of an armed demonstration, but the organizers of that same event testified that the accused was against such a show of force and the event was never actually held. If so, the attorney cynically pondered, what law was the General Guide accused of breaking? Earlier in the proceedings, Judge Salem remarked that, if the demonstration had come to pass, there may very well have been grave repercussions. Mazen now responded that the court was best advised to stay clear of conjecture, for the judges' sole mandate was to examine the evidence that was submitted before them, and the fact remained that the demonstration was not held.

At this point, Mazen arrived at one of his principal arguments: The fact that Hudaybi is the General Guide does not mean that he can be blamed for every single action or statement of the MB. It is incumbent upon the court to draw a distinction between general and personal responsibility. In this particular context, the lawyer asserted, collective responsibility has its limitations. Furthermore, a case for direct liability can only be made if the prosecution can show that the defendant collaborated with the perpetrators. The attorney Mazen made this point while discussing Hudaybi's support for the July Revolution. "Does he [the General Guide] indeed oppose the revolution?" the advocate wondered. "Was he not a partner" in this enterprise? "You know better than I [do] that, from the first day [of the coup, the accused] made statements in which he expressed his full support for the revolution, namely that every person is obligated to support this revolution."[12] Conversely, the prosecution had failed, in his estimation, to provide any evidence that warrants their suspicions as to his client's opposition to the end of the monarchy.

In summation, attorney Mazen asked, "With what are we left?" There was an assassination attempt, he noted, and it is the government's obligation to conduct a thorough investigation to determine who stood behind this crime. "It is the duty of the revolution and not only its privilege to" safeguard the country. However, the judges must bear in mind that Hudaybi condemned the assassination attempt, and none of his actions as General Guide imply that he wished to embroil the country in a civil war (*fitna*). This very recrimination, he added, has caused the defendant a great deal of harm. Mazen then concluded that, in light of the points raised in his closing arguments, he expects *Mahkamat al-Sha'b* to serve justice and acquit Hudaybi. Not only is the General Guide a patriotic citizen and a devout Muslim, but he firmly upholds the principle of "commanding right and forbidding wrong" (*amr bi-l-ma'aruf wa-nahy 'an al-munkar*).[13]

Immediately following the defense's closing arguments, the prosecutor asked to take the floor. The judges sustained the motion but not before giving Hudaybi an opportunity to clear up some loose ends of his own. To begin, the defendant stressed that he had no idea the SA possessed weapons. However, his chief priority was to direct the court's attention to his poor health. With this in mind, he presented a medical record indicating that he had suffered a stroke, which left him partially paralyzed and impaired his memory and speech. Lastly, he swore that he was completely unaware of the plot against the prime minister and would never have consented to such a plan.[14]

After Hudaybi's comments, Judge Salem called a short recess, whereupon the prosecution began its rebuttal. It stands to reason that senior officials in the Attorney General Office realized the strong impression that Mazen's closing arguments had made on the journalists and radio audience. Despite the late hour, the deputy attorney general spoke for approximately sixty minutes.[15] His main point was that the prosecution had proven beyond the shadow of a doubt that the General Guide was guilty of all the counts brought against him. Thereafter, the litigator expanded on the claim that the MB had exploited the Islamic faith for the purpose of, inter alia, manipulating broad segments of the Egyptian populace. The movement's objective, he declared, was not to advance the greater good but to seize power.

At this juncture, he confirmed Mazen's observation that the legal code calls for personal responsibility. However, he reminded the judges that the law also stipulates that an individual abetting a crime is guilty as well. In addition, he noted that, according to section 48 of the Penal Code, a conspiracy to violate the law is an action involving two or more persons. The deputy attorney general then derisively claimed that there is no basis to the defense's argument that the prosecution had failed to note the specific offenses Hudaybi was accused of committing. "Does the advocate mean so say," he added, "that the law . . . permits an individual to set up a private army [*jaysh khas*]within the state?" In addition, the Penal Code forbids "the establishment of an armed gang" and instructs judges to punish severely those found guilty of planning a coup or of illegal arms possession.[16]

The prosecutor then took issue with Mazen's argument concerning the 1952 Party Law. He admitted that the law called for the dispersal of political parties, while leaving associations (the heading under which the MB fell) to continue their operations. Nonetheless, the statue was applicable to the MB the moment it decided to launch an armed insurrection. According to the deputy attorney general, some of the witnesses and a number of the organization's manifestos alluded to this plot. For example, one communiqué, which even "bore the signature of the General Guide," urged activists to prepare for war against the "heretical' regime."[17] Toward the end of the rebuttal, he scoffed at Hudaybi's alleged health impediments. Finally, he reiterated the state's case that the General Guide was involved in a conspiracy to murder the prime minister. Before adjourning the court, Judge Salem announced that the verdict and sentencing in the Hudaybi trial would be announced within a few days. In the meantime, *Mahkamat al-Sha'b* would deliberate over several other bills of indictment that were on its docket.

At 11:00 am, on December 4, 1954, the verdicts were announced in the trials of 'Abd al-Latif and six senior MB activists, including the General Guide. The judges convicted the defendants of all counts and sentenced them to death by hanging. Pursuant to the decree establishing *Mahkamat al-Sha'b*, the RCC had the authority to overrule these sentences. While most of the punishments were approved, Hudaybi's sentence was immediately commuted to life in prison with hard labor. The rest of the convicts were executed just two days later. In photographs taken minutes before the first hanging, the six condemned men are barefoot and attired in the red uniforms of death row. A black flag was raised atop the jail house in Cairo. At precisely six in the morning, the noose was lowered around the neck of 'Abd al-Latif. Over the next three hours, all the men were put to death.[18]

The Hudaybi trial's importance stems from the fundamental issues that were raised during its hearings and, all the more so, from the insatiable public interest in the proceedings against the head of the MB. Despite their egregiously hostile attitude toward Hudaybi, the judges made an exception and allowed the defendant and his counselor, Sami Mazen, to present their case at length and even to criticize publicly the work of *Mahkamat al-Sha'b*. The fascinating exchange over whether the General Guide was personally responsible for every action carried out by the organization's members is an example. Despite the evidence to the contrary, the judges accepted the prosecution's argument that Hudaybi was liable for the crimes perpetrated by the SA, on the grounds that he had ignored the FO's demand to terminate the armed wing.

Moreover, the judges upheld the claim that the attempt on the prime minister's life was the opening shot of a campaign to overthrow violently the legitimate government. Not surprisingly, the defense centered on the prosecution's unfounded statements, thereby prompting a discursive exchange in which each side directly responded to the other's contentions. The attorney

Mazen revealed a spate of legal flaws both in the indictment and the prosecution's arguments. In this respect, the People's Court was a platform for views that the regime otherwise sought to exclude from the public discourse. However, this criticism of the tribunal's functioning was summarily rejected by the judges.

By this stage, it was evident that the government was in firm control of the local media. Consequently, Hudaybi and Mazen's objections found only marginal and fragmented expression in the intensive coverage of this trial, while the narrative of the judges and prosecution was embraced by the local press. From the perspective of the latter, the eight shots that ʿAbd al-Latif had fired at the prime minister symbolized the MB leadership's radical interpretation of the Quran, particularly the concept of jihad. Egyptian op-ed writers repeatedly claimed that the dangers the MB posed to the regime and greater society left the RCC with little choice but to prosecute its activists before a special court and mete out harsh punishments. The affinity between the underlying messages of the tribunal and the public discourse corroborates that the rhetoric generated by the special courts was among the main objective behind their establishment.

Constructing Categories

In a long row of academic and semi-academic works, the MB is deemed to be a self-understood movement, namely, one that does not necessitate in-depth analysis. This essentialist approach imputes characteristics to the organization that are supposedly inherent of all groups that fall under the rubric of political Islam. Similarly, the leaders of these bodies are deemed to be adherents of a religio-ideological platform, and their activities tend to be examined in this narrow context. As a result, such studies often understate the influence of political forces and related developments on the MB's positions and actions. In addition, this school of thought turns a blind eye to internal power struggles over the movement's goals and the means for achieving them.

On the basis of comprehensive examination of the People's Court, it appears as though the enduring labels of "political Islam" and "religious extremism" that have long been associated with the MB stem mostly from the political struggle that was waged against the movement by the RCC. Although Egypt's monarchical regime and liberal parties also considered the organization a threat and the former took harsh measures against it, the pressure that the FOs brought to bear on the movement in 1954 was unprecedented in scope, and the far-reaching repercussions thereof are manifest to this day. *Mahkamat al-Shaʿb* played a critical role in lodging these categories into the public consciousness.[19] The trials that were conducted in the revolutionary setting of the early 1950s and the attendant public discourse constituted the framework in which the labels of political Islam and religious extremism were fashioned. It was against this backdrop that the objectives of the regime and the MB as well as their mutual understanding of one another took form. In the ensuing decades, the political discourse in Egypt and throughout the Middle East has indeed revolved around these same categories.

The rhetoric that was generated by the People's Court served two highly significant and inextricably linked purposes: these categories were the lens through which the MB and the regime viewed each other, and the rhetoric perpetuated the emergency atmosphere at a critical stage in the forging of the republican regime. The special tribunal's pseudo-juridical framework and the public discourse on its trials brought the RCC's attempts to sully the MB's reputation to new heights, as the court painted the movement as a reactionary force that jeopardized the well-being of the entire country. The MB was repeatedly depicted as a terrorist organization that, under the guise of a tolerant religious enterprise, sought to overthrow a legitimate regime and transform Egypt into a benighted theocracy.

The movement's top brass was also accused of espousing a radical interpretation of scriptural texts. In addition, the FOs claimed that MB officials would stop at nothing to advance their "despicable" goals, including the deception of innocent citizens and initiating acts of murder and sabotage. By means of the evidence they presented, the defendants' confessions, and the witnesses' testimony, the judges and prosecution sought to demonstrate that the organization's leaders were directly responsible for a long row of serious offenses. Similarly, they contended that the Brothers' positions were unethical and contravened the tenets of Islam, which the movement professed to represent. Finally, this unwavering assault on the MB was portrayed as an unavoidable step in the regime's efforts to defend society against the dangers, foremost among them civil war (*fitna*), that the movement posed to the Egyptian public.

The delegitimation of the MB was essentially a campaign to "de-Islamitize" a movement whose motto was and remains "Islam is the solution." For example, *Mahkamat al-Sha'b*'s rhetoric revolved around the following contention: while the MB might profess to embody the values of Islam, in practice its conduct stands in stark contradistinction to the principles of this same faith. Time and again, the prosecution and judges enjoined the defendants to explain their outlook on the balance between religion and state. On the other hand, the regime sought to accentuate its commitment to instituting a modern ruling order that anchors civil rights in a progressive constitution, which also faithfully expresses the values of Islam. In contrast, it depicted the MB as a radical force that is striving to transform Egypt into a dark theocracy that would consign the people to the tribulations of anarchy, poverty, backwardness, and violence.

The court goaded many witnesses into declaring their unswerving commitment to Islam's scriptures in an attempt to draw a correlation between these statements and the MB's alleged estrangement from the laws of the land. To the question of what guides the movement's conduct, ʿAbdallah al-Ris responded, "Among our principles is a government in accordance with the Quran, which is our constitution." Within this framework, he continued, there is perhaps room for other civil and criminal codes but only under the condition that they conform to the precepts of the Quran.[20] In an effort to expose the movement's radical interpretation of canonical texts, the judges and prosecution asked some of the defendants to state their views on the prohibitions against drinking wine and charging interest. The central motif in the court's rhetoric was that the MB's positions and activities constitute an outright deviation (*khuruj*) from Islam. In asking the defendants to outline the lineaments of what they believed to be a worthy Islamic ruler and government, the judges and prosecution adopted a binary narrative according to which modernity and progress are fundamentally incompatible with the Muslim faith as well as local customs and tradition.

The over one thousand pages of transcripts from the trials and the comprehensive newspaper coverage of these proceedings shed light on the court's efforts to paint and disseminate a negative image of the MB—for example, Judge Salem's occasional interactions with the audience, most of whom were journalists. Developments at *Mahkamat al-Shaʿb* made the front pages of the country's newspapers on a daily basis. As evidenced by the slant of the press reports and commentary, most of the papers were already under the authorities' prying supervision. An examination of the relevant media coverage shows that the journalists' emphasis was on the bills of indictment, the words of the judges and the prosecution, and the defendants' admissions. For example, declarations such as "I admit that I was wrong" or "I regret what I did," along with accompanying photographs, usually made headlines in the next day's papers.[21] Regardless of whether they actually came up in the contexts in which they were presented, these sort of declarations were a recurrent theme in the government's narrative, which received top billing in the press.

In those rare instances when points raised by MB representatives were covered, their statements were usually cited in an abridged manner without any reference to the actual context in which they were made. Likewise, the press completely ignored the legal irregularities that informed the hearings. Most of the writers simply regurgitated the official position that the court is a special tribunal and thus exempt from standard procedure.

On the other hand, the court transcripts attest to the fact that the General Guide and his capable attorney raised a litany of arguments that revealed the shaky legal grounds on which MB members were indicted. For instance, they reminded the judges that the Egyptian Penal Code clearly stipulates that personal responsibility must be proven to convict someone of a crime. This requirement notwithstanding, according to Hudaybi and Mazen, *Mahkamat al-Shaʿb*'s objective was to pass collective judgment on thousands of citizens who had nothing to do with the attempt on ʿAbd al-Nasser's life and, in fact, had no prior knowledge of the existence of the assassination plot. The General Guide and his counsel did not deny the assassination attempt but emphasized that the court's job was to convict only those involved in its planning and execution. Moreover, they asserted that there is no legal basis for adjudicating every last MB activist. On several occasions, Hudaybi also reprimanded the court for improper generalizations (e.g., "the MB did") and endeavored—albeit without success—to convince the judges that they had misread the way in which the movement conducted its affairs.[22]

One of the study's less-than-surprising revelations was that *al-Jumhuriya*, the newspaper founded by the RCC and run by Anwar al-Sadat (its editor-in-chief), served as the organ of the revolutionary government. This, then, accounts for its journalists' complete identification with the narrative that was spun by the judges (including Sadat) and the prosecution. Much more troublesome was the fact that the established and independent newspapers largely sympathized with the regime's positions. Although they continued to provide a platform for several unbiased writers, nonhegemonic views were few and far between. For example, the legal coverage and editorials on the People's Court in *Ruz al-Yusuf* (established 1925) from the latter half of 1954 offered a one-sided picture of the RCC's struggle with the MB. The front and first few pages of the popular weekly magazine exemplify the importance that the period's editors placed on illustrations and caricatures. Within this framework, prominent figures or occurrences merited a regular illustrated image on the magazine's pages.

As in the past, the nation was represented by the "Egyptian *effendi*"—a heavy-set and balding man with a penchant for Western attire (a three-piece suit, a tie, leather shoes, and round glasses) along with a tarbush on his head and prayer beads in his hand. *Ruz al-Yusuf*'s lead op-ed column carried the byline "The Egyptian Citizen." As the RCC government steadily consolidated its power, the revolution was symbolized by a man in military attire. From the beginning of 1954, this anonymous figure was replaced with a caricature of 'Abd al-Nasser. The glaring absence of Naguib, who was still serving as president, reflected the leanings of most media outlets with respect to the internal struggle at the upper reaches of government. During the period under review, the dimensions of 'Abd al-Nasser's illustrated body were appreciably expanded. Moreover, they stress the prime minister's upright stance and his athletic, muscular physique. He sports an army uniform with full insignia but does not tote a weapon. His body language exudes power and determination.

Throughout that year, *Ruz al-Yusuf* frequently depicted the revolution and Egyptian society as partners whose objectives and intentions were one and the same. Conversely, the MB's leaders were displayed as the polar opposite of the nation and government. In most of the magazine's 1954 editions, the movement was symbolized by one of two new illustrated figures. The first was dubbed "Shaykh Matluf." Although a human being, the Shaykh possessed the head of a bird. In addition to cultivating a pointy goatee, Matluf donned a turban, glasses, a *galabiya* (cloak), and cloth shoes.

The second figure was not given a name. By virtue of his external features, I call him the "Islamist *effendi.*" While dressed in a similar fashion to the Egyptian *effendi*, his jacket is shabby, his turban is overadorned, and he forgoes a necktie. Weighed down by a corpulent body, the Islamist *effendi*'s thick beard covers most of his face. These negative traits make for a shady, repulsive, and menacing figure. Compared to the naïve Egyptian *effendi* who aspires to progress and good, his Islamist counterpart hatches plots, which he hopes to conceal by dressing like a respectable citizen and uttering ambiguous statements. However, to leave no doubts as to his true intentions, the Islamist is often depicted brandishing a bomb or another weapon at his enemies: the Egyptian *effendi* and the heads of the revolution.

As the crisis between the regime and the MB escalated, the textual and visual accounts in the Egyptian press did little to sugarcoat the all-out struggle between the two. The nation and the revolution's leaders were now depicted as standing shoulder to shoulder in the vanguard of a judicious campaign against the forces of darkness, that is, the MB and its helmsmen. For example *Ruz al-Yusuf* came out with an edition following the Manshiya incident in which the entire cover page is taken up by an illustration of ʿAbd al-Nasser wearing a suit of armor, which is labeled "the people." The suit is repelling bullets that are being fired by the assassin, who appears in the form of the Islamist *effendi*. Like many other illustrations published during this stage of the revolution, ʿAbd al-Nasser is portrayed as a giant, whereas the terrorist is a mere Lilliputian. The central theme of this particular edition is that the attempt on the prime minister's life was an act of treason. ʿAbd al-Nasser and the people are portrayed as a unified body that is firmly arrayed against the MB, which threatens to undermine the revolution and harm the Egyptian people.[23]

This same point is made in the front-page illustration gracing the edition that came out following the execution of the six convicts. The Islamist *effendi*'s oversized corpse, which includes a tag reading "terrorism," is pictured strewn across the highway, while his kitschy tarbush, a machine gun, and a chain of bullets are scattered all around. In front of the body is the Egyptian *effendi* wearing full military attire, and a sword is sheathed to his waist. He is peering through binoculars at the bright sun on the horizon, which symbolizes "the future." Summing up the scene, the bottom caption reads "the Egyptian citizen—I believe that now the way is secure!!"[24]

The MB and the special tribunal dominated the November and December 1954 editions of *Ruz al-Yusuf*. An analysis of the written and visual content points to an exceedingly unfavorable representation of the movement. The written commentary focused on the issues that surfaced during the hearings, while the defendant's gaffes were highlighted by the caricaturists. In both the text and illustrations, *Mahkamat al-Sha'b* and the people formed a united front against the MB. On one occasion, it is the court that protects society against terrorists, and the next time it is the nation that shields the judges of the special tribunal. After the opening of the 'Abd al-Latif trial, *Ruz al-Yusuf*'s editors published an op-ed piece under "the Egyptian Citizen" byline stating that the objective behind these proceedings is to defend Egyptian society and the achievements of the July Revolution. That said, they candidly expressed their hope that "the circumstances that compelled the revolution to reopen the doors of this court will end as quickly as possible." The editorial concluded that one must not attribute more significance to the work of these special tribunals than to that of "the regular courts, which adjudicate hundreds of cases and hundreds of defendants" each and every day.[25]

After the first week of the 'Abd al-Latif trial, "the Egyptian Citizen" penned another essay titled "Truths from *Mahkamat al-Sha'b*." The writer(s) praised the special tribunal for revealing the great lengths to which the MB's leaders ("terrorists" and "an armed gang") had gone to hide the fact "that their main goal is to attain seats in government at all costs." They are not interested in disseminating Islam (*al-da'wa*) but rather ensconcing the ten members of the Guidance Office in government offices. Under the veil of religious enterprise, "they are trying to set [Egypt] back five hundred years to the age in which the nations were controlled by the churches and by the hands of the clergy." If they were to succeed, the editors surmised, the age-old struggle for self-rule will have been for naught.[26]

In the next edition (November 22), the emphasis was placed on the regime and Egyptian society's concerted effort against the machinations of the MB. While the RCC was usually portrayed as shielding the nation, this time around it was society propping up the special tribunal. This motif was exemplified by a front-page illustration of a colossal Egyptian *effendi* protecting the judges of *Mahkamat al-Sha'b*. At the foot of the judges' desk, the Islamist *effendi* has taken to one knee and is begging for his life. Next to the illustration is the following Quran verse: "Verily those who believed, then disbelieved, again believed, and again disbelieved, then increased in [their] disbelief, Allah will not forgive them, nor will He guide them to the [right] way."[27] In that same edition, the lead editorial bemoans the attempts by MB figures to wash their hands clean of the assassination:

> 'Abd al-Latif said that he is not responsible and so did Hindawi [Duwayr], and Khamis Humayda, and Yusuf Tal'at. And then came Hudaybi, the MB's General Guide, and he also said that he is not responsible. If so, who in the MB is responsible for everything that has happened? Who is responsible for the deadly plans, the weapon caches, the explosive belts, and the detonation charges?[28]

Commenting on the essence of *Mahkamat al-Sha'b*, the editorial staff opined that it was not to bring the MB's leadership to justice but rather to pass judgment on "the idea that has taken shape in this movement" that it is possible to oppose the government and "force its will on society" by any and all means, be it terrorism, liquidations, or provoking civil war. The MB's plan was "predicated not on reason but pistols, not on persuasion but dynamite." This observation led the editors to the conclusion that the People's Court was not seeking to punish any individual in particular, but to expose "the principles" governing the conduct of the movement and its top officials and "to eliminate these principles" lest "other people" embrace the path of violence.[29] The MB was also portrayed as a terrorist organization in an illustration of the Islamist *effendi* addressing the court. To the astonishment of the judges, he is pointing to a bomb while declaring that "my intentions are honorable."[30]

Revolutionary Justice—The Closing Arguments

The establishment of the July Revolution's special tribunals coincided with the most serious political crisis between the RCC and the mélange of groups composing the opposition, especially the Wafd and the MB. One year after the coup the euphoria surrounding Faruq's exile and the untempered public adoration for the heroes of the revolution had subsided. At the heart of this crisis stood the army's continued rule. This pivotal issue was not only a matter of controversy between the FO and its rivals, but it unsettled the upper echelons of government. The public debate over this topic corresponded with the trials against 'Abd al-Hadi, 'Abd al-Latif, and Hudaybi. In fact, the argument can be made that *Mahkamat al-Thawra* primarily contended with the rudimentary question of whether it was absolutely necessary for the FO to intervene in politics and overthrow the monarchial regime. *Mahkamat al-Sha'b* also dealt with this issue, within the context of the political struggle that followed in the wake of the coup. In the process, another burning question surfaced over the course of its hearings: Some two years after toppling King Faruq, why had the army yet to return to the barracks?

Pursuant to the decrees setting up these courts, the trials were open to the public. Moreover, their hearings garnered extensive coverage in the Egyptian media. The developments at these tribunals loomed large in the discourse over the most pressing issues of the day. Likewise, the court rhetoric percolated down to the public and played a role in the construction of the categories that were employed in the general discourse and by both the RCC and its rivals to articulate their respective views of each other.[31] It thus stands to reason that the decision to open the special courts to the public was largely meant to influence popular opinion. Besides adjudicating defendants, the tribunals and their oratory was a means for controlling and deterring the populace. Moreover, the very functioning of these tribunals heightened the emergency atmosphere by triggering a vicious cycle: the establishment of these courts was made possible by the state of emergency, while their hearings fanned the flames.

Against this backdrop, the FO raised two principal arguments. First, the military coup was an absolute necessity given the catastrophic situation that the monarchy had brought upon the Land of the Nile. Second, the RCC's continued hold on the reins of government, along with the exceptional measures that it took, were ineluctable due to attempts by "reactionary forces" (e.g., the Wafd, the MB, and powerful figures in the old regime) to disrupt the revolution, which the military was spearheading on the people's behalf. The FO provided myriad justifications for establishing *Mahkamat al-Thawra* and *Mahkamat al-Sha'b*, which all boiled down to the following claim: domestic and foreign elements pose a tangible threat to Egyptian society and the revolution. The overthrow of the monarchy was presented as the first step on a treacherous path toward a national renaissance. If the army yielded to its rivals' demands and returned to the barracks, the junta claimed, those same individuals who formed the backbone of the old dispensation would reclaim the helm. According to the revolution's speakers, the very fact that these same "reactionaries" are still active demonstrates that this scenario is not far-fetched.

In making this case, the regime was also intimating that the circumstances in Egypt were so dire that the public had good reason for worry. During the trials against MB activists, the judges and prosecution repeatedly argued that the movement's activities are liable to spark a *fitna* ("civil war"). The use of this freighted Islamic term was hardly a coincidence, as the Quran deems this sort of internecine to be one of the gravest threats to the *umma* (nation of believers). The integration of prevalent religious terms into the emergency rhetoric was aimed at convincing the public that Egypt was on the brink of disaster and that only exceptional measures on the part of the RCC could avert such a catastrophe. This dark forecast was a logical prelude to another pillar of the courts' prime message: the military and people share a basic common interest. It is in this context that one must understand the ensuing words of Deputy Prosecutor General Ahmad Mu'afi before the Revolution's Court:

> The revolution is a covenant between you [i.e., the judges and, by extension, the rest of the RCC top brass] and the people. You executed it on their behalf and not for your own sake; consequently, they are entitled [to demand] that you wipe out the corruption Egypt has suffered from. . . . As it now stands, you are the just law of Allah in the land. By sitting in judgment, you are currently writing glorious pages in the annals of

> Egypt in that you are hereby punishing the traitors and despots who oppressed the public and the country.[32]

Implicit in the FO's resort to special courts was the belief that the rhetoric of these institutions was superior to that of the civil justice system. In turning to these exceptional frameworks, the regime signaled that it was going to identify itself with an alternative arm of the judiciary.

Throughout the July Revolution's decisive transition stages, the junta often resorted to rule by fiat. On the face of things, the judiciary and law enforcement continued to abide by the existing civil and criminal codes, but irregular legal measures, such as the Treason Law and the establishment of special courts, were implemented by dint of recently minted decrees. From the very first day of the coup, the FO endeavored to legitimize or, according to its detractors, "whitewash" the new government's controversial steps, including its use of aberrant means against political rivals, under a veneer of lawfulness. This process, which has thus far eluded the attention of scholars, was headed by two prominent jurists: Supreme Court President ʿAbd al-Razzaq al-Sanhuri, a renowned jurist who steered the drafting of civil codes for a number of Arab states, and his deputy Sulayman Hafiz.

Regardless of their public displays of homage to the justice system and its professional staff, the RCC reiterated the argument that the emergency state justifies its turn to "revolutionary justice," namely, to special tribunals. On the occasion of *Mahkamat al-Thawra*'s dedication ceremony in September of 1953, Minister of National Guidance Salah Salem remarked:

> In the history of all revolutions, it has not happened that the fate of any revolution is deliberated in an ordinary trial. The regular laws have constraints and limitations that its judges cannot breach, and the reason for this is that these [checks] were legislated for the circumstances of normal life.[33]

In addition, the FO stated that it would use whatever means necessary to fulfill its solemn duty of protecting the nation.

The Revolution's Court and the People's Court hailed the events surrounding the monarchy's removal as a dramatic transformation in the annals of the Egyptian nation. In their constitutive decrees and hearings, a correlation was drawn between the tribunals' exceptional powers and the aberrant circumstances in Egypt. The RCC claimed that its efforts to forge a new political and social order were a complete departure from the state of affairs before the coup. This same conception of revolutionary time was also manifest in the judges' preoccupation with episodes from the country's not too distant past. References to such events were part and parcel of the junta's new historical narrative that, among other things, justified the monarchy's ouster. The rewriting history is a routine and well-documented phenomenon during revolutions. Nevertheless, the unique role of these particular courts in the formulation and dissemination of the RCC's narratives barely comes up in the plethora of historiographical and socio-legal works chronicling modern Egypt.

Mahkamat al-Thawra and *Mahkamat al-Sha'b* left their mark on the FO's new hegemonic narrative of the monarchial era. In collecting and assessing written and oral testimony on a wide range of events, the judges basically filled the role of historian. While inspired by Carlo Ginzburg's critical analysis of the similarities and differences between what judges and historians view as facts, the present study demonstrates how the state's representatives at these courts, essentially acted as if they were historians.[34] This new historical narrative was commensurate with the tribunal's defamatory claim against the FO's past and present rivals. At the same time, the judges echoed the government's self-aggrandizement and sanguine predictions of a brighter future.

That is, the delegitimization campaign against the junta's adversaries was, for all purposes, the flip side of its efforts to burnish the government's credentials. Therefore, it comes as no surprise that the defendants were portrayed as "traitors" and "enemies of the people," rather than political opponents who in criticizing the government's policies were merely doing their jobs. From the RCC's standpoint, the court's quasi-juridical investigations substantiated its case that the accused had undermined national interests by sabotaging the legitimate goals of the revolution. The military was touted as the only Egyptian institution capable of bringing these goals to fruition and preventing the reemergence of the corrupt *ancien régime*. As a result, the FO claimed, it is imperative for the military to preside over what could very well be a prolonged transition period.

9

Trapped between Two Revolutions

At least at the outset, ʿAbd al-Nasser and the FO attempted to replace the monarchy with a democratic system of government that raised the banner of justice. Its social and political achievements notwithstanding, during the post-revolution transitional period, the RCC laid the foundations for the authoritarian regime that has ruled Egypt in the decades to come. Within two and half years of the coup, both the 1923 Constitution and the political pluralism of the monarchial era were out of commission. Moreover, the cosmopolitan atmosphere that had hitherto pervaded urban life vanished, as nationalist rhetoric and sanctions pushed hundreds of thousands of Greeks, Italians, and Jews out of the Nile Valley. Finally, the absolute power of the executive branch enabled the president and the security apparatus to dominate the public sphere.

The military, the police, and the internal security forces (led by the *mukhabarat*) formed the backbone of the regime. Their deep involvement in every facet of government and Egyptian society was rather conspicuous. The unrestrained police committed blatant human rights violations. Owing to its long reach, the regime was able to detect any sign of organized political opposition. The State of Emergency Law of 1958 authorized the government and security forces to take extraordinary measures against domestic opponents, without any judicial or public oversight. Parliamentary life was paralyzed, and the legislative functions were in the hands of the ruling elite. Dictating the local media's coverage, the authorities created the illusion of total synergy between the regime and the people. Furthermore, the judiciary's independence was compromised. More specifically, the legal system and law enforcement bodies were mere agents of the regime whose primary goal was to keep the public under wraps.

The Revolution's Court and the People's Court were dissolved at the end of the July Revolution's transitional period. However, the long-standing Egyptian practice of adjudicating citizens before special courts would reach new heights. Although the names given to these institutions changed over the years (a present-day version is the Emergency State Security Court), they were all conferred with exceptional powers. The widespread use of these tribunals, including the military variety, turned that exception into the rule. In conjunction with these tribunals, the notorious "special wards" of the country's prison system were an integral part of the apparatus through which the state sought to maintain its dominance over the political arena.[1] The physical and mental torture of inmates has been thoroughly documented in memoirs, diaries, popular poems, prose, and historical studies. Although the objective behind these incarcerations was to remove the opposition from the public sphere and force the government's critics to abandon their anti-establishment views, the years in prison only bolstered their ideological commitment to the struggle against the authoritarian regime. Due to its failure to win the backing of civil society, the ruling elite became ever more reliant on the "iron fist" of the security apparatus. Consequently, Egypt steadily took on the attributes of a police state that intimidated its citizens and depoliticized society.

Domestic criticism of the regime's nondemocratic facets was attenuated by, inter alia, the government's effective performance at the outset. The agrarian reform extricated millions of peasants from the suffocating yoke of landowners. Illiteracy was significantly reduced, and an entire generation enjoyed greater access to schools and higher education. Between 1956 and 1967, 'Abd al-Nasser established himself as a prominent leader on the international stage. His decision to nationalize the Suez Canal took a heavy toll on Egypt in the form of the Suez War. When the smoke had cleared, though, the regime was able to point to significant political and economic achievements: the regime had survived an invasion by two colonial powers (Britain and France) and Israel, enemy forces completely withdrew from Egyptian territory, and the war paved the way for the construction of the Aswan High Dam.

In the Global South, the charismatic president's actions were viewed as a paradigm for decolonization. The Egyptian–Syrian union (UAR, 1958–61) won the hearts of millions of Arabs, who saw Nasserism as an alternative to the conservative Middle Eastern regimes that were established under the auspices of and remained in thrall to Western powers. Nasserite rhetoric portrayed the liberation of Palestine and the Arab world's conflict with Israel as the frontlines in the struggle against imperialism.

While Syria's departure from the UAR certainly hurt, it was two regional wars that led to the movement-cum-ideology's downfall. First, 'Abd al-Nasser's support for the rebels in Yemen mired his army in a protracted campaign. Not only did tens of thousands of combatants perish in this war, but Cairo was ultimately forced to bow to the dictates of Saudi Arabia and the Yemenite Sultan. Second, the defeat in the 1967 War against Israel was the swan song of revolutionary Egypt. Harsh criticism of the broken system and the search for alternatives headlined the public debate and even found expression in works of art. 'Abd al-Nasser still enjoyed broad support in his own and other Arab countries, but these two enormous setbacks left deep scars. Within three years, the beleaguered president would succumb to a rash of health ailments. Despite mounting disappointment with the regime, the huge crowds at 'Abd al-Nasser's funeral and the dark veil of mourning that descended over the entire country testified to his immense popularity.

The *Infitah* Era

Upon succeeding 'Abd al-Nasser as head of the republic, Anwar al-Sadat ordered the release of political prisoners. Soon after, he consolidated his rule by purging left-wing and pro-Soviet officials from the upper echelons of government and the security apparatus—the so-called corrective revolution (*al-thawra al-tashihiya*). At the same time, the MB was allowed to resume its activities in public. More specifically, the movement reinaugurated its publications as well as projects in the fields of welfare, social work, and education. During that time, Egypt was inundated with books and articles on how the 'Abd al-Nasser regime had trammeled parliamentary life and infringed upon human rights.[2] Under the heading of the *infitah* (openness) program, Sadat vigorously revamped Egypt's economic policy and national security doctrine over the course of his eleven-year tenure (1970–81). This new strategy was premised on the assumption of a symbiotic relationship between the country's social, economic, and demographic realities on the one hand and its political course and security policies on the other. Within this framework, Sadat steered the republic in the direction of a market economy in the hope of lifting tens of millions of citizens out of poverty. In other words, he sought to expand the private sector, reduce the sprawling public sector, and encourage foreign investment.

Two decades of special relations with the Soviet Union gave way to cooperation with the United States in a wide range of areas. Seeking to end the state of "neither war nor peace" with the neighbors up north, Sadat launched an invasion of Israeli-controlled territory. Buoyed by his army's considerable gains in the 1973 War, the president embarked on a bold political gambit that ultimately paid dividends in the form of his historic speech before the Knesset in Jerusalem, the negotiations at Camp David, and the signing of a peace treaty between the two countries on March 26, 1979. Highly controversial on the domestic front, the accord with Israel also severely damaged Egypt's relations with Arab states and the Palestine Liberation Organization.

In the long run, the decision to limit the *infitah* program to economic and political-security issues was misguided. Although Sadat frequently spoke of his commitment to reforming the political sphere, he proceeded at a glacial pace to keep his government in firm control. The Arab Socialist Union—the only political organization that was allowed to function during the revolutionary period—was replaced by three "platforms" (left, right, and center), which set the stage for the resumption of party life. However, this reform did not blunt the authoritarian regime. To begin, the new Constitution of 1971 gave the president broad powers. The ruling party, the National Democratic Party (NDP), ran the show in parliament, which enacted legislation that consolidated the regime's power and limited the opposition's room for protest to tolerable levels. Other laws enabled the government to keep its adversaries—including parties and nongovernmental organizations—under constant surveillance and onerous censorship. The constitution ostensibly guaranteed freedom of expression, but restrictions on the media rendered this guarantee meaningless.

The clashes between the regime and its domestic rivals escalated in the fall of 1981. Ratcheting up its criticism of domestic and foreign policy, the opposition argued that the leadership was severely compromising national interests. In the hope of curbing the opposition, Sadat resorted to draconian measures, including the confinement of thousands of activists for unspecified periods of time. Since the mid-1970s, militant Islamist groups had been lashing out at the regime. They claimed that the government's policy was in violation of Islamic law and that "Sadat the infidel" was unworthy of living. On October 6, 1981, members of the Egyptian Islamic Jihad assassinated the president at a military parade marking the army's gains in the 1973 War, which for many Egyptians symbolized the high point of his reign. The assassins were tried before a military tribunal. At the hearings, the government and the defendants hurled accusations at each other. The latter justified the killing on the grounds that Sadat had led a heretical tyranny. Khalid al-Islambuli, the leader of the assassination squad, even declared, "We killed the Pharaoh!"[3]

Vice-President Hosni Mubarak, who had been sitting next to Sadat at the time of the assassination, was sworn in as the fourth president of the republic. At his behest, a state of emergency was declared. This measure granted the regime extraordinary powers, including the right to arbitrarily detain citizens for indefinite periods and bring them to justice before military courts. In addition, Mubarak launched an all-out war against militant Islamist groups. As part of a sweeping crackdown, hundreds of defendants were tried in a manner that was reminiscent of the hearings at *Mahkamat al-Sha'b*. In parallel, thousands of political activists who had been incarcerated toward the end of Sadat's reign were freed. In so doing, the new president sent a message of reconciliation, signaling that the regime was opening a clean slate in its relations with the opposition. However, it soon became evident that Mubarak was picking up where his predecessor had left off in all that concerned the deceased ruler's authoritarian approach to governance, neoliberal economic tendencies, the strategic partnership with the United States, and the peace treaty with Israel.

The vast expansion of the private sector under the *infitah* program triggered appreciable macro-economic changes. From the early 1980s onward, the gross national product consistently rose. The Egyptian economy's growth far exceeded that of the population, whose birth rate fell to two percent a year. Generous foreign aid (mostly from the United States) and an impressive uptick in foreign investment lined the treasury with billions of dollars. By virtue of the tourism industry's unprecedented growth and the enhanced profitability of the Suez Canal Company, Egypt was awash in foreign currency. The government and its supporters among the elite attributed these developments to the *infitah*. In any event, the average Egyptian's quality of life was improving, as the increasing revenues allowed the government to upgrade the infrastructure and services for the ever-growing population.

Despite these positive developments, the negative aspects of the openness policy could not be long ignored. Prices rose at a much faster rate than wages; subsidies on consumer goods, fuel, and services were gradually reduced; and unemployment climbed to dangerous levels, especially among young college graduates. Moreover, the gap between rich and poor was widening, as various groups that previously belonged to the middle class fell below the poverty line.[4] An inefficient bureaucracy, shoddy planning, and mounting corruption also made themselves felt. While Egyptian exports surged thanks to the private sector's growth, imports increased at a much higher pace. As a result, the trade deficit ballooned, and the national debt correspondingly swelled to about fifty billion dollars in the early 1990s. To make matters worse, the purchasing power of the Egyptian pound was losing ground. Moderate GDP growth and limited resources condemned Egypt to a chronic dependency on foreign (mostly American) aid and loans from the World Bank and the IMF. These shortcomings only exacerbated the pressure on the country's less than adequate infrastructure and services.

A Soft Police State

While there was a greater degree of openness in the political arena under Mubarak, like other authoritarian regimes, the government cultivated a political reality in which most citizens belonged to the "silent majority" that refrained from voicing political opinions. Similarly, a "regime of fear" distanced the opposition parties from the public sphere. Buttressed by several new laws, the parties did expand their activities, but they remained under the control of the security forces, which were empowered by the state of emergency. The NDP's supremacy in parliament and the local councils went unchallenged. Although the MB's request to be recognized as a political party was repeatedly denied, the movement's representatives were elected to the legislature by dint of a constitutional clause permitting candidates to run independently for public office. MB activists also rose to the top of various professional associations and trade unions. The movement established itself as the country's leading opposition group. Expressions of resistance to the continuation of the despotic order stood out in novels, poems, plays, films, and other art forms. The famed Egyptian sense of humor provided a daily, if indirect, outlet for letting off steam.

As such, there were a few available channels for voicing objections to Mubarak's economic policy and its grave social consequences. The detractors pointed to the spike in inequality, the growing number of destitute Egyptians, and the ineptitude of social and public services. Furthermore, they argued that given the country's large population and dearth of resources, capital, and scientific-cum-technological know-how, the *infitah* program and globalization have turned Egypt into a supplier of cheap labor and mass consumer of goods and commodities produced by Western multinational companies, which keep the bulk of the profits for themselves. This economic dependency on external players, the opposition contended, harms national interests, for it comes at a high political price. In this same context, the burgeoning strategic alliance with the United States and the peace with Israel drew a substantial amount of heat.

By the early 1980s, the army and the internal security forces had solidified their role as the central cog in the regime. Owing to their near omnipotence, a "soft police state" had taken form in Egypt. The Constitution of 1971 set the president's term of office at six years, but did not limit the number of terms he could serve (Article 77). Moreover, parliament was charged with selecting the president (by two-thirds majority), whereupon its candidate would be put before a public referendum. Under this system, Mubarak was elected president five times. Time and again, the legislature rubber-stamped the government's requests to extend the state of emergency, so that it became the norm over Mubarak's thirty-year reign. Under the pretext of maintaining public order and security, the regime severely violated the constitution's protections of human rights and civil liberties. Arrests, humiliation, and torture in police stations and prisons had become routine. Seeking to further their political, security, and economic interests, the world powers cossetted the authoritarian regime in a blanket of international support. Stability was, in fact, the top priority of the regime and its foreign allies. While successive American administrations funded civil society projects in Egypt and urged the Mubarak regime to promote democratization, Washington's overriding concern was to safeguard its political and security interests in the region.

The period from 2005 to 2010 constituted a major crossroads in the struggle over the regime's fate. The debate revolved around the possibility that Mubarak would bequeath the presidency to his son Gamal. By this stage, the latter had already become the most influential figure in the ruling party. The semi-establishment press not only showered Gamal with prime coverage, but nurtured his image as a reformer striving to lead Egypt into the twenty-first century. That said, the consensus among observers was that he would not garner the requisite support from the military and security brass. Resistance to the younger Mubarak's candidacy was ratcheted up, and many Egyptians identified with the *Kifaya* (Enough) movement's rallying cry: "No to [Gamal's] succession and no to an extension of [Hosni's] fifth term in office" (*la' lil-tawrith . . . la' lil-tamdid li-fatrat ri'asa khamisa*).[5] The opposition also demanded an amendment to the constitution that would bar the ruling party and the president from exerting undue influence over the political sphere. Moreover, they pressed for the termination of the never-ending state of emergency and the weighty government control over the media. In an effort to mollify the public, the regime did make an unprecedented concession, allowing a number of candidates to run for president in the 2005 race. While Mubarak prevailed over a dozen challengers, the tension between the regime and the opposition skyrocketed during his fifth term in office.

The NDP's poor showing in the 2005 parliamentary elections underscored the public discontent with the country's state of affairs. In the opening round, the MB candidates won eighty-eight seats—nearly six times the movement's output in the previous elections. Security forces disrupted the next two rounds of voting, thereby preventing the opposition from gaining control of the house for the first time.[6] By virtue of the struggles it waged in public and in the legislature, the MB cemented its reputation as the leading force for change. However, the movement's electoral gains were a cause for concern among wide swathes of Egyptian society, particularly the large Coptic minority. Over the next five years, the security forces waged an aggressive campaign against the entire opposition, but the focus was on the MB. Official government statements intentionally blurred the significant differences between the latter and militant jihadist groups. In addition, the movement's funds and property were confiscated and hundreds of activists, including some high-ranking leaders, were tried before military courts. At the end of swift and highly controversial proceedings, the judges meted out stiff punishments.

At the beginning of 2010, President Mubarak's health began to deteriorate. By early March, he was hospitalized for three weeks in Germany for gall bladder surgery. These developments reignited the campaign against Gamal Mubarak's succession. For their part, the regime's spokespersons let it be known that they would do whatever it took to remain at the helm. In the run-up to November 28, 2010 parliamentary elections, over a thousand MB activists were arrested, hundreds of demonstrators were injured in clashes with the security forces, and quite a few of the movement's candidates were disqualified on various grounds. Government supporters argued that the MB's activities threaten to divide Egyptian society because the group intended on overthrowing the government by unlawful means and transforming Egypt into a theocracy. On the eve of the elections, the confrontations between the security forces and opposition groups intensified. Citing rampant tampering, several parties announced that they were boycotting the ballot. Monitors concluded that election fraud had been committed on a huge scale. When the dust had settled, though, the NDP and its political allies had won a landslide victory.

Economic hardships further galvanized anti-regime sentiments, as ever more Egyptians began demanding immediate change. By this juncture, different sectors were holding regular protests. The crackdown against old-fashioned demonstrations in the public squares turned the Internet and other technologies into prime catalysts for resistance. Social networks, blogs, YouTube, text messages, twitter, and mobile phone cameras turned out to be effective outlets for fostering political solidarity and drawing millions of young Egyptians into the fray. Attempts to throw a wrench into the networking activities blew up in the regime's face, as security personnel were no match for the internet-savvy protest leaders. Footage of *mukhabarat* agents beating of a popular blogger, Khaled Sa'id, to death on a main street of Alexandria (June 6, 2010) set off a wave of virtual protests that was unprecedented in scope.

Against this backdrop, a rally was planned for Police Day, January 25, 2011, at Tahrir Square. Tens of thousands of young Egyptians had already visited the Facebook page "We Are All Khaled Sa'id."[7] The protestors were further galvanized by the dramatic events in Tunisia following the self-immolation of a street vendor and the flight of the dictator, Zein al-'Abidine Ben 'Ali. A YouTube video by Asmaa Mahfouz—a young, female founder of the April 6 Youth Movement—is indicative of the spirit and *modus operandi* of the Egyptian organizers. In an emotional appeal uploaded on the eve of the said rally, Mahfouz urged her fellow citizens to take to the street:

> We want to go down to Tahrir Square on January 25. If we still have honor and want to live in dignity in this land, we have to go down on January 25. We'll go down and demand our rights, our international human rights. . . . Whoever says it's not worth it coz there will be only a handful of people,I want to tell him, you are the reason behind this. . . . Your presence with us will make a difference. A big difference. Come and protect me, and other girls in the protest.[8]

Civil Uprising

The massive turnout surprised even the organizers, and nobody could have foreseen the events that unfolded in the days ahead. When the uprising began, the public sphere was dominated by the *nabūt* (baton) of the security forces and their hired thugs (*baltajiya*). However, the first wave of protesters—mainly young men and women—were determined to stand their ground. The more brutal the repression became, the greater the support that the protest attracted from the "masses," who steadily joined the ranks of demonstrators on the square. Within a few days, the regime's "wall of fear" came crumbling down, thereby upending the distribution of power in the public sphere. The demonstrations mushroomed into a popular insurrection numbering millions of people. The fact that the massive uprising was not associated with any specific party or sector made it easier for Egyptians of all stripes to identify with its goals and enter the fray. However, it was, in fact, the younger generation—both men and women—who spearheaded the revolution. Modern communication and information technologies contributed to their efforts in a variety of ways. Online social networks, text messaging, and mobile phone cameras were used not only to establish vital contacts and mobilize supporters but also as a platform to create solidarity. [9]In addition, satellite TV channels (led by al-Jazeera) provided sympathetic coverage of the Arab Spring.

However, the Tahrir Square protest would not have evolved into a popular uprising without the backing of other sectors, whose members were not necessarily Internet savvy or, for that matter, the owners of mobile devices. Tens of millions of protesters expressed themselves by traditional means: marching, chanting slogans, and confronting security forces.[10] Horrifying as it may be, the main impetus behind the mass attendance at this pivotal demonstration was the authorities' brutal repression of the participants. In the eyes of many Egyptians, this heavy-handed approach was emblematic of the regime's illegitimacy. As the violence picked up, more and more Egyptians from all walks of life identified with the aims of the struggle. It was this turn of events that provided the critical mass of support that enabled the organizers to speak in the name of "the people."

The solidarity that was formed between the demonstrators during the uprising provided them with inexhaustible reserves of energy for carrying on with the struggle. This unity of purpose among individuals and groups was achieved without intermediaries, at a unique "moment" of the peaceful civil uprising. The protestors' daring and rage bespoke their awareness that this time there was a realistic chance for appreciable gains in the battle for freedom, social justice, and life with dignity. Allegedly "passive" and "submissive," the Egyptian populace steadfastly demanded its rights.

Tahrir Square became the heart of the struggle as well as the blueprint for resistance throughout the country. "Egypt's young sit-in protesters" (*shabab misr al-muʿtasimin*) hung a gigantic banner across the façade of a twelve-story building overlooking the square listing their seven principal demands: the president's removal, the dissolution of parliament, an end to the state of emergency, the establishment of a transitional unity government, legislation paving the way for the president to be elected directly by the citizens (rather than parliament), and the prosecution of corrupt officials along with those responsible for the lethal violence against protesters. From Alexandria in the north to Aswan in the south, millions of demonstrators from all walks of life shouted in unison: "The people want to topple the president [*al-ra'is*]" and "The people want to topple the regime [*al-niẓam*]." In public spaces throughout the country, there were riveting spectacles of popular revolt. Protesters responded to Mubarak's desperate attempts to propose reforms by screaming "Go away" (*irhal*). This formidable display of civic power caught the entire world off guard. Some looked on in breathless admiration, while others were aghast.

On the eighteenth day of the uprising, the military high command forced the long-serving autocratic president to step down. This dramatic decision was only taken after millions of Egyptians had risked life and limb against the security forces. Mubarak's ouster signaled the beginning of the January Revolution's transition phase, which was destined to tread down a rocky and circuitous path. The ensuing struggles over the new dispensation triggered heavy crises that buffeted society and the institutions of government to the point of undermining Egypt's economic stability and national security.

In parallel, the solidarity that informed the protests was rapidly fading. New and established parties and groups that had previously joined forces to overthrow the Mubarak regime were now fighting each other over positions of power and public support. Despite the infighting, a wide range of civic organizations labored to advance the goals of the January Revolution, especially in all that concerns freedom and social justice. On the other hand, the army, the security forces, and the administrative bases of power, which pundits refer collectively to as the "deep state" (*al-dawla al-'amiqa*), put up a relentless fight to protect their interests.

As the political crisis intensified, a fascinating public debate was waged over the similarities and differences between the July 1952 Revolution and the one in the making.[11] Both cases shared the following elements: the fall of a strongman raised hopes among many Egyptians that a "new era" was just around the corner; a military council assumed control over the daily running of government; a state of emergency was declared; a fierce political struggle erupted over the contours of the new political order; the constitution was suspended; parliament was disbanded; thousands of people were summarily arrested; and the leadership promulgated a wide assortment of laws by means of constitutional decrees.

Similar to the July Revolution, the judicial system and the courts loomed large in the on-going, all-out struggle over the new dispensation. With Mubarak's resignation, the Supreme Council of the Armed Forces (SCAF) assumed both executive and legislative powers. At the height of the uprising, the police and security forces evacuated the streets, leaving chaos in their wake. The army was called upon to fill this void. Though cautious about blemishing its reputation among the general public, military units took up positions in urban protest zones. In parallel, hundreds of officials in the bureaucracy and security apparatus were removed from their posts. The July Revolution had begun with a bloodless military coup and ended with an authoritarian regime. Conversely, the January Revolution was led by civil society forces, under the slogan "The people want the overthrow of the regime." Mubarak's presidency was a direct continuation of the one established by 'Abd al-Nasser and the FO six decades earlier. During the 2011 uprising, about 850 civilians were killed and thousands more wounded. Although the SCAF declared that they had no intention of running the government for long, the young leaders of the struggle (the representatives of, inter alia, the April 6 Youth Movement and the Coalition of the Revolution's Youth) insisted that the army commanders were undermining the revolution's goals.

The SCAF's "road map"—a constitutional declaration that was issued on March 30, 2011—was the tipping point in the public debate over the January Revolution's transition stage.[12] While the majority of the political parties and groups that were associated with the uprising clamored for the drafting of a new constitution *before* the next elections, the interim government decided to proceed in the opposite order. By virtue of the MB's support, the SCAF ultimately managed to push off the deadline for a new constitution until after the elections. For its part, the MB was motivated by its own electoral prospects. Given its effective organizational apparatus and considerable financial resources, the movement's leaders saw the road map as an opportunity to wrest the reins of government away from the generals and oversee the construction of a new order in Egypt. In turn, the revolutionary camp viewed the MB leadership's support for early elections to be a power play that threatened to derail the January Revolution soon after it left the station.

Muslim Brothers at the Helm

For the next three years, the battle for primacy in the land of the Nile gradually intensified. Resistance to the SCAF's continuing rule took the form of daily confrontations, which exacted a great deal of violence and bloodshed. The victory of the MB's Freedom and Justice Party (*hizb al-hurriya wa-l-'adala*) in the January 2012 elections to the "revolutionary parliament" and the legislature's subsequent dispersal a mere five months later by order of the Supreme Constitutional Court were the opening salvoes in a heated struggle between the MB and a broad coalition of its rivals. While some of the powers of government were transferred to an elected civilian leadership, the SCAF continued to stir the seething political cauldron. Two of the key moments in this confrontation were Muhammad Morsi's triumph in the June 2012 presidential elections and his dismissal a year later. Morsi, a senior MB leader, was the first Egyptian president to be elected in a free and fair campaign. In large part, he owed his victory to the support of millions of citizens who do not identify with "political Islam." Instead, they voted against his opponent, Ahmad Shafik—a retired general and confidant of Mubarak—because he was seen as a representative of the "counter-revolution." For his part, Morsi had pledged to realize the January Revolution's goals, establish a civilian government and state apparatus, and protect the interests of the entire populace.

It soon became evident that there was a copious gap between the new ruler's professed commitments and the agenda that he pursued as head of state. To begin, Morsi adopted an authoritarian style that reminded many of his predecessors. Moreover, there was concern that his chief priority was the Brotherhoodization of the state (*ikhwanat al-dawla*). On November 22, 2012, Morsi issued a presidential decree that conferred extraordinary powers upon the executive branch. Thereafter, he appointed hundreds of MB members to senior government posts, some of which wield crucial authority within the state apparatus. In addition, the president directly intervened in the work of the committee that was appointed to draft a new constitution. Despite the fierce resistance from opposition parties and various sectors, he also decided to have the draft constitution approved by referendum. (When Morsi began his tenure, there was no valid constitution defining the executive powers.) Moreover, a supplementary constitutional declaration that was promulgated before his election left a sizeable amount of power in the hands of the SCAF, appreciably diminishing the bailiwick of the legislative and executive branches.

Morsi attempted to tip the scales back in favor of the civilian leadership. On this matter, he relied on broad public dissent to the military leadership's efforts to mold the revolution in accordance with the interests of the "deep state." To this end, Morsi issued a constitutional declaration of his own that scaled back the SCAF's province. Some of the president's statements and especially his orders drew the ire of the judiciary's senior ranks. His next step was even more dramatic. At Morsi's behest, most of the SCAF's members were removed from their posts. In a backroom deal, Field Marshal Muhammad Husayn Tantawi and Chief of Staff Sami ʿAnan agreed to retire. Furthermore, the military high command was entrusted to ʿAbd al-Fattah al-Sisi—the youngest general on the SCAF.

The opposition argued that Morsi had made no headway whatsoever in solving the country's internal problems. In their estimation, the president had failed to rebuild the economy, and internal security had gone from bad to worse. More specifically, there was a shortage of essential goods on the market, including petrol and diesel. The cost of living index, inflation, and unemployment were skyrocketing. To make matters worse, the local currency and the Cairo stock exchange were in a free fall. External aid, much of which was then coming from Qatar, barely alleviated the budget deficit, which had climbed to an alarming twelve percent of the GDP. With respect to public safety, the conflict between the security forces and militant Islamist groups on the Sinai Peninsula spilled over into major cities, particularly the capital. Hundreds of people in uniform were killed in attacks by insurgents, heightening the average Egyptian's foreboding. At the vanguard of the sharp anti-government criticism was the National Salvation Front (*jabhat al-inqaẓ al-watani*), a coalition of several political parties that were united by their opposition to Morsi's presidency and the MB's involvement in the shaping of the new dispensation. However, this group had difficulties agreeing on an effective plan of action.

In the meantime, the public arena was being altered by a new, anonymous organization comprised of young Egyptians who were unaffiliated with any particular party. This "start-up" embarked on a grass roots campaign, which was called "rebellion" (*tamarrūd*), to unseat Muhammad Morsi. Within a few weeks, millions of Egyptians had signed the group's petition calling for early presidential elections. As the drama built up, the campaign's organizers announced that a mass demonstration would be held at the entrance to the presidential palace on June 30—a year to the day that Morsi assumed the helm. Encouraged by their success, the leaders announced the founding of the June 30 Front (*jabhat 30 yuniyu*). Furthermore, they unveiled a road map for running the affairs of state once the Morsi regime was overthrown. As far as the Islamic camp was concerned, these steps were no less than an attempted coup against the democratically elected, legitimate government. Consequently, the president's supporters declared that they would do whatever it takes to thwart this plot. From their standpoint, not only was the fate of the Morsi government at stake but also the future of the entire MB movement.

The Return of the Generals

This nerve-wracking crisis came to a head toward the end of June. Some twenty million people demonstrated throughout the country either in support of or against the president, thereby raising alarm bells that violence and chaos were imminent. As could be expected, Morsi summarily refused to step down. From a legal standpoint, he noted that the constitution stipulates that early elections can only be triggered by the president's resignation. This stance reflected the fundamental difference between how the MB and their political adversaries viewed the situation. Whereas the former argued that the government was constitutionally sound and that Morsi had triumphed in free and fair elections, the latter maintained that in these extraordinary times the decisive factor was "legitimacy of the revolution" (*shar'iyat al-thwara*). Put differently, the government is only legitimate inasmuch as it works to bring the revolution's goals to fruition. The army brass eventually called on the feuding parties to reach an understanding within a couple of days, but its arm-twisting did not bear fruit. In a speech to the nation (June 26), Morsi reiterated his determination to remain in office and dubbed his opponents "traitors." Furthermore, he reminded his audience, which included the upper echelons of the military, that, according to the constitution, "the president of the republic is the supreme commander of the armed forces."[13]

Soon after, the SCAF issued an ultimatum whose main thrust was that the generals have lost confidence in the president and are switching their allegiance to the MB's opponents. Forty-eight hours later (July 3), Sisi ordered Morsi to relinquish his post, whereupon the latter was detained in an undisclosed location and held incommunicado. From that point on, the ambitious defense minister reshuffled the playing cards of the January Revolution. Initially unhinged by the military's intervention, the MB leadership quickly regained its bearings and organized a battery of protests demanding Morsi's reinstatement. The movement announced that it would fight tooth and nail against the perpetrators of "the military coup" (*al-inqilab al-ʿaskari*) and called on the judiciary to prosecute those responsible for this crime, foremost among them General Sisi. MB spokespersons accused the organization's political adversaries of being Mubarak's lackeys. Lastly, they claimed that the military commanders were "traitors" who were not only in breach of the constitution but had also betrayed the trust that the president had placed in them.

Immediately following Morsi's dismissal, an interim government was formed and ʿAdly Mansur, the head of the Supreme Constitutional Court, was sworn in as interim president. The newfangled civilian and military leadership declared that it was committed to getting the January Revolution back on the right track. More specifically, the government would advance the revolution's original objectives, restore security, and resuscitate the stagnant economy. However, intentions aside, the deep chasm within Egyptian society rendered it impossible to pursue these goals.

The situation took a turn for the worse on August 14, 2013, when Sisi, the strong man who had latterly been promoted to field marshal, had the security forces brutally disperse a massive sit-in. Already in its sixth week, the demonstration attracted tens of thousands of Morsi's supporters to Rabiʿa al-ʿAdawiyya Mosque in Cairo. During the crackdown, at least 1,150 civilians were killed and some 5,000 are estimated to have been wounded and/or detained.[14] In the weeks to come, thousands of other MB activists found themselves behind bars. Accused of serious offenses, such as treason, the movement's leaders were put on trial. As part of this crackdown, the government officially classified the MB a terrorist organization, ordered the confiscation of its assets and funds, and set out to delegitimize the movement. More generally, a curfew was put into effect in large cities and a rigid "anti-protest law" was enacted for the purpose of stymieing the protests.

Sisi's heavy-handed tactics received accolades from many in the liberal camp, sectors associated with the Mubarak regime, and the vast majority of the local press. Foreign journalists reported that the entire country was stricken with "Sisi-mania." Christened "Egypt's savior," the new commander-in-chief quickly amassed a veritable cult following.[15] The steadily mounting fears among the groups most identified with the January Revolution that the police state was back in business were not far-fetched. To begin, the security forces exhibited little patience for attempts at organizing protests. Human rights groups published reports on widespread abuses, such as the torturing of detainees. In addition, civilian and military courts punished thousands of citizens for failing to comply with the notorious "anti-protest law."[16]

Presidents in the Metal Cage

The prosecution of Mubarak and Morsi were momentous developments in the annals of the January Revolution, as the uprising of 2011 was dubbed in Egypt. Notwithstanding the dubious legal procedures, what stand out most from these political trials are the historical insights that they offer concerning revolutionary transition periods. To this point, both trials were held in civilian criminal courts as per standard Egyptian procedure. In contrast, the cases against the FO's opponents were adjudicated in special tribunals at the behest of the RCC. Similar to the trials held in the tribunals of the July 1952 Revolution, the prosecution of both Morsi and Mubarak were highly political, and their rhetoric helped shape the categories with which the regime and its rivals perceived one another. The serious charges that were put forth by the attorney general and the interrogation of the defendants contributed to the prolonging of the state of emergency that was in force at the time. In turn, the freighted atmosphere justified the SCAF's reluctance to cede the helm as well as the extraordinary measures that the regime took against its opponents. The judicial process also laid the groundwork for a new hegemonic discourse on Egyptian history. Conversely, the defendants, their counselors, and supporters repeatedly exposed the weaknesses in the "official" version of past and present events.

In the immediate aftermath of Mubarak's resignation, a fiery public debate erupted over what to do with the former president. The revolutionaries agreed that Mubarak, members of his family, and senior government officials must be brought to justice. However, there were vast differences over the venue and procedures: What sort of juridical body should prosecute the leaders of the deposed regime? And under which of the country's law codes should they be indicted? One school of thought focused on revenge. Its proponents insisted that the defendants be tried before a revolutionary court that would operate on the basis of the Treason Law, which has remained on the books since the July 1952 Revolution. On the other hand, many Egyptians felt that the trials should be held in a civilian court that adhered to the Egyptian criminal code. In other words, the hearings should exemplify the democratic nature and aspirations of the January Revolution. The SCAF, whose generals still viewed Mubarak as a comrade in arms, ultimately instructed the attorney general to prosecute Mubarak and dozens of other suspects in the state's criminal courts, where the rulings are grounded on the penal code.[17]

The Mubarak trial was presided over by Ahmad Rif'at, one of Egypt's most prominent judges. The hearings, which took place at the Cairo Police Academy, lasted about six months. Following the closing arguments, Rif'at announced that he would need at least three months to digest the thousands of pages of trial minutes and formulate his ruling. This timeframe stands in stark contradistinction to that of the July Revolution's special courts, whose judges usually cranked out harsh sentences within a matter of days. On June 2, 2012, the verdict against Mubarak was unveiled. Convicted of "enabling the manslaughter" of over 850 peaceful protestors, the ex-president was sentenced to life behind bars. Seven months later, though, his defense team successfully appealed to the Court of Cassation, and a retrial opened on May 11, 2013. The so-called trial of the century (*mahkamat al-qarn*) aroused enormous public interest, both domestically and abroad. Its importance clearly emanates from the social and political processes that were triggered by the January Revolution as well as from the symbolism of a former omnipotent ruler brought to his knees by the judiciary.

On November 4, 2013, the trial of Muhammad Morsi got underway. The opening session was fittingly held in the same auditorium as his predecessor's trial. From within the defendants' cage, Morsi demanded a microphone. Upon realizing his voice would remain muted, the incensed ex-ruler shouted: "There is a military coup . . . I am the President of the Republic according to the Constitution, and I am being forcibly detained!"[18] The indictment against Egypt's first freely elected president was replete with serious offenses. Besides treason, Morsi was accused of inciting the security forces to kill demonstrators outside the *Ittihadiya* presidential palace on December 4, 2012. Moreover, he was charged with escaping from prison, with the help of Hamas members who had allegedly broken into the facility. While Mubarak was accused of enabling manslaughter, his successor faced the more serious charge of incitement and direct involvement in the killing of civilians. Other MB leaders, including the General Guide, were also imputed with grave offences during this period. Not one member of the security forces that were involved in the crackdown was so much as charged.

Exactly six decades after the trials at *Mahkamat al-Sha'b*, Egyptian courts once again produced rhetoric that denigrated the MB and justified the draconian measures the regime took against the movement's assorted members. The toppling of President Morsi and the army's intervention in civilian affairs were deemed to be necessary steps, for the MB's actions were liable to ignite a deadly civil war (*fitna*). Generally speaking, the SCAF's prosecution of the organization's leaders is reminiscent of the "vicious cycle" of the mid-1950s trials. Given the state of emergency, so the argument went, there was "no choice" but to remove President Morsi from office and outlaw the MB. Documents and other evidence presented at the trials ostensibly proved that the Islamist movement and its leader posed a tangible threat to Egypt's well-being. The onerous punishments, including hundreds of death sentences that were imposed on MB activists fanned the flames of the "emergency" atmosphere.

At the height of the proceedings against Morsi, a verdict was reached in the Mubarak retrial (on November 29, 2014). The court dropped the main charge against the latter—complicity in the death of hundreds of demonstrators. In practice, Mubarak was neither convicted nor acquitted of this count, as Chief Justice Mahmud Kamel al-Rashidi ruled that the addition of charges against the ex-president to the bill of indictment against the minister of the interior and his subordinates was legally flawed. In addition, the senior officials of the internal security apparatus were fully exonerated of criminal involvement in this case. In short, despite the abundance of evidence documenting the security forces' violence against protestors, not one high-ranking figure was held responsible for the thousands of casualties. The judge did, however, call upon the government authorities to compensate the victims' families. As part of the same ruling, Mubarak was found not guilty of corruption. More than anything else, the dramatic twists and turns in "the trial of the century" attested to the difficulty of shielding the legal process from on-going political developments.

The reactions to the verdict laid bare the unprecedentedly gaping chasms in Egyptian society. Mubarak's well-wishers—the vast majority of whom backed President Sisi—claimed that Rashidi's verdict had done historic justice to an Egyptian hero. As soon as the decision was announced, a spontaneous rally in support of the deposed head of state was held opposite the military hospital in which he is confined. On the other hand, the victims' families and groups identified with the January Revolution were outraged by the court's ruling. Opposition figures argued that the verdict epitomized the fact that the justice system is beholden to the executive branch. The dissidents also proclaimed that they are determined to carry on with the struggle against the restoration of the authoritarian regime. Lastly, the attorney general announced that he would appeal the decision before the Court of Cassation, which has the power to order a second retrial.

Egypt and Beyond

While this study has focused on the transition stage of the July 1952 Revolution in Egypt, the insights gleaned from the two case studies are also germane to other instances of abrupt regime change. Prime examples of such succession include the dramatic events that have been transpiring in the Middle East since December 2010. Of course, local conditions in each society make for a unique tapestry. In other words, developments in one state by and large do not recur elsewhere: Egypt is not Syria; Tunisia is not Libya; and so on. Nevertheless, the despotic regimes that took root in these countries during the post-Second World War era have clear similarities. Roger Owen has deftly described the shared attributes of "presidents for life" in the Arab republics that entered the world stage from the 1950s onward: pervasive centralization, which is exemplified by the public's complete identification of the regime with the president; an all-powerful internal security apparatus that guarantees political stability at the price of serious civil rights violations, by instilling an atmosphere of fear that muffles the local population; a personality cult surrounding the leader; bequeathing of power from father to son; and a venal governing system rife with cronyism.[19]

Hamid Dabashi contends that the successions triggered by the Arab Spring mark "the end of coloniality." The revolutions in Tunisia, Egypt, Libya, and Yemen are not," he contends, "a radical and sudden shift of political power with an accompanying social and economic restructuring of society." On the contrary, they are "historic revolutions" because their fomenters have emphatically jettisoned the systems of rule and ideologies that the Western powers sought to implant in the region. As evidenced by the transformation in political consciousness and the demands for universal rights, the seeds for long-term change have been sown.[20]

The phenomenon of millions of citizens rising up against the oppressive regimes of Ben ʿAli and Mubarak has merited considerable attention in the research literature. Within this framework, scholars have explored various manifestations of these revolutions: street politics; the use of public space; the meaningful role played by media outlets and social networks; the participation of unions, women, and various other sectors; and the emergence of a new vocabulary and political groupings, especially those falling under the rubric of political Islam.[21]

Intentionally or otherwise, an array of scholars from different fields have bolstered Hannah Arendt's pioneering argument that freedom is the ultimate objective of any contemporary revolution and that the decision by an appreciable percentage of the citizen body to join an open-ended, full-blown struggle emanates from the belief that these deeds constitute the start of a new chapter in their country's annals. As Arendt put it in *On Revolution*:

> Crucial, then, to any understanding of revolutions in the modern age is that the idea of freedom and the experience of a new beginning should coincide. . . . What the revolutions brought to the fore was this experience of being free . . . this ever-repeated insistence that nothing comparable in grandeur and significance had ever happened. . . . Only where

> this pathos of novelty is present and where novelty is connected with the idea of freedom are we entitled to speak of revolution. This means of course that revolutions are more than successful insurrections and that we are not justified in calling every *coup d'état* a revolution or even in detecting one in each civil war.[22]

Arendt also contended that revolutions involve a fair share of violence, which insurrectionists resort to pave the way for a new dispensation and usher in an age of freedom.[23] To succeed, then, a critical mass of the population must keep up the fight. This is only possible if the revolutionaries are motivated by a sense of "novelty," which continues to shape their lives even after the ruler is deposed.

In addition, the esteemed philosopher distinguished between the concepts of "liberation" and "freedom." Liberation does not entail a major transformation of the ruling order. Consequently, it does not engender true freedom because the latter cannot be achieved until a new body politic has materialized. Yet another of Arendt's central arguments is that revolutionary situations are characterized by spontaneous action, namely, a lack of both leadership and a well-conceived agenda. Latent in this claim is one of the main differences between a revolution and a coup d'état. Whereas the former gives rise to a new dispensation, the heads of a coup merely replace the government and, more often than not, its head.[24]

As thought-provoking as these insights may be, they do not shed light on the critical issue of the *creation* and *perpetuation* of what Arendt referred to as the sense of "break and rupture from the past." This process commences when people start to believe that the overthrow of the existing government is an attainable goal. In parallel, the ruling order, along with the hegemonic narrative of past and present, is reshaped. At the height of the "revolutionary moment," Arendt observed, "[s]uddenly an entirely new imagery begins to cluster around the old metaphor and an entirely new vocabulary is introduced into political language."[25] The weakest link in this hypothesis is that the staying power of the new image of reality—its conceptualization and emergence as a defining element of the revolution—is far from assured. Therefore, the "new vocabulary" is best viewed as a process. Like many scholars writing about the Arab Spring, Arendt's key argument eschewed the dynamics that shape transition phases, which begin "the day after" the regime's ouster, and the actions of the revolution's helmsmen.

The crux of the enigmatic "revolutionary transition phase" is embodied by two of the more prominent slogans that were voiced during the anti-Mubarak uprising. At first, the demonstrators' general plaint was encapsulated by the call "The people want to topple the president [*al-sha'b yurid isqat al-ra'is*]." On second thought, the masses switched to the following rallying cry: "The people want to topple the regime [*al-sha'b yurid isqat al-niẓam*]." To wit, the legions of protestors intuited that ridding themselves of the president would not suffice if the "regime" were to survive; for as Owen has shown, it is impossible to separate between the "chief" and the "state" in governments headed by "presidents for life." For this reason, the edited slogan became the principal rallying cry of the January Revolution. The toppling of a leader is often a formative event, but the termination of a regime is a process. It is at this juncture that a revolution enters its transition phase. While the efforts to dispose of, say, Mubarak or Bashar al-Assad were bloody affairs, the creation of a new regime has turned out to be a much more complex and painstaking enterprise.

The revolutionary transition period in Egypt, which at the time of this writing is well into its fifth year, is akin to a series of tidal waves, each of which has shaped the country anew. The first was the civil uprising in January 2011. Eighteen days after the Tsunami hit, the thirty-year reign of Hosni Mubarak was over and done with. The second tidal wave struck a year and a half later, when the army overthrew the new head of state, Morsi, and Sisi stepped into the void.

The 2011 uprising was a historical moment that led millions of Egyptians to believe in the possibility of revolution. Expectations aside, the civil uprising and the toppling of Mubarak were just the beginning of a transition phase, the fate of which no one can predict even now, five years later. The unpredictable manner of the transition stage is to determine the fate of any uprising or coup. On the very day in July 14, 1789 when the Bastille was taken, or on July 23, 1952, when King Faruq was ousted, no one could have known that a Great Revolution was born in France or a revolution in Egypt. Despite President Sisi's initial popularity, the army's continued involvement in civilian matters is tenuous. All told, the January Revolution jolted the political awareness of millions of people from different walks of life, particularly Egyptian millennials. Many of them oppose the restoration of the authoritarian regime and fear that Sisi is but another dictatorial pharaoh. Although the field marshal's meteoric rise to power constitutes a major milestone, it is doubtful that this was the last tidal wave of the January Revolution.

APPENDIX I

Decree on the Crime of Treason—Law No. 344 of 1952

In the name of the King of Egypt and the Sudan
Prince Regent
After reviewing the declaration of the Commander-in-Chief of the Armed Forces on December 10, 1952, in his capacity as head of the Army Movement [*harakat al-jaysh*];
And based on what the Prime Minister presented and on the approval of the Cabinet of Ministers, The following is decreed:

Article (1)

In the implementation of the provisions of this law, the perpetrator of a crime of treason is any public employee, whether a minister or not, any member of parliament or of a municipal or rural council or of the directorate councils; and in general, any person holding public office, who committed any of the following acts after September 1, 1939:

(a) Collaborating to corrupt the regime or political life by harming or neglecting the country's supreme interests, or by breaching the law for his own political advantage.
(b) Abuse of power [*istighlal al-nufudh*], even by pretending to have influence, in order to obtain special privileges for himself or for others from any public authority or body or company or institution.
(c) Abuse of power to obtain an appointment in government or a position in a public institution or in any other body or company,

or private company, for himself or for someone to whom he is related through family ties or marriage or political party membership, or to obtain an advantage or a benefit granting him exemption from the applicable rules in such bodies.

(d) Abuse of power to conduct acts to influence directly, or indirectly, the price of real estate, goods, crops, or government securities or securities listed in the stock market or offered for dealing in the stock market, for his own benefit or that of others.
(e) Any act or conduct intended to influence judges or members of anybody legally vested with the authority to adjudicate or to counsel.
(f) [Any act of] interference that is harmful to the public interest, by those who do not have the authority [to interfere], and acceptance of such interference.

Interference by those who are not mentioned in this article shall fall under the crime of treason, if the interferer has exploited his relation to any public authority.

Article (2)

Without prejudice to criminal and disciplinary penalties, treason shall be punishable by one or all of the following measures:

(a) Dismissal from public office.
(b) Ban from membership in both houses of parliament or municipal councils or village or directorate councils.
(c) Revocation of the right to vote or to be elected to any of the bodies stated in [Article 2/b] above for a period of at least five years from the date of conviction.
(d) Revocation of the right to hold public office for a minimum period of five years from the date of conviction.
(e) Revocation of the right to membership in any political party for at least five years from the date of conviction.
(f) Revocation of the right to membership in board of directors of any bodies or companies or institutions that are under the supervision of the public authorities, and of the right to hold any position in such entities for a period of at least five years from the date of conviction.
(g) Revocation of the right to entitlement to pension, wholly or partially.

The Egyptian citizenship may also be revoked from the person who committed treason, and he may be ordered to reimburse the amounts he gained by means of treason. The estimation of the amount [of such reimbursement] shall be decided by the court.

Article (3)

Any perpetrator of the crime of treason shall be judged by a special court [*mahkama khasa*] headed by a judge from the Court of Cessation [*mahkamat al-naqd*] and having, as members, two judges from the Cairo Appeals Court [*mahkamat al-isti'naf*] to be appointed by the Minster of Justice, and four army officers with the rank of no less than a Major, appointed by the Commander-in-Chief of the Armed Forces. The headquarters of this court shall be in Cairo, and its jurisdiction shall extend to all parts of the Kingdom of Egypt.

The General Prosecutor's Office shall prosecute the case before the court.

Article (4)

The case shall be referred to the court based on a decision from one of the Purge Committees [*lijan al-taṭhir*] established pursuant to Decree-Law No. 130 of 1952 on the Purification of the Government Apparatus, or based on a request by the General Prosecution's Office on its own. The president of the court shall determine the date in which the case shall be prosecuted provided that this date shall be within 15 days of the day the indictment was issued.

The defendant shall be notified to appear before the court at least eight days in advance. The defendant has the right to be represented by one lawyer only.

Consideration of the case shall not be deferred more than twice and for a period of no more than a week each time. Judgement shall be pronounced justified by its reasons.

Article (5)

Should the defendant fail to appear before the court despite being summoned and should a lawyer representing him fail to appear before the court, the court shall proceed with the case and shall pronounce its judgement in absentia.

Article (6)

The court's judgements shall not be subject to ordinary or extraordinary appeals.

The judgment shall be published in the Official Gazette and in two wide-circulation newspapers within a week of its issuance.

Article (7)

Without prejudice to the preceding provisions, the applicable provisions of the Code of Criminal Proceedings for Misdemeanors shall apply to the self-removal of judges and objection to judges with regard to reviewing the case and witnesses and other evidence, provided that the court itself will decide on any objection to the judges.

Article (8)

Any person convicted shall be punished for each violation of the provisions of Article 2 [sic] by imprisonment and a fine of no less than two hundred Egyptian Pounds and no more than two thousand Egyptian Pounds or by any [one] of these two punishments.

The same punishment shall apply to anyone who was an accomplice in any manner in the offense [of crime] committed.

Article (9)

Ministers, each according to his competence, undertake to implement the law that shall enter into effect as of the date of its publication in the Official Gazette.

Issued at ʿAbdin Palace on 5 Rabiʿ al-Thani 1372 [December 22, 1952].

APPENDIX II

Decree on the Establishment of the Revolution's Court (1953)

After reviewing Article 8 of the Provisional Constitution, the following has been decided:

Article (1)

The Revolution's Court shall be created as stipulated in the Revolution Command Council decree dated September 16, 1953. The court shall be composed of:

Wing Commander 'Abd al-Latif al-Baghdadi, member of the Revolution Command Council—head;
Major Anwar al-Sadat, member of the Revolution Command Council—member;
Flight Commander Hasan Ibrahim, member of the Revolution Command Council—member.

Article (2)

The Court shall have jurisdiction to examine and adjudicate actions deemed to constitute an act of treason against the homeland [*khiyanat al-watan*], or against its well-being, from within and from abroad; and actions directed against the present government or against the foundation upon which the revolution was instituted. The court shall also examine actions that aided government corruption and enabled [the penetration] of colonialism into the country, and all that has caused the rotting of political life, or the exploitation of influence without taking into account the good of the homeland whether through evading the applicable provisions of the previous constitution or through other similar means, even if such acts were carried out before the present decree came into force.

The Court shall also have jurisdiction to try matters referred to it by the Revolution Command Council whatever these matters may be, even if they have already been [tried] before regular courts or before other judicial authorities, so long as a verdict has not been handed down in the matter. Such regular courts or judicial bodies shall be deemed to have deferred the said case. The case shall thus immediately be referred to the Revolution's Court pursuant to an order from the Revolution Command Council.

Article (3)

The actions tried by the Court shall be punishable by death penalty, life or temporary imprisonment with hard labor, or imprisonment for a period determined by the Court. The Court may order the defendant—in addition to the aforementioned punishment—to reimburse the State's General Treasury for [the harm] resulting from his actions or for the loss of revenues incurred to the General Treasury due to such actions.

The Court may decide to confiscate [*musadara*] all or part of the defendant's assets, if the Court discovered that these were due to an illicit gain.

The Court shall decide the manner in which a judgment is to be executed.

Article (4)

In the headquarters of the Revolution Command Council, an Investigation and Prosecution Bureau shall be established. Military and public prosecutors shall be appointed to this [bureau] by the Revolution Command Council to investigate, file indictments and prosecute pursuant to the jurisdiction of this Court, and they shall have the authority to detain the defendants and hold them for designated periods pending the investigation. Objection to this regulation is not permitted.

Article (5)

The Prosecutor shall notify the defendant of the charges and the trial date at least 24 hours in advance.

A trial may not be deferred for more than once for a period of no more than 72 hours.

The defendant shall appear in person before the Court. Should he fail to do so, he may be subject to arrest and imprisonment. The defendant may represent himself before the Court or he may appoint an attorney to act as his representative concerning all charges brought against him.

Article (6)

The trial shall begin by asking the defendant about the actions attributed to him, then it [the Court] shall hear the Prosecution's witness or witnesses, if any. The Court may hear the witnesses for the defense [*suhud al-naf'i*], if it deems it fit. Then the court shall hear the Prosecutor's statement and the defendant's defense.

The Court may follow another procedural sequence if it deems it appropriate, and objections to the court's stuff or [to] one of its members will not be allowed.

Article (7)

The hearings before this Court will be conducted in a public manner [*bi-tariqa 'alaniya*], unless the Court decides to hold a secret hearing [*jalsa sir-riya*] for reasons that it sees fit. The Court's sentence will be handed down in an open session, and this after its approval [*tasdiq*] by the Revolution Command Council that reserves the right to commute the punishment to a level that it sees fit.

Article (8)

The verdicts of this Court are final and no appeal will be accepted in any way or before any authority whatsoever, and appeals will not be permitted on court procedures or their implementation.

Article (9)

This order shall enter into force as of the date of its issuance.
Cairo, 7 Muharram 1373 [September 16, 1953]

[Signatures]
Muhammad Naguib, 'Abd al-Hakim 'Amr, Anwar al-Sadat, Khalid Muhyi al-Din, Hasan Ibrahim, Husayn Kamal al-Din, 'Abd al-Latif al-Baghdadi, Gamal 'Abd al-Nasser, Husayn al-Shafi'i, Gamal Salem, Zakariya Muhyi al-Din

APPENDIX III

Decree on the Establishment of the People's Court (1954)

On November 1, 1954, The Revolution Command Council issued the following decree establishing a Special Court [*mahkama makhsusa*]:

After reviewing Article 8 of the Provisional Constitution, the Revolution Command Council decided:

Article (1)

The establishment of a court [composed of] the following:

Wing Commander Gamal Mustafa Salem, member of the Revolution Command Council—head;
Major Anwar al-Sadat, member of the Revolution Command Council—member;
Lieutenant Colonel, Husayn al-Shafi'i, member of the Revolution Command Council -member.

The Court shall convene in the headquarters of the Revolution Command Council in al-Jazira, Cairo, or in any other venue or time designated by the Court's president.

Article (2)

The Court shall have jurisdiction to adjudicate domestic or foreign actions that are deemed to constitute treason against the homeland [*khiyana lil-watan*] or are detrimental to its well-being both from within and abroad as well as actions directed against the governing order [*niẓam al-hukm*] or the foundations [*usus*] upon which the revolution was instituted, even if such actions were carried out before the present decree came into force.

The Court shall have jurisdiction to try any person who conceals, by himself or through another person, anyone that abets in any way the acts stated in the previous clause and [was] summoned by the court. In addition [the Court has jurisdiction] over any person helping someone to escape legal prosecution.

The Court has jurisdiction over any case referred to it by the Revolution Command Council regardless of its kind, even if another court or other legal bodies are adjudicating it, provided that no verdict was issued on the matter. Such court or legal bodies shall refer the case to the Special Court as soon as the Revolution Command Council issues the order to refer it.

Article (3)

The acts prosecuted by the court shall be punishable by the death penalty, life in prison, life in prison with hard labor or limited hard labor, imprisonment for various durations, or any other penalties as seen fit by the Court.

Article (4)

An investigating office will be set up in the Revolution Command Council headquarters. The office shall include military representatives and members from the Public Prosecution, headed by Lieutenant Colonel Zakariya Muhyi al-Din, member of the Revolution Command Council, and attorney Lieutenant Colonel Muhammad al-Tabʿi, attorney Lieutenant Colonel Ibrahim Sami Jad al-Haq, attorney Lieutenant Colonel Sayyid Jad, and Mr. ʿAbd al-Rahman Salah of the Public Prosecution office.

They will undertake the investigation, the indictment and the prosecution on behalf of the [Revolution Command] Council with regard to acts that fall under the jurisdiction of the Court. They have the right to arrest the accused and hold them under provisional detention; this right cannot be opposed.

Article (5)

With the knowledge of the Prosecutor, the defendant shall be notified of the charges brought against him and the date of the trial at least twenty-four hours prior to the trial. The trial cannot be postponed more than once and for a maximum of forty-eight hours, even in cases of dire need. The defendant must attend court in person, and in the case of his non-attendance, he shall be subject to arrest and imprisonment.

Article (6)

The Court shall follow the procedures deemed necessary to advance the course of the case's prosecution. No challenge shall be made as to the composition of the court or any of its members.

Article (7)

The hearings before the Court shall be public, unless the Court, for its own reasons, decides to make it secret.

Article (8)

The verdicts [*ahkam*] of the Court are final, and they cannot be appealed by any means, or in front of any authority. It is also forbidden to appeal against the Court's procedures or their implementation.

Article (9)

This decree shall come into force as of its date of issue.
Cairo, November 1, 1954.

NOTES

Introduction

1. *Mahkamat al-Thawra*, vol. 1, 46. See Appendix II.

2. The special courts of the July Revolution also dealt with other cases of public importance, including the trials of the Wafd leaders Mustafa al-Nahhas and Fu'ad Siraj al-Din. However, because the full transcripts of the deliberations in these trials were not published, I chose not to deal with these major cases. I discuss the central importance that I attach to the transcripts of the special tribunals later on in this introduction.

3. It is worth noting that only a few libraries in the world hold the entire collection of these transcripts. Thanks to the efforts of several used book stores in Cairo, I was fortunate enough to acquire the original volumes as well as Kirah's abridged version.

4. *Mahkamat al-Thawra*, vol. 1, 3–4. The comparison with the French Revolution had become common in revolutions of the modern times, including in Egypt. The 1919 popular uprising against British rule in Egypt was coined in the public debate a "revolution" and compared by local writers to the French Revolution.

5. *Mahkamat al-Sha'b*, vol. 3, 483, 718.

6. *Mahkamat al-Sha'b*, vol. 3, 723, 972.

7. *Mahkamat al-Sha'b*, vol. 5, 980.

8. Kirah, *Mahkamat al-Sha'b*, dedication page, no number. The editor interjected his hostile attitude toward the MB in various places throughout this work. For example, the heading of the page that precedes the chapter on the movement reads "Not Brothers . . . Not Muslims" in large font. Kirah, *Mahkamat al-Sha'b*, 31.

9. Stagh, *The Limits of Freedom of Speech*.

10. Levi, "On Microhistory," 107.

Chapter 1

1. The leading purveyor of this approach is P. J. Vatikiotis. In fact, the countless references to his work attest to his status as the preeminent Western scholar of Nasserism. Vatikiotis, *Nasser and His Generation*; Vatikiotis, *Egypt since the Revolution*; Issawi, *Egypt in Revolution*; Kerr, *The Arab Cold War*; Baer, *Studies in the Social History*; Shamir (ed.), *Egypt from Monarchy to Republic*. Vatikiotis's analysis and accounts of the July Revolution are included in the majority of textbooks on the modern Middle East, including those authored by Malcolm Yapp, Albert Hourani, Afaf Lutfi al-Sayyid Marsot, and Arthur Goldschmidt.

2. 'A. Ramadan, *Tahtim al-āliha*; Murad, *Man kana yahkum misr?*; Binder, *The Ideological Revolution*; Dekmejian, *Egypt under Nasir*; Sharabi, *Nationalism and Revolution*; Sayyid Ahmad, *Thawrat al-jiniral*; Mansfield, *Nasser*; Stephens, *Nasser*; Rejwan, *Nasserist Ideology*; St. John, *The Boss*.

3. Klein, " ha-Intelektu'alim ba-mitsrayim ha-natserit."

4. Gordon, *Nasser's Blessed Movement.*

5. Johansen, *Contingency in a Sacred Law*; Asad, *Formations of the Secular*; Salim, *al-niẓam al-qada'i*; al-Bishri, *al-Shari'a al-islamiya*; S. al-'Ashmawi, *al-Shari'a al-islamiya*; Cuno, *Modernizing Marriage*; Skovgaard-Petersen, *Defining Islam*; Hill, *Mahkama!*; Brown, *The Rule of Law.*

6. Their efforts are discussed in greater detail later on in this chapter.

7. al-Sanhuri and al-Shawi (eds.), *Al-Sanhuri*, 287–8.

8. Hafiz, *Dhikkrayati 'an al-thawra.*

9. al-Rafi'i, *Thawrat 23 yuliyu*, 10. For a comprehensive study on modern Egyptian historiography, see Di-Capua, *Gatekeepers of the Arab Past.* The historian Amin Sa'id, who defined himself as a "nationalist," wrote a twenty-three-part series on the history of Egypt, from Napoleon's invasion to the latter stages of the 1950s. Three of the volumes are about the July Revolution. While these books draw heavily on source material, they are informed by an idyllic approach that gives the FO the benefit of the doubt. For example, Sa'id described Egyptian policy during the years of revolutionary experimentation as a long chain of achievements that bolster the exceptional standing of the July Revolution in the annals of the Arab nations. One of these volumes is dedicated "to the great president Gamal 'Abd al-Nasser," who is lionized as the "creator of the Arabs' modern political history and the one who brought it to fruition. You are an honest and loyal *rasul* [emissary] of Arab nationalism. You are the one who liberated the Arabs and delivered them from the oppression of imperialism to the light of freedom." Sa'id, *al-Thawra*, 5.

10. Ra'fat, *Fusul min thawrat 23 juliyu.*

11. Ra'fat, *Dirasat*, 12–13.

12. al-Bishri, *al-Dimuqratiya wa-niẓam*, 74–5, 85–8.

13. al-Bishri, *al-Dimuqratiya wa-l-nasiriya*, 76.

14. al-Bishri, *al-Dimuqratiya wa-niẓam*, 169.

15. Brown, *The Rule of Law*, 44–6.

16. Brown, *The Rule of Law*, 48.

17. Brown, *The Rule of Law*, 57–8.

18. In his important study on colonial Egypt and the 'Urabi rebellion, Cole analyzes the developments that precipitated this urban protest. Between January 1879 and June 1882, discontent and tensions mounted because "Britain and France had decisively entered the arena of domestic Egyptian politics. Policies that might once have simply elicited popular hatred of the viceroy now conjured up anti-European protesters." Cole, *Colonialism and Revolution*, 210. According to Cole, Britain was not simply "drawn into" Egypt by the turn of events, but its penetration was a calculated move "to ensure that a process of state formation did not succeed in creating a new sort of stable order that would end European privileges and threaten the security of European property and investments." Ibid., 17.

19. Asad, *Formations of the Secular*, 235, 240.

20. Asad, *Formations of the Secular*, 216, 227. For a comprehensive review of the modern Egyptian judicial system, see Cannon, *Politics of Law.* A critical review of the common premise that Egypt's khedivial-Shari'a legal system before the reforms of the 1870s was unjust and arbitrary, see Fahmy, "Justice, Law and Pain."

21. Esmeir's overarching claim regarding the "rupture" tends to minimize the historical fact that a certain version of positive law had been in use in pre-modern Ottoman

Empire in the form of *kanuns* and in a more systematic way in the form of nineteenth-century codification, which was evident also in Egypt. The Egyptian (Khedive Sa'id) and Ottoman land codes, for instance, were positive law for all purposes and intents, in addition to other codified laws.

22. While discussing the juridical reforms in which London was interested, Alfred Milner, a British statesman and the undersecretary of finance in Egypt from 1890 to 1892, noted, "Our task, therefore, included something more than new principles and new methods. It ultimately involved new man." Cited in Esmeir, *Juridical Humanity*, 69. On the ignorance of British observers when reporting on local law, see Rubin, "British Perceptions."

23. Esmeir, *Juridical Humanity*, 40–61, esp. 59. This development coincided with a steady decline in the power of the 'Ulama (the educated Islamic legal scholars). Cole, *Colonialism and Revolution*, 38.

24. Esmeir, *Juridical Humanity*, 270–1. Cromer also described the two sides of Egypt's "old" legal order; see Baring, *Modern Egypt*, 316–20, 514–23. However, more recent works have cast serious doubt on these accounts. Fahmy and Peters, "The Legal History of Ottoman Egypt." In her comprehensive study on law in the imperial world between 1400 and 1900, Benton repeatedly shows how the imperial powers asserted their jurisdiction in territories under their control by creating multiple systems of law and jurisprudence within a single expanse. During the modern era, the local sovereignty of the colonies was all but a facade. Benton, *Law and Colonial Cultures*.

25. Esmeir, *Juridical Humanity*, 257.

26. For more on the Mixed Courts, see Brinton, *The Mixed Courts*.

27. Cole, *Colonialism and Revolution*, 235. While many historical studies on the 1881–2 revolt against Khedive Tewfik placed an emphasis on senior commanders and junior officers, Cole focuses on other players, especially the urban populace, along with the structure, organization, and ideology of the different political parties. He contends that 'Urabi headed a farrago of sectors that shared an interest in displacing the ruling elites and putting an end to what they deemed to be colonial occupation. Ibid., Chapters 4–7.

28. Britain's representatives thrust criticism at the special committees' work, arguing that the conduct of a fair trial necessitates public transparency and the right to legal counsel. In the absence of these principles, they opined, it is impossible to determine whether 'Urabi is a political or criminal offender. A report by the British representative at the trial listed the following irregularities: the collection of evidence was flawed; testimony was not given under oath; witnesses were not cross-examined; the chief judge provided testimony against the same defendants that he was adjudicating; and some of the affidavits raised heavy suspicion that the witnesses had coordinated their accounts ahead of time. In addition, a few of the defendants were poorly treated; some were even held in solitary confinement for approximately two months.

29. Cited from Esmeir, *Juridical Humanity*, 248. In Esmeir's view, the 'Urabi trial exposed the "division of labor" between the Egyptian government (whose representatives judged and convicted the rebels) and Britain (whose representatives served as advisers). Attended by hundreds of Egyptian officers, the ceremony stripping 'Urabi of his rank was held at the Qasr al-Nil base, near Tahrir Square (then known as Isma'iliya Square). An assortment of punishments were handed down to the 157 other defendants who were found to have participated in the 'Urabi rebellion.

30. Cannon, *Politics of Law*, 158–62.

31. Esmeir, *Juridical Humanity*, 254.

32. In his memoirs, Charles Coles Pasha, a British officer who served for decades in the colonial apparatus, including a stint as Egypt's inspector-general of prisons, described pigeon hunts in India and Egypt as a most popular form of recreation. Coles, *Recollections and Reflections*, 7–8.

33. R. Owen, *Lord Cromer*, 335–6.

34. R. Owen, *Lord Cromer*, 336. In Owen's estimation, "Cromer realized that a mistake had been made," but nevertheless publically supported the harsh sentences. Ibid., 337.

35. For a standard Egyptian version of the Dinshaway incident, see al-Rafi'i, *Mustafa Kamil*, 197–235.

36. Badrawi, *Political Violence in Egypt*, 41. For a detailed description of al-Wardani's trial, see ibid., 22–47. See also Seikaly, "Prime Minister and Assassin."

37. As cited in R. Owen, *Lord Cromer*, 341.

38. Esmeir, *Juridical Humanity*, 266.

39. Kedourie, "Revolutionary Justice."

40. Brown, *The Rule of Law*, 77–8.

41. Gordon, *Nasser's Blessed Movement*, 182.

42. 'A. Ramadan, *al-Ikhwan al-muslimun*, 247–309. Excerpts from the minutes of the People's Court have been integrated into Egyptian-authored works of history. In his comprehensive study on 'Abd al-Nasser and the bitter struggles his regime waged against domestic rivals, Rif'at Sayyid Ahmad cites extensively from the minutes of Hasan al-Hudaybi's trial, which is discussed in chapter 8. However, like the authors of similar publications, Sayyid Ahmad offers no analysis of the trials' political and legal context. Sayyid Ahmad, *Thawrat al-jiniral*, 216–70.

43. 'A. Ramadan, *al-Ikhwan al-muslimun*, 283.

44. Mitchell, *The Society of the Muslim Brothers*, 157.

45. In his memoirs, which were published some thirty years after the coup, 'Abd al-Hadi claimed that this platform marks the first time he is publically revealing the motives behind his silence throughout most of the trial. *Ruz al-Yusuf* 2839 (November 8, 1982): 36.

46. This narrative was reinforced by MB activists in al-Jazeera's special investigation piece (December 22, 2006) on the failed attempts on 'Abd al-Nasser's life; http://www.aljazeera.net/NR/exeres/870EB471-AFDD-4DBC-88FD-A62629EF0E26.htm#L2. Accusations of conducting a show trial are hardly alien to other societies. See Djilas, *Memoir of a Revolutionary*, 127–30. For example, the American left claimed that the McCarthy hearings were an American show trial. Moreover, they argued that McCarthy was doing exactly what Stalin did with the same goals in mind: to generate public hysteria and fear.

47. Qa'ud, *'Umar al-tilmissani*, 115–25; quote on p. 123. For more on the trials "that were run without any legal [basis]," see the organ of the MB, *al-Da'wa* 30 (November 1978): 34–5.

48. Grunwald, *Courtroom to Revolutionary Stage*, 4.

49. Grunwald, *Courtroom to Revolutionary Stage*, 216.

50. Grunwald, *Courtroom to Revolutionary Stage*, vii.

51. Grunwald, *Courtroom to Revolutionary Stage*, vii. Moreover, Grunwald claims that "the legal outcome" of the Weimar trials "was subordinated to the propagandistic impact,

and the interest of the individual defendants had to yield to those of the party they represented." Ibid., 2.

52. Grunwald, *Courtroom to Revolutionary Stage*, 90.

53. Schmitt, *Political Theology*; Schmitt, *The Concept of the Political*. The exploitation of states of exception is much more commonplace in authoritarian regimes, but the widespread assumption that democratic regimes eschew such means is unfounded. An illuminating example of this is the extraordinary powers that Franklin Roosevelt aggregated over the course of the Second World War, which led to, inter alia, the internment of more than 110,000 people of Japanese descent. Likewise, President Bush took exceptional measures in the wake of al-Qaeda's attacks on September 11, 2001. The same can be said for France's brutal campaign to thwart the FLN's efforts to achieve independence in Algeria. Lastly, Israel has controlled the Occupied Territories for tens of years by dint of emergency regulations. Also, note that Schmitt was the principal theoretician of the Nazi regime. Even the results of the Second World War did not prompt the German jurist to renounce his views.

54. Agamben, *State of Exception*, 1, 5, 39.

55. Agamben, *State of Exception*, 33, 4.

56. Schmitt, *The Concept of the Political*, 36, 26–7. Agamben claims that the friend–foe dichotomy was expressed in the imprisonment of thousands of political rivals and by setting up "special tribunals [that were] authorized to pronounce capital sentences." Agamben, *State of Exception*, 15.

Chapter 2

1. Rafi'i, *Thawrat 23 yuliyu*, 32–3.

2. As described in his memoirs, Muhammad Husayn Haykal attended a meeting of senior politicians from the liberal stream (including the former prime minister, Ibrahim 'Abd al-Hadi). Later on, the participants initiated a meeting with Muhammad Naguib in which they expressed their backing for the coup. The general thanked them for their heartfelt support and added that the military is seeking to advance the very same policy that his liberal interlocutors had been advocating in recent years. Haykal, *Mudhakkirat*, vol. 2, 376.

3. *al-Ahram*, July 28, 1952. The MB's declaration of support was issued only five days after the coup. In so doing, the General Guide hoped to secure a commitment from the military leaders regarding their plans for the future.

4. *al-Masri*, August 20, 1952. A thick fog of uncertainty hung over the country in the aftermath of the military coup. In light of this uncertainty, Ahmad Abu al-Fatah, the editor of the liberal newspaper *al-Masri*, published a series of articles under the heading "Where To?" On September 7, he wrote, "Only God himself knows how happy I was on the day that the coup succeeded. Alongside the king's ouster, my happiness stemmed from the [blessed] movement's determination to safeguard the constitution."

5. Law No. 181 (September 14, 1952). Purge committees were also established in the local councils, pursuant to Law No. 130 of 1952. For an in-depth look at this topic, see Gordon, *Nasser's Blessed Movement*, 68–75.

6. For more on the Kafr al-Dawwar incident, see Gordon, *Nasser's Blessed Movement*, 62–2, 93–5.

7. Rafi'i, *Thawrat 23 yuliyu*, 54–5. Cf., Naguib, *Masir misr*, 101–3; Beinin and Lockman, *Workers on the Nile*, 421–7.

8. Quoted from Jawadi, *Qādat al-shurtah*, 335. As in the colonial period, this apparatus was under the Ministry of the Interior's authority. The Ministry would also control *al-Mukhabarat* (the General Intelligence Service), which was established some two years later. Over the years, the General Investigations unit spread its wrath on the Egyptian populace.

9. Hafiz, *Dhikkrayati*, 90. Laws No. 130 and 132 of 1952 paved the way for the adjudication of state workers who were suspected of corruption. Pursuant to Law No. 181 of September 14, 1952, hundreds of employees were forced into early retirement. For a disquisition on the purge committees' activity, especially their efforts to bring officials of various ranks to justice, see Bishri, *al-dimuqratiya wa-niẓam*, 90–2.

10. In fact, a wide purge within the army and other security apparatuses took place immediately following the coup. See a report in *al-Ahram*, July 27, 1952.

11. Sayyid Ahmad, *Thawrat al-jiniral*, 131. These protestations aside, in early October 1952, the Wafd named Nahhas its honorary president—a position that precluded him from serving in government—and completely removed a number of other senior officials. In so doing, the party hoped to placate the authorities' demands. For an account of the political feud between the Wafd and the FO, see Bishri, *al-dimuqratiya wa-niẓam*, ch. 3; Ra'fat, *Dirasat*, 17–18. Sulayman Hafiz's memoirs well reflect his deep-seated animosity to the Wafd, especially Nahhas. See Hafiz, *Dhikkrayati*, 32, 74–8.

12. Rafi'i, *Thawrat 23 yuliyu*, 51–4. For more on the demand to purge the parties' ranks, see Sayyid Ahmad, *Thawrat al-jiniral*, 130–1. Bishri claims that the tightening of government supervision over the parties within the framework of the "purge" seriously trammeled political freedom in Egypt; Bishri, *al-dimuqratiya wa-l-nasiriya*, 69–70.

13. Rafi'i examines the agricultural sector and the imbalance in land ownership. Rafi'i, *Thawrat 23 yuliyu*, 60–8. Compared to the government's expectations, the agrarian reform's achievements were ultimately quite limited. Baer took stock of why the agricultural sector's problems were ignored during the monarchial age. Drawing on statistics, he showed that most of arable land was held by the most affluent ten percent of Egyptian society, either on an individual basis or through companies. Furthermore, these same plots were tended by peasant farmers who were essentially struggling sharecroppers. In other words, the *fellahin* did not own the fields on which they worked and lived. Baer, *A History of Landownership*; Abbas and El-Dessouky, *The Large Landowning*; Adams, *Development and Social Change*.

14. The Republic of Egypt, *Social Development*, 20.

15. On the social background of the FO, see Be'eri, *Army Officers*, 293–9, 305–25.

16. The dispute over the agrarian reform drove the Wafd and the FO even farther apart. The latter claimed that the Wafd leaders' opposition stemmed from the fact that many of them owned vast agricultural estates. In his in-depth discussion on this topic, Salah 'Isá shows that the party tied its support for the legislation to several conditions, one of which was that the reform must be introduced over a five-year period. 'Isá, *Muhakamat*, 65–8.

17. Bishri sheds light on the functioning of the committee that oversaw the agrarian reform. In addition, he argues that this law was the first significant step in the FO's efforts to consolidate power gradually. Bishri, *al-dimuqratiya wa-niẓam*, 85–8. Sayyid Mar'i,

who had earned a reputation as an agricultural expert, was the government's point man on the reform initiative. His appointment bears witness to the fact that technocrats placed themselves at the disposal of the new regime, which even welcomed some professionals who had filled senior roles in the monarchial regime. See Marʿi, *Awraq siyasiya*.

18. For an analysis of the new party law, see Ra'fat, *Fusul*, 74–7. The first clause of the law determines that any association or organization whose calling is "scientific, cultural, or religious" shall not be considered a political party.

19. *al-Masri*, August 20, 1952.

20. Naguib, *Kalimati lil-ta'rikh*, 53–70. For more on the fears that were triggered by these incarcerations, see Ra'fat, *Fusul*, 77.

21. The coup merited the backing of other top jurists, such as ʿAbd al-Rahman al-Rafiʿi and Muhsen ʿAbd al-Hafiz. Conversely, Wahid Ra'fat and Shawkat al-Tuni, inter alios, felt that their colleagues' public support of the coup was detrimental to the legal system, the Supreme Court, and the principles of justice.

22. Klein identified some of the clerisy as opinion makers and journalists. Klein, *ha-Intelektu'alim*, 155–8. For Ramadan's words, see ibid., 155. See also Bishri, *al-dimuqratiya wa-niẓam*, 73.

23. For the document, see *al-Ahram*, July 27, 1952.

24. Hafiz, *Dhikkrayati*, 73–4.

25. For an analysis of this legal opinion, see Bishri, *al-dimuqratiya wa-niẓam*, 73.

26. Hafiz discussed his role in forging the RCC's response to "the legal emergency situation" that was set in motion by the coup; Hafiz, *Dhikkrayati*, 11–12, 21–30.

27. Hill, "Al-Sanhuri and Islamic Law: The Place," 192–9; Bechor, *The Sanhuri Code*; Hamad, "When the Gavel Speaks," 80–4.

28. Further biographical details on Hafiz can be found in the introductory chapter of his memoirs, which was written by the historian Latifa Muhammad Salem. This chapter emphasizes his complete identification with the July Revolution and his role in helping the FO to navigate "the legal emergency situation" in the aftermath of the coup. Hafiz, *Dhikkrayati*, 11–12, 21–30.

29. While clothed in allegory, Sanhuri's diary gives voice to his frustration with the new regime. An example is his poem *al-shahid* (the martyr), which was written the day after the execution of MB activists who were implicated in the attempt on ʿAbd al-Nasser's life. Sanhuri and Shawi, *al-Sanhuri*, 286–7.

30. Sanhuri's beating has merited considerable attention in the literature on the July Revolution. See Brown, *The Rule of Law*, 74–5; Hill, "Al-Sanhuri and Islamic Law," 104.

31. Hafiz's memoirs well reflect his deep-seated animosity toward the Wafd, especially Nahhas. For instance, he repeatedly claims that it played a central role in the monarchy's venal ruling apparatus. Hafiz, *Dhikkrayati*, 32, 74–8.

32. Hafiz, *Dhikkrayati*, 74.

33. Ra'fat, *Dirasat*, 17–18. Elsewhere, Ra'fat noted that he is the author of the legal opinion upon which this memorandum is based. Ra'fat, *Fusul*, 78–9.

34. See Rafiʿi, *Thawrat 23 yuliyu*, 77. An unabridged version of the law can be found in *al-Ahram*, November 14, 1952.

35. For the distinction between "rule by law" and "rule of law," see Neumann, *The Rule of Law*; Tamanaha, *Law as a Means to an End*; Tamanaha, *Beyond the Formalist–Realist Divide*.

36. *Royal Decree No. 43 of 1923*; I used the copy held in the library of the Law School, Harvard University. The two jurists also leaned on article 55 of the constitution whereby the powers of a king who dies without heirs are transferred to the government.

37. Hafiz, *Dhikkrayati*, 89.

38. Hafiz, *Dhikkrayati*, 89–90.

39. As Rubin eloquently showed, legal positivism had considerable roots in the region, going back to the early stages of the Ottoman *Tanzimat* (1839–76). Rubin, *Ottoman Nizamiye Courts*, 83–132.

40. Hafiz, *Dhikkrayati*, 92. For more on the decision to adopt a new constitution and the reactions it elicited, see Gordon, *Nasser's Blessed Movement*, 74–5. The jurist Tariq al-Bishri claims that this move stemmed from an accurate reading of the circumstances. More specifically, it was absurd to continue using the 1923 Constitution in the wake of the coup given the fundamental changes to the governing institutions and the tectonic shift in the distribution of power. Bishri, *al-Dimuqratiya wa-l-nasiriya*, 14.

41. Hafiz, *Dhikkrayati*, 90–2. 'Abd al-Hafiz went on to become a prominent constitutional scholar.

42. In an op-ed piece titled "The Revolutionary Law" (*al-fiqh al-thawri*), Sayyid Sabri, a jurist at Cairo University's Faculty of Law, argued that the Constitution of 1923 had been rendered null and void with the king's ouster. *al-Ahram*, July 31, 1952. In a three-part series, Ra'fat took issue with this contention. *al-Ahram*, August 24, September 5, and September 13, 1952.

43. *al-Ahram*, September 13, 1952. Bishri also describes the political context of the debate over the fate of the 1923 Constitution. See Bishri, *al-Dimuqratiya wa-niẓam*, 71–5.

44. Bishri examines the declaration and the reactions to this declaration in his *al-Dimuqratiya wa-l-nasiriya*, 72–3. The document states that "the constitution was rife with loopholes." Therefore, it is necessary to replace it "with another constitution that will enable the nation to achieve its goals, so that it will duly be the source of government." Ra'fat, *Fusul*, 43.

45. *Mahkamat al-Thawra*, vol. 1, 16–18; for an English version (my translation of the original Arabic text), see Appendix I.

46. The interpretation in the law's codicil notes that the court's special authority and legal procedures are designed to "streamline the process and finish the trial within a short time." *Mahkamat al-Thawra*, vol. 1, 15.

47. *Mahkamat al-Thawra*, vol. 1, 15.

48. For the appendix text, see *Mahkamat al-Thawra*, vol. 1, 12–15.

49. Rafi'i, *Thawrat 23 yuliyu*, 88–9; Ra'fat, *Fusul*, 82–7. The decree did not refer to the MB, on the technical grounds that it was a religious society rather than a political party.

50. Bishri, *al-Dimuqratiya wa-l-nasiriya*, 74–6.

51. All quotes were taken from the Arabic text "*I'alan dusturi min al-qa'id al-'amm lil-quwat al-musallaha wa-qa'id thawrat al-jaysh*."

52. For a discussion on the activity of the parties and the legislature during the monarchial period, see 'A. Ramadan, *Tatawwur al-haraka al-wataniya*; Deeb, *Party Politics in Egypt*; Sayyid Marsot, *Egypt's Liberal Experiment*.

53. The fraying of this unwritten pact stands at the heart of the discussion in chapter 7.

54. The Liberation Rally's members took an active part in pro-regime demonstrations. However, this bid to create an alternative to the multiparty system was an unmitigated

failure. Several years later, the Liberation Rally was replaced by the National Unity (*al-itihad al-qawmi*) organization, but this step did not produce the coveted results either. With the publication of "the National Covenant" (*al-mithaq al-watani*) in 1962, yet another umbrella organization was rolled out—the Arab Socialist Unity (*al-itihad al-ishtiraki al-ʿarabi*). These organizations are fleshed out in al-Jumhuriya al-ʿArabiya al-Mutahida, *al-Tanẓim al-siyasi*; idem, *al-Dimuqratiya*.

55. K. Sayyid, *al-Mujtamaʿa wa-l-siyasa*, 97.

56. *al-Thaqafa*, August 18, 1952. In another article, the union leader described the revolution as a step forward after a corrupt, feudal era. See *al-Hilal* (January 1953): 82–5.

57. At this point significant changes were introduced in the curriculum and textbooks; see Meital, "School Textbooks."

58. For an account of the events leading up to the committee's establishment and an analysis of its composition, see ʿIsá, *Dustur*, 25–34.

59. Rafiʿi, *Thawrat 23 yuliyu*, 79–87. Ra'fat cited extensively from the central subcommittee's report. Most important, he elucidates its member's reasons for proposing a republican regime over a monarchial one. Ra'fat, *Fusul*, 139–44.

60. Rafiʿi, *Thawrat 23 yuliyu*, 79. ʿIsá expands on the discussion that was held on March 24; ʿIsá, *Dustur*, 120–1.

61. Ra'fat, *Fusul*, 144.

62. The committee of fifty continued working for another year or so, but the draft of the constitution that it submitted to the government in August 1954 was a no go, or what ʿIsá referred to, in the title of his book on this very topic, as "a constitution in a trash can" (*dustur fi sunduq al-qimamah*). For decades, the text of this draft proposal did not see the light of day. Therefore, the publication of its full version is one of the achievements of ʿIsá's work. See ʿIsá, *Dustur*, 151–87. Many of the draft's articles pertain to general liberties and civil rights, such as the freedom to organize in political parties and hold demonstrations. Other articles enshrine the principle of the separation of powers. In addition to terminating the RCC, the proposed constitution bars the army from intervening in the political sphere, presidential elections included.

63. In the years ahead, this sort of rhetoric was a key part of the revolutionary discourse. The identification of the revolution with the "people" looms large in the popular culture as well. For example, the song "We Are the People" (*nahnu al-shaʿb*) was performed by ʿAbd al-Halim Hafiz—the so-called voice of the revolution. He first sang this song at the celebrations marking ʿAbd al-Nasser's victory in the 1956 presidential elections.

64. For a handwritten facsimile of the original decree, which includes the signatures of all the RCC's members, see http://nasser.bibalex.org/Decisions/DECcontent.aspx?src=Search&lang=ar. The text can also be found in Rafiʿi, *Thawrat 23 yuliyu*, 97.

65. For the wording of this declaration, see *al-Ahram*, June 19, 1953.

66. *al-Ahram*, June 19, 1953. On this same occasion, Hafiz was appointed to the newly created position of the president's assistant for legal affairs.

67. The monarchial government had interspersed many aspects of its official historical narrative into the Egyptian landscape, most notably central Cairo. With the declaration of the republic, steps were taken to remove the trappings of the "old order" and replace them with symbols of the revolution. Changes to the names of streets and squares, the unveiling of public statues, and ceremonies held in downtown Cairo reflected this turn of

events. These steps manifested the revolution's nascent historical and national hegemonic narrative. They exemplified the RCC's aspirations to draw a clear distinction between itself and the monarchial order. The government's speakers and followers trumpeted the idea of a "new dawn," according to which the republic's path and values were a clean break from the serious flaws of the Muhammad 'Ali dynasty. A case in point was the renaming of the capital's streets and squares, especially in the vicinity of Midan al-Isma'iliya, during the early years of the republic. I have expounded on this development in Meital, "Central Cairo."

68. For an English version of the six objectives, see The Republic of Egypt, *Goals of the Egyptian Revolution*, dedication page, no number.

69. For example, see the article by RCC member Husayn al-Shafi'i in *al-Hilal* (July 1953): 36–7.

70. Ahmad Amin, "Khaw'tir fi al-inqilab al-hadith," *al-Hilal* (July 1953): 24–5.

71. 'Isá, *Muhakamat*, 74–5.

Chapter 3

1. *al-Ahram*, September 16, 1953. The lead headline from the next day's edition of *al-Ahram* boasted that "200 Thousand Egyptians" took part in the rally. Beneath the headline was a large photograph of the square packed with demonstrators. Similar to revolutions in other societies, the new heads of Egypt made intensive use of the public sphere. While Faruq's ouster continued to serve as a source of legitimacy for the FO's hold on government, the RCC was desperate for broad public support for the new regime. In the absence of functioning representative institutions, like political parties and a legislature, which were dispersed following the military coup, the top brass regularly held mass rallies in which they would unveil all sorts of initiatives.

2. *Mahkamat al-Thawra*, vol. 1, 23; *al-Ahram*, September 16, 1953.

3. *Mahkamat al-Thawra*, vol. 1, 27, 29.

4. *Mahkamat al-Thawra*, vol. 1, 33. Several months later, in a speech marking the revolution's second anniversary, 'Abd al-Nasser drew a correlation between remembering the past and the current political struggles: "Some of us are beginning to forget the past, and the hardships we suffered. To forget is to yield to our enemies, and hence to surrender. We must, therefore, always remember the terrible past and to have faith in the revolution." See The Republic of Egypt, *Goals of the Egyptian Revolution*, 59–60.

5. *Mahkamat al-Thawra*, vol. 1, 38–9.

6. *Mahkamat al-Thawra*, vol. 1, 34.

7. *Mahkamat al-Thawra*, vol. 1, 31. He also claimed that, since the Revolution of 1919, lack of unity had worked to the detriment of Egyptian society. For example, this was the reason why the earlier revolution had failed to live up to the "people's expectations." Ibid., 32.

8. *Mahkamat al-Thawra*, vol. 1, 44.

9. *Mahkamat al-Thawra*, vol. 1, 45. A day after the rally, *al-Ahram*'s headline read: "The Establishment of the Court of the Revolution for Judging the Homeland's Enemies." The reports and photographs in this edition concentrated on two principal messages: the unequivocal public support for the leadership's decisions and putting to rest the rumors of discord within the revolution's top ranks. A picture of the RCC's members joining

hands at the end of the rally before thousands of onlookers was prominently displayed. However, this facade of unity soon collapsed. This tense atmosphere served as the backdrop for the court's opening hearings.

10. *Mahkamat al-Thawra*, vol. 1, 46–8. For an English translation, see Appendix II.

11. Born in Kafar Shakr (1918), a village in the region of Mit Ghamar, Muhyi al-Din was a graduate of the Military Academy (1938). He saw action in hard-fought battles in southern Palestine during the 1948 War. The RCC member published, along with ʿAbd al-Nasser, the FO's initial post-coup proclamations and reorganized the secret service (*al-mukhabarat*). Kirah describes him as possessing nerves of steel, a stickler for detail who assiduously plots out his next moves, and a man of action, not talk. Kirah, *Muhakamat al-Thawra*, vol. 1, 11.

12. According to Kirah, Hilbawi (b. 1917) was a dynamic litigator with a reputation for moral rectitude. The son of the Egyptian Bar Association's first chief officer, he stood out thanks to his towering height and fair skin. After twelve years as an attorney and prosecutor, Hilbawi served as a judge in Alexandria. By virtue of his support for the revolution and its goals, he quickly became one of the top officials at the Attorney General's Office. In addition, the jurist sat on the RCC's "purge" committee and served as the prosecutor in the Treason Court. His two colleagues had similar career paths. Kirah, *Muhakamat al-Thawra*, vol. 1, 14.

13. Kirah describes ʿAbd al-Rahman Salah as a reserved man who "respects every opinion, but only believes in his own." Together with Sami Jad al-Haq, a colleague from the Military Prosecutors' Office, he headed the prosecution team in the trial of Fu'ad Siraj al-Din (a prominent leader of the Wafd)—"the largest case that was heard by the Revolution's Court." Kirah, *Muhakamat al-Thawra*, vol. 1, 12.

14. According to a biography of Baghdadi, "he was the first pilot" in the Palestine War "to rain down bombs on Tel Aviv and participated in 'the death flights'—aerial raids of Tel Aviv in the light of day." Kirah, *Muhakamat al-Thawra*, vol. 1, 7. Kirah describes him as possessing peace of mind, a pragmatist, and cautious about jumping to conclusions. After a short stint as defense minister (1953–4), he filled a long row of economic and planning posts. Ibid., viii. Baghdadi's memoirs provide a comprehensive account on the July Revolution but dedicated only a few sentences to the Revolution's Court on which he presided. Baghdadi, *Mudhakkirat*, vol. 1, 79–80.

15. Kirah writes that Sadat (1918–81) was blessed with a pleasant disposition and tended to express himself in a calm manner. He was also "a proficient writer who frequently published his views in writing." Kirah, *Muhakamat al-Thawra*, vol. 1, 8. See also Sadat, *In Search of Identity*. Sadat's memoirs say nothing on his role as a member of the Revolution's Court.

16. *Mahkamat al-Thawra*, vol. 1, 51. Kirah emphasized Ibrahim's sensitivity and trademark smile. The judge's statements attest to his forgiving nature. Moreover, Kirah describes him as a self-effacing person "who does not believe in anything but justice and does not know anything but common sense." It also bears noting that Ibrahim was "drawn to Nazism" during his studies at the Military Academy—"an hour in which he saw Germany and Italy advancing toward progress." Kirah, *Muhakamat al-Thawra*, vol. 1, 9.

17. Marʿi, *Awraq siyasiya*, 174–5.

18. Marʿi, *Awraq siyasiya*, 219.

19. *Mahkamat al-Thawra*, vol. 1, 53–4.

20. In his memoirs, 'Abd al-Hadi claimed that the investigators and prison guards were disrespectful: "No good morning and no hello and how do you do." He also wrote that they were afraid to be seen in his company and thus kept their distance. *Ruz al-Yusuf* 2839 (8 November, 1982): 37–8.

21. Mustafa Mar'i (1902–87) was a prominent jurist during the latter stages of the monarchial era. Furthermore, he served as a member of Egypt's upper house, the Council of Dignitaries (*majlis al-shuyukh*). In this capacity, he placed government corruption and the army's defective weapons in the 1948 War on the public agenda.

22. For the entire text of the bill of indictment, see *Mahkamat al-Thawra*, vol. 1, 63.

23. *Mahkamat al-Thawra*, vol. 1, 66. Kirah notes that, two days before the opening of the trial, the attorney general presented before 'Abd al-Hadi the counts of which he was suspected.

24. *Mahkamat al-Thawra*, vol. 1, 68.

25. Muawi commanded the Egyptian forces in Palestine from the eve of the invasion until November 1948. At this juncture, he was replaced by Sadiq, who served in this capacity until the signing of the Egyptian–Israeli armistice agreement on February 24, 1949.

26. *Mahkamat al-Thawra*, vol. 1, 69–70.

27. *Mahkamat al-Thawra*, vol. 1, 71–2.

28. *Mahkamat al-Thawra*, vol. 1, 75.

29. For the text of this document, see *Mahkamat al-Thawra*, vol. 1, 76–7.

30. *Mahkamat al-Thawra*, vol. 1, 78–80.

31. *Mahkamat al-Thawra*, vol. 1, 82–3.

32. *Mahkamat al-Thawra*, vol. 1, 86.

33. *Mahkamat al-Thawra*, vol. 1, 86–7.

34. *Mahkamat al-Thawra*, vol. 1, 87.

35. *Mahkamat al-Thawra*, vol. 1, 88.

36. *Mahkamat al-Thawra*, vol. 1, 89–91.

37. *Mahkamat al-Thawra*, vol. 1, 92. The court records are completely devoid of references to what transpired in the secret hearing. 'Abd al-Hadi briefly touched upon this session in his memoirs. According to the ex-premier, Zakariya Muhyi al-Din (the minister of the interior and head of military intelligence) claimed that the accused was "in contact with a foreign country." As evidence, he testified that an English diplomat's car was spotted "parking close to your house" on a number of occasions. 'Abd al-Hadi replied that foreign diplomats live on his small block, and they hold a variety of events. Therefore, it could very well be that the British representative was in the vicinity, but not for the reasons the minister believes. At this point, Judge Hasan Ibrahim asked whether the defendant took part in a particular reception at the British Embassy in Cairo. 'Abd al-Hadi answered that he had indeed been there, but it was not a secret meeting. On the contrary, it was an official function that was also attended by Prime Minister 'Ali Mahir, Muhammad Husayn Haykal, and several leaders of the revolution. In addition, the authorities had given him permission to attend the reception. 'Abd al-Hadi then cynically wrote that this was the evidence that was submitted in the closed hearing on "my betrayal of my country, and which led the court to sentence me to death. No other proof beyond this was presented." *Ruz al-Yusuf* 2839 (November 8, 1982): 38–9.

38. *Mahkamat al-Thawra*, vol. 1, 116. The emphases in the citation are my own.

39. *Mahkamat al-Thawra*, vol. 1, 183.

40. *Mahkamat al-Thawra*, vol. 1, 156. Tab'i contended that the Revolution's Court was immeasurably fairer to the opposition than the previous regime: "We heard the testimony on the rough interrogations, torture, and the unjustified incarcerations [during the monarchial era], some of which the accused was responsible for." Ibid.

41. For the bill of indictment against Sunbati, see *Mahkamat al-Thawra*, vol. 1, 191–2; for the charges against Maligi, see ibid., 237.

42. *Mahkamat al-Thawra*, vol. 1, 240–1.

43. *Mahkamat al-Thawra*, vol. 1, 239.

44. *Mahkamat al-Thawra*, vol. 1, 235–6, 241–2.

Chapter 4

1. *Mahkamat al-Thawra*, vol. 1, 109.

2. *Mahkamat al-Thawra*, vol. 1, 96.

3. *Mahkamat al-Thawra*, vol. 1, 92–3.

4. *Mahkamat al-Thawra*, vol. 1, 92–7. Standard procedures required ministers initially to coordinate their appointments with the king via the Prime Minister's Office and then the Royal Divan. 'Abd al-Hadi testified that, in practice, Haidar had "a special standing and everyone knew it." Ibid., 95.

5. Abd el-Nasser, *The Philosophy of the Revolution*, 60–1.

6. In his comprehensive study on the 1948 War, Shakib describes the intense pressure that university students wielded through campus demonstrations and other platforms. For instance, he cites from a memorandum that was formulated by student unions demanding that the government either unleash the army or resign immediately. Shakib, *Harb filastin 1948*, 62–4, 114–16.

7. *Mahkamat al-Thawra*, vol. 1, 141–2. A similar account can be found in 'Abd al-Hadi's memoirs; see *Ruz al-Yusuf* 2831 (September 13, 1982).

8. *Mahkamat al-Thawra*, vol. 1, 98.

9. *Mahkamat al-Thawra*, vol. 1, 98–9.

10. *Mahkamat al-Thawra*, vol. 1, 99.

11. *Mahkamat al-Thawra*, vol. 1, 98–101.

12. For the full text of the manifestos, see Nusayr et al., *Thawrat yuliyu*, 141–3.

13. *Mahkamat al-Thawra*, vol. 1, 102.

14. This embarrassing and mendacious answer bolstered the prosecution's claim as to the corrupt and feckless nature of the previous regime.

15. *Mahkamat al-Thawra*, vol. 1, 102–3.

16. The works of Benny Morris, Avi Shlaim, and Ilan Pappé are among the most prominent in the historiography of the 1948 War. However, none of these scholars refer to the discussions that were held at the upper echelons of the Egyptian government on whether to launch the invasion.

17. *Mahkamat al-Thawra*, vol. 1, 103–5. I refer to this meeting again in my discussion of the Muawi affidavit.

18. Haidar noted that the atmosphere was extremely tense. From the very outset of this hearing, there were noticeable discrepancies between the war minister and the premier in all that concerned the run-up to the war. According to Haidar, the tension heightened when the war minister demanded to present the army's position after Nuqrashi's survey.

19. *Mahkamat al-Thawra*, vol. 1, 110. The military historian Ibrahim Shakib wrote an in-depth study on this topic that is largely predicated on original documents from hearings on the eve of the war. According to his work, a commission of inquiry consisting of representatives from *Majlis al-Shuyukh* was established on May 1, 1948 at the prime minister's behest to examine the merits of launching an invasion. In a secret meeting the very next day, the commission's report was presented before the plenum of the Egyptian Senate. "In entering Palestine," the document read, "the Egyptian army will fulfill the most noble military mission of restoring the peace to the land of peace, and it [i.e., the army] has the courage, the strength, and the preparation that will allow it to fulfill this mission within the constraints set for it by the Egyptian government." Shakib, *Harb Filastin 1948*, 125. During this hearing, Isma'il Sidqi, the controversial former prime minister, expressed the most resolute opposition to entering the war. More specifically, he posed fourteen questions to Nuqrashi that basically cast doubt on the army's readiness for and the state's financial ability to fund a protracted campaign. While expressing his concerns, Sidqi was apparently interrupted time and again with hostile remarks. In contrast, the premier's pro-war statements drew several rounds of applause. For the full version of the protocol, see Kamil, *Harb filastin 48*, 102–26. Shakib notes that some of the parliamentarians were influenced by Sidqi's piercing questions. That said, all the parties, including the oppositional Wafd, ultimately supported the government's proclamation in favor of having the Egyptian standing army join the fray. The next day parliament, the Chamber of Deputies (*majlis al-nu'ab*), passed a similar resolution. Shakib, *Harb Filastin 1948*, 128–9.

20. *Mahkamat al-Thawra*, vol. 1, 103. It must be remembered, Haidar stated, that the prime minister headed a parliamentary coalition and that the latter and the chief of the Royal Divan were members of the same political movement. If the two would have demurred, he continued, they could have convinced the legislature to pass a resolution against an invasion. In addition, had an anti-war front emerged, the king may very well have backed down. Ibid., 110.

21. *Mahkamat al-Thawra*, vol. 1, 104–6, 109–10. Jumay'i enumerates several domestic and external reasons behind the king's decision to enter the war, foremost among them his assumption that it would rehabilitate his standing both in Egypt and among the Arab heads of state. Jumay'i, *al-Asliha al-fasida*, 91–2.

22. *Mahkamat al-Thawra*, vol. 1, 105–6.

23. *Mahkamat al-Thawra*, vol. 1, 140–2. Years later, 'Abd al-Hadi similarly claimed that Nuqrashi had absolutely no desire to enter the fray, stating, "I am certain about this. He feared for the future of the Egyptian army." *Ruz al-Yusuf* 2831 (September 13, 1982). In a historical study on the 1948 War, Jumay'i took stock of Nuqrashi's about-face. Jumay'i, *al-Asliha al-fasida*, 87–92.

24. *Mahkamat al-Thawra*, vol. 1, 142–3. Iskandar testified that over the course of the war Haidar reported to the government that the Egyptian army is carrying the day. In retrospect, these reports were far-fetched.

25. Israel moved its capital from Tel-Aviv to Jerusalem in December 13, 1949.

26. Haykal, *Mudhakkirat*, vol. 2, 321, 336–7. In his memoirs, published after his death, 'Abd al-Hadi confirmed that the decision to enter the war was never duly approved by the government. *Ruz al-Yusuf* 2831 (September 13, 1982): 36–7.

27. For the version of the affidavit that was presented before the court, see *Mahkamat al-Thawra*, vol. 1, 112–15. According to Shakib, Muawi provided factual, accurate, and

trustworthy accounts of the campaign and the situation of the troops on the southern front to the general command in Cairo. After the war, he was promoted to the rank of major general and retired from the military in December of 1950. Shakib, *Harb Filastin 1948*, 593–4.

28. *Mahkamat al-Thawra*, vol. 1, 112.

29. *Mahkamat al-Thawra*, vol. 1, 113–15.

30. In his detailed study, Jumay'i asserted that during this meeting, part of the military command—including the chief of staff—opined that, given the army's present state, it was best to hold off on an invasion. However, the political echelon ignored them. Shakib's comprehensive study deals at length with the Egyptian army's readiness on the eve of the war. His disquisition is based on a memorandum that competently documents the shortage in weapon systems, logistics, and skilled manpower. Shakib, *Harb filastin 1948*, 149–58. Although Chief of Staff al-Mahdi forwarded this illuminating memorandum to War Minister Haidar on March 31, 1948, it is not cited in the historiography of the 1948 War.

31. *Mahkamat al-Thawra*, vol. 1, 115.

32. *Mahkamat al-Thawra*, vol. 1, 157–8.

33. *Mahkamat al-Thawra*, vol. 1, 161-162.

34. *Mahkamat al-Thawra*, vol. 1, 162.

35. *Mahkamat al-Thawra*, vol. 1, 158.

36. *Mahkamat al-Thawra*, vol. 1, 161.

Chapter 5

1. *Mahkamat al-Thawra*, vol. 1, 115–6.

2. Years later, 'Abd al-Hadi asserted that investigations conducted some time before the July Revolution found that he had nothing to do with the General Guide's liquidation. According to the ex-premier, al-Banna was murdered by one Muhammad Wasfi, an army officer who was known to have ties with the palace. Ruz al-Yusuf 2839 (November 8, 1982): 37–8.

3. *Mahkamat al-Thawra*, vol. 1, 161, 167-8.

4. *Mahkamat al-Thawra*, vol. 1, 116-17.

5. *Mahkamat al-Thawra*, vol. 1, 117.

6. *Mahkamat al-Thawra*, vol. 1, 117, 120.

7. *Mahkamat al-Thawra*, vol. 1, 117. This remark concerning the witness's "language" attests to the public relations in which the special tribunal engaged. It is worth noting, this part of the 'Abd al-Hadi trial was broadcast live on Egyptian radio.

8. *Mahkamat al-Thawra*, vol. 1, 121–3.

9. *Mahkamat al-Thawra*, vol. 1, 191–208, 210.

10. Mitchell, *The Society of the Muslim Brothers*, 70–9.

11. Muhammad Husayn Haykal argued that the premier was murdered (December 28, 1948) against the backdrop of the decree outlawing the movement and confiscating its assets. According to Haykal, it was only natural that 'Abd al-Hadi was elected to succeed Nuqrashi as the leader of the Sa'dist party and Egypt's prime minister. In the capacity, he was expected to continue his predecessor's clamp down on both the MB and the communists. Haykal, *Mudhakkirat*, vol. 2, 340–1.

12. *Mahkamat al-Thawra*, vol. 1, 169–76.

13. *Mahkamat al-Thawra*, vol. 1, 124–5. Likewise, the attorney general contended that the overriding purpose behind this wave of arrests was to isolate the General Guide from his confidantes and thus leave him susceptible to an assassination attempt. Correspondingly, the authorities removed the security that had protected Banna for years. Hilbawi also asserted that the main objective behind the vigil was to keep track of the shaykh's movements. Ibid., 170–1.

14. *Mahkamat al-Thawra*, vol. 1, 131–2, 163–4. During the prosecution's closing arguments, Hilbawi claimed that the low point that the regime had reached during 'Abd al-Hadi's tenure as prime minister was epitomized by the fact that the police were ordered to arrest citizens whose only crime was their desire to pay their final respects to Banna by his graveside.

15. Although the witness served as police chief at the time of Banna's assassination, the prosecution did not ask him for any details about the incident. *Mahkamat al-Thawra*, vol. 1, 145–6.

16. *Mahkamat al-Thawra*, vol. 1, 146.

17. *Mahkamat al-Thawra*, vol. 1, 148–9, 152. 'Abd al-Hadi took advantage of his right to remain silent throughout most of the trial. For example, at the end of the previous witness's questioning, he declared, "Your honor, I prefer to keep silent. And you should handle my matter as you see fit. And may Allah be with you." Ibid., 134. By this point in the trial, these words did not garner a response from the judges. In his memoirs, 'Abd al-Hadi devoted an entire chapter to his relations with the MB. "I waged a struggle against the Secret Apparatus of the Brothers by dint of my position and with the objective of maintaining the security and well-being of society." *Ruz al-Yusuf* 2835 (October 11, 1982): 35.

18. Haykal, *Mudhakkirat*, vol. 2, 328–30, 355–7. In his own trial before the Revolution's Court, Karim Thabit, Faruq's close advisor, denied the vast majority of the charges that were leveled at his boss. However, he asserted that the king's purported indiscretions were the primary factor behind his ouster. According to Thabit, the monarch was well aware of these accusations but was determined to carry on with his lifestyle even at the expense of his throne. Thabit, *Mudhakkirat*, 291, 399; *Mahkamat al-Thawra*, vol. 2, 291, 399.

19. Haykal, *Mudhakkirat*, vol. 2, 358–60.

20. *Mahkamat al-Thawra*, vol. 1, 134.

21. *Mahkamat al-Thawra*, vol. 1, 137–8.

22. By the time the treasury committed to the renovations, the prosecutor claimed in his closing arguments, it was obvious that the price had increased fourfold, if not more. The green light was given, he added, despite the fact that the war effort had emptied the state coffers. *Mahkamat al-Thawra*, vol. 1, 179.

23. *Mahkamat al-Thawra*, vol. 1, 138–9.

24. *Mahkamat al-Thawra*, vol. 1, 139.

25. *Mahkamat al-Thawra*, vol. 1, 150. Following the appearance of the first two defense witnesses, the prosecutor called Husayn Ra'fat, the final person on counselor Mar'i's list, to the stand. As noted, the details that these so-called defense witnesses submitted did not help the accused and, for the most part, corroborated the prosecution's case. For example, Ra'fat, the former director-general of the Ministry of the Interior, claimed that the defendant regularly intervened in an illegitimate manner in the office's work during his tenure as chief of the Royal Divan.

26. *Mahkamat al-Thawra*, vol. 1, 153–6.

27. *Mahkamat al-Thawra*, vol. 1, 184. In his memoirs, 'Abd al-Hadi noted that the death penalty was commuted to a life sentence "after Major General Muhammad Naguib, the president of the republic at the time, refused to approve the verdict." *Ruz al-Yusuf* 2839 (November 8, 1982): 39.

28. *Mahkamat al-Thawra*, vol. 1, 188–9.

29. Siraj al-Din's trial opened on December 8, 1953 and lasted approximately three months. The counts against the large landowner and politician of the Wafd were similar to those brought against 'Abd al-Hadi. Wafd speakers lashed out against the revolutionaries for continuing to hold onto power. In response, the RCC persecuted its leaders and activists. For sharp criticism of the regime's campaign against the Wafd, see 'Isá, *Muhakamat*.

30. *Mahkamat al-Thawra*, vol. 1, 208-9. Hamān is the main evil protagonist in the Book of Esther. During the prosecution's closing arguments, Hilbawi invoked Quranic passages that lash out against the corrupt. For example, Ibid., 163.

31. *Mahkamat al-Thawra*, vol. 1, 161–2.

32. *Mahkamat al-Thawra*, vol. 1, 155.

33. *Mahkamat al-Thawra*, vol. 1, 155. The emphasis in the citation is my own. Jumay'i concluded that, given the army's deficiencies in equipment, ammunition, and training, the RCC was justified in its efforts to bring the politicians who embroiled the country in the 1948 War to justice. In his estimation, "the responsibility [for the defeat] was political more than it was military." Jumay'i, *al-Asliha al-fasida*, 91–2.

34. *Mahkamat al-Thawra*, vol. 1, 207.

35. The proceedings also included references to defective lorries and trucks. The claims on that were published soon after the coup. *al-Ahram*, July 31, 1952.

36. Haykal, *Mudhakkirat*, vol. 2, 352–5; Mar'i, *Awraq siyasiya*, vol. 1, 166–70.

37. The four articles that opened the series bore the title "Trial of Palestine War Criminals." See *Ruz al-Yusuf*, June 6, 13, 20, and 27, 1950. 'Abd al-Quddous asserted that information on this topic started reaching his desk right after the war, but he was moved to write these pieces by the heated session in Senate.

38. Kamil, *Harb filastin 48*, 196–7.

39. For example, the historian Falah Khaled claimed that "the reason for the Egyptian army's rout, if one can define it as such, stemmed first and foremost from the defective weapons that they used." As quoted by Jumay'i, *al-Asliha al-fasida*, 95–6.

40. The full text in Rafi'i, *Thawrat 23 yuliyu*, 40–1.

41. A synopsis of this narrative turns up in the autobiography of Sayyid Mar'i, one of the civilians that managed to crack the top ranks of the Nasserite regime. In the chapter "The Explosion of the Defective Weaponry," Mar'i averred that "the rout in Palestine was not military, but first and foremost political." The decision making in the run-up to the war starkly "revealed to anyone with eyes on his head the [magnitude] of the corruption of the political regime in Egypt." Mar'i, *Awraq siyasiya*, vol. 1, 166. For my analysis of the official narratives in Egypt's education system, see Meital, "School Textbooks."

42. Among the sources cited in Jumay'i's work are the personal papers of Husayn Sirri 'Amr, who commanded the Egyptian Border Patrol during the war and was tried by a military court for his part in unscrupulous arms deals.

43. Jumay'i, *al-Asliha al-fasida*, 98–100.

44. For the text of this announcement, see Rafi'i, *Thawrat 23 yuliyu*, 32–3.

45. *Majalat al-Katiba al-Thamina* 4 (October 1953): 46. For an in-depth look at the changes to Egypt's cultural sphere and public space under the republican regime, see Meital, "Central Cairo."

46. Ottoman rule along the Nile was described as a protracted occupation that began in 1517 and ended with the Napoleonic invasion some 280 years later. The *wali*—the Ottoman governors of Egypt—were blamed for the deterioration of government institutions, the economy, trade, and even the nation's culture. This period was regarded as a nadir in the country's annals in one of the first textbooks that was published in the aftermath of the July Revolution. See Jumhuriyat Misr, Wizarat al-Ma'arif al-'Umumiya, *al-Mutala'a al-'arabiya*, 16.

47. Jumhuriyat Misr, Wizarat al-Ma'arif al-'Umumiya, *al-Mutala'a al-'arabiya*, 16. For an identical narrative, see Al-Jumhuriya al-'Arabiya al-Mutahida, *al-Ta'rikh al-hadith*, 39–45.

48. In a nuanced analysis of various publications by these historians, Di-Capua argues "that the hermeneutic process of analyzing historical evidence was replaced with the tendency to demonstrate the historic value of present political acts." Di-Capua, *Gatekeepers of the Arab Past*, ch. 7; quotation, p. 248.

49. *al-Hilal* (August 1953): 40–3; quotation, p. 41. See also his article in *al-Hilal*, February 1953, 20, and his renowned book *Muqaddamat*. For similar claims see: Anis, *Madrasat al-ta'rikh*; Sa'id, *al-Thawra*; Tamawi, *Thawrat*.

50. al-Jumhuriya al-'Arabiya al-Mutahida, *al-Ta'rikh al-hadith*, 45.

51. "The Egyptian Revolution," *Foreign Affairs* 33 (October 1954–July 1955): 200–1. Furthermore, 'Abd al-Nasser emphasized, "The nation had sworn allegiance to Mohammad 'Ali in the attempt to overthrow the rule of the Mamelukes, but Mohammad 'Ali and his descendants unfortunately forfeited this loyalty, embarking on despotic enterprises and usurping the rights of the people." Ibid., 203.

52. The text of announcing Egypt as a republic, see Rafi'i, *Thawrat 23 yuliyu*, 97–8.

53. Khijawi and 'Abd al-'Aziz, *Malik ḍid sha'b*, 102. The motto that the monarchial regime worked against the interests of both the Egyptian state and society was also emphasized in the memoirs of General Naguib. See his *Kalimati*, 11–35. Similar arguments were raised in Hamrush, *Qisat thawrat yuliyu*, vol. 1, 43–52; Rafi'i, *Muqaddamat*, 158–9, 176–215.

54. For a nuance study of the funeral procession, see Gershoni and Jankowski, *Commemorating the Nation*, 203–14.

55. *al-Ahram*, February 11, 1953. Kamil was known as an orator, fervent patriot, politician and editor. He is considered by many as the first to launch a public campaign aimed at evacuating of the British forces from Egypt.

56. *al-Ahram*, November 16, 1953.

57. In one textbook, the pupils are asked to "take stock of the meanings that are included" in an illustration bearing the caption "'Urabi demands the people's rights." al-Jumhuriya al-'Arabiya al-Mutahida, *al-Tilmidh wa-watanihi*, 65–6.

58. al-Jumhuriya al-'Arabiya al-Mutahida, *al-Ta'rikh al-hadith*, 58. "Freer" (*ahrar*) was one of the common nicknames of the FO and the revolutionaries. According to this same outlook, the plot that the khedive hatched with the British and French is solely to blame for 'Urabi's disenfranchisement, his arraignment, conviction, and exile. The authors also tied these developments to the British occupation of Egypt.

59. 'Abd al-Rahman al-Rafi'i, "al-'Urabi wa-muhammad naguib," *al-Hilal*, September 1952, 9–12.

60. Rafi'i, *Thawrat 23 yuliyu*, 10. Sa'id Amin published a series consisting of twenty-three volumes on the annals of Egypt from the Napoleonic invasion until the late 1950s. In the three volumes on the July Revolution, Egypt's new policy is described as a long chain of achievements that buttress the July Revolution's lofty standing in the modern history of the Arab nations. The scholar's admiration for 'Abd al-Nasser is evident in the lengthy preface wherein the revolutionary is described as the "champion of the Arab people, the architect of Arab unity, the leader who significantly advanced the interests of both Arabs and Muslims, and led them to historical victory in the struggle against the oppressed regime at home and the forces of imperialism." Sa'id, *al-Thawra*, 5.

61. *"Makan al-thawra fi ta'rikh misr al-hadith," al-Hilal* (July 1953): 34. Ghurbal also proposed an alternative to the teleological approach that informed the linear narrative of the July Revolution. Moreover, he adamantly contested the FO's representation of Muhammad 'Ali and his successors as inept rulers. As in his books on modern Egypt, Ghurbal averred that it was Muhammad 'Ali's policies and projects that laid the foundations, both in theory and in practice, for the establishment of modern Egypt. He also argued that the collapse of the order that was ushered in by the Anglo-Egyptian Agreement of 1936 was the true catalyst behind the July Revolution. In all likelihood, the primary target audience of Ghurbal's article was not the revolutionaries, who were striving to reshape the picture of the past, but his fellow historians from the opposing camp.

Chapter 6

1. For the draft of the charge sheet, see *Mahkamat al-Sha'b*, vol. 1, 4.

2. For the text of the decree, see *al-Ahram*, November 2, 1954. For a translation to English of "Decree on the Establishment of the People's Court (1954)," see Appendix III.

3. Signed by Muhammad Naguib, the document opens: "Constitutional declaration of the Commander-in-Chief of the Armed Forces and the Commander of the Army's Revolution." It also states that this document is no less than "the constitutional order [*al-niẓam al-dusturi*] by which Egypt shall be ruled during the transitional period." See *"I'alan dusturi min al-qa'id al-'amm li'l-quwat al-musallaha wa-qa'id thawrat al-jaysh."*

4. The constitutional declaration of February 10, 1953, determines that "the judiciary is independent and solely subordinated to the law, and its decisions shall be promulgated and executed in accordance to the law and in the name of the nation" (article 7). See *"I'alan dusturi min al-qa'id al-'amm li'l-quwat al-musallaha wa-qa'id thawrat al-jaysh."*

5. As explained by Egypt's State Information Service, these three colors symbolize the July Revolution's stature as a key turning point in Egyptian history: http://www.sis.gov.eg/en/lastpage.aspx?category_id=18.

6. The new *effendiya* strata, which increasingly prospered from the early 1930s onward, is mostly identified with the sons and daughters of the urban middle class. These educated teens and young adults sought to forge a modern and independent nation-state. They saw themselves as the authentic representatives of Egyptian nationalism. In addition, most of them assumed that these goals could not be achieved without an uncompromising

struggle against British occupation, which they saw as the primary cause behind the hardships faced by the country's steadily growing population. In his penetrating study on the interwar period in Egypt, Gershoni takes stock of the *effendiya* strata's growing impact on the country's political, social, and cultural enterprise. As he demonstrates, its members firmly believed that the time had come for rapid change and that they possessed the wherewithal to bring it to fruition. See Gershoni, *Confronting Fascism in Egypt*, 51–5; Ryzova, *The Age of the Efendiyya*.

7. Kirah, *Mahkamat al-Sha'b*, 13. Although Sadat dedicates a fair share of his autobiography to the July Revolution and the power struggles in which the FO was immersed at the time (including the confrontation with the MB), the book completely ignores his tenure on the People's Court. Sadat, *In Search of Identity*.

8. *Mahkamat al-Sha'b*, vol. 1, 193, 206, 219–20. Cf. Kirah, *Mahkamat al-Sha'b*, 89, 121–4.

9. These citations are taken from *Mahkamat al-Sha'b*, vol. 2, 390; vol. 4, 770–8; Kirah, *Mahkamat al-Sha'b*, 144–5, 154.

10. Kirah, *Mahkamat al-Sha'b*, 16–18. Later on, Kirah expands on senior-level assistants who were active in the court's prosecution office. Ibid., 27–8.

11. See *al-Akhbar*, November 11, 1954.

12. Kirah, *Mahkamat al-Sha'b*, 87. For the responses of those lawyers who were unwilling to represent 'Abd al-Latif, see *al-Akhbar*, November 10, 1954. Once these candidates had turned down the job, the special tribunal, according to Kirah, appointed Nahil.

13. Ramadan, *al-Ikhwan al-muslimun*, 265–6.

14. This line of defense constitutes a mirror image of the narrative that was championed by the regime's speakers, including 'Abd al-Nasser. At a speech in Cairo's Republic Square on October 29, 1954, the prime minister described 'Abd al-Latif as "the poor man for the sake of whom we labored and invested our energy; and for the sake of whose children and for his and his children's future, we are working . . . to remove . . . from a [life of] poverty and provide his children a better education, health, and standard of living than we received." Thereafter, he portrayed the would-be assassin as a victim who fell into the net of the General Guide [Hudaybi] and his accomplices. According to 'Abd al-Nasser, the MB leaders made a fool of 'Abd al-Latif and many other citizens in the name of the Islamic faith. See http://nasser.bibalex.org/Speeches/browser.aspx?SID=273&lang=ar.

15. In this context, Kirah attributes comments to 'Abd al-Latif that do not appear in the official transcripts or, for that matter, any other source. For example, the accused described how Hindawi Duwayr ordered him to assassinate the prime minister, telling him that "the Brothers' leadership has sanctioned the killing of Gamal 'Abd al-Nasser." The defendant went ahead with the plot on the assumption that he was "serving Islam . . . but I did not understand that they had used us [*ghradu*] as pawns, as I have realized from the testimonies here. Had I known, it wouldn't have crossed my mind to act in this way. Praise be Allah that the blood of 'Abd al-Nasser was not spilled by our hands." Kirah, *Mahkamat al-Sha'b*, 208.

16. Kirah, *Mahkamat al-Sha'b*, 82.

17. The testimony of 'Abdallah al-Ris, a history student, before *Mahkamat al-Sha'b* indicates that there were SA activists (like him) who were opposed to the truculent approach that was championed by Ibrahim al-Tayyib. Instead, they called for a nonviolent, public struggle against the treaty with Britain. *Mahkamat al-Sha'b*, vol. 1, 119–23.

18. As per a comprehensive investigation by al-Jazeera Network, the assassin was supposed to work in cahoots with Sa'd Hajaj, a member of his cell. However, a short time before their departure, Hajaj did not receive a weapon, so 'Abd al-Latif set out for Alexandria on his own. *Hadith al-manshiya*, December 22, 2006.

19. At the end of a long day of hearings, Tayyib asserted that the plot came in response to the regime's hostility toward the MB. By this point, Judge Salem's patience was wearing thin: "Your deeds are harming the state in a serious manner and they are serving the interests of Egypt's enemies—the English and Israel. You presented Egypt as weak and on the brink of civil war." Cited from Tayyib's testimony on Monday, November 15, 1954, 7:00 pm. *Mahkamat al-Sha'b*, vol. 3, 487, 492. It bears noting that the Lavon Affair (the exposure of an Israeli spy ring in Egypt involving members of the local Jewish community) was unfolding at that time. The defense attorney made reference to the similarities between the MB's offenses and the acts of sabotage that were carried out by a terrorist cell operated by Israeli intelligence (the perpetrators had recently been captured by the Egyptian authorities). As the defense attorney pointed out, both sides were operating against the government. Ibid., 550–3.

20. *Mahkamat al-Sha'b*, vol. 1, 34. Duwayr then described how the MB had planned to unleash a period of chaos by means of "terrorist acts" [*'amaliyat irhabiya*], with the objective of helping Naguib replace the members of the RCC at the helm. Ibid., 36. Duwayr's testimony was unusual from the standpoint of its length and content. In essence, he incriminated himself and the movement's entire leadership of all the counts that were brought against them. Over the years, many MB activists have claimed that Duwayr had closed a deal with the prosecution. In return for testifying against the movement's leadership and admitting to his own involvement in the conspiracy, the regime would reduce his punishment. Nonetheless, Duwayr was convicted and ultimately put to death. There are those who interpret his cries of "It was not supposed to happen this way" as a grouse against the state for failing to follow through on its end of the bargain. *Hadith al-manshiya*, December 29, 2006.

21. *Hadith al-manshiya*, December 22, 2006. As mentioned, there is reason to believe that Duwayr tailored his account to fit the prosecution's narrative.

22. According to Kirah, whose account is predicated on interviews with officers involved in the interrogation of 'Abd al-Latif, the latter stated that he came to Duwayr's house two days before the assassination attempt. His commander proposed that the job be executed by means of an explosive belt, but 'Abd al-Latif refused. Consequently, Duwayr handed him a gun, bullets, and two Egyptian pounds for travel expenses. The two then parted ways with tidings of success (*'alā barakat Allah*). Kirah, *Mahkamat al-Sha'b*, 81–2. 'Ali 'Abd al-Fatah Nuwyto, an MB activist, claimed that while both were incarcerated in a military prison, 'Abd al-Latif told him that the confession was extracted from him under duress: if the defendant refused to sign, his pregnant wife would pay the price. *Hadith al-manshiya*, December 29, 2006. The first photo of 'Abd al-Latif in the Egyptian press appeared five days after the Manshiya incident. The picture features a skinny man with a swollen face and other signs of torture. *Al-Ahram*, November 1, 1954. Calvert cites from a British Embassy report on the trials. This source describes the poor state of the accused due to the harsh conditions in jail and the torture to which they were subjected. Calvert, *Sayyid Qutb*, 193.

23. The official 'Abd al-Nasser website includes a daily news program of this sort. *Hadith al-manshiya*, http://nasser.bibalex.org/home/main.aspx?lang=ar#. The press

coverage of this trip well reflected the regime's "public relations" campaign. On the front page of the popular magazine *Ruz al-Yusuf* (October 25, 1954) is a caricature portraying RCC officers lined up at an honor guard. Instead of guns, they are carrying letters that together spell the word "Evacuation" (*jalā'*). The picture also contains an *effendi* marching on a red carpet while contently saluting the regime's officials. Ibid. As in previous and subsequent editions of this publication, the *jalā'* treaty garnered immensely favorable press and was depicted as a historic achievement.

24. For the full draft of "'Abd al-Nasser's speech in Manshiya Square on October 26, 1954," see http://nasser.bibalex.org/Speeches/browser.aspx?SID=263&lang=ar. For the interview in the *Sunday Times*, see "Sunday Times Reporter Interview with President Gamal Abdel Nasser," http://nasser.bibalex.org/Common/pictures01-%20sira3_en.htm. On Sidqi's first government and the public protest, see Badrawi, *Ismail Sidqi*, 58–83.

25. *Hadith al-manshiya*, December 29, 2006.

26. *Mahkamat al-Sha'b*, vol. 1, 8–9. From al-Desuki's testimony, it also turns out that, although 'Abd al-Latif's name does turn up in their files, the *mukhabarat* lacked any concrete information on the plot to kill 'Abd al-Nasser. *Hadith al-manshiya*, December 22, 2006.

27. See "'Abd al-Nasser's speech in Manshiya Square on October 26, 1954," http://nasser.bibalex.org/Speeches/browser.aspx?SID=263&lang=ar.

28. As per Kirah's account, 'Abd al-Latif disclosed details about the run-up to the assassination during his interrogation: He reached Alexandria the day before 'Abd al-Nasser's speech and stayed at the al-Sa'da Hotel. In 'Abd al-Latif's words, he opened fire with the objective of killing the prime minister, as per the orders of his handlers. Kirah, *Mahkamat al-Sha'b*, 64–5. An extensive description of the assassination attempt and the perpetrator's capture was given during the prosecution's closing arguments. *Mahkamat al-Sha'b*, vol. 4, 959–62.

29. For a discussion on the MB's investigation of the arson, see *al-Da'wa* 5 (November 1976): 30–1, 57.

30. "Abd al-Nasser's Speech at Cairo's Republic Square on October 29, 1954," http://nasser.bibalex.org/Speeches/browser.aspx?SID=273&lang=ar.

31. Since its inception (December 9, 1952) the new ministry played a major role at deconstructing the old narrative and in disseminating the new one. For a thorough account on the work of this ministry, including the production of the transcripts of the Revolution's Court and the People's Court, see Klein, "*ha-Intelektu'alim*, 30–41; Hamrush, *Qisat thawrat 23 yuliyu*, vol. 4, 44–9; Ayubi, *Bureaucracy and Politics*, 347–9.

32. *al-Ahram*, October 30, 1954.

33. "'Abd al-Nasser's Words to the Delegation of Imbaba Residents, November 4, 1954," http://nasser.bibalex.org/Speeches/browser.aspx?SID=277&lang=ar.

34. Under the heading "School for terrorism" (*madrasat al-irhab*), Kirah expanded on the purview of the "Secret" Apparatus. His description corroborates the position of *Mahkamat al Sha'b*'s Investigations Bureau whereby the military wing was a clandestine operation that possessed a huge arms cache and trained its personnel to kill and carry out sabotage missions. Moreover, according to Kirah, a supreme council, which was comprised of five senior-level MB activists, oversaw the Apparatus's operations. The members of this board demanded that their subordinates maintain absolute secrecy and fully comply with orders from on high. Kirah, *Mahkamat al-Sha'b*, 83–4.

35. Lia, *The Society of the Muslim Brothers*, 180–1. Banna's efforts to defuse the militants had failed, and the MB got involved in a cycle of political violence between 1945 and 1949. Ibid., 270–1. In another comprehensive study on the SA, ʿAbd al-ʿAzim Ramadan surmised that it was established around 1942. However, he suggested that the MB was involved in clandestine activity, albeit to a limited extent, since 1937. Ramadan, *al-Ikhwan al-muslimun*, 44–53. Mahmud Sabbagh, who was among the very first to join the military wing, provides a detailed account on the formation of the Apparatus and implicitly marked 1939 as the year of its inception. Sabbagh, *Haqiqat al-tanẓim al-khass*, 65–7, 126–7. For a disquisition on the movement's views on the Palestine issue and its members' participation in the 1948 War, see ʿUwaysi, *The Muslim Brothers;* Hammudah, *Asrar harakat*, 47–70.

36. For example, a popular weekly magazine opined that the intrigues of the Secret Apparatus were not aimed exclusively at the regime, but against the entire nation. *Ruz al-Yusuf* 1379 (November 15, 1954): 6. Although the movement's activists repeatedly asked the prosecution to use the name Special Apparatus, these requests fell on deaf ears, save for a single episode: During his testimony, the General Guide noted that he is unfamiliar with the term *Secret* Apparatus. Consequently, the prosecutor deigned to refer to the wing as the *Special* Apparatus a few times. *Mahkamat al-Shaʿb*, vol. 4, 823.

37. Ibrahim al-Tayyib, among the heads of the SA, asserted that everyone knew about its existence, so that it can hardly be considered "secret." *Mahkamat al-Shaʿb*, vol. 2, 429–30.

38. *Mahkamat al-Shaʿb*, vol. 1, 52.

39. *Mahkamat al-Shaʿb*, vol. 1, 48–51. Mitchell examines the order to disband the MB and takes stock of the scathing campaign that the regime subsequently waged against Hudaybi, who was publicly accused of plotting to overthrow the government. Mitchell, *The Society of the Muslim Brothers*, 126–7. For the text of the edict and a discussion on its main clauses, see al-Rafiʿi, *Thawrat 23 yuliyu*, 105–14. Mitchell offers an English translation of the order on p. 127, n. 61. The historian Rifʿat Sayyid Ahmad notes that Naguib was the only member of the RCC to oppose this decision. Sayyid Ahmad, *Thawrat al-jiniral*, 202. According to Kirah, one of the high points of the MB–RCC crisis was the regime's declaration that the movement is a political party; for in taking this step, it was essentially ordering the Brothers to shut down—a fate that was imposed on all political parties a year earlier. After releasing this edict, the regime seized the organization's assets and terminated its activities. Moreover, the RCC arrested a number of its senior members, including the General Guide.

40. The exchange appears in Kirah, *Mahkamat al-Shaʿb*, 170.

41. Kirah, *Mahkamat al-Shaʿb*, 34–8. A list of fourteen major acts of sabotage has been appended to the fourth volume that Kirah edited. For more on these operations, see Ramadan, *al-Ikhwan al-muslimun*, 75–6. For the text of the decree that ordered the dissolution of the MB, see Sabbagh, *Haqiqat al-tanẓim al-khass*, 189–91.

42. At the time, a similar assumption prevailed among the Israeli intelligence community. This outlook entangled Israel in the Lavon Affair—a spy and sabotage ring that carried out attacks against targets in Egypt (July 1954) with the objective of forcing Britain to reconsider its decision to withdraw its troops from the country. For a discussion of this affair and its ramifications on Egypt and Israel, see Beinin, *The Dispersion of Egyptian Jewry*, 94–117.

43. ʿAbd al-Ra'uf, *Arghamtu Faruq*, 179–87.

44. *Mahkamat al-Shaʿb*, vol. 4, 847, 854.

45. For biographical information on Hudaybi, see Zollner, *The Muslim Brotherhood*, 21–49. Zollner's study does not solve the riddle of when exactly Hudaybi joined the MB. She wrote: "While there is some verifiable information about his career, not much is known about his early contact with the Brotherhood or the nature of his relations with Hasan al-Banna." Ibid., 22.

46. Hudaybi added that he adjudicated interest-related cases only when there was no choice, for he realized that the secular codes run counter to the *Shariʿa* in this particular matter. *Mahkamat al-Shaʿb*, vol. 4, 808–10.

47. Hudaybi listed a number of "offenses" that the movement committed before he was appointed General Guide. *Mahkamat al-Shaʿb*, vol. 4, 780–9. The reaction of the Apparatus's chiefs, including ʿAbd al-Rahman al-Sanadi, to Hudaybi's appointment sheds light on the personnel changes that he implemented. In his testimony, Muhammad Farghali, a member of the Guidance Office, dwelled on the power struggles over the selection of the next General Guide. He also noted that this struggle spilled over into the first months of Hudaybi's tenure. Kirah, *Mahkamat al-Shaʿb*, 189. For more on this development, see Ramadan, *al-Ikhwan al-muslimun*, 89–101; Zollner, *The Muslim Brotherhood*, 32–3.

48. Talʿat was among the first to participate in the activities that were initiated by Hasan al-Banna, the movement's founder, in the city of Ismaʿiliya. Unlike other senior Apparatus figures (e.g., Tayyib and Duwayr), Talʿat only possessed a rudimentary education. Formerly a carpenter, at the time of the trial he was trading in wheat. For a disquisition on the wing's reorganization under Talʿat's leadership, see Ramadan, *al-Ikhwan al-muslimun*, 153–86.

49. *Mahkamat al-Shaʿb*, vol. 4, 817.

50. Kirah, *Mahkamat al-Shaʿb*, 205–6. For Hudaybi's testimony on Talʿat's words, see *Mahkamat al-Shaʿb*, vol. 4, 843–5.

51. Kirah, *Mahkamat al-Shaʿb*, 200. Mahmud al-Huwatki testified that he chose to leave the MB and the SA when the tension between the movement and the regime boiled over. In response, Salem derisively called him Akhenaten II. Thereafter, the judge called to the stand another MB activist who declared: "Mahmud al-Huwatki, you are a liar"—you never left the MB. At this point, Salem forced Huwatki to swear to Allah that the previous witness was lying. Ibid., 131.

52. *Mahkamat al-Shaʿb*, vol. 4, 824.

53. *Mahkamat al-Shaʿb*, vol. 4, 824. Later on, the General Guide was asked to explain the weapons that the authorities found in the home of Hasan al-ʿAshmawi. He noted that an internal MB inquiry found that "the weapons were transferred to [the movement] by several members of the revolution" during an event that was dubbed the Cairo Fire (or Black Saturday; January 26, 1952), but he was unsure why the arms were not returned to their owner. Ibid., 872–3.

54. Hudaybi also stated that he had refrained from disbanding the SA because he had no idea they possessed arms or harbored violent intentions. *Mahkamat al-Shaʿb*, vol. 4, 868. Senior and low-level MB activists described the SA's mission in a similar fashion. See, for example, the testimony of Muhammad Khamis Humayda, November 16, 1954. Ibid., vol. 3, 558. ʿAbd al-Fatah Nuwyto testified that he joined the SA to "defend the Islamic idea

and fight the English in the canal and the Jews in Palestine." Ibid., vol. 1, 156. Similarly, Isma'il 'Arif Rizq, a twenty-six-year-old agriculture student at Cairo University and an MB activist since 1947, noted that the weapons were slated for operations like the ones that were carried out against the Zionists and the British. Ibid., vol. 2, 415.

55. *Mahkamat al-Sha'b*, vol. 2, 233. Duwayr—among the leaders of the Apparatus's hardline camp—listed similar reasons for joining the National Guard, as did Salah al-Din 'Ali Abu al-Khayr, another senior activist in the SA. Kirah, *Mahkamat al-Sha'b*, 97, 135.

56. *Mahkamat al-Sha'b*, vol. 2, 237–8.

57. *Mahkamat al-Sha'b*, vol. 3, 536; vol. 4, 818.

58. For more on these two issues, see the testimony of Muhammad Farghali, *Mahkamat al-Sha'b*, vol. 4, 751–78.

59. Zollner, *The Muslim Brotherhood*, 16–21.

60. Over the first twenty-five years of its existence, the Brothers expanded into many fields, including professional unions, student associations, welfare, and education. Mitchell, *The Society of the Muslim Brothers*, 170–4. An illuminating survey of the movement's chain of command was presented to the court by Husayn Abu Salem, among the heads of the SA in Cairo. *Mahkamat al-Sha'b*, vol. 2, 334–40.

61. Kirah, *Mahkamat al-Sha'b*, 173–5. In an investigative report that was conducted by al-Jazeera, Mohammed al-Mahdi 'Akef (the General Guide from 2004 to 2010) claimed that, in practice, he ran the Apparatus, not Tal'at. *Hadith al-manshiya*, December 22, 2006.

62. This initiative did not garner the full support of the wing's activists. For example, 'Abdallah al-Ris, a history student and veteran member of the SA, testified that he was opposed to this policy. *Mahkamat al-Sha'b*, vol. 1, 123.

63. *Mahkamat al-Sha'b*, vol. 4, 885.

64. In the court's transcripts, he bears the title *wakil al-ikhwan al-muslimun*, but his actual title was the Deputy General Guide. Hudaybi testified that the authority over the movement's daily operations, including administrative and financial matters, was placed in the hands of Humayda. *Mahkamat al-Sha'b*, vol. 4, 804–6. Also see Kirah, *Mahkamat al-Sha'b*, 200. For a more in-depth discussion of Humayda's appointment and his responsibilities *vis-à-vis* those of the General Guide, see Mitchell, *The Society of the Muslim Brothers*, 87–8.

65. Duwayr also mentioned that internal disagreements hampered the organization's functioning and created an atmosphere in which the Guidance Office's members struggled to present a united front with respect to critical topics on its agenda. The heads of the various departments formulated positions and took actions independently of the movement's leadership. *Mahkamat al-Sha'b*, vol. 1, 46. Muhammad 'Ali al-Nusyri, an activist in the SA, also made note of a number of irreconcilable positions within the organization. Ibid., 88. Likewise, Mahmud al-Huwatki testified that the MB was incapable of forging coherent views on major issues that commanded widespread internal support. Among the examples that he gave was the movement's outlook toward the present government; the question of whether to collaborate with the regime; and, later on, if the movement should resort to violence against the RCC. Ibid., vol. 2, 254.

66. Kirah, *Mahkamat al-Sha'b*, 182–3.

67. *Mahkamat al-Sha'b*, vol. 4, 898.

68. *Mahkamat al-Sha'b*, vol. 1, 10, 30.

69. *Mahkamat al-Sha'b*, vol. 2, 429–32. For a disquisition on the MB's training camps as of 1937, see Ramadan, *al-Ikhwan al-muslimun*, 37–42.

70. *Mahkamat al-Sha'b*, vol. 4, 896, 927.

71. *Mahkamat al-Sha'b*, vol. 4, 757–8.

72. Kirah, *Mahkamat al-Sha'b*, 141.

73. *Mahkamat al-Sha'b*, vol. 3, 697–8.

74. During the fourth session of the trial, another member of the Imbaba cell, 'Ali 'Abd al-Fatah Nuwyto, testified that the group's principal activity was the memorization of Quran verses. The cell's most popular chapter was *al-'Imran*, which constitutes one of the main sources for interpreting the commandment of Jihad. For the perspectives of radical Islamic thinkers on this matter, see Calvert, *Sayyid Qutb*, ch. 7; 'Abd al-Salam Faraj, *al-Farida al-gha'iba*, later issued as a book by Jamal al-Banna, *al-Farida al-gha'iba*. For an English translation of the pamphlet with introductory chapters, see Jansen, *The Neglected Duty*.

75. *Mahkamat al-Sha'b*, vol. 1, 8–9, 13, 18–21.

76. *Mahkamat al-Sha'b*, vol. 1, 23; Kirah, *Mahkamat al-Sha'b*, 87.

Chapter 7

1. Schmitt, *The Concept of the Political*, 26–7.

2. Killearn, *The Killearn Diaries*, 209–13. For a comprehensive discussion of the February 4 episode, see Ramadan, *Tatawwur al-haraka al-wataniya*, vol. 4, 125–218; Smith, "4 February 1942"; Jankowski, "The View from the Embassy"; H. 'Abd al-Nasir, *Britain and the Egyptian Nationalist Movement*, 69–90.

3. Abd al-Nasser, *The Philosophy of the Revolution*, 16. 'Abd al-Nasser's description mirrored the FO's new narrative on the February 1942 incident. For a comprehensive historical account, see Ramadan, *Tatawwur al-haraka al-wataniya*, vol. 4, 192–218. Despite fundamental differences, the MB under Banna cooperated with the Nahhas cabinet of 1942–4. Lia, *The Society of the Muslim Brothers*, 268–9.

4. On the establishment of the MB and its diverse array of activities during the first twenty years of its existence, see Lia, *The Society of the Muslim Brothers*; Mitchell, *The Society of the Muslim Brothers*, 1–79.

5. 'Umar al-Tilmissani, who would go on to become the third General Guide, referred to the movement's operations in Palestine at length in his autobiography: Qa'ud, *'Umar al-tilmissani*, 59–71. 'Abd al-Ra'uf, a member of the FO, commanded a battalion (*katiba*) of MB volunteers. In his autobiography, he expanded on both their training and the battles in which they took part. 'Abd al-Ra'uf, *Arghamtu faruq*, 47–59.

6. For the statements by the MB's founder see al-Banna, *Majmu'at rasa'il*. For Althusser's thesis and a discussion on his contribution, see Althusser, "Ideology and Ideological State Apparatus"; Jameson, *The Political Unconscious*.

7. Zubaida, *Islam, the People and the State*, 155.

8. The manifestos that both the MB and the FO published attest to the similarities between their views. For the original wording of the FO's manifestos, see Nusayr et al., *Thawrat yuliyu*, 141–3, 223–5. Compare with MB manifestos, ibid., 242–6.

9. Gordon, *Nasser's Blessed Movement*, 44–5. Gordon claims that "by 1948 this activity lapsed," and officers who were in touch with the MB "did so on a purely personal basis." He argues that "Nasser secretly helped train irregulars." When 'Abd al-Nasser

established the core of the FO in late 1949, he "turned first to four comrades from his cell in the Muslim Brotherhood." Ibid, 47.

10. 'Abd al-Ra'uf describes how he was forced to retire from the army due to his past support for the MB. A short time later, he was detained and tried before a military tribunal (May 1954). After making up his mind to escape, he got in touch with MB officials who helped the officer and his family. While on the run, 'Abd al-Ra'uf was put up for some time at Hindawi Duwayr's home in Imbaba. 'Abd al-Ra'uf, *Arghamtu faruq*, 41–6, 63–8. For a similar account by another member of this group, who would eventually joined the FO, see Hammudah, *Asrar harakat*, 25–37. Hammudah listed the names of seven army officers, including 'Abd al-Nasser, who took an oath to join the SA and subsequently joined the FO; ibid., 33–7. In her memoirs, Tahiya 'Abd al-Nasser recalled helping her spouse hide an assortment of weapons in their home during this period. Alongside pistols and bombs, which were ordinarily stored in closets, they concealed large pieces in a special room "where they would remain for [only] a short time. . . . After a day or two they would disappear and I would calm down, but others would immediately arrive." On one occasion, "Gamal told me that the weapons I saw in the house were transported to the Suez Canal and other places that the British were present in order to kill them and cause them to fear that their lives are in jeopardy in our country. And he added that [operational] plans are established in our home, and whoever goes out to [fight in] Suez passes through him before departing." T. J. 'Abd al-Nasir, *Dhikkrayat*, 45–8. It is unclear as to when 'Abd al-Nasser hid weapons in his home, as Tahiya's account does not provide dates.

11. Zollner, *The Muslim Brotherhood*, 26.

12. For the citations from the autobiography, see Sadat, *In Search of Identity*, 22–4, 59, 69–70. With respect to Sadat's support for the MB, he noted: "Let me put [it] on record here, incidentally, that I had joined every single political party in Egypt, either out of curiosity or in [the] hope that it might provide a way out of our predicament." Ibid., 59. Officer Hammudah reflected on a meeting that he had with Banna under similar circumstances: "I was completely persuaded by the Islamic thought as it was explained to me by the imam, the martyr Hasan al-Banna, and I was determined to operate within the framework of the Muslim Brothers association to achieve the goals of the revival of Islam's glory and the liberation of our land." Hammudah, *Asrar harakat*, 31.

13. Sadat expounded on this affair in his memoirs; Sadat, *In Search of Identity*, 59. According to his account, he was released after the judge ruled that he was "not guilty;" ibid., 92. For an account of 'Uthman's involvement in the intricate web of relations between Egypt and Great Britain as well as a description of his assassination, see Hamouda, "The Reed Phenomenon," 120–4.

14. Be'eri, *Army Officers*, 78, 86–8.

15. In his memoirs, Tilmissani expanded on the coordination between the leaders of the revolution, including 'Abd al-Nasser, and the MB. From his standpoint, the decision by those officers who were members of the MB not to insist on joining the FO's leadership ranks was a big mistake, especially in light of their critical role in the military coup. See Qa'ud, *'Umar al-tilmissani*, 93–5.

16. Ginzburg, "Killing a Chinese Mandarin," 49. He further elaborated on this in his *Wooden Eyes*.

17. In fact, the situation within the movement's ranks was much more complex. While Hudaybi "remained cautious," Zollner argues, "many Brothers welcomed the coup

d'état." This inner tension might explain why the MB only released its official statement backing the "blessed movement of the army" a week after the king's removal. Zollner, *The Muslim Brotherhood*, 25–7.

18. 'Ali Sabri, who held senior positions in the revolutionary regime, including the head of *mukhabarat*, presents the RCC's outlook on the deteriorating relations with the MB. The FO leadership's principal argument was that the MB sought to take advantage of the coup for the purpose of forcing its radical agenda on the entire country. See Imam, *'Ali sabri yatadhkar*, 23–39.

19. Zollner, *The Muslim Brotherhood*, 25–7.

20. *al-Masri*, July 31, 1952.

21. Upon submitting the memorandum to the RCC, the MB requested the government's permission to disseminate this communication in public, but the censor turned down the request. References to this missive turn up in various publications, including Mitchell's study. Ghada Osman cited large excerpts from the text. Twenty-five years later, the movement's organ published the full version; *al-Da'wa* 17 (October 1977): 32–4. This edition contains the Hijri date of writing, *Dhu al-Qi'da* 11, 1371, which is apparently the source for those researchers, who have dated it to August 1 or 2, 1952. Osman, the daughter of one of the MB's senior members during the period in question, has examined the memorandum. In her estimation, besides general declarations in favor of social justice, the document recommends measures that specifically pertain to the country's priorities during the March crisis: "The brothers detailed some priorities. First, a thorough cleansing was necessary, with previous politicians tried and prevented from reappointment, the state of emergency abolished, and political prisoners freed. After that, a series of comprehensive reforms had to be carried out. Moral reform had to take place through religious education based on spiritual, ethical and national principles, and government banning of what had been forbidden by Islam, such as gambling, liquor, play houses, and explicit movies and magazines. Constitutional reform needed to take place via a Consultative Assembly that would create a new constitution, benefiting from previous constitutional experience, and reflecting the will of the people and the Islamic dictate that all should be equal before the law." Osman, *A Journey in Islamic Thought*, 112–13.

22. The quotations henceforth are based on the document that was published in the MB's official organ: *al-Da'wa* 17 (October 1977): 32–4.

23. At this early phase of the new government, the MB was mired in a leadership crisis that hindered its ability to function. To wit, in the three and a half years since the murder of Banna, the position of General Guide had yet to be filled and the Guidance Office struggled to impose it authority on all the organization's departments.

24. The regime offered to appoint the MB's Shaykh Ahmad Hasan al-Baquri to a ministerial post. However, Hudaybi insisted on having the movement select its own officials—a demand that RCC rejected. For his part, Baquri accepted the Council's offer and was thus expelled from the organization's ranks. Husayn Abu Salem, a senior figure in the SA, also spoke about the close ties between the two bodies: "On the day that the revolution began, there was full cooperation with the Muslim Brothers." In his estimation, the rift began with the dispute over the inclusion of MB representatives in the new government. *Mahkamat al-Sha'b*, vol. 2, 342. Surveying these developments from the vantage point of the movement's senior officials, Tilmissani believed that the General Guide was correct

in assuming that 'Abd al-Nasser was uninterested in a true partnership with the MB. See Qa'ud, *'Umar al-tilmissani*, 96–100.

25. Rafi'i, *Thawrat 23 yuliyu*, 73. For the full version of the memorandum, see *al-Da'wa* 15 (August 1977): 32–3. According to the original MB charter, the movement is an "Islamic authority" (*hayah islamiya*) committed to disseminating the Islamic faith. Sulayman Hafiz expanded on his efforts to formulate the law dispersing the political parties; Hafiz, *Dhikkrayati*, 74–9.

26. *al-Da'wa* 21 (February 1978): 32–3.

27. *al-Da'wa* 38 (July 1979): 50.

28. Calvert, *Sayyid Qutb*, 182–3. From late 1952 onward, Qutb's suspicions concerning the regime steadily grew. Like many, he feared that the RCC was planning to monopolize the public sphere and short-change the Islamic agenda. His ties with the regime were severed, and he officially joined the MB in February 1953.

29. Gordon, *Nasser's Blessed Movement*, 110–18.

30. In a letter the General Guide sent to President Naguib from his jail cell in March of 1954, he claimed that the decision to dismantle the MB is legally flawed. It was also detached from reality, Hudaybi argued, because it is impossible to disband a movement whose members are linked by a deep commitment to Allah and the dissemination of Islam. "Missive from Hasan al-Hudaybi, the General Guide of the Muslim Brothers to Muhammad Naguib, the President of the Republic," reprinted by *al-Da'wa* 10 (March 1977): 32–3. Most of the detainees were freed after ten weeks behind bars.

31. The text of this announcement can be found in *al-Ahram*, February 25, 1954. For a complete transcript, see *Misr al-Mahrusa* 25 (October 2002): 34–8.

32. Ramadan, *al-Ikhwan al-muslimun*, 133. For the wording of the RCC's declaration, see http://nasser.bibalex.org/Common/pictures01-%20sira.htm#6.

33. *Mahkamat al-Sha'b*, vol. 3, 643–4. In response, Judge Salem claimed that the MB's own institutions fly in the face of the consultation principle.

34. *Mahkamat al-Sha'b*, vol. 4, 739–40, 753–4.

35. *Mahkamat al-Sha'b*, vol. 3, 637. Judge Salem directed a series of questions to the witness aimed at wrenching an admission that the SA not only runs counter to the values of Islam but is also liable to instigate a civil war. Ibid., 638–40.

36. Throughout the proceedings, Judge Salem noted that, upon seizing power, the heads of the RCC advocated restoring parliament once the parties had been purged of reactionary elements. Moreover, he claimed that it became clear during the regime's contacts with the MB that the movement's top brass was actually in favor of extending military rule and suspending parliament for at least ten years. "Citizens," Salem concluded, "this is a dictatorship." *Mahkamat al-Sha'b*, vol. 2, 442, 474.

37. Naguib noted that, although he formally held all the key positions at the time, "in practice all decisions were subject to a majority vote in the RCC." For this quotation and the letter of resignation, see Naguib, *Masir misr*, 125. See also Gordon, *Nasser's Blessed Movement*, 127–56. For a description of the demonstrations, see Shalabi, *'Ishruna yawman*, 10–12.

38. For the full text of 'Abd al-Nasser's announcement on March 25, 1954, see Shalabi, *'Ishruna yawman*, 4–5; *Misr al-Mahrusa* 25 (October 2002): 53–9.

39. The main headline of the March 26, 1954 edition of *al-Ahram* read thus: "Hasan al-Hudaybi, 'Abd al-Qadir 'Awda and Two Hundred Brothers Freed." In the days that

followed, the MB leadership publicly called on all the relevant parties to open talks aimed at resolving the March crisis. Years later, the text of the Guidance Office's initiative was published in the organization's mouthpiece; *al-Da'wa* 10 (March 1977): 34.

40. *al-Masri*, March 26, 1954. A few days later, the newspaper reported that the MB members who had been released from jail were surprised by the strife within the RCC as well as the tribulations that the country was going through. Consequently, these leaders announced that they would attempt to "fulfill their duty" and help rescue the country from this serious crisis. "There is no choice," they asserted, "but to preserve our relationship with the sides to this dispute and to secure a timeout to alleviate the tension." In addition, the paper reported that a MB delegation had met with 'Abd al-Nasser and Naguib. *al-Masri*, March 29, 1954.

41. For a typical personal account on this, see 'Awad, *Li-misr wa-l-hurriya*. Cf. Stagh, *The Limits of Freedom of Speech*.

42. "Letter of Hasan al-Hudaybi, the General Guide of the Muslim Brothers, to Gamal 'Abd al-Nasser," reprinted in *al-Da'wa* 8 (January 1977): 32–3.

43. *Mahkamat al-Sha'b*, vol. 1, 46. Kirah also refers to this dispute over how the movement should approach the RCC; Kirah, *Mahkamat al-Sha'b*, 89. According to Duwayr, the third group may have been headed by the General Guide. However, the witness admitted that he was not privy to all the information concerning the leaders of this camp. Muhammad 'Ali Nusyri, an activist in the SA, also testified on this matter; *Mahkamat al-Sha'b*, vol. 1, 88. In addition, Muhammad al-Huwatki discussed the lack of coherent, movement-wide positions on key issues, such as the mindset of the present government, cooperation with the regime, and, later on, the question of whether to adopt violent means against the FO. Ibid., vol. 2, 254.

44. Kirah, *Mahkamat al-Sha'b*, 154. Al-Tilmissani raised similar claims in his memoirs; see Qa'ud, *'Umar al-tilmissani*, 108–10.

45. *Mahkamat al-Sha'b*, vol. 4, 847–51.

46. *Mahkamat al-Sha'b*, vol. 4, 768–70.

47. Kirah, *Mahkamat al-Sha'b*, 177. On October 8, 1953, the Founding Authority held a marathon session. The main topic was the candidates for the Guidance Office that were put forth by Hudaybi, but the delegates also discussed the movement's budget and its activities. For more on this important meeting, see *al-Da'wa* 41 (October 1979): 44.

48. For a disquisition on how important the issue of relations with Britain was to Egyptian national parties and streams, see H. Abd al-Nasir, *Britain and the Egyptian Nationalist Movement*; Cohen and Kolinsky (eds.), *Demise of the British Empire*; Ramadan, *Tatawwur al-haraka al-wataniya*. For studies on the political and geostrategic level, see Morewood, "Prelude to the Suez Crisis."

49. For the citations from the Hudaybi interview and the Guidance Office's memorandum, see *al-Da'wa* 11 (April 1977): 32–3.

50. 'Abd al-Nasser raised this argument in a speech before members of the Liberation Rally in Cairo on September 5, 1954. *Khutub wa-tasrihat al-ra'is*, vol. 3, 513–17. He expressed similar sentiments in a speech on September 20, 1954. Ibid., 526–9.

51. "Missive from Hasan al-Hudaybi to the Muslim Brothers," reprinted in *al-Da'wa* 9 (February 1977): 42–4.

52. For the text of the Evacuation Treaty, see "*The Anglo-Egyptian Agreement*." President Naguib's glaring absence from the signing ceremony was consistent with his exclusion from the pivotal stages of the negotiations.

53. Husayn Abu Salem, the previously mentioned customs official and veteran activist in the SA, took part in movement-wide senior-level discussions on the treaty's "weak points." Within this framework, a decision was made to "turn the nation's attention to" these flaws by publishing the Guidance Office's memorandum. According to Abu Salem, the MB asked for the government's permission to publish this document, but the censor turned down the request. Nevertheless, "the memorandum was printed at the [movement's] headquarters in the form of a manifesto and circulated among the people." *Mahkamat al-Sha'b*, vol. 2, 345. The witness did not mention who gave the order to distribute this communiqué. Hamed 'Abd al-Fatah Nuwyto's testimony provides some general insights on how the movement printed and circulated its missives. As a student worker at a university printing press, Nuwyto was heavily involved in this process. For instance, the MB activist helped disseminate anti-government material that was critical of the Anglo–Egyptian Treaty. Kirah, *Mahkamat al-Sha'b*, 117–18. While on the topic, it is worth noting that a dispute over the content of the organization's manifestos also erupted between the MB leadership and a few of the SA's operatives. During his testimony, Farghali mentioned that he had taken part in a Guidance Office meeting wherein the leaders condemned the dissemination of secret manifestos. As part of the tribunal's attempt to document the MB's illegal activities, the witness was asked for his take on the matter; however, Nuwyto's answer bolstered the case that the movement was awash in internal disputes. Ibid., 191.

54. *Mahkamat al-Sha'b*, vol. 1, 10. 'Abd al-Latif was alluding to an earlier Anglo–Egyptian Treaty (signed on August 8, 1936) that allowed Britain to maintain troops and bases in the Suez Canal Zone for a period of twenty years. While the previous agreement put an end to the formal occupation, Laila Morsy claims that, in practice, it enabled London to maintain the status quo. Morsy, "The Military Clauses of the Anglo–Egyptian Treaty."

55. *Mahkamat al-Sha'b*, vol. 2, 472.

56. The details and arguments that were included in this memorandum shed light on how the MB's leaders formulated their positions amid the imbroglio with the regime. *al-Da'wa* 11 (April 1977): 32.

57. Kirah posits that news of these contacts came to the RCC's attention in May 1953. As a consequence, 'Abd al-Nasser issued the following warning to Hasan al-'Ashmawi, a senior MB official: "We will not sit with our hands crossed opposite this behavior, which must cease at once." The next day 'Abd al-Nasser reiterated this point to Khamis Humayda, who promised to forward the message to the movement's top brass. Kirah, *Mahkamat al-Sha'b*, 46.

58. Kirah, *Mahkamat al-Sha'b*, 180, 193.

59. *Mahkamat al-Sha'b*, vol. 3, 597-8, 611-12. Salem's turn to the audience calls to mind scenes from Charles Dickens, *A Tale of Two Cities*, on the revolutionary court in the aftermath of the French Revolution.

60. *Mahkamat al-Sha'b*, vol. 3, 609. Humayda is referring to the Guidance Office's memorandum that was sent to 'Abd al-Nasser immediately following the signing ceremony. The text was reprinted in *al-Da'wa* 11 (April 1977): 32.

61. *Mahkamat al-Sha'b*, vol. 3, 610.

62. For a disquisition on the hegemonic Egyptian narrative of the treaty, see Rafi'i, *Thawrat 23 yuliyu*, 179–95.

63. The ensuing passages from the prosecution's argument are taken from *Mahkamat al-Sha'b*, vol. 4, 894–9, 902–23, 927–44, 958–74.

64. For the passages of the defense's closing arguments cited herein, see *Mahkamat al-Sha'b*, vol. 5, 984–96, 1005–23.

65. Whether intentional, the defense counsel's terminology bears a striking resemblance to section 87 of the Egyptian Penal Code, which pertains to the formation of an armed gang (*'isbah musallaha*) operating against the existing government.

Chapter 8

1. Hudaybi was appointed General Guide on October 19, 1951. According to Zollner, the distinguished judge had steadily advanced through the ranks of the Egyptian "judicial system." From his entry-level judgeship in 1924, he would go on to hold senior posts by the end of the 1940s. For several years he served as Director of the High Court's Department of Public Prosecution and as the Advisor to the Chamber of Appeal. Zollner, *The Muslim Brotherhood*, 22. According to Kirah, Hudaybi was arrested by the police on October 30, 1954 in Alexandria, where he was hiding in a villa. The property was rented under the pseudonym Dr. Hasan Sabri. See Kirah, *Mahkamat al-Sha'b*, 71.

2. *Mahkamat al-Sha'b*, vol. 5, 1025.

3. Carlo Ginzburg takes stock of this problematic phenomenon in his *The Judge and the Historian*, 7–9.

4. For the portions of the prosecution's closing arguments cited herein, see *Mahkamat al-Sha'b*, vol. 6, 1363–1400.

5. *Mahkamat al-Sha'b*, vol. 6, 1399–1400.

6. *Mahkamat al-Sha'b*, vol. 6, 1400.

7. For attorney Sami Mazen's closing arguments, see *Mahkamat al-Sha'b*, vol. 7, 1414–41.

8. *Mahkamat al-Sha'b*, vol. 7, 1428–9

9. *Mahkamat al-Sha'b*, vol. 7, 1429–30.

10. *Mahkamat al-Sha'b*, vol. 7, 1432–3.

11. *Mahkamat al-Sha'b*, vol. 7, 1440.

12. *Mahkamat al-Sha'b*, vol. 7, 1436. In fact, the General Guide adopted a cautious approach to the revolution in the immediate aftermath of the coup.

13. *Mahkamat al-Sha'b*, vol. 7, 1422.

14. For the full text of Hudaybi's statement, see *Mahkamat al-Sha'b*, vol. 7, 1443–6.

15. For the remarks of the deputy attorney general quoted herein, see *Mahkamat al-Sha'b*, vol. 7, 1446–66.

16. *Mahkamat al-Sha'b*, vol. 7, 1457.

17. *Mahkamat al-Sha'b*, vol. 4, 904–5, 916–18. The deputy claimed to possess a report on the MB's manifestos and their dissemination, which was based on the findings from an interrogation of Sayyid Qutb on August 20, 1954. According to the prosecutor, the aforementioned communiqué enjoins activists to do whatever it takes to ready themselves for the difficult struggle against its enemies, including "the rulers of this dear homeland." Later on, the prosecution submitted as evidence an MB publication that was said to contain lies about the government. For example, the document allegedly hinted that the regime was holding secret discussions with Israel over an agreement between the two countries. During the hearings, Qutb was referred to as the person responsible for the movement's publications and a member of the SA. In written testimony made public

after the trial, Qutb vehemently denied these allegations. Qutb, *Limadha*, 76–7. Qutb was sentenced to a life in prison with hard labor. However, he was released from prison after five years due to his poor health, which was exacerbated by the torture he endured over the course of his interrogation. Ibid., 33.

18. For the details and rare photos of the execution, see *al-Daʿwa* 31 (December 1978): 34–5. Cf. Kirah, *Mahkamat al-Shaʿb*, 217. According to a secret report by the British Embassy (dated December 29, 1954), ʿAbd al-Nasser and Gamal Salem disagreed over the punishment. The former was in favor of exhibiting leniency, whereas the judge demanded that the original sentences be carried out in full. *Hadith al-manshiya*, Decemer 29, 2006.

19. For an erudite and illuminating discussion on the artificiality of this sort of branding, see Mahmood, "Is Liberalism Islam's Only Answer?"

20. *Mahkamat al-Shaʿb*, vol. 1, 144–6.

21. Hindawi Duwayr, the assassin's direct supervisor, admitted before the court, "I made a mistake." *Mahkamat al-Shaʿb*, vol. 1, 55. ʿAbdallah al-Ris (a twenty-six-year-old engineering student) expressed regret for having joined the movement and especially for having served in the SA. As a loyal citizen, he claimed, it did not even cross his mind to harm the homeland. When Ris realized that an anti-government bent was taking form, he objected to this approach in writing. He then said that his entire tenure in the MB had been one big mistake. Kirah, *Mahkamat al-Shʿab*, 109–11.

22. *Mahkamat al-Shaʿb*, vol. 4, 828, 887.

23. *Ruz al-Yusuf* 1374 (November 1, 1954): 18.

24. *Ruz al-Yusuf* 1383 (December 13, 1954). A more ambiguous message concerning the nation's future and its revolutionary path is expressed by an illustration that graced the front page of the magazine's Christmas Eve edition. Dressed up as Santa Claus, ʿAbd al-Nasser is carrying a handful of precious gifts: factories, the High Dam, the withdrawal agreement, and more. Next to him is the Egyptian *effendi* stretched out on a bed. The caption beneath reads "Father Gamal: 'You [i.e., the *effendi*] will only be able to use these gifts after awakening from your coma!'" *Ruz al-Yusuf* 1385 (December 27, 1954).

25. *Ruz al-Yusuf* 1378 (November 8, 1954): 6.

26. *Ruz al-Yusuf* 1379 (November 15, 1954): 6.

27. Quran, Sura 4 (*al-nisāʾ*): 137. This front-page illustration graced the following edition of the magazine. *Ruz al-Yusuf* 1380 (November 22, 1954).

28. *Ruz al-Yusuf* 1380 (November 22, 1954): 6.

29. *Ruz al-Yusuf* 1380 (November 22, 1954): 6.

30. *Ruz al-Yusuf* 1380 (November 22, 1954): 9. The weekly continued to deal with the MB leaders' supposed refusal to hold themselves accountable for the movement's actions. For instance, a front-page illustration depicts the prominent defendants standing on their colleague's shoulders; the caption reads "I don't know a thing about the Secret Apparatus!!" *Ruz al-Yusuf* 1381 (November 29, 1954).

31. Like any show trial, these hearings also had a pedagogic dimension, which is a hallmark of modern jurisprudence. For an illuminating analysis of an Ottoman show trial in the 1880s, see Rubin, "The Trial of the Prosecutor Hamdi Bey."

32. Kirah, *Muhakamat al-Thawra*, vol. 2, 263.

33. *Mahkamat al-Thawra*, vol. 1, 45.

34. Ginzburg, *The Judge and the Historian*.

Chapter 9

1. Hamad, "When the Gavel Speaks," 91–146.

2. Within this framework, a controversy was sparked by Tawfiq al-Hakim's small book, *'Awdat al-wa'i* (Return of Consciousness). For a Nasserite response to Hakim's work, see Karrum, *Suqut al-hakim* (The Fall of Hakim).

3. Khalid, *Mahkamat fir'aun*, esp. chapters 11 and 13.

4. For multidimensional studies on the relations between economic growth, income distribution, and poverty in Egypt, see Kheir-El-Din, *The Egyptian Economy*; Farah, *Egypt's Political Economy*, 30–52; Salamah, *al-Infitah al-iqtisadi*; Amin, *Whatever Happened to the Egyptians*, 7–30, 45–54; Abdel Khalek, "The Open Door Economic Policy."

5. *Kifaya*, the catchy slogan that was chosen by the founders of the Egyptian Movement for Change (*al-haraka al-misriya lil-taghyir*), quickly captured the Egyptian public's imagination. On the movement and its slogans, see Kifaya's official Facebook page: https://ar-ar.facebook.com/Kefaya.Movement.

6. Meital, "The Struggle over Political Order."

7. Ghonim, *Revolution 2.0*, 58–121; Khamis and Vaughn, "'We Are All Khaled Said.'"

8. "Meet Asmaa Mahfouz and the Blog that Helped Spark the Revolution," at http://www.youtube.com/watch?v=SgjIgMdsEuk.

9. Herrera, *Revolution*; El-Nawawy and Khamis, *Egyptian Revolution 2.0*; Abu-Lughod, "Living the 'Revolution.'"

10. Shayib, *Daftar al-ghadab*; Hasan, *'Ishtu ma jarā;* 'Abd al-'Alim, *Yawmiyat al-ghadab*; Baybars, *Nisā' min al-maydan*; Sa'dawi, *Nawal al-sa'dawi*; Soueif, *Cairo*; Ashraf, *Liberation Square*; Idle and Nunns, *Tweets from Tahrir.*

11. Hashim, *Durus min thawrat yuliyu*; Waheed Abdel-Maguid, "The 23 July and 25 January Revolutions," *Ahram Online*, July 29, 2012, http://english.ahram.org.eg/NewsContentP/4/48999/Opinion/The--July-and--January-revolutions.aspx; Ahmad Shokr, "Reflections on Two Revolutions."

12. See "Constitutional Declaration 2011." Nathan Brown delves into the legal and political aspects of this crucial document in "Landmines in Egypt's Constitutional Roadmap."

13. President Morsi's last speech in https://www.youtube.com/watch?v=-sxfvuuzxCA.

14. Human Rights Watch, *All according to Plan.*

15. Chakravarti, "From Strongman to Superman."

16. "New Presidential Decree Stokes Fears of State Intervention in Universities," *Ahram Online*, June 25, 2014: http://english.ahram.org.eg/NewsContent/1/64/104762/Egypt/Politics-/New-presidential-decree-stokes-fears-of-state-inte.aspx; "Hundreds of Writers, Intellectuals Endorse Call to Rescind Egypt's Protest Law," *Ahram Online*, July 6, 2014: http://english.ahram.org.eg/NewsContent/1/64/105561/Egypt/Politics-/Hundreds-of-writers,-intellectuals-endorse-call-to.aspx; "Crackdown on Civil Society Groups Now Worse than under Mubarak, Warn Rights Activists," *Mada Masr*, December 19, 2013: http://www.madamasr.com/content/crackdown-civil-society-groups-now-worse-under-mubarak-warn-rights-activists.

17. During the January Revolution's transitional period, thousands of civilians were tried in military courts that were informed by dubious legal proceedings. For example, some of the defendants were tortured during their confinement and interrogation. Many

of these trials ended with long prison sentences. These grave human rights violations contradict the SCAF and the government's statements that normative juridical procedures are compulsory. See Amnesty International, *Broken Promises*, 24–33. Also see idem., *Brutality Unpunished and Unchecked.*

18. Yasmine Saleh and Yara Bayoumy "In Court, Defiant Mursi Says He Is Still Egypt's President," Reuters, November 4, 2013. http://www.reuters.com/article/us-egypt-mursi-trial-idUSBRE9A303P20131104.

19. R. Owen, *The Rise and Fall of Arab Presidents for Life.* Cf. Stacher, *Adaptable Autocrats.*

20. Dabashi, *The Arab Spring*, 5.

21. Amin, *Egypt in the Era of Hosni Mubarak*; Lesch, "Concentrated Power"; El-Houdaiby, "Islamism in and after Egypt's Revolution"; Mehrez, *Translating Egypt's Revolution*; Beinin, "Workers, Trade Unions and Egypt's Political Future"; Sowers and Toensing (eds.), *The Journey to Tahrir*; Ghobashy, "The Praxis of the Egyptian Revolution"; T. Ramadan, *Islam and the Arab Awakening.* For accounts by Egyptian activists who took part in the uprising and the struggles that ensued, see note 10.

22. Arendt, *On Revolution*, 19, 24. The first Arabic translation of *On Revolution*, whose introduction is not without criticism of Arendt's ideas, came out in 1964. Since then, the most illuminating work by an Arab intellectual on this book is Jens Hanssen, "Translating Revolution." In an illuminating article on the dynamics of revolutionary settings, Vaclav Havel described "the power of the masses." He concluded that this power is grounded on the people's refusal to continue abiding by the rules of the game that were forced on them by an oppressive regime. Havel, *The Power of the Powerless.*

23. Arendt, *On Revolution*, 25. Arendt further elaborated on this issue in her *On Violence.*

24. The theoretical issue of what constitutes a revolution is vast. For a comprehensive analysis, see Stone, "Theories of Revolution." For a nuanced study on revolutions in non-Western nations, see Foran, *Taking Power.* For a short summary on the key differences between "revolution" and "rebellion," see Selbin, *Revolution, Rebellion, Resistance*, 10–18.

25. Arendt, *On Revolution*, 39.

BIBLIOGRAPHY

Official Egyptian Publications/Documents

The Anglo-Egyptian Agreement, Cairo, October 19, 1954. Alexandria: Journal du Commerce et de la Marine, 1954[?].

Constitutional Declaration 2011. Cairo: Egyptian Government Services, 2015. http://www.egypt.gov.eg/english/laws/constitution.

al-Dimuqratiya. Cairo: al-Jumhuriya al-ʿArabiya al-Mutahida, 1963.

Dustur 1923. Facsimile. Minneapolis: Human Rights Center, University of Minnesota Law School. https://www1.umn.edu/humanrts/arabic/Egyptian_Constitution/EG-CON.1923-1.pdf

Dustur 1923: Taʿliqat ʿalá mawaḍihi bi-l-aʿmal al-tahḍiriya wa-l-munaqashat al-barlamaniya. Cairo: Matbʿat Misr, 1940.

Goals of the Egyptian Revolution. Cairo: The Republic of Egypt, The Information Administration, 1955[?].

Iʿalan dusturi min al-qa'id al-ʿamm li'l-quwat al-musallaha wa-qa'id thawrat al-jaysh. Facsimile. Minneapolis: Human Rights Center, University of Minnesota Law School. https://www1.umn.edu/humanrts/arabic/Egyptian_Constitution/EG-CON.1953-2.pdf.

Khutub wa-tasrihat al-ra'is jamal ʿabd al-nasir min sanat 1952–1959. Vols. 1–13. Cairo: Matabiʿa Shirkat al-Iʿalanat al-Sharqiya, 1960[?].

Mahkamat al-Shaʿb. Edited by al-Kirah ʿAbd al-Hamid Kamal. Cairo: Shirkat al-Nil lil-Nashr wa-l-Tawziʿa, 1954[?].

Mahkamat al-Shaʿb: Al-maḍbata al-rasmiya li-mahaḍir jalasat mahkamat al-shaʿb. 7 vols. Cairo: Maslahat al-Istiʿlamat, 1954–5.

Mahkamat al-Thawra, 3 vols. Cairo: Matbaʿat Misr, 1953–4.

Mahkamat al-Thawra, 7 vols. Edited by al-Kirah ʿAbd al-Hamid Kamal. Cairo: Maktab Shu'un Mahkamat al-Thawra, 1954–5.

al-Mutalaʿa al-ʿarabiya lil-madaris al-thanawiya. Cairo: Jumhuriyat Misr, Wizarat al-Maʿarif al-ʿUmumiya, 1953.

al-Nashra al-tashriʿiya li-sanat 1953. Cairo: Wizarat al-ʿAdl, 1954.

Royal Decree No. 43 of 1923 on Building a Constitutional System for the Egyptian State. Cairo: ʿAbdin Palace, April 19, 1923. Repr. Translated by International Institute for Democracy and Electoral Assistance. Stockholm: ConstitutionNet. http://www.constitutionnet.org/files/1923_-_egyptian_constitution_english_1.pdf

Social Development under the New Regime. Cairo: The Republic of Egypt, 1954[?].

al-Taʿabiya al-ʿammah wa-l-'amn al-qawmi wa-l-difʿa wa-l-tawarī. Cairo: al-Hayah al-ʿAmmah li-Shu'un al-Matabiʿa al-Amiriya, 1986.

al-Tanẓim al-siyasi. Cairo: al-Jumhuriya al-ʿArabiya al-Mutahida, Maslahat al-Istiʿlamat, 1962[?].

al-Ta'rikh al-hadith lil-watan al-ʿarabi al-kabir lil-saf al-thalith al-ibtid'ī. Cairo: Al-Jumhuriya al-ʿArabiya al-Mutahida, Wizarat al-Tarbiya wa-l-Taʿalim, 1965.

al-Tilmidh wa-watanihi. Cairo: al-Jumhuriya al-ʿArabiya al-Mutahida, Wizarat al-Tarbiya wa-l-Taʿalim, 1961.

Newspapers, Magazines and Media Websites

al-Ahram

Ahram online (English)

al-Akhbar

al-Daʿwa

Foreign Affairs

al-Hilal

al-Jazeera.net

al-Jumhuriya

Mada Masr

Majalat al-Katiba al-Thamina

al-Masri

Misr al-Mahrusa

Ruz al-Yusuf

Sunday Times Magazine (London)

al-Thaqafa

Other Publications

Abbas, Raouf, and Assem El-Dessouky. *The Large Landowning Class and the Peasantry in Egypt, 1837–1952*. Syracuse, NY: Syracuse University Press, 2011.

ʿAbd al-ʿAlim, Hibah. *Yawmiyat al-ghadab: Shahadat haya min mayadin misr al-thawra*. Cairo: Dar al-Hayah lil-Nashr wa-l-Tawziʿa, 2012.

ʿAbd al-Ghani, Mustafa. *Mudhakkirat wa-watha'iq sirriya li-thawrat yuliyu*. Cairo: Atlas lil-Nashr wa-l-Intaj al-Iʿlami, 2004.

ʿAbd al-Hadi, Masʿūd. *al-Thawrat al-haditha fi al-sharq al-awsat*. Cairo: 1959.

ʿAbd al-Halim, Mahmud. *al-Ikhwan al-muslimun: Ru'ya min al-dakhil*. Alexandria: Dar al-Daʿwa, 1985.

ʿAbd al-Nasir, Huda. *Britain and the Egyptian Nationalist Movement, 1936–1952*. Reading, MA: Ithaca, 1994.

ʿAbd al-Nasir, Tahiya Jamal. *Dhikkrayat maʿahu*. Cairo: Dar al-Shuruq, 2011.

Abd al-Nasser, Gamal. *The Philosophy of the Revolution*. Cairo: Dar al-Maʿarif, 1955[?].

ʿAbd Rabbih, Nabih. *Hasan al-Hudaybi: al-Murshid al-thani lil-ikhwan al-muslimun*. Amman: Dar al-Diyā, 1987.

ʿAbd al-Ra'uf, ʿAbd al-Munʿim. *Arghamtu faruq ʿalá al-tanazul ʿan al-ʿarsh: Mudhakkirat*. Cairo: al-Zahra' lil-Iʿlam al-ʿArabi, 1988.

ʿAbd al-Salam, Muhammad. *Sanawat ʿasibah: Dhikkrayat na'ib ʿamm*. Cairo: Dar al-Shuruq, 1975.

Abdel Khalek, Gouda. "The Open Door Economic Policy in Egypt: A Search for Meaning, Interpretation and Implication." *Cairo Papers in Social Science* 2.3 (July 1983): 73–100.

Abdel-Malek, Anouar. *Egypt: Military Society*. New York: Random House, 1968.

Abdel Nasser, Jamal. "Nasser's Memoires of the First Palestine War." *Journal of Palestine Studies* 2.2 (1973): 3–32.

Abu al-Fadl, 'Abd al-Fattah. *Kuntu na'iban li-ra'is al-mukhabarat*. Cairo: Dar al-Hurriya, 1986.

Abu-Lughod, Lila. "Living the 'Revolution' in an Egyptian Village: Moral Action in a National Space." *American Ethnologist* 39 (2012): 21–5.

Aburish, Said. *Nasser: The Last Arab*. New York: St. Martin's, 2004.

Adams, Richard. *Development and Social Change in Rural Egypt*. Syracuse, NY: Syracuse University Press, 1986.

al-'Afifi, 'Abd al-Hakim Mahmud. *Ta'rikh al-ightiyalat al-siyasiya fi misr*. Cairo: al-Dar al-Misriya al-Lubnaniya, 1992.

al-'Afifi, 'Abd al-Hakim Mahmud. *Mawsu'at ta'rikh al-i'dam al-siyasi fi misr*. Cairo: Maktabat Madbuli al-Saghir, 1997.

Agamben, Giorgione. *State of Exception*. Chicago: University of Chicago Press, 2005.

Agmon, Iris. *Family and Court: Legal Culture and Modernity in Late Ottoman Palestine*. Syracuse, NY: Syracuse University Press, 2006.

Althusser, Louis. "Ideology and Ideological State Apparatus." In *Lenin and Philosophy and Other Essays*. By Louis Althusser. Translated from the French by Ben Brewster, 85–126. New York: Monthly Review, 2001.

Amin, Galal. *Whatever Happened to the Egyptians? Changes in Egyptian Society from 1950 to the Present*. Cairo: American University in Cairo Press, 2000.

Amin, Galal. *Egypt in the Era of Hosni Mubarak*. Cairo: American University in Cairo Press, 2011.

Amnesty International. "Broken Promises: Egypt's Military Rulers Erode Human Rights," November 22, 2011. http://www.amnesty.org/en/library/asset/MDE12/053/2011/en/47be269e-b67a-42f4-835b-787f91044e04/mde120532011en.pdf.

Amnesty International. "Brutality Unpunished and Unchecked: Egypt's Military Kill and Torture Protesters with Impunity," October 2, 2012. http://www.amnestyusa.org/research/reports/brutality-unpunished-and-unchecked-egypt-s-military-kill-and-torture-protesters-with-impunity.

Anis, Muhammad. *Madrasat al-ta'rikh al-misri fi al-'asr al-'uthmani*. Cairo: Jami'at al-Duwal al-'Arabiya, Ma'had al-Dirasat al-'Arabiya al-'Aliya, 1962.

al-Ansari, Nasir. *Ta'rikh anẓimat al-shurtah fi misr*. Cairo: Dar al-Shuruq, 1990.

Arendt, Hannah. *On Violence*. New York: Harcourt, 1970.

Arendt, Hannah. *On Revolution*. New York: Penguin, 2006.

al-'Arusi, Mahmud Kamil. *Muhakamat sayyid qutb: Wathiqat muhakamat al-shaykh sayyid qutb wa-rifaqihi fi al-fatra 1959–1965*. Cairo: Matba'at al-Jumhuriya al-Haditha, 1995.

Asad, Talal. *Formations of the Secular: Christianity, Islam, Modernity*. Stanford, CA: Stanford University Press, 2003.

al-'Ashmawi, Hasan. *al-Ikhwan al-muslimun wa-l-thawra*. Cairo: al-Maktab al-Misri al-Hadith, 1977.

al-ʿAshmawi, Hasan. *Hasad al-ayyam: Mudhakkirat harib*. Cairo: Dar al-Tawziʿa wa-l-Nashr al-Islamiya, 1991.
al-ʿAshmawi, Saʿid. *al-Shariʿa al-islamiya wa-l-qanun al-misri*. Cairo: Madbuli, 1996.
Ashraf, Khalil. *Liberation Square: Inside the Egyptian Revolution and the Rebirth of a Nation*. New York: St. Martin's, 2012.
al-Aswany, Alaa. *On the State of Egypt*. Cairo: American University in Cairo Press, 2011.
ʿAwad, Luwis. *Aqniʿat al-nasiriya al-sabʿah: Munaqashat tawfiq al-hakim wa-muhammad hasanayn haykal*. Beirut: Dar al-Qadaya, 1975.
ʿAwad, Luwis. *Li-misr wa-l-hurriya: mawaqif siyasiya*. Beirut: Dar al-Qaḍaya, 1977.
ʿAwdah, ʿAbd al-Qadir. *al-Islam wa-awdaʿuna al-qanuniya*. Amman: Arwiqa, 2012.
Ayubi, Nazih. *Bureaucracy and Politics in Contemporary Egypt*. London: Ithaca, 1980.
Badrawi, Malak. *Ismail Sidqi 1875–1950: Pragmatism and Vision in Twentieth-Century Egypt*. Surrey, UK: Curzon, 1996.
Badrawi, Malak. *Political Violence in Egypt 1910–1924: Secret Societies, Plots and Assassinations*. London: Curzon, 2000.
Baer, Gabriel. *A History of Landownership in Modern Egypt, 1800–1950*. London: Oxford University Press, 1962.
Baer, Gabriel. *Studies in the Social History of Modern Egypt*. Chicago: University of Chicago Press, 1969.
al-Baghdadi, ʿAbd al-Latif. *Mudhakkirat ʿAbd al-latif al-baghdadi*, 2 vols. Cairo: al-Maktab al-Misri al-Hadith, 1977.
Bakr, ʿAbd al-Wahhab. *al-Bulis al-misri 1922–1952*. Cairo: Maktabat Madbuli, 1988.
al-Banna, Hasan. *Majmuʿat rasa'il al-imam al-shahid hasan al-banna*. Cairo: Dar al-Daʿwa, 1990.
al-Banna, Hasan. *Mudhakkirat al-daʿwa wa-l-daʿiya*. Cairo: Dar al-Shihab, 1978[?].
al-Banna, Jamal. *al-Farida al-gha'iba: Jihad al-sayf am jihad al-ʿaql?* Cairo: Dar al-Thabit, 1984.
Baring, Evelyn (The Earl of Cromer). *Modern Egypt*. London: Macmillan, 1908.
Baybars, Iman. *Nisā' min al-maydan*. Cairo: Dar Akhbar al-Yawm, 2011.
Beattie, Kirk. *Egypt during the Nasser Years: Ideology, Politics, and Civil Society*. Boulder, CO: Westview, 1994.
Bechor, Guy. *The Sanhuri Code and the Emergence of Modern Arab Civil Law, 1932 to 1949*. Leiden: Brill, 2007.
Be'eri, Eliezer. *Army Officers in Arab Politics and Society*. New York: Praeger, 1970.
Beinin, Joel. *The Dispersion of Egyptian Jewry: Culture, Politics, and the Formation of a Modern Diaspora*. Cairo: American University in Cairo Press, 2005.
Beinin, Joel. "Workers, Trade Unions and Egypt's Political Future." Middle East Research and Information Project, January 18, 2013. http://www.merip.org/mero/mero011813
Beinin, Joel, and Zachary Lockman. *Workers on the Nile: Nationalism, Communism, Islam, and the Egyptian Working Class, 1882–1954*. Princeton, NJ: Princeton University Press, 1987.
Benton, Lauren. *Law and Colonial Cultures: Legal Regimes in World History, 1400–1900*. Cambridge, UK: Cambridge University Press, 2002.
Bernard-Maugiron, Nathalie, ed. *Judges and Political Reforms in Egypt*. Cairo: American University in Cairo Press, 2008.

Bhutta, Nehal. "Between Liberal Legal Didactics and Political Manichaeism: The Politics and Law of the Iraqi Special Tribunal." *Melbourne Journal of International Law* 6.2 (2005): 1–25.

Binder, Leonard. *The Ideological Revolution in the Middle East.* New York: Wiley, 1964.

Binder, Leonard. *In a Moment of Enthusiasm: Political Power and the Second Stratum in Egypt.* Chicago: University of Chicago Press, 1978.

al-Bishri, Tariq. *al-Dimuqratiya wa-l-nasiriya.* Cairo: Dar al-Thaqafa, 1975.

al-Bishri, Tariq. *al-Dimuqratiya wa-niẓam thawrat yuliyu 1952–1970.* Beirut: Mu'asasat al-Abhath al-'Arabiya, 1987a.

al-Bishri, Tariq. *Dirasat fi al-dimuqratiya al-misriya.* Cairo: Dar al-Shuruq, 1987b.

al-Bishri, Tariq. *al-Shari'a al-islamiya wa-l-qanun al-wad'i.* Cairo: Dar al-Shuruq, 1996.

Botman, Selma. *Egypt from Independence to Revolution, 1919–1952.* Syracuse, NY: Syracuse University Press, 1991.

Brinton, Jasper Yeates. *The Mixed Courts of Egypt.* New Haven, CT: Yale University Press, 1968.

Brown, Nathan. *The Rule of Law in the Arab World: Courts in Egypt and the Gulf.* Cambridge, UK: Cambridge University Press, 1997.

Brown, Nathan. "Landmines in Egypt's Constitutional Roadmap." Carnegie Endowment for International Peace, December 7, 2011. http://carnegieendowment.org/2011/12/07/landmines-in-egypt-s-constitutional-roadmap

Burchell, Graham, Colin Gordon, and Peter Miller, eds. *The Foucault Effect: Studies in Governmentality.* Chicago: University of Chicago Press, 1991.

Calvert, John. *Sayyid Qutb and the Origins of Radical Islam.* New York: Columbia University Press, 2010.

Cambanis, Thanassis. *Once Upon a Revolution: An Egyptian Story.* New York: Simon & Schuster, 2015.

Cannon, Byron. *Politics of Law and the Courts in Nineteen Century Egypt.* Salt Lake City: University of Utah Press, 1988.

Chakravarti, Leila Zaki, "From Strongman to Superman: Sisi the Saviour of Egypt." Open Democracy, April 28, 2014. https://www.opendemocracy.net/5050/leila-zaki-chakravarti/from-strongman-to-superman-sisi-saviour-of-egypt

Christenson, Ron. *Political Trials in History from Antiquity to the Present.* New Brunswick, NJ: Transaction, 1991.

Cohen, Michael J., and Martin Kolinsky, eds. *Demise of the British Empire in the Middle East: Britain's Responses to Nationalist Movements, 1943–55.* London: Frank Cass, 1998.

Cole, Juan. *Colonialism and Revolution in the Middle East: Social and Cultural Origins of Egypt's 'Urabi Movement.* Cairo: American University in Cairo Press, 1999.

Coles Pasha, Charles. *Recollections and Reflections.* London: Saint Catherine, 1918.

Crabbs, Jack. "Politics, History, and Culture in Nasser's Egypt." *International Journal of Middle East Studies* 6 (1975): 386–420.

Cuno, Kenneth. *Modernizing Marriage: Family, Ideology, and Law in Nineteenth- and Early Twentieth-Century Egypt.* Syracuse, NY: Syracuse University Press, 2015.

Dabashi, Hamid. *The Arab Spring: The End of Postcolonialism.* London: Zed, 2012.

Deeb, Marius. *Party Politics in Egypt: The Wafd and its Rivals, 1919–1939.* London: Ithaca, 1979.

Dekmejian, Harir. *Egypt under Nasir.* Albany, NY: State University of New York Press, 1971.

Di-Capua, Yoav. *Gatekeepers of the Arab Past: Historians and History Writing in Twentieth-Century Egypt*. Berkeley: University of California Press, 2009.

Djilas, Milovan. *Memoir of a Revolutionary*. New York: Harcourt Brace Jovanovich, 1973.

Doran, Michael. *Pan-Arabism before Nasser: Egyptian Power Politics and the Palestine Question*. New York: Oxford University Press, 1999.

Eisenstadt, Shmuel. *Revolution and the Transformation of Societies: A Comparative Study of Civilizations*. New York: Free Press, 1978.

Esmeir, Samera. *Juridical Humanity: A Colonial History*. Stanford, CA: Stanford University Press, 2012.

Ewick, Patricia, and Susan Silbey. "Subversive Stories and Hegemonic Tales: Toward a Sociology of Narrative." *Law and Society Review* 29.2 (1995): 197–226.

Fahmy, Khaled. "Justice, Law and Pain in Khedival Egypt." In *Standing Trial: Law and the Person in the Modern Middle East*. Edited by Baudouin Dupret, 85–116. London: I. B. Tauris, 2004.

Fahmy, Khaled, and Rudolph Peters. "The Legal History of Ottoman Egypt." *Islamic Law and Society* 6.2 (1999): 224–71.

Farah, Nadia Ramsis. *Egypt's Political Economy: Power Relations in Development*. Cairo: American University in Cairo Press, 2009.

Fellman, Susanna, and Marjatta Rahikainen, eds. *Historical Knowledge: In Quest of Theory, Method and Evidence*. Newcastle upon Tyne: Cambridge Scholars Publishing, 2012.

Fleur, Johns. "Guantanamo Bay and the Annihilation of the Exception." *European Journal of International Law* 16.4 (2005): 613–35.

Foran John. *Taking Power: On the Origins of Third World Revolutions*. Cambridge, UK: Cambridge University Press, 2005.

Foran, John. "Theorizing the Cuban Revolution." *Latin American Perspectives* 36.2 (2009): 16–30.

Foucault, Michel. "The Subject and Power." *Critical Inquiry* 8.4 (Summer 1982): 777–95.

Foucault, Michel. *The History of Sexuality*. New York: Vintage, 1988.

Foucault, Michel. "Governmentality." In *The Foucault Effect: Studies in Governmentality*. Edited by Graham Burchell, Colin Gordon, and Peter Miller, 87–104. Chicago: University of Chicago Press, 1991.

Foucault, Michel. *Discipline and Punish: The Birth of the Prison*. New York: Vintage, 1995.

Foucault, Michel. *The Essential Foucault: Selections from Essential Works of Foucault, 1954–1984*. Edited by Paul Rabinow and Nikolas Rose. New York: New Press, 2003.

Gershoni, Israel. *Confronting Fascism in Egypt: Dictatorship versus Democracy in the 1930s*. Stanford, CA: Stanford University Press, 2010.

Gershoni, Israel, ed. *Arab Responses to Fascism and Nazism: Attraction and Repulsion*. Austin: University of Texas Press, 2014.

Gershoni, Israel, and Jankowski James. *Commemorating the Nation: Collective Memory, Public Commemoration, and National Identity in Twentieth-Century Egypt*. Chicago: Middle East Documentation Center, 2004.

al-Ghazali, Muhammad. *al-Islam wa-l-istibdād al-siyasi*. Cairo: Dar Nahdat Misr, 1997.

Ghobashy, Mona. "The Praxis of the Egyptian Revolution." *Middle East Report* 258 (Spring 2011): 2–13.

Ghonim, Wael. *Revolution 2.0: The Power of the People Is Greater than the People in Power—A Memoir*. Boston: Houghton Mifflin Harcourt, 2012.

Ginzburg, Carlo. "Killing a Chinese Mandarin: The Moral Implications of Distance." *Critical Inquiry* 21.1 (Autumn 1994): 46–60.

Ginzburg, Carlo. *Wooden Eyes: Nine Reflections on Distance*. New York: Columbia University Press, 2001.

Ginzburg, Carlo. *The Judge and the Historian: Marginal Notes on a Late-Twentieth-Century Miscarriage of Justice*. London: Verso, 2002.

Ginzburg, Carlo. *The Cheese and the Worms: The Cosmos of a Sixteenth-Century Miller*. Baltimore: Johns Hopkins University Press, 2013a.

Ginzburg, Carlo. *The Night Battles: Witchcraft and Agrarian Cults in the Sixteenth and Seventeenth Centuries*. Baltimore: Johns Hopkins University Press, 2013b.

Goldschmidt, Arthur. *Modern Egypt: The Formation of a Nation State*. Boulder, CO: Westview, 1988.

Goldschmidt, Arthur, Amy Johnson, and Barak Salmoni, eds. *Re-envisioning Egypt, 1919–1952*. New York: American University in Cairo Press, 2005.

Gordon, Joel. *Nasser's Blessed Movement: Egypt's Free Officers and the July Revolution*. New York: Oxford University Press, 1992.

Grunwald, Henning. *Courtroom to Revolutionary Stage: Performance and Ideology in Weimar Political Trials*. Oxford: Oxford University Press, 2012.

Hadith al-manshiya. Part 1. al-Jazeera, December 22, 2006. http://www.aljazeera.net/NR/exeres/870EB471-AFDD-4DBC-88FD-A62629EF0E26.htm#L2

Hadith al-manshiya. Part 2. al-Jazeera, December 29, 2006. http://www.aljazeera.net/NR/EXERES/F6453271-354A-4DE1-9226-76D5769363BF.htm.

Hafiz, Sulayman. *Dhikkrayati ʿan al-thawra*. Cairo: Dar al-Shuruq, 2010.

al-Hakim, Tawfiq. *ʿAwdat al-waʿi*. Beirut: Dar al-Shuruq, 1974.

Hamad, Mahmoud. "When the Gavel Speaks: Judicial Politics in Modern Egypt." Ph.D. dissertation, University of Utah, 2008.

Hammudah, Muhammad Ahmad. *Asrar harakat al-ḍubat al-ahrar wa-l-ikhwan al-muslimun*. Cairo: al-Zahra' lil-Iʿlam al-ʿArabi, 1985.

Hamouda, Sahar. "The Reed Phenomenon." In *Victoria College: A History Revealed*. Edited by Sahar Hamouda and Colin Clement, 63–136. Cairo: American University in Cairo Press, 2002.

Hamrush, Ahmad. *Qissat thawrat 23 yuliyu*. 5 vols. Cairo: Maktabat Madbuli, 1983–4.

Hanssen, Jens. "Translating Revolution: Hannah Arendt in Arab Political Culture." *HannahArendt.net: Zeitschrift für politisches Denken* 7.1 (November 2013). http://www.hannaharendt.net/index.php/han/article/view/301/437

Hasan, ʿAmmar ʿAli. *ʿIshtu ma jarā: Shahadati ʿalá thawrat yanayir*. Cairo: Al-Hayah al-ʿAmmah li-Qusur al-Thaqafa, 2013.

Hashim, Muhammad Yunus. *Durus min thawrat yuliyu li-thawrat yanayir*. Cairo: Dar Zuhur al-Maʿrifa wa-l-Baraka, 2012.

Havel, Vaclav. *The Power of the Powerless: Citizens Against the State in Central-Eastern Europe*. London: Routledge, 2009.

Haykal, Muhammad Husayn. *Mudhakkirat fi al-siyasa al-misriya*, 2 vols. Cairo: Dar al-Maʿarif, 1978.

Herrera, Linda. *Revolution in the Age of Social Media*. London: Verso, 2014.

Hill, Enid. *Mahkama! Studies in the Egyptian Legal System: Courts and Crimes, Law and Society*. London: Ithaca, 1979.

Hill, Enid. "Al-Sanhuri and Islamic Law." *Cairo Papers in Social Science* 10 (Summer 1987a): Monograph 2.

Hill, Enid. *Al-Sanhuri and Islamic Law: The Place and Significance of Islamic Law in the Life and Work of 'Abd al-Razzaq Ahmad al-Sanhuri, Egyptian Jurist and Scholar, 1895–1971*. Cairo: American University in Cairo Press, 1987b.

Hill, Enid. "Al-Sanhuri and Islamic Law: The Place and Significance of Islamic Law in the Life and Work of 'Abd al-Razzaq Ahmad al-Sanhuri, Egyptian Jurist and Scholar, 1895–1971 (Part II)." *Arab Law Quarterly* 3.2 (May 1988): 182–218.

Hill, Enid. "The Golden Anniversary of Egypt's National Courts." In *Historians in Cairo*. Edited by Jill Edwards, 203–22. New York: American University in Cairo Press, 2002.

El-Houdaiby, Ibrahim. "Islamism in and after Egypt's Revolution." In *Arab Spring in Egypt: Revolution and beyond*. Edited by Bahgat Korany and Rabab el-Mahdi, 125–51. Cairo: American University in Cairo Press, 2012.

Hourani, Albert. *A History of the Arab Peoples*. New York: Warner, 1992.

Human Rights Watch. "All according to Plan: The Rab'a Massacre and Mass Killings of Protesters in Egypt," August 2014. http://www.hrw.org/sites/default/files/reports/egypt0814_ForUpload_0.pdf.

Hussain, Nasser. *The Jurisprudence of Emergency: Colonialism and the Rule of Law*. Ann Arbor: University of Michigan Press, 2003.

Huysmans, Jef. "The Jargon of Exception: On Schmitt, Agamben and the Absence of Political Society." *International Political Sociology* 2 (2008): 163–83.

Idle, Nadine, and Alex Nunns. *Tweets from Tahrir: Egypt's Revolution as It Unfolded in the Words of the People Who Made It*. New York: OR, 2011.

Imam, 'Abdallah. *'Ali sabri yatadhkkar*. Beirut: Dar al-Wahda, 1988.

Imam, 'Abdallah. *'Abd al-nasir wa-l-ikhwan al-muslimun*. Cairo: Dar al-Khayyal, 1996.

'Isá, Salah. *Dustur fi sunduq al-qimamah—qissat mashru'a dustur 1954: Dirasa wa-wathiqa*. Cairo: Markaz al-Qahira li-Dirasat Huquq al-Insan, 2001.

'Isá, Salah. *Muhakamat fu'ad siraj al-din basha: Tahqiq wa-dirasat*. Cairo: Madbuli, 1983.

'Isá, Salah. *Sha'ir takdir al-'amn al-'amm: al-Milaffat al-qada'iya lil-sha'ir ahmad fu'ad nejam—dirasa wa-watha'iq*. Cairo: Dar al-Shuruq, 2007.

al-'Isawi, 'Ali 'Abdel 'Al. *Asrar al-muhakamat al-siyasiya min waqā'i sijillat al-mahakim*. Beirut: al-Maktaba al-Thaqafiya, 1994.

Issawi, Charles. *Egypt in Revolution: An Economic Analysis*. London: Oxford University Press, 1963.

Jameson, Frederic. *The Political Unconscious: Narrative as a Social Symbolic Act*. Ithaca, NY: Cornell University Press, 1981.

Jankowski, James. "The View from the Embassy: British Assessment of Egyptian Attitudes during World War II." In *Arab Responses to Fascism and Nazism: Attraction and Repulsion*. Edited by Israel Gershoni, 171–94. Austin: University of Texas Press, 2014.

Jansen, Johannes. *The Neglected Duty: The Creed of Sadat's Assassins and Islamic Resurgence in the Middle East*. New York: Macmillan, 1986.

al-Jawadi, Muhammad. *Mudhakkirat qādat al-mukhabarat wa-l-mabahith: al-'Amn al-qawmi li-Misr*. Cairo: Dar al-Khayyal, 1999.

al-Jawadi, Muhammad. *Mudhakkirat al-ḍubat al-ahrar: al-Thawra fawqa al-dimuqratiya—nahwa hukm al-fard*. Cairo: Dar al-Khayyal, 2003a.

al-Jawadi, Muhammad. *Qādat al-shurtah al-misriya*. Cairo: Madbuli, 2003b.

Johansen, Baber. *Contingency in a Sacred Law: Legal and Ethical Norms in the Muslim Fiqh*. Leiden: Brill, 1999.

al-Jumay'i, 'Abd al-Mun'im al-Dusuqi. *al-Asliha al-fasida wa-dawruha fi harb filastin 1948*. Cairo: al-Hay'ah al-Misriya al-'Ammah lil-Kitab, 1990.

Kamil, Rashad. *Harb filastin 48: al-khayba wa-l-khadi'a—hadith al-watha'iq*. Cairo: Dar Nashr, 1998.

Karrum, Hasanayn. *Suqut al-hakim: Al-radd 'alá kitab watha'iq fi tariq 'awdat al-wa'i*. Cairo: Dar Ma'mun lil-Tiba'ah, 1975.

Kassem, Maye. *Egyptian Politics: The Dynamics of Authoritarian Rule*. Boulder, CO: Lynne Rienner, 2004.

Kedourie, Elie. "Revolutionary Justice in Egypt: The Trials of 1953." *The Political Quarterly* 29.4 (October 1958): 389–96.

Kerboeuf, Anne-Claire. "The Cairo Fire of 26 January 1952 and the Interpretations of History." In *Re-envisioning Egypt, 1919–1952*. Edited by Arthur Goldschmidt, Amy Johnson, and Barak Salmoni, 194–216. Cairo: American University in Cairo Press, 2005.

Kerr, Malcolm. *The Arab Cold War*. London: Oxford University Press, 1971.

Khalid, Shawqi. *Mahkamat fir'aun*. Cairo: Sina' lil-Nashr, 1986.

Khalil, Ashraf. *Liberation Square: Inside the Egyptian Revolution and the Rebirth of a Nation*. New York: St. Martin's, 2012.

Khamis, Sahar, and Katherine Vaughn. "'We are All Khaled Said': The Potentials and Limitations of Cyber Activism in Triggering Public Mobilization and Promoting Political Change." *Journal of Arab and Muslim Media Research* 4 (2012): 145–63.

Kheir-El-Din, Hanaa. *The Egyptian Economy: Current Challenges and Future Prospects*. Cairo: American University in Cairo Press, 2008.

al-Khijawi, Zakariya, and 'Abd al-'Aziz Jaber. *Malik ḍid sh'ab*. Cairo: Sharikat al-Tawzi'a al-Misriya, 1953[?].

al-Kilani, Najib. *Lamahat min hayati*. Beirut: Mu'asasat al-Risala, 1985.

al-Kilani, Najib. *Mudhakkirat al-duktur najib al-kilani*. Cairo: Kitab al-Mukhtar, 2006.

Killearn, Miles Lampson. *The Killearn Diaries, 1934–1946: The Diplomatic and Personal Record of Lord Killearn (Sir Miles Lampson), High Commissioner and Ambassador, Egypt*. Edited by Trefor Evans. London: Sidgwick and Jackson, 1972.

Killearn, Miles Lampson. *Politics and Diplomacy in Egypt: The Diaries of Sir Miles Lampson, 1935–1937*. Edited by Malcolm Yapp. Oxford: Oxford University Press, 1997.

Kirchheimer, Otto. *Political Justice: The Use of Legal Procedure for Political Ends*. New Jersey: Princeton University Press, 1961.

Klein, Menachem. "ha-Intelektu'alim ba-mitsrayim ha-natserit". Ph.D. diss., Hebrew University of Jerusalem, 1992.

Korany, Bahgat, and Rabab el-Mahdi, eds. *Arab Spring in Egypt: Revolution and Beyond*. Cairo: American University in Cairo Press, 2012.

LaCapra, Dominick. *History and Criticism*. Ithaca, NY: Cornel University Press, 1985.

Lesch, Ann. "Concentrated Power Breeds Corruption, Repression, and Resistance." In *Arab Spring in Egypt: Revolution and beyond*. Edited by Bahgat Korany and Rabab el-Mahdi, 17–39. Cairo: American University in Cairo Press, 2012.

Levi, Giovanni. "On Microhistory." In *Historical Writings*. Edited by Peter Burke, 93–113. Philadelphia: University of Pennsylvania Press, 1995.

Levi, Giovanni. "Microhistory and the Recovery of Complexity." In *Historical Knowledge: In Quest of Theory, Method and Evidence*. Edited by Susanna Fellman and Marjatta Rahikainen, 121–32. Newcastle upon Tyne, UK: Cambridge Scholars Publishing, 2012.

Lia, Brynjar. *The Society of the Muslim Brothers in Egypt: The Rise of an Islamic Mass Movement, 1928–1942*. Reading, UK: Ithaca, 1998.

Lombardi, Clark. *State Law as Islamic Law in Modern Egypt: The Incorporation of the Sharia into Egyptian Constitutional Law*. Leiden, The Netherlands: Brill, 2006.

Lutz, Ellen, and Caitlin Reiger, eds. *Prosecuting Heads of State*. New York: Cambridge University Press, 2009.

Maghraoui, Abdeslam. *Liberalism without Democracy: Nationhood and Citizenship in Egypt, 1922–1936*. Durham, NC: Duke University Press, 2006.

Magnússon, Gylfi Sigurður, and IstvánI Szíjártó. *What Is Microhistory? Theory and Practice*. London: Routledge, 2013.

Mahmood, Saba. "Is Liberalism Islam's Only Answer?" In *Islam and the Challenge of Democracy*. Edited by Joshua Cohen and Deborah Chasman, 74–7. Princeton, NJ: Princeton University Press, 2004.

Mahmud, ʿAbd al-Halim. *al-Ikhwan al-muslimun, ahdath sanaʿat al-taʾrikh: Ruʾya min al-dakhil*. 3 vols. Alexandria, Egypt: Dar al-Daʿwa, 1979–86.

Mangan, J.A., ed. *Making Imperial Mentalities: Socialisation and British Imperialism*. London: Routledge, 2010.

Mansfield, Peter. *Nasser*. London: Methuen, 1969.

Marʿi, Sayyid. *Awraq siyasiya: Min al-qarya ilā al-islah*. Cairo: al-Ahram, 1978.

Mayer, Thomas. "Egypt's 1948 Invasion of Palestine." *Middle Eastern Studies* 22.1 (1986): 20–35.

McLeave, Hugh. *The Last Pharaoh: Farouk of Egypt*. New York: McCall, 1970.

McLoughlin, Leslie. *In a Sea of Knowledge: British Arabists in the Twentieth Century*. Reading, MA: Ithaca, 2002.

Mehrez, Samia. *Translating Egypt's Revolution: The Language of Tahrir*. Cairo: American University in Cairo Press, 2012.

Meital, Yoram. "School Textbooks and Assembling the Puzzle of the Past in Revolutionary Egypt." *Middle Eastern Studies* 42.2 (Winter 2006a): 255–70.

Meital, Yoram. "The Struggle over Political Order in Egypt: The 2005 Elections." *Middle East Journal* 60 (2006b): 257–79.

Meital, Yoram. "Central Cairo: Street Naming and the Struggle over Historical Representation." *Middle Eastern Studies* 43.6 (November 2007): 857–78.

Merry, Sally Engle. "Resistance and the Cultural Power of Law." *Law and Society Review* 29.1 (1995): 11–26.

Mitchell, Richard. *The Society of the Muslim Brothers*. Oxford: Oxford University Press, 1969; repr. 1993.

Mohi el-Din Khaled. *Memoirs of Revolution: Egypt 1952*. Cairo: American University in Cairo Press, 1995.

Morewood, Steve. "Prelude to the Suez Crisis: The Rise and Fall of British Dominance over the Suez Canal, 1869–1956." In *Reassessing Suez 1956: New Perspectives on the Crisis and Its Aftermath*. Edited by Simon Smith, 13–52. Burlington, UK: Ashgate, 2008.

Morsy, Laila. "The Military Clauses of the Anglo–Egyptian Treaty of Friendship and Alliance, 1936." *International Journal of Middle East Studies* 16 (1984): 67–97.

Morris, Benny. *Righteous victims: A history of the Zionist-Arab conflict, 1881-1999*. London: John Murray, 2000.

Murad, Mahmud. *Man kana yahkum misr? Shahadat watha'iqiya*. Cairo: Madbuli, 1975.

Muti'i, Lam'i. *Ha'ula hum rijal yuliyu: Ma'a adwā 'alá mudhakkirat Yusuf Siddiq wa-'Abd al-Mun'im 'Abd al-Ra'uf*. Cairo: Madbuli, 1989.

Naguib, Muhammad. *Kalimati lil-ta'rikh*. Cairo: Dar al-Kitab, 1975.

Naguib, Muhammad. *Masir misr*. Cairo: Dar Diwan, 1995.

Nasr, Salah. *Mudhakkirat Salah Nasr*, 3 vols. Cairo: Dar al-Khayyal, 1999.

El-Nawawy, Mohammed, and Sahar Khamis. *Egyptian Revolution 2.0: Political Blogging, Civic Engagement, and Citizen Journalism*. New York: Palgrave Macmillan, 2013.

Neocleous, Mark. "The Problem with Normality: Taking Exception to Permanent Emergency." *Alternatives* 31 (2006): 191–213.

Neumann, Michael. *The Rule of Law: Politicizing Ethics*. Aldershot, UK: Ashgate, 2002.

Nusayr, Mustafa 'Abd al-Majid, 'Abd al-Hamid Kafafi, Sa'd 'Abd al-Hafiz, and Jamal Mansur. *Thawrat yuliyu wa-l-haqiqa al-gha'iba*. Cairo: al-Hay'ah al-Misriya al-'Ammah lil-Kitab, 1997.

Osman, Ghada. *A Journey in Islamic Thought: The Life of Fathi Osman*. London: I. B. Tauris, 2011.

Owen, Roger. *Lord Cromer: Victorian Imperialist*. Oxford: Oxford University Press, 2004.

Owen, Roger. *The Rise and Fall of Arab Presidents for Life*. Cambridge, MA: Harvard University Press, 2012.

Owen, Sirrs. *A History of the Egyptian Intelligence Service: A History of the Mukhabarat, 1910–2009*. New York: Routledge, 2010.

Pappé, Ilan. The making of the Arab-Israeli conflict, 1947–51. London; I. B. Tauris, 1994.

Pierce, Leslie. *Morality Tales: Law and Gender in the Ottoman Court of Aintab*. Berkeley: University of California Press, 2003.

Qa'ud, Ibrahim. *'Umar al-tilmissani shahidan 'alá al-'asr: al-Ikwan al-muslimun fi da'irat al-haqiqa al-ghaiba*. Cairo: al-Mukhtar al-Islami, 1985.

Qutb, Sayyid. *Limadha a'damuni?* Cairo: Manshurat Nun, 2007.

Ra'fat, Wahid. *Fusul min thawrat 23 juliyu*. Cairo: Dar al-Shuruq, 1978.

Ra'fat, Wahid. *Dirasat fi ba'd al-qawanin al-munazima lil-hurriyat*. Alexandria, Egypt: Munsh'at al-Ma'arif, 1981.

al-Rafi'i, 'Abd al-Rahman. *Muqaddamat thawrat 23 yuliyu sanat 1952*. Cairo: Maktabat al-Nahdah al-Misriya, 1957.

al-Rafi'i, 'Abd al-Rahman. *Thawrat 23 yuliyu: Ta'rikhuna al-qawmi fi sab'a sanawat, 1952–1959*. Cairo: Maktabat al-Nahdah al-Misriya, 1959.

al-Rafi'i, 'Abd al-Rahman. *Mustafa Kamil*. Cairo: Maktabat al-Nahdah al-Misriya, 1962.

Ramadan, 'Abd al-'Azim. *al-Ikhwan al-muslimun wa-l-tanẓim al-sirri*. Cairo: Maktabat Ruz al-Yusuf, 1982.

Ramadan, 'Abd al-'Azim. *'Abd al-Nasir wa-azmat mars*. Cairo: Madbuli, 1977.

Ramadan, 'Abd al-'Azim. *Tahtim al-āliha*. Cairo: Madbuli, 1986.

Ramadan, 'Abd al-'Azim. *Tatawwur al-haraka al-wataniya fi misr min sanat 1937 ilā sanat 1948*. 4 vols. Cairo: al-Hay'ah al-Misriya al-'Ammah lil-Kitab, 1998.

Ramadan, Tariq. *Islam and the Arab Awakening*. Oxford: Oxford University Press, 2012.

Reid, Donald. *Lawyers and Politics in the Arab world, 1880–1960*. Minneapolis: Bibliotheca Islamica, 1981.

Rejwan, Nissim. *Nasserist Ideology: Its Exponents and Critics*. New York: Wiley, 1974.

Reynolds, Nancy. *A City Consumed: Urban Commerce, the Cairo Fire, and the Politics of Decolonization in Egypt*. Stanford, CA: Stanford University Press, 2012.

Reza, Sadiq. "Endless Emergency: The Case of Egypt." *New Criminal Law Review* 10 (Fall 2007): 532–53.

Roberts, Richard. "History and Memory: The Power of Statist Narratives." *International Journal of African Historical Studies* 33.3 (2000): 513–22.

Rosberg, James. "The Emergence of an Independent Judiciary in Contemporary Egypt." Ph.D. dissertation, Massachusetts Institute of Technology, 1995.

Rubin, Avi. "British Perceptions of Ottoman Judicial Reform in the Late Nineteenth Century: Some Preliminary Insights." *Law and Social Inquiry* 37 (2012): 991–1012.

Rubin, Avi. *Ottoman Nizamiye Courts: Law and Modernity*. New York: Palgrave Macmillan, 2011.

Rubin, Avi. "The Trial of the Prosecutor Hamdi Bey: Inside and Out of the Ottoman Nizamiye Court." *Journal of Social History* 45 (2011): 757–79.

Russell, Sir Thomas. *Egyptian Service, 1902–1946*. London: John Murray, 1949.

Ryzova, Lucie. "Egyptianizing Modernity through the 'New *Effendiya*': Social and Cultural Constructions of the Middle Class in Egypt under the Monarchy." In *Re-Envisioning Egypt, 1919–1952*. Edited by Arthur Goldschmidt, Amy Johnson, and Barak Salmoni, 124–63. Cairo: American University in Cairo Press, 2005.

Ryzova, Lucie. *The Age of the Efendiyya: Passages to Modernity in National–Colonial Egypt*. Oxford: Oxford University Press, 2014.

Sabbagh, Mahmud. *Haqiqat al-tanẓim al-khas wa-dawruhu fi da'wat al-ikhwan al-muslimun*. Cairo: Dar al-I'tisam, 1988.

Sadat, Anwar. *In Search of Identity: An Autobiography*. New York: Harper & Row, 1978.

Sa'dawi, Nawal. *Nawal al-sa'dawi wa-l-thawrat al-'arabiya*. Bayrut: Sharikat al-Matbu'at lil-Tawzi'a wa-l-Nashr, 2013.

Sa'id, Amin. *al-Thawra min 23 yuliyu ilā 29 uktobir 1956*. Cairo: 'Isa al-Halabi, 1959.

Salim, Latifa. *al-Niẓam al-qada'i al-misri al-hadith, 1914–1952*. Cairo: al-Hay'ah al-Misriyah al-'Ammah lil-Kitab, 2001.

Salim, Latifa. *Ta'rikh al-qada' al-misri al-hadith*. Cairo: al-Hay'ah al-Misriya al-'Ammah lil-Kitab, 1991.

Salamah, Muhammad 'Ali. *al-Infitah al-iqtisadi wa-atharuhu al-ijtima'iya 'alá al-āusra*. Alexandria: Dar al-Wafa' li-Dunya al-Tiba'ah wa-l-Nashr, 2002.

al-Sanhuri, Nadya, and Tawfiq al-Shawi, eds. *Al-Sanhuri min khilal awraqihi al-shakhsiya*. Cairo: Dar al-Shuruq, 2005.

Sayyid Ahmad, Rif'at. *Thawrat al-jiniral: Qissat jamal 'abd al-nasir kamila, min al-milad ilā al-mawt, 1918–1970*. Cairo: Dar al-Huda, 1993.

al-Sayyid, Mustafa Kamil. *al-Mujtama'a wa-l-siyasa fi misr: Dawr jama'at al-masalih fi al-niẓam al-siyasi al-misri, 1952–1981*. Cairo: Dar al-Mustaqbal al-'Arabi, 1983.

al-Sayyid Marsot, Afaf Lutfi. *A History of Egypt: From the Arab Conquest to the Present*. Cambridge, UK: Cambridge University Press, 2007.

al-Sayyid Marsot, Afaf Lutfi. *Egypt's Liberal Experiment, 1922–1936*. Berkeley: University of California Press, 1977.

Schmitt, Carl. *The Concept of the Political*. Chicago: University of Chicago Press, 1996.
Schmitt, Carl. *Political Theology: Four Chapters on the Concept of Sovereignty*. Cambridge: Massachusetts Institute of Technology Press, 1985.
Scott, James. *Domination and the Arts of Resistance: Hidden Transcripts*. New Haven, CT: Yale University Press, 1990.
Seikaly, Samir. "Prime Minister and Assassin: Butrus Ghali and Wardani." *Middle Eastern Studies* 13.1 (1977): 112–23.
Selbin, Eric. *Revolution, Rebellion, Resistance: The Power of Story*. New York: Palgrave, 2010.
Shahar, Ido. "Palestinians in an Israeli Court: Culture, Control, and Resistance in the Shari'a Court of West Jerusalem." MA thesis, Hebrew University of Jerusalem, 2000.
Shakib, Ibrahim. *Harb filastin 1948: Ru'ya misriya*. Cairo: al-Zahra' lil-I'lam al-'Arabi, 1986.
Shalabi, Karam. *'Ishruna yawman hazzat misr: Dirasa wa-watha'iq fi azmat mars*. Cairo: Dar Usamah lil-Tiba'ah wa-l-Nashr, 1976.
Shamir, Shimon, ed., *Egypt from Monarchy to Republic: A Reassessment of Revolution and Change*. Boulder, CO: Westview, 1995.
Shlaim, Avi. *The Iron Wall: Israel and the Arab World*. London: Penguin Press, 2000.
Sharabi, Hisham. *Nationalism and Revolution in the Arab World*. Princeton, NJ: Van Nostrand, 1966.
Sharaf, Sami. *'Abd al-Nasir kayfa hakama misr?* Cairo: Maktabat Madbuli al-Saghir, 1996.
al-Sharqawi, Jamal. *Hariq al-qahira*. Cairo: Dar al-Thaqafa al-Jadida, 1976.
al-Shayib, Jalal. *Daftar al-ghadab: Yawmiyat shakhs 'adi sharaka fi al-thawra, 2010–2012*. Cairo: Dar Nahdat Misr lil-Nashr, 2013.
Shenhav, Yehuda. "Beyond 'Instrumental Rationality': Lord Cromer and the Imperial Roots of Eichmann's Bureaucracy." *Journal of Genocide Research* 15.4 (2013): 379–99.
Shokr, Ahmad. "Reflections on Two Revolutions." *Middle East Report* 265 (Winter 2012). http://www.merip.org/mer/mer265/reflections-two-revolutions
Siraj al-Din, Fadiyah. *al-Tahrir al-watani: al-Qadiya al-misriya fi al-marhala al-akhira, 1950–1954*. Cairo: 'Ayn lil-Dirasat wa-l-Buhuth al-Insaniya wa-l-Ijtima'iya, 1995.
Skocpol, Theda. *States and Social Revolutions: A Comparative Analysis of France, Russia, and China*. New York: Cambridge University Press, 1979.
Skovgaard-Petersen, Jakob. *Defining Islam for the Egyptian State: Muftis and Fatwas of the Dar al-Ifta*. Leiden: Brill, 1997.
Smith, Charles D. "4 February 1942: Its Causes and Its Influence on Egyptian Politics and on the Future of Anglo-Egyptian Relations, 1937–1945." *International Journal of Middle East Studies* 10 (1979): 453–79.
Smith, Simon, ed. *Reassessing Suez 1956: New Perspectives on the Crisis and Its Aftermath*. Burlington, UK: Ashgate, 2008.
Soueif, Ahdaf. *Cairo: My City, Our Revolution*. London: Bloomsbury, 2012.
Sowers, Jeannie, and Chris Toensing, eds. *The Journey to Tahrir: Revolution, Protest and Social Change in Egypt*. New York: Verso, 2012.
St. John, Robert. *The Boss: The Story of Gamal Abdel Nasser*. New York: McGraw-Hill, 1960.
Stacher, Joshua. *Adaptable Autocrats: Regime Power in Egypt and Syria*. Stanford, CA: Stanford University Press, 2013.
Stagh, Marina. *The Limits of Freedom of Speech: Prose Literature and Prose Writers in Egypt under Nasser and Sadat*. Stockholm: Almqvist & Wiksell International, 1993.
Stephens, Robert. *Nasser: A Political Biography*. London: Allen Lane, 1971.

Stone, Lawrence. "Theories of Revolution." *World Politics* 18.2 (January 1966): 159–76.
Tamanaha, Brian. *Law as a Means to an End: Threat to the Rule of Law.* Cambridge, UK: Cambridge University Press, 2007.
Tamanaha, Brian. *Beyond the Formalist-Realist Divide: The Role of Politics in Judging.* Princeton, NJ: Princeton University Press, 2009.
al-Tamawi, Sulayman Muhammad. *Thawrat 23 yuliyu sanat 1952 bayna thawarat al-ʿalam.* Cairo: Dar al-Fikr al-ʿArabi, 1964.
Thabit, Karim. *Mudhakkirat karim thabit.* Cairo: Dar al-Shuruq, 2000.
al-Tilmissani, ʿUmar. *Dhikkrayat la mudhakkirat.* Cairo: Dar al-Tibaʿah wa-l-Nashr al-Islamiya, 1985.
Tollefson, Harold. *Policing Islam: The British Occupation of Egypt and the Anglo-Egyptian Struggle over Control of the Police, 1882–1914.* Westport, CT: Greenwood, 1999.
Trimberger, Ellen Kay. *Revolution from Above: Military Bureaucrats and Development in Japan, Turkey, Egypt, and Peru.* New Brunswick, NJ: Transaction, 1978.
al-Tuni, Muhammad Shawkat. *Suwar min al-mahkama: Nas wa-ahdath fi tariq al-khuṭā al-mafquda.* Cairo: Maktabat al-Anjlu al-Misriya, 1964.
al-Tuni, Muhammad Shawkat. *Muhakamat al-dijawi.* Cairo: Mu'asasat Dar al-Shaʿb, 1975.
ʿUwaysi, ʿAbd al-Fattah. *The Muslim Brothers and the Palestine Question, 1928–1947.* London: Tauris, 1998.
Vatikiotis, P.J. *Nasser and His Generation.* New York: St. Martin's, 1978.
Vatikiotis, P.J. *Egypt since the Revolution.* New York: Praeger, 1968.
Zemon Davis, Natalie. *The Return of Martin Guerre.* Cambridge, MA: Harvard University Press, 1983.
Zollner, Barbara. *The Muslim Brotherhood: Hasan al-Hudaybi and Ideology.* London: Routledge 2009.
Zubaida, Sami. *Islam, the People and the State: Political Ideas and Movements in the Middle East.* London: I. B. Tauris, 2009.

INDEX

The manufacturer's authorised representative in the EU for product safety is Oxford University Press España S.A. of El Parque Empresarial San Fernando de Henares, Avenida de Castilla, 2 - 28830 Madrid (www.oup.es/en or product.safety@oup.com). OUP España S.A. also acts as importer into Spain of products made by the manufacturer.
Printed and bound by CPI Group (UK) Ltd, Croydon, CR0 4YY
14/09/2026
02216307-0019